LEGITIMACY

Legitimacy

The State and Beyond

Edited by
WOJCIECH SADURSKI
MICHAEL SEVEL
and
KEVIN WALTON

OXFORD
UNIVERSITY PRESS

OXFORD
UNIVERSITY PRESS

Great Clarendon Street, Oxford, OX2 6DP,
United Kingdom

Oxford University Press is a department of the University of Oxford.
It furthers the University's objective of excellence in research, scholarship,
and education by publishing worldwide. Oxford is a registered trade mark of
Oxford University Press in the UK and in certain other countries

First Edition published in 2019

Published in the United States of America by Oxford University Press
198 Madison Avenue, New York, NY 10016, United States of America

British Library Cataloguing in Publication Data
Data available

Library of Congress Control Number: 2018965754

ISBN 978–0–19–882526–5

Contents

Notes on the Contributors

Cormac Mac Amhlaigh, University of Edinburgh

Andreas Follesdal, University of Oslo

Martin Krygier, University of New South Wales

Fabienne Peter, University of Warwick

Philip Pettit, Princeton University/Australian National University

Jiří Přibáň, Cardiff University

Joseph Raz, Columbia University/King's College London

Nicole Roughan, University of Auckland

Wojciech Sadurski, University of Sydney/University of Warsaw

Michael Sevel, University of Sydney

Kevin Walton, University of Sydney

Paul Weithman, University of Notre Dame

Introduction

Wojciech Sadurski, Michael Sevel, and Kevin Walton

Traditionally, discussions of legitimacy have been about states. The present volume engages with this tradition, but goes beyond it to examine, in addition, the legitimacy of suprastate institutions and norms. Yet consideration of legitimacy in these two contexts obviously raises another issue: what is legitimacy? Part One focuses on this general inquiry. But every contributor is concerned, even if only implicitly, with it.

Here is one aspect of this general inquiry: what *sort* of problem is legitimacy? Some, most notably Max Weber,[1] consider it empirical, some think of it as moral, and some believe it to be both. Philip Pettit, the author of the first chapter, is among those for whom it is a moral problem. According to Pettit, a state is legitimate if its exercise of power over its citizens is morally justified. One contributor who takes legitimacy to be a matter of social fact is Jiří Přibáň, whose chapter is a sociological study of the ambiguous role of values in legitimation of the state. Martin Krygier thinks that both moral and empirical tests must be met for an institution to be legitimate. For Krygier, the legitimacy of the state depends on the perceptions of its citizens plus its moral character.

Pettit not only adopts a moral conception of legitimacy; he also separates the issue of legitimacy from those of justice and authority. The distinction between legitimacy and justice is familiar. Wojciech Sadurski also makes it in his chapter. On this common view, a state can be legitimate without being entirely just and can be illegitimate while being broadly just. The question of legitimacy, Pettit explains, is about the vertical relation between the state and its citizens, whereas the question of justice is about the horizontal relations established by the state between its citizens. In making the further distinction between legitimacy and authority, Pettit gives the former priority over the latter. He takes the question of legitimacy to be more fundamental than the matter of authority and, therefore, crucial for any moral obligation owed to the state by citizens.

What is this moral obligation? It is, Pettit supposes, an obligation on citizens who contest the law to do so in a way that does not involve changing the regime. But most

[1] See Max Weber, *Economy and Society: An Outline of Interpretive Sociology* (Guenther Roth and Claus Wittich eds, Ephraim Fischoff and others trs, University of California Press 1968) 212–301.

Legitimacy: The State and Beyond. First Edition. Edited by Wojciech Sadurski, Michael Sevel, and Kevin Walton. Published 2019 by Oxford University Press.

theorists take a different view: they assume that the obligation is to *obey* the law. For Sadurski, the majority view is ill-suited to the supranational realm, where it should be replaced, in his opinion, by a weaker alternative, according to which those subject to legitimate norms have a moral obligation merely to *respect* them.

Among the many theorists for whom the legitimacy of an authority entails a moral obligation to obey its directives is Joseph Raz, the author of the opening chapter of Part Two. His earlier work features in the contributions of several others, most obviously in Fabienne Peter's response to the objection that Raz's view of legitimate political authority fails to distinguish authority adequately from expertise, in Michael Sevel's extension of Raz's perfectionist-liberal theory of legitimacy to international law, and in Andreas Follesdal's reliance on Raz's conception of authority in his chapter on the legitimacy of international courts.

Another theorist who is mentioned in more than one chapter is John Rawls. Indeed, his treatment of legitimacy in his later work is the exclusive concern of Paul Weithman's contribution, which offers an interpretation of his view. More critical is Sadurski, who dismisses Rawls's account of public reason as a conception of legitimacy in the supranational sphere. Sevel considers his work, too, albeit less directly, when defending Raz's perfectionist brand of liberalism against Martha Nussbaum's Rawlsian critique.

Besides these general issues and the writings of Raz and Rawls, what else do the contributors discuss? Short summaries of their chapters follow.

From the perspective of republicanism, which he defends elsewhere, Pettit looks at theories of state legitimacy of three types: benefit-, merit-, and will-based. Since benefits can be provided by dictators and the merits of a leader cannot be guaranteed, the third, according to which the will of the state must not be dominating for those who live under it, is best, says Pettit. Yet he does not regard all will-based approaches as equal. Of the three that he examines, only the 'control' approach ensures that individuals are not dominated, which means, in his view, that its unwelcome decisions should not be resented, but viewed instead as just 'tough luck'.

In her chapter, Peter replies to Stephen Darwall, who accuses Raz of conflating expertise and legitimate political authority. According to Darwall, such authority depends on a mode of justification involving mutual accountability, which public reason approaches exemplify. The main point of disagreement between Darwall and Raz, says Peter, is not whether expertise is sufficient for legitimate political authority—Raz admits that it is not—but whether, as Raz thinks but Darwall denies, it is necessary. Having clarified the debate, Peter defends the possibility of grounding legitimate political authority in expertise. She thus dismisses Darwall's critique. She concludes, however, that the mode of justification on which he insists is nevertheless important in democratic societies, in which, on many issues, expertise is not available.

The third chapter is, as stated above, an attempt by Weithman to make sense of Rawls's account of legitimacy in his later work. Weithman thinks that the answers to the questions raised by this account are to be found in Rawls's claim, familiar from social contract theory, that political power is the power of the public as a corporate body. In so claiming, Weithman suggests, Rawls follows Immanuel Kant, not

John Locke. Understood as Kantian, his conception of legitimacy is less puzzling, says Weithman, even if some questions persist.

Raz's contribution, which keeps its original character as a talk, is the first of four to focus on the legitimacy of the state. It starts with a question: Do increasing challenges to state sovereignty require legal theory to be re-thought? In response, Raz observes that, despite these challenges, state sovereignty persists, since no alternative is available. He argues that the success of the assortment of international organizations that challenge state sovereignty depends on their ability to attract loyalty, which depends, in turn, on their ability to recognize the truth of pluralism and respond to diverse interests, preferences, and traditions. Perhaps such value-pluralism is best protected by sovereign states, he says.

In the fifth chapter, Nicole Roughan argues that, to be complete, an account of a state's legitimacy must evaluate not only its powers and its institutions, but also its officials. She gives three reasons for separate consideration of the third: officials are not only institutional, but also moral agents; important aspects of legitimacy will be missed unless the legitimacy of officials is examined; and the identity of those who exercise powers and control institutions is a normative matter. She proceeds to indicate that, to be legitimate, officials, having claimed a state's authority, must seek to improve the legitimacy of both its powers and its institutions and, in exercising its authority, must try to behave respectfully towards those subject to its powers and institutions. Roughan finishes by emphasizing that an assessment of the 'micro-legitimacy' of officials is not all that matters in evaluating the legitimacy of a state as one among many claimants of authority.

Krygier begins his chapter on the rule of law and state legitimacy by pointing out that how the rule of law contributes to state legitimacy turns on how the rule of law is understood. Drawing on earlier work, he recommends looking first to its point, which is, in his opinion, to temper the arbitrary exercise of power. Such tempering, he thinks, even if Marxists and others do not, is something without which a state cannot be legitimate. Krygier then queries the assumption of lawyers and legal philosophers that the rule of law depends simply on the formal rules and procedures of states; it also depends, he insists, on the actual and perceived functioning of those rules and procedures, on tempering non-state arbitrariness, and on passing 'Hobbes's test' of effectiveness.

Part Two ends with Přibáň's inquiry into the legitimation of the nation state in a post-national world. He employs systems theory, according to which law is one of many normative systems and the state is one of many societal organizations, to make sense of the role of values in the state's legitimation. He argues that processes of legitimation are constituted by systemic communication between law and politics within and beyond the nation state, communication that involves the internalization of values that are external to these systems. Yet, stresses Přibáň, such values are not transcendental foundations; they are instead internally generated expectations that differentiate between legitimacy and illegitimacies in both politics and law.

Legitimacy beyond the state is the subject of Part Three. In his chapter, Sadurski contends that legitimacy in this sphere should be understood, given the democratic deficit of supranational authorities, as a subject-conferred attribute of specific norms that generates, as previously mentioned, no more than a duty to respect those norms. The conception of this concept of legitimacy that he favours is a public reason one. It is not Rawls's view of public reason in the supranational sphere, which, points out Sadurski, cannot be understood as a conception of legitimacy. Rather, it is what he calls Supranational Public Reason *sensu stricto*, which, he says, not only can be so understood, but can also be detected in the legitimating strategies of supranational bodies such as the European Court of Human Rights.

In the ninth chapter, Cormac Mac Amhlaigh replies to critics of attempts to ground the legitimacy of suprastate institutions in constitutionalism. More specifically, he responds to the objection that suprastate constitutionalism is idealistic due to the improbability of a demos beyond the state. He makes two points: first, the objection relies on a normative understanding of the idea of a demos that is *itself* potentially idealistic and, second, the objection assumes that idealism in normative theory is problematic, which might be doubted.

As already indicated, Sevel examines Raz's perfectionist liberalism, an alternative to liberal neutrality. Sevel notes that perfectionists, unlike neutralists, have done little to extend their view beyond the state to international law and institutions. He wonders whether perfectionist liberalism can be a theory of legitimacy in this sphere. His discussion focuses on the neutralist worry that the moral pluralism and the conception of autonomy that are aspects of Raz's view fail to respect moral diversity and the equal standing of citizens across state boundaries. In particular, he looks at Nussbaum's claim that Raz's liberalism is less stable than Rawls's because it is incompatible with the moral views of many people. Sevel argues that this critique is not persuasive in the state context and, even if it were compelling, it would be less so in the suprastate context, due to well-known attributes of international institutions, including their limited jurisdiction and their limited capacity to enforce their decisions.

Follesdal's contribution concludes Part Three and the volume as a whole. In it, he tries to bring some order to debates about the legitimacy of international courts. His attempt draws on Raz's conception of authority and on cosmopolitan theory. Follesdal argues that this approach can reduce apparent confusion about the legitimacy of international courts by explaining the significance of considerations such as states' consent, states' compliance, and the legality of courts' decisions.

These chapters represent a wide diversity of both established and emerging approaches to the problem of legitimacy. They raise the question of what sort of problem it is. They also explore whether an account of the legitimacy of states is adequate for assessing the legitimacy of suprastate institutions. Do the latter have such distinctive features that a different account is needed? As suprastate institutions evolve, as they have rapidly over the last half-century, further reflection will surely be necessary. That reflection will, we hope, be facilitated by these chapters.

PART I

THEORY OF LEGITIMACY

I

The Control Theory of Legitimacy

*Philip Pettit**

This chapter addresses the problem of legitimacy that every state poses and looks at different grounds on which a state might be thought to be legitimate. As I use the term, the problem of legitimacy is that of morally justifying the way a state exercises monopoly power over its adult, able-minded, more or less permanently resident members: in short, its citizens.[1] It may be that this exercise of power cannot be justified, of course, in which case we can only view the state in question, despite any good qualities it may possess, as an organization on a moral par with a mafia-like agency. But most of us think that it is at least possible for states to wield political power in a more or less legitimate or justifiable way and the challenge is to identify what would make for their legitimacy.

In focusing on this problem, the chapter assumes that there is no issue about whether or not the system under which the world is divided into states is itself justified. History has left us with that system, which is now close to irreversible. Individual states might choose in principle to renounce their power, but in practice none dares to do so, for fear that others would take over its population and territory.[2] They might choose to fuse into larger states, of course—at an unlikely limit, a single world-state—or divide into smaller. But those choices would still preserve the system. That system would cease to obtain only in the vanishingly unlikely event that existing states could agree and entrench an arrangement to let world society operate without anyone exercising political power.

Thus, it makes only speculative sense to ask whether it is justifiable that states should possess the power that they have under the system of states. We have no

* I was greatly helped in revising this chapter by discussion at the conference in Sydney Law School in which the volume originated. I learned in particular from the many astute observations of my commentator, Paul Patton.

[1] I put aside here the difficult issues as to how the citizenry ought to be determined, how those who are not adult or able-minded should be identified, and how the state ought to behave towards them.

[2] Thus, to anticipate later discussion, the choice of a state to remain in existence is not voluntary—there is no acceptable alternative to its doing so—and so it does not impose its own will on its members and does not dominate them by doing so. See Serena Olsaretti, *Liberty, Desert and the Market* (Cambridge University Press 2004); Philip Pettit, *On the People's Terms: A Republican Theory and Model of Democracy* (Cambridge University Press 2012); Philip Pettit, *Just Freedom: A Moral Compass for a Complex World* (WW Norton & Co 2014).

Legitimacy: The State and Beyond. First Edition. Edited by Wojciech Sadurski, Michael Sevel, and Kevin Walton. © Philip Pettit 2019. Published 2019 by Oxford University Press.

practical as distinct from theoretical interest in arguing that the system of states ought or ought not to be in place—that *the* state ought or ought not to exist, as it is often put—since there is no corresponding 'can'; there is no agent to which we can address a suitable prescription.[3] It makes good practical sense, by contrast, to ask whether a particular state is justified in how it exercises the power it has under the system of states. We have a practical interest in knowing the answer, after all, since here there is a 'can' that answers to the implied 'ought': in saying that it ought to exercise its power in a certain manner, we assume that it can be made to do so.

As the focus on morally justifying how a state exercises its power is distinct from an interest in whether the existence of the state is justified, so it is distinct from a concern with how far the social structure that the state uses its power to establish is morally appealing or just. It is possible for a legitimate state not to establish a fully just order and for an illegitimate state to establish an order that is just in broad outline.[4] And so, the two concerns are relatively distinct. Both may be expressed, of course, as concerns with justice. But ours is a concern for the political or vertical justice of the state exercising monopoly power over its citizens, the other a concern with the social or horizontal justice of the relations that the state sets up among its citizenry.[5]

This chapter is in three progressively longer sections. The first distinguishes the legitimacy of a state from the authority that is sometimes ascribed to the state and explains the sort of obligation—the sort of political obligation—that legitimacy imposes on citizens. The second sketches the case for what I describe as a will-based approach to the problem of legitimacy, indicating its advantages over benefit-based and merit-based alternatives. And the third looks at the different forms that this approach may assume.

This last and longest section argues in favour of a version of the will-based approach that has two characteristics: it takes the state to be a proper agency, not just an apparatus that mediates the agency of individuals; and it takes legitimacy to require not that citizens individually consent to the state or enjoy collective command over the state, but that they share equally in imposing a controlling discipline on what the state does in their name. I have defended this control theory elsewhere on premises drawn from the republican tradition of thought.[6] The aim here is not to recapitulate

[3] Of course, we might conceivably want to know whether we should welcome the existence of the system of states on the ground that if it is not the best possible system, it is at least better than the state of nature. It is possible to read Kant's discussion of the state in *The Doctrine of Right* on these lines. See Arthur Ripstein, *Force and Freedom: Kant's Legal and Political Philosophy* (Harvard University Press 2009); Kyla Ebels-Duggan, 'Kant's Political Philosophy' (2012) 7 Philosophy Compass 896.

[4] See A John Simmons, 'Justification and Legitimacy' (1999) 109 Ethics 739; Philip Pettit, 'Justice, Social and Political' in David Sobel, Peter Vallentyne, and Steven Wall (eds), *Oxford Studies in Political Philosophy*, vol 1 (Oxford University Press 2015); Anna Stilz, 'The Value of Self-Determination' in David Sobel, Peter Vallentyne, and Steven Wall (eds), *Oxford Studies in Political Philosophy*, vol 2 (Oxford University Press 2016).

[5] As Martin Krygier points out, the word 'arbitrary' is often used to indict a system of law on both counts: on the one side, for being imposed on an unjustified, wilful basis; on the other, for having an unjustified character or content. See Martin Krygier, 'The Rule of Law: Pasts, Presents, and Two Possible Futures' (2016) 12 Annual Review of Law and Social Science 199.

[6] See Pettit, *On the People's Terms* (n 2); Pettit, *Just Freedom* (n 2); Philip Pettit, 'The General Will, the Common Good, and a Democracy of Standards' in Yiftah Elazar and Geneviève Rousselière (eds), *Republicanism and the Future of Democracy* (Cambridge University Press 2019).

that defence so much as to show that the theory compares favourably with both the alternatives outside and the alternatives inside the will-based family of theories.

A. Legitimacy, Authority, and Political Obligation

1. Legitimacy and authority

The problem of whether a state's exercise of monopoly power is justified or legitimate is distinct from the question as to whether it has the right, on an independent basis, to exercise such power: that is, the right to coerce its citizens into obeying its laws, punish them for disobedience, tax them for resources, and do all of this to the exclusion of any competitor. If its exercise of power can be morally justified, of course, then it may be right that the state should act as it does. And under one or another morally justified system of rights, it may be said then to have the right or authority to impose on members in that particular way. But that is not to ascribe an independent right or authority to the state, only a right relative to that system of rights and that justification.[7]

I take the issue of whether the state's exercise of monopoly power is justified or legitimate, not only to be distinct from the question of whether the state has the independent right to exercise such power, but also to be more basic. On this assumption, the state has a certain authority because it is legitimate, and not the other way around. The assumption marks a difference from any approaches that first try to establish the authority of the state and then aim to derive its legitimacy from its authority.[8]

Those who want to put authority first often do so out of a wish to argue that on that same independent basis citizens have a certain duty or obligation to their state: that they have a duty akin to the directed obligation debtors have to their creditor, or children to their parents. But even if the state is an agent in its own right, as I argue later, the idea that citizens have this sort of independent obligation or duty towards it is not immediately intuitive. They may have a duty of obligation to the state, as we shall now see, only to the extent that the state is legitimate.

2. Legitimacy and political obligation

Suppose that the state exercises its monopoly power legitimately or justifiably; put aside for the moment the fact that legitimacy is bound to come in degrees. What follows about how citizens morally ought to behave: about how it is right that they should treat the state and the state's initiatives? What is the political obligation that goes with the legitimacy of a state?

[7] See Allen Buchanan, *Justice, Legitimacy, and Self-Determination: Moral Foundations for International Law* (Oxford University Press 2002).

[8] See Fabienne Peter, 'Political Legitimacy' in Edward N Zalta (ed), *The Stanford Encyclopedia of Philosophy* (summer 2017 edn) <https://plato.stanford.edu/archives/sum2017/entries/legitimacy/> accessed 16 March 2018.

One possibility is particularly salient, and commonly invoked in the literature.[9] We might say that other things being equal the citizens of a legitimate state ought to obey its laws: that while they may not be obligated towards the state in the directed manner associated with an independent authority, they are obliged in a more general sense to display obedience. The idea is that if the way the state makes and applies law is legitimate, then the compliance of citizens with that law is required *pro tanto*—required other things being equal. On this account, political obligation is nothing more than legal obligation: the obligation to obey the law.

The identification of political with legal obligation is hardly persuasive, however. For the legal obligation of citizens seems to derive from the character of the laws imposed rather than from the legitimacy of the state that imposes them. Even if the state failed to be legitimate, citizens would be plausibly required *pro tanto* to obey established, relatively fair laws. The fairness of the laws would argue in itself for conformity; and this, all the more so, when those laws provide a basis for mutual expectation and coordination among the citizenry. Indeed, if the laws established by a legitimate state were unfair—if they imposed unjust or unequal requirements—then it is not clear that citizens would necessarily be required to obey them; if they were required to obey, that could only be because the unfairness was not significant and the laws played an important coordinating role.[10]

The pairing of legal obligation with the fairness of the laws rather than with the legitimacy of the state is further supported by the fact that non-citizens who reside in the state are obliged equally with citizens to obey the law. There is a sense in which a state does not impose monopoly power on such non-citizens, since they are formally free to leave, assuming they are citizens of another state. And so, we should not expect the legitimacy of the state to be relevant to whether or not they are obliged to obey the law of the country they live in. In their case, then, it is more likely to be the fairness of the established laws, or their role in establishing mutual expectations, that grounds an obligation to obey the law. And if that is the ground of the obligation in their case, it is plausibly the ground in the case of citizens too.[11]

If the state exercises its monopoly power in a way that is justified, then, is there any more distinctive obligation than the obligation to obey the law supported by this legitimacy? Under almost any conceivable political regime, people are going to differ in how far they are satisfied with the laws imposed, having rival interests in what laws there should be and diverging in their opinions about the justice or fairness of competing candidates.[12] The circumstances of politics, as Jeremy Waldron

[9] See Christopher Heath Wellman and A John Simmons, *Is There a Duty to Obey the Law? For and Against* (Cambridge University Press 2005).

[10] There may be a range of reasons apart from the fairness of the laws and their role in grounding mutual expectations for why citizens and other residents should obey the law. See Buchanan, *Justice, Legitimacy, and Self-Determination* (n 7).

[11] Admittedly, there is another possible ground of obligation in the case of non-citizen residents. It may be said that those who choose to reside in a state where they are not citizens, with the permission of the authorities, commit implicitly to conforming with the local laws and regulations. In that case, their commitment to conform would help to explain why they are obliged to obey the laws, and perhaps even to obey unfair laws.

[12] See Thomas Nagel, 'Moral Conflict and Political Legitimacy' (1987) 16 Philosophy and Public Affairs 215.

says, are circumstances of disagreement.[13] That raises a question about the obligations that fall on citizens who disagree with some laws and are disposed to contest them. And it is plausible that the legitimacy of the state has implications for the obligation of citizens in this domain.

If the state were illegitimate, so that its exercise of monopoly power were not justified, then we might say that other things being equal—collateral costs being intuitively acceptable, for example—it would be permissible for citizens to look for radical regime change. If the state was legitimate, however, then changing the regime would seem to be ruled out: it would amount to overthrowing a body that by hypothesis was justified in how it acted. And so, a plausible proposal is that the legitimacy of a state imposes on citizens the conditional obligation, if they contest the law, to contest it within the system: that is, to contest it in a manner that does not require regime change.[14]

We have been putting aside the fact that legitimacy is bound to come in degrees. Taking that fact into account, the proposal supported here is that to the extent to which the state is legitimate, there is an obligation on citizens to contest any public laws or decisions they regard as unjust—or indeed illegitimate in their particular genesis—only within the system. I shall assume in what follows that this conditional, contestatory obligation is the correlate for citizens of any legitimacy enjoyed by their state. That this is the correlated obligation does not presuppose that people ought to contest the laws or decisions with which they disagree, but merely that such contestation is unobjectionable or permissible. And, as noted, it does not presuppose that people ought to seek the overthrow of any illegitimate regime; collateral costs might argue for trying to work for change within the system rather than outside it.

In presupposing the permissibility of contesting a legitimate state only within the system, the proposal naturally suggests that the more or less legitimate state ought to establish ways in which citizens may contest the laws that it enacts or proposes. While any plausible regime will offer citizens many different ways in which they may challenge its laws, there is always one mode of contestation—civil disobedience—that any system is required by its very design to leave in place. This might consist in publicly breaking the law to which you object, and not protesting about your conviction and punishment; such behaviour would communicate, on the basis of shared assumptions, that you oppose the law in question and hold that it should be changed. Or, in a slight variant, it might consist in publicly breaking some other law, not protesting your conviction or punishment, and communicating explicitly that

[13] Jeremy Waldron, *Law and Disagreement* (Oxford University Press 1999).

[14] See Pettit, *On the People's Terms* (n 2) ch 2. Overthrowing the state and achieving radical regime change need not involve armed rebellion. It might take the form, for example, that it took when the American founders proposed the new constitution of 1787 and established it with popular, electoral support; no such change of constitution was possible under the regime as it stood: that is, under the Articles of Confederation that had united the states. But it is possible to take a narrower or wider view of the processes for amending a constitution that are allowed within it. Thus, while a narrower view would suggest that the US constitution can only be amended under Article 5, Akil Amar argues that it would not amount to a rejection of that constitution to amend it under a countrywide majority vote. See Akil Amar, 'Philadelphia Revisited: Amending the Constitution outside Article V' (1988) 55 University of Chicago Law Review 1043.

you are doing this as a means of challenging the law to which you object. Such civil disobedience constitutes a form of contestation within the system, since it does not challenge the power exercised by the state in convicting or punishing you; it does not suggest that the state is illegitimate.

To sum up these observations, then, the legitimacy of a state is fixed by how far its exercise of power over citizens is morally justified. Such legitimacy is distinct from, and more basic than, any independent authority that a state might claim to exercise this power and any independent duty that citizens might be said to have towards the state; and the duty with which it correlates is not an obligation to obey the law, but an obligation on the part of citizens to contest the law, if they contest it, within the system.

B. Benefit-Based, Merit-Based, and Will-Based Theories

1. Three candidate legitimators

Any legitimator of a state, any justifier of how a state exercises its power, should explain why the citizens ought to contest its laws only within the system: why they should seek amendments only in a way that does not require starting again from scratch. Thus, it should explain why citizens ought to seek a change in the constitutional order only under the accepted ways of amending the constitution. Assuming an electoral democracy, it should explain why they ought to seek other changes only at the ballot box or in the courts, in the media, in public demonstrations, or in acts of civil disobedience.

Very broadly, there are three kinds of candidates that might be proposed for the role of state legitimator: the role of providing on its own a sufficient ground for determining legitimacy. One is that the state delivers some significant benefit to citizens, whatever that may be taken to be. A second is that the state is guided by personnel who are suitably meritorious: they enjoy appropriate expertise in the issues they confront and, being equally responsive to every member of the citizenry, they display appropriate virtue. And a third is that the state does not impose an independent will on its citizens: it does not hold them in its power.

In each case, the legitimator may come in degrees and confer legitimacy only in a corresponding measure. But again, for convenience, I shall generally speak as if legitimacy is an on-off property: a feature that the state has or fails to have, period.

2. The republican tradition

There is a long republican tradition of thought under which the first two approaches, respectively benefit-based and merit-based, are not plausible candidates for legitimating the state. I shall draw here on this tradition in order to identify a common failure in the approaches and to provide ground for exploring the will-based approach instead.

The republican tradition begins with figures like Polybius, Cicero, and Livy, who defended the Roman Republic. And it is associated with those in later ages—for example, in the Italian Renaissance, the English revolution, the American war of independence—who took that republic to hold out an ideal for how the state should be organized in their own era. The paramount ideal in these writers was that in a republic all citizens should count as equally free persons. And their guiding institutional assumption was that citizens could only achieve that status if they were protected in the same range of personal choices—the basic liberties, as these were often known—under a mixed constitution: that is, before a law over which they maintain a multi-centred, multi-level, form of more or less equally shared control.[15]

In the Renaissance period, these writers included Machiavelli of the *Discourses on Livy's History*; in the period of the English revolutions, authors such as James Harrington, John Milton, and Algernon Sidney; and in the eighteenth century, radicals like the authors of *Cato's Letters*, American rebels like John Adams and James Madison, and English supporters of the American cause like Joseph Priestley and Richard Price. They uniformly celebrate the idea that being a free citizen means enjoying independence from others in the exercise of the basic liberties that any law should recognize. And they equally support the multi-modular system of government associated with the mixed constitution. Variously interpreted in the tradition, this is an arrangement that distributes power among different authorities, puts those authorities in a position to check and balance one another, and exposes them to the electoral and contestatory power of the people as a whole.

[15] There is now an extended literature on the history and nature of republican thought and on the break that classical liberal modes of thought initiated; for an overview, see Frank Lovett and Philip Pettit, 'Neo-Republicanism: A Normative and Institutional Research Program' (2009) 12 Annual Review of Political Science 18. Contemporary republicanism has its origins in Zera S Fink, *The Classical Republicans: An Essay in the Recovery of a Pattern of Thought in Seventeenth Century England* (Northwestern University Press 1962); Caroline Robbins, *The Eighteenth Century Commonwealthman* (Harvard University Press 1959); and especially JGA Pocock, *The Machiavellian Moment: Florentine Political Theory and the Atlantic Republican Tradition* (Princeton University Press 1975), which first revived interest in the classical republican writers and charted the historical continuity of their political ideas. Quentin Skinner argued in a number of essays, later collected (and somewhat revised) in Quentin Skinner, *Visions of Politics*, vol 2: *Renaissance Virtues* (Cambridge University Press 2002), that these works had failed to recognize that classical republicanism did not endorse an allegedly 'positive' view of freedom as equivalent to a right of participation in government. And building on this insight, Pettit—and Skinner himself—cast the republican conception of freedom as one according to which it is the absence of domination or dependence on the arbitrary will of another, and not the absence of mere interference, that matters. See Philip Pettit, 'Freedom and Antipower' (1996) 106 Ethics 576; Philip Pettit, *Republicanism: A Theory of Freedom and Government* (Oxford University Press 1997); Quentin Skinner, *Liberty before Liberalism* (Cambridge University Press 1998). This idea of freedom as non-domination has become the crucial unifying theme for those who work within the neo-republican framework, although of course within that frame there are also some differences of emphasis and detail. See Philip Pettit, 'Keeping Republican Freedom Simple: On a Difference with Quentin Skinner' (2002) 30 Political Theory 339. For a recent, alternative history of thinking about freedom, see David Schmidtz and Jason Brennan, *A Brief History of Liberty* (Wiley Blackwell 2010).

3. Against the benefit-based approach

The benefit-based approach to legitimating the state is rejected in this long tradition on the basis of a spectre that became particularly salient in the eighteenth century: that of the benevolent despot. The idea was that if the benefit provided by a state could legitimate it as a regime, then the dictatorship of a well-disposed monarch—say, a dictatorship that delivered a just and efficient system of law—would be legitimate. And that was taken in this tradition to be utterly implausible, even absurd.

Freedom in the sense in which it requires independence from others in the exercise of the basic liberties implies that no slave can be free, not even one whose master is wholly benevolent; if the slave may choose to act as he or she wishes, this is only possible so long as that is the wish of the master. Any master or *dominus*, no matter how indulgent, has the power to interfere at will with his or her slaves in the exercise of their basic liberties. And this *dominatio*, as the Romans called it,[16] is enough to put the will of the master in control. Freedom requires the absence of such domination, then, not just the absence of the interference it might make possible. It requires that so far as possible no one has the power of interfering at will in a person's exercise of their basic liberties: that is, in the exercise of suitably established, suitably extensive choices that each can exercise without detriment or disadvantage to others.[17] Thus, in the words of Algernon Sidney, writing in the seventeenth century, 'he is a slave who serves the best and gentlest man in the world, as well as he who serves the worst'.[18]

This republican understanding of freedom implies that to live under a dictator, no matter how benevolent, is to be effectively a slave of that authority. Even if you can exercise a suitable range of basic liberties under such a regime, your access to those liberties—your access to a law that defines and defends them—is dependent on the willingness of the ruler to establish them. And, of course, your unhindered exercise of the liberties that are actually established is dependent equally on the ruler's willingness to allow you in particular to benefit from them in the same manner as others. This means that in relation to the ruler you are in the position of a slave: a lucky slave, to be sure, but still a slave.

The supporters of the American cause in the eighteenth century took up this theme when they challenged the legitimacy of British Colonial Rule, as it had come to be conceptualized and practised in the previous decade. The Westminster Parliament may have proved itself to be gentle and benevolent when, in response to American complaints, it withdrew the Stamp Act in 1766. But at the same time, it claimed in the Declaratory Act, as it was called, that it enjoyed the status of a master; it asserted as 'of right' that it had 'full power and authority to make laws and statutes' to bind the Americans. This is one of the things that particularly enraged the colonists, conscious as they would have been that as a people they were then no

[16] See Frank Lovett, *A General Theory of Domination and Justice* (Oxford University Press 2010) app.
[17] See Pettit, *On the People's Terms* (n 2).
[18] Algernon Sidney, *Discourses Concerning Government* (Liberty Classics 1990) 441.

better than slaves in relation to the British. Richard Price expressed their grievance particularly well. Commenting that individuals under the power of masters 'cannot be denominated free, however equitably and kindly they may be treated', he argued that the same lesson applied to societies like Great Britain and its colonies: 'This is strictly true of communities', he said, 'as well as of individuals'.[19]

Assuming a suitable conception of the basic liberties, it is surely plausible that freedom in the republican sense, freedom as non-domination in the exercise of these liberties, is an ideal we ought all to cherish.[20] And it is equally plausible that the benevolent dictatorship, whether it be that of an individual, an elite, or a colonial power, is a form of subjection or slavery that compromises people's freedom. This being so, it is hard to see how the mere fact that a state produces various benefits can justify the way in which it exercises power and thereby establish its legitimacy.

No matter what the benefits it produces, then, a state may resemble a benevolent dictatorship in the way in which it exercises power and may count as a dominating presence in its people's lives. And when a state has this profile, it is hard to see why the subjects should be morally obliged to operate within the system, even when there are no collateral reasons to refrain from seeking regime change. Perhaps Kant is the only otherwise liberal philosopher who ever held that, regardless of domination by the state, its people were always obliged to operate within the system. He argued that the subjects of any government, even a government that behaves 'tyrannically', should only enjoy the freedom of the pen: the freedom to try to persuade the ruler to act differently, but not to call 'by word or deed' for a change of regime.[21]

The complaint about the benevolent dictator supports a critique of many different sorts of arrangements, each identifying a different benefit that a state might achieve for its citizenry. The fact that a particular state promotes the aims of citizens more effectively than those citizens could themselves promote them;[22] the fact that the state is epistemically reliable in the judgements of fact and value that it makes;[23] the fact that by selecting rulers by lottery it allows power to rotate on an impartial basis;[24] or the fact that it delivers a form of governance that could be justified to reasonable citizens:[25] these will all fail, at least on their own, to justify the state's exercise of power.[26] For, regardless of the advantages for citizens, the state's exercise

[19] Richard Price, *Political Writings* (Cambridge University Press 1991) 77–78.

[20] Whether or not non-domination is used to define freedom, of course, it may still be regarded as an ideal worth promoting in social life. The argument in the chapter is strictly independent, then, of the republican linkage between non-domination and freedom.

[21] Immanuel Kant, *Practical Philosophy* (Mary J Gregor tr and ed, Cambridge University Press 1996) 298–392. For an argument in support of a more congenial reading of Kant, see Ripstein, *Force and Freedom* (n 3).

[22] See Joseph Raz, *The Morality of Freedom* (Oxford University Press 1986).

[23] See David Estlund, *Democratic Authority: A Philosophical Framework* (Princeton University Press 2007).

[24] See Alexander A Guerrero, 'Against Elections: The Lottocratic Alternative' (2014) 42 Philosophy and Public Affairs 135.

[25] See John Rawls, *Political Liberalism* (Columbia University Press 1993).

[26] The different proposals gestured at in this paragraph are loosely characterized as legitimating the state by reference to a benefit it provides, and the different authors cited are only loosely associated with those proposals. The list is meant to be indicative only of the different directions that a benefit-based approach might take.

of power may still be objectionable on the most basic of grounds, namely, that it puts those citizens severally as well as collectively under the rule of an independent will; it makes them into slaves, albeit slaves of a relatively benign master.[27]

While these and other benefits might not be sufficient for legitimating a state, however, it might be asked if they are necessary for legitimacy. Without considering the question properly, it is worth noting that on the approach defended later in the chapter, they are not necessary in one sense, but they are in another. They are not necessary in the sense that they are not part of what determines or grounds legitimacy: the fact, according to the line taken, that the state is under the equally shared control of the people. But, still, some of them may be necessary in the sense that it is barely conceivable that the state might be controlled in that way without delivering such benefits. They may not themselves help to ground legitimacy, but still be entailed by the realization of its proper ground.

4. Against the virtue-based approach

As resources provided by the republican tradition enable us to challenge any benefit-based candidate for legitimating a state, so they also make it possible to challenge any merit-based candidate for that role. An example of such a candidate is provided recently by Daniel Bell in his defence of what he describes as the China model.[28] This is a model of how state authorities might be selected that idealizes current practices in the People's Republic of China. The idea is that a state's exercise of power would be justified if it was guided by those who proved meritorious or worthy by the standard of such practices: they proved not only to have the expertise required for governing well, but also the virtue to govern impartially.

Assume for the moment that we could rely on a ruler or set of rulers to be suitably expert and, in particular, to be virtuous or impartial. Would that really support the claim that the state is legitimate? The suggestion is that even if the benevolence of a dictatorial ruler or set of rulers—presumptively, expert or knowledgeable rulers—would not be enough to make the state legitimate, their virtue would.

There is indeed a difference worth registering between the benevolent and the virtuous ruler. For a ruler might be benevolent as a result of certain contingencies: for example, the happy accident of wanting to be remembered kindly in history. But a ruler would not be virtuous if the benevolence they displayed were dependent on that sort of contingency. In order to count as virtuous, we may suppose, they would have to be disposed to be benevolent, not just as things actually stand—not just so long as they want to enjoy historical esteem—but robustly over variations in the personal attraction or ease of displaying such goodwill. In short, they would have

[27] A critique that converges with this complaint is that in benignly imposing on its citizens the state usurps their judgements about what is in their interest and, assuming a paternalistic role, does not recognize or respect them as autonomous subjects. See Seana Shiffrin, 'Paternalism, Unconscionability Doctrine, and Accommodation' (2000) 29 Philosophy and Public Affairs 205.

[28] Daniel A Bell, *The China Model: Political Meritocracy and the Limits of Democracy* (Princeton University Press 2015).

to be robustly benevolent.[29] In a phrase of Niko Kolodny's, they would have to be 'resolutely disposed',[30] not just disposed in a more or less adventitious manner, to deal benevolently with subjects.

Would this virtue in rulers do more than mere benevolence to secure the freedom of citizens who live under their power, gaining access to a protected range of basic liberties by grace of their goodwill? The problem with the benevolent dictator is that citizens depend on the ruling will remaining unchanged in order to enjoy their basic liberties, so that in that sense they are subject to that will; let it change and their access to the basic liberties may cease. Is there a similar problem with the virtuous dictator? Or does the dispositional robustness of virtue make for a crucial difference?

I do not think that it does. For even if the rulers were virtuously or robustly disposed to deal well and fairly with the citizens, they would still be liable to lose that disposition or liable not to manifest it on this or that occasion. Consistently with deserving the name of virtue, it could not be hard-wired into their make-up and could not deprive them of choice, making them into involuntary do-gooders. Thus, like the rest of us, they would be exposed to the possibility of corruption, on the one side, and more or less spasmodic episodes of *akrasia*—weakness of will—on the other. And that means that the citizenry would still depend on the will of the rulers for being able to access and exercise the basic liberties established in law. If that will failed to be virtuous, whether permanently or occasionally, they would cease to enjoy that benefit. The virtuous dictator may behave well more reliably than the merely benevolent counterpart, but citizens would still depend on the survival of the dictator's goodwill and still be subject to domination.

This critique of the virtuous dictator extends to any regime where the exercise of power is supposed to be legitimated by the virtue of those in authority. As mentioned, it would lose force if the authorities were supposed to be incapable of losing their virtue, or acting against it, and in that respect not to be as other human beings. But such a supposition would be fantastical. And in any case, it is a long republican theme that far from the power of office tending to support or even elicit virtue in rulers, it usually has the effect of corrupting them. Providing new opportunities for abuse, and often providing a better prospect for hiding any abuse practised, power tends to destroy virtue rather than maintain it. Lord Acton gave expression to a lesson long rehearsed in the tradition when he said: 'Power tends to corrupt, and absolute power corrupts absolutely.'[31]

This lesson about the effects of power has strong empirical support in the social science of regulation.[32] And equally it is borne out in the long history of politics, where patrimonial interests have always threatened to corrupt politics.[33] While most

[29] See Philip Pettit, *The Robust Demands of the Good: Ethics with Attachment, Virtue, and Respect* (Oxford University Press 2015).

[30] Niko Kolodny, 'Rule over None II: Social Equality and the Justification of Democracy' (2014) 42 Philosophy and Public Affairs 287, 295.

[31] Letter from Lord Acton to Archbishop Creighton (5 April 1887) accessed 10 October 2018.

[32] See Pettit, *Republicanism* (n 15) ch 7.

[33] See Francis Fukuyama, *The Origins of Political Order: From Prehuman Times to the French Revolution* (Farrar, Straus and Girous 2011).

republican thinkers celebrated the presence of civic virtue in rulers, none thought that we could rely on its surviving in the presence of unchecked power. Part of the reason for seeking a multi-modular, contestatory form of constitution, indeed, was that it promised to keep the authorities in check, even if their civic virtue wilted. It was with this in mind that republicans endorsed the idea, in an eighteenth-century phrase, that the price of liberty is eternal vigilance: that freedom can prosper only when citizens relentlessly interrogate and invigilate those in authority.

5. Towards a will-based approach

You do not have to sign up to the republican way of thinking in order to appreciate the problems cited in these critiques. All you have do is to endorse the central idea that it is hard to see how the state's exercise of power over its citizens is going to be justified, if things are organized so that the state can interfere at will in determining people's liberties or protecting the exercise of those liberties. The only point in rehearsing the long republican support for this idea is to indicate that it is not a contemporary invention, let alone an idea that I am proposing on the basis of special insight. There is a natural disposition in our species to resent subjection to the will of others.[34] And it is important to be able to show that we join an established way of thinking about legitimacy when we argue that, regardless of its commitment to benevolence or virtue, no state can be justified in its exercise of power if the constitution of that power means that it dominates its people: it enjoys a position where, notwithstanding any benevolence or virtue in the rulers, it can interfere at will in their lives.

This critique not only teaches a negative lesson for benefit-based and virtue-based theories of legitimacy. It also supports a positive lesson for how legitimacy may be achieved. It suggests that a state is going to count as legitimate if the will it enacts is not dominating for any of the individuals who live under it. Such a state has to establish a suitable range of basic liberties for each—otherwise its citizens will certainly be dominated by it—and for that same reason it must entrench these against its own capacity to interfere at will in how they are defined or exercised. And while it may pursue other objectives too, it must also pursue these in a non-dominating way.

But how could a state do its job and not dominate its citizens? One abstract possibility might be that it does not operate on the basis of will at all, only as a natural force or only under the impetus of an invisible hand. That possibility can be rapidly dismissed, however, since nothing of that kind could carry out the tasks of the state in enacting and adjusting law, in administering the application of that law, and in adjudicating and penalizing breaches.[35]

[34] See Philip Pettit, 'The Domination Complaint' (2005) 86 Nomos 87; Philip Pettit, 'Republicanism across Cultures' in Jun-Hyeok Kwak and Leigh Jenco (eds), *Republicanism in Northeast Asia* (Routledge 2014).

[35] Some thinkers occasionally idealize the rule of common law on the grounds that it operates in the manner of a non-intentional force for good. See FA Hayek, *The Fatal Conceit: The Errors of Socialism* (WW Bartley III ed, University of Chicago Press 1988).

Another abstract possibility is that the state might operate under the direction of a robot that does not have a will of any kind, but is designed to do all that citizens might wish.[36] But this also is a possibility we can dismiss. The most ideally designed robot could not possibly keep up to date in adjusting the law to cope with cultural and technological changes, and changes in people's sense of their own interests: for example, their interest in being able to enjoy this or that sort of liberty. And even if it could do these things, there would still be an issue of legitimacy about how such a robotic rule should be established and, once it is in place, how questions may be raised and decisions made about whether to keep it in place: unless this is possible, then later generations will be subject to the will of those who introduced robotic rule in the first place.

With these abstract possibilities put aside, we turn in the final section to explore the possibility that while there is a will behind what the state does, that will need not be a dominating presence in the lives of citizens. But before we do so, it is important to identify and defend an assumption on the basis of which the inquiry will proceed. This is the assumption that the state is an agent in its own right and, in particular, an agent capable of dominating its citizens.[37]

6. The state as agent

There are good reasons for assuming that the state has agential status.[38] An agent is any system that forms more or less reliable representations of the environment it can affect and more or less reliably acts for the realization of identifiable goals in the environment as it represents it. Thus, it generally takes advantage of the opportunities that present themselves for action and takes account of the means and obstacles in view. Even a little household robot that scans its surrounds and acts on the basis of its representations or judgements to effect one single purpose—say, to put the furniture in a particular order at the end of each day—counts in that sense as an agent.

[36] For consideration of this possibility, see Jake Zuehl, *Collective Self-Determination* (PhD thesis, Princeton University 2016); Rainer Forst, 'Die neue republikanische Maschine. Zue Unabdinbarkeit des kantischen Republikanismus' in Violetta L Waibel and Margit Ruffing (eds), *Nature and Freedom: Proceedings of the 12th International Kant Congress* (Walter De Gruyter 2018).

[37] This assumption is not accepted on all sides, although it is all too rarely addressed. Allen Buchanan may reject it when he maintains that the state is an 'institutional structure', such that it would be conceptually incoherent to imagine that subjects might owe obedience to it. See Buchanan, *Justice, Legitimacy, and Self-Determination* (n 7) 691. And Niko Kolodny may reject it in voicing the thought—misleading though he takes it in certain ways to be—that 'the state, once the robes and badges are peeled off, is just other people'. See Niko Kolodny, 'Political Rule and its Discontents' in David Sobel, Peter Vallentyne, and Steven Wall (eds), *Oxford Studies in Political Philosophy*, vol 2 (Oxford University Press 2015) 65. Elsewhere, however, Kolodny argues that it is subordination or social inferiority that is objectionable, not domination as such, and social inferiority would not be threatened by the power of the state as such, only by the power of individuals. See Kolodny, 'Rule over None II' (n 30); Niko Kolodny, 'Rule over None I: What Justifies Democracy?' (2014) 42 Philosophy and Public Affairs 287. From my perspective, that in itself should raise doubts about the importance of non-subordination as distinct from non-domination.

[38] See Christian List and Philip Pettit, *Group Agency: The Possibility, Design and Status of Corporate Agents* (Oxford University Press 2011).

Without going into the theory of how group agents can form, it should be clear that groups can incorporate as agents insofar as members go along with a procedure for determining group purposes and judgements, and commit to acting as required of them individually, under accepted protocols. The state clearly displays this sort of agential pattern in both the national and international arenas, with its officials seeking—perhaps conditional on the acquiescence of citizens—to act for identifiable purposes according to suitably formed judgements about the world it occupies. It will do this insofar as it ensures that the law assumes a coherent form across constitutional, statutory, judicial, and executive determinations. And it will do it, more generally, insofar as it pursues various objectives or policies, domestic and global.[39]

Not every agent is capable of dominating others, in particular individuals like us. In order to have the power of interfering at will—or more or less at will—in your choices, an agent will have to know what choice is, will have to be able to identify the options before you in any choice, and will have to have the capacity to choose to interfere with those options, depending on what it wishes. Thus, it will have to have the ability, depending on its wishes, to decide for or against removing an option, for or against replacing it by a penalized alternative, or for or against misrepresenting it to you, whether by deception or manipulation.

Any individual is liable to have this ability in relation to one or another choice on your part. And so, any number of individuals who are incorporated as an agent are liable to have this ability too. They will inherit the required conceptual capacities from their members, being able to recognize that you face choices in which interference is possible, and they may very well have the ability to interfere as a group, particularly in light of the power conferred by incorporation. Being group agents of this character, then, states are certainly liable to have the ability to interfere in your choices, especially if you are a citizen, as they are liable to have an ability to interfere in the choices of other states and of group agents besides states.

It may be thought that any dominating power of interference that the state has in your life as a citizen is bound ultimately to involve a dominating power on the part of one or another particular agent. And if that thought is sound, then it would follow that in order for a state to be legitimate—in order for it not to enjoy dominating power—all that is needed is that no individuals, in particular no officials of the state, have such power.

Without going into the theory of group agency, it should be clear that this thought is misleading. In order to dominate others, officials would have to have a power of interfering at will in their lives; they would have to have a choice about whether to interfere or not. That means that they would have to be able to interfere voluntarily: they would have to be able to practise or refrain from interference, depending on their wishes: neither option involves significant difficulties or incurs significant costs.[40] But where the state requires officials on pain of its incoherence as an agent to impose a certain law or policy, they will not generally impose it on a voluntary

[39] On the theory of group agency assumed here, see ibid; Philip Pettit, 'Group Agents are not Expressive, Pragmatic or Theoretical Fictions' (2014) 11 Erkenntnis 79.

[40] See Olsaretti, *Liberty, Desert and the Market* (n 2).

basis. The alternative of not imposing it would presumably trigger significant costs for them, putting their very position in peril. Thus, they will be in the position exemplified by judges who say that they have no choice but to interpret the law thus and so or to impose such and such a sentence: they do so involuntarily and, as it well may be, with great reluctance.

This being so, it is going to be necessary to ensure not just that the exercise of state power does not entail the domination of some by the will of one or another official, but also that it does not entail domination by the state itself. Individual officials might not dominate people even when the state they serve does dominate them. The laws and regulations of a dominating state might evolve, as under an independent will, without any of its agents having the power as individuals to exercise interference according to their own wishes.

C. Mapping the Will-Based Approach

There are many approaches that acknowledge the presence of will in the actions of the state, but still maintain that the state need not dominate its citizens. These divide on lines familiar from the history of political theory. One approach says that the state will be un-dominating and legitimate just in case individuals consent to its rule in their lives. Another says that it will be un-dominating and legitimate just in case the people as a body—the people as a group agent—enjoy command over everything the state does, or at least over everything it does in the domain of legislation, which has traditionally been taken to be more important than other domains. And a third, my favoured approach, holds that it will pass those tests just in case individuals share equally in controlling what the state does: specifically, in controlling it to the point where no one has ground for resentment when it happens to pass unwelcome initiatives.

1. The consent version

The consent approach to the legitimacy issue supposes, in a tag from Roman law, that no one is injured or wronged—and so no one suffers dominating interference—when they consent to what is done to them: *injuria non fit volenti*.[41] There are two variants of the approach. One insists on the importance of consensually entering a relevant arrangement; the other emphasizes the importance of consensually staying there, where this is ensured by the permanent possibility of exit.

The pure form of the entry-centred approach would require citizens to endorse unanimously every action of the state or at least every legislative action: this, because

[41] The Roman tag presupposes under a natural interpretation that the injury done is done intentionally. Domination is not an intentional injury, since you may dominate me by virtue of your power of interference without wanting to have such power. But interference is presumptively intentional, of course, and if it does not constitute an injury then that must be because it is not imposed in a dominating way.

of an assumption that legislation is at the source of all other state activity. It would give every individual a power of veto over any relevant initiative taken by the state. This is clearly infeasible under real-world conditions and we may put it aside.

An alternative form of the entry-centred approach would require citizens not to endorse every action of the state unanimously, legislative or otherwise, but to endorse unanimously the majoritarian rule of a sovereign assembly of the citizens, or the rule of an individual or committee that is established as sovereign by a majority vote of the assembly. Hobbes,[42] Locke,[43] and Rousseau[44] all adopt this approach, although they differ on associated requirements.[45] Their main difference consists in the fact that Hobbes allows the assembly to transfer its sovereignty to an elite committee or an individual monarch; Locke thinks that such a transfer—not his word—can always be retracted when a majority rise up against such a sovereign; and Rousseau denies that a transfer would ever be acceptable.

The requirement of such indirect unanimity is as infeasible as the requirement of direct unanimity. And it is subject to the added difficulty that entering a contract voluntarily does not guard against being dominated within the relationship set up by that contract. This lesson was traditionally illustrated by the possibility of the slave contract, which had had a marginal presence in classical Rome. Someone would enter the contract more or less voluntarily in order to achieve a certain benefit—say, the benefit for a foreigner of being taken to live in Rome. But in subjecting themselves to the domination of the other they would trade away their freedom. The slave contract made vivid the possibility of suffering domination in a relationship, despite having consented to entering that relationship.

These unanimity-based proposals, direct and indirect, all put emphasis on the ways in which individuals enter into relations with the state, whether in submitting to a particular law, or submitting to an arrangement for law-making. An alternative sort of proposal would invest, not in any such entry condition, but rather in a condition of exit. The idea would be that if citizens are free to leave a state in the event of its proving objectionable—in particular, to leave it for a state that was not similarly objectionable—it follows that when they stay, they stay consensually. They effectively consent, if not to every law and policy, at least to the general arrangement for making law and policy.

This proposal parallels the familiar claim that in a market where workers could exit any particular employment relationship—this, of course, might be only a

[42] Thomas Hobbes, *Human Nature and De Corpore Politico: The Elements of Law, Natural and Politic* (Oxford University Press 1994); Thomas Hobbes, *On the Citizen* (Richard Tuck and Michael Silverthorne trs and eds, Cambridge University Press 1998).

[43] John Locke, *Two Treatises of Government* (Cambridge University Press 1960).

[44] Jean-Jacques Rousseau, *The Social Contract and Other Later Political Writings* (Victor Gourevitch ed, Cambridge University Press 1997).

[45] Strictly, Hobbes takes the approach ascribed only in *Human Nature and De Corpore Politico* (n 42) and *On the Citizen* (n 42). In the later *Leviathan* (Richard Tuck ed, Cambridge University Press 1991), he also seems to envisage the possibility of individuals unanimously consenting to be ruled by an individual or a committee without recourse to majority voting in an assembly of the whole.

utopian possibility—they would not be subject to domination by any employer; if they stayed with an employer, that would be by their own continuing consent.[46]

The proposal might work in principle, but it is utterly infeasible in practice. Whatever difficulties there may be with the idea of a market where workers could freely move between jobs, they are overwhelmed by the difficulties facing any proposal that would rely on citizens being able to move between countries. As in the market case, there would likely be great costs associated with moving, so that the employer or state would have the upper hand. But every country has to control its borders, since it could not otherwise maintain the monopoly power of a state. And so, things would actually be worse here than in the market case. In a world where there are no stateless territories, people cannot possibly be guaranteed the capacity, should they wish, to move elsewhere.

But even if every state gave its citizens freedom of exit, and every state allowed anyone to enter, that might still not help individuals. For every state might dominate its members, as every firm in a market might dominate its workers.[47] In such a world, things would be organized so that domination was inevitable among people; their only choice would be a choice between living under this or that dominating regime. The arrangement might not be dominating as such, not being imposed by anyone's will, but it would facilitate, indeed necessitate, domination; it would be structurally, not agentially, dominating.[48]

2. The command version

The approaches that invoke consent all require that how the state operates should conform to the wills of its individual citizens, thereby ensuring against domination. But there is another approach according to which it is going to be enough if the citizens establish a shared will about how the state should exercise its power and impose that will on the state.

Rousseau is at the origin of this approach too, for he thinks that it is necessary not only that the majority vote of the assembly should rule on the basis of unanimous consent, but also that it should rule in such a way that it expresses what he describes as the general will of the people.[49] Thus he moves the focus from individual will to collective will, arguing that what is also needed in order for people to control the will of the state, and to escape an illegitimate form of political domination, is that they form a general will and let this determine what the state does, at least in the sphere of

[46] See Philip Pettit, 'Freedom in the Market' (2006) 5 Politics, Philosophy and Economics 131; Robert S Taylor, 'Market Freedom as Antipower' (2013) 107 American Political Science Review 593; Robert S Taylor, *Exit Left: Markets and Mobility in Republican Thought* (Oxford University Press 2017).

[47] See Alex Gourevitch, *From Slavery to the Cooperative Commonwealth: Labor and Republican Liberty in the Nineteenth Century* (Cambridge University Press 2014).

[48] See Pettit, *On the People's Terms* (n 2); Pettit, *Just Freedom* (n 2).

[49] See Jean-Jacques Rousseau, *The Discourses and Other Early Political Writings* (Victor Gourevitch ed, Cambridge University Press 1997). For an argument that the two parts of this package pull against one another, raising the spectre of a dilemma, see Philip Pettit, 'Rousseau's Dilemma' in Avi Lifschitz (ed), *Engaging with Rousseau: Reception and Interpretation from the Eighteenth Century to the Present* (Cambridge University Press 2016).

legislation. The command approach to legitimacy, as envisaged here, would suggest that such command over the state is not just necessary for its legitimacy, but sufficient too; it does not have to be based in unanimous consent.

The main problem with this approach is well recognized in the literature. On any conceivable way of determining the shared will of the people—the general will, in Rousseau's terminology—it is almost certain that some individuals will not share in that will. And that means that while the state may be governed by the collective will of the people—while it may not dominate them collectively—it is likely to dominate at least some of them individually. Certainly, it will dominate those who do not share in the purportedly collective will.[50]

Rousseau thought that the general will could be determined by majority voting provided that three conditions were met: (1) voting is confined to matters of general law where personal or factional interests are less likely to influence citizens; (2) the citizens are well advised and informed on all relevant issues; and (3) when they vote, they think as members of the people, not as self-interested or faction-bound individuals. When these conditions are fulfilled, he holds that the general will expressed in majority voting is likely to be the will of each individual, existing side by side with his or her particular will, and that members of the defeated minority can think of themselves as having been mistaken about the general aspect of their will. If in such a case 'the opinion contrary to my own prevails', he writes in *The Social Contract*, 'it proves nothing more than that I made a mistake and that what I took to be the general will was not'.[51]

There are a number of problems with this proposal. One is that majority voting among individually consistent voters does not guarantee consistency of judgement when the issues in question are logically connected with one another, as many laws will be.[52] But even if that were not a problem, it is hard to see why the members of a minority on any issue should have to regard the will of the majority as truly their will: this, at any rate, without endorsing a dubious doctrine of what constitutes someone's 'real' or 'true' will.[53] And even if this in turn were not problematic—even if minority voters could be persuaded of the effect alleged in a case where Rousseau's

[50] The problem discussed here does not affect those who want to argue, like Anna Stilz, that there is a workable sense of self-determination that should be taken as a relevant value, at least in matters of international justice. See Stilz, 'The Value of Self-Determination' (n 4).

[51] Rousseau, *The Social Contract* (n 44) IV.2.8. This reading of Rousseau, under which it is important that the general will is my will, is not uncontroversial, of course. But I am interested primarily in the view that each of us can share in the will behind the law, whether or not Rousseau was explicitly committed to it.

[52] See Philip Pettit, 'Deliberative Democracy and the Discursive Dilemma' (2001) 11 Philosophical Issues 268. This is the discursive dilemma, as I have called it. Suppose you, Mary, and I vote on whether p, whether q, and whether p&q. Mary and you may vote for p, Mary and I for q, and only Mary for p&q, yielding the inconsistent majority judgements that p, that q, and that not-p&q. For a generalization to an impossibility theorem in the aggregation of judgements, see Christian List and Philip Pettit, 'Aggregating Sets of Judgments: An Impossibility Result' (2002) 18 Economics and Philosophy 89; and for later work in this area, see Christian List and Ben Polak, 'Symposium on Judgment Aggregation' (2010) 145 Journal of Economic Theory 441. For background to the discursive dilemma, see Lewis A Kornhauser and Lawrence A Sager, 'The One and the Many: Adjudication in Collegial Courts' (1991) 81 California Law Review 1 on the doctrinal paradox in law.

[53] See Isaiah Berlin, *Two Concepts of Liberty* (Oxford University Press 1958).

conditions are satisfied—they would surely have good reason in many situations to think that the conditions are not satisfied: that the majority vote is driven by factional interests and is not in any sense their will.[54]

3. The control version

We have looked at two broad versions of the will-based approach to legitimacy. Under the consent account, citizens have to give their individual consent to how the state rules, whether by voluntarily entering it or by voluntarily staying put: that is, staying put in the presence of a viable exit option. Under the command account, citizens have to share in a single will as to what laws should be in place and install this in the operation of the state: ideally, they should establish their assembly as the legislature.

Neither the entry-centred consent approach nor the command approach would seem to deliver what is required: a guarantee that individuals are not dominated under state rule. And even if the exit-centred consent approach would guarantee this, it shares with the other proposals the problem that it is manifestly infeasible. The fact that someone is allowed to leave their state does not imply that they will be allowed to enter any other state, and in a state-bound Earth, that means that they cannot have an effective right of exit. In any case exit would enable them to avoid domination, only if there were a non-dominating regime that they were in a position to enter; it would not be enough to have the freedom to enter dominating alternatives.

But there is a third way of thinking about how a state might be forced to conform to the wills of its members. This requires that the citizens should share equally in controlling the state: that is, in imposing suitable constraints or terms on how the state exercises its power over them. The idea is that such constraints can ensure that the state's power of interfering in the lives of citizens is not dominating. The state may impose laws coercively and exclusively of rival authorities, it may dictate the basic liberties that citizens are to enjoy under those laws, and it may forcibly tax citizens for the resources it needs to pursue its goals. But it would do these things, so the idea goes, under such constraints that it does not dominate its citizens.

4. The guiding idea in the approach

The idea behind the control version of the will-based theory of legitimacy is motivated by examples of everyday relationships in which you allow someone to make certain decisions for you without that person counting as a dominator. Suppose that you no longer want to indulge your occasional impulses to travel at weekends to foreign places—it is costing you more than you would like—and that you give me your passport, instructing me to return it to you only at a week's notice. In such a case, I have and exercise a certain power over you when in response to

[54] See Pettit, 'Rousseau's Dilemma' (n 49).

your impulsive request I refuse to hand over the passport and thereby stop you flying abroad on a particular weekend. Do I dominate you in virtue of having that power? Surely not. My power is constrained according to your will, so that my interference in refusing you the passport does not impose an independent will in your life.

One dis-analogy between this case and the case of the state is that none of us sets up the state as an entity with a power of interfering in our lives. In that respect, your relationship to the state is very different from the relationship with me in the passport case. But even if you do not set up that relationship, the existence of the relationship is the irreversible legacy of history, not the effect of anyone's interference or domination, whether in the past or the present. And given that you need have no problem about the existence of the relationship, you may hope to achieve in your dealings with the state the same sort of un-dominated status that you enjoy in dealing with me. There is a possibility, at least in principle, that how the state behaves towards you can be constrained in the same way, and to the same welcome effect, as my behaviour in relation to you.

But a second dis-analogy suggests that this possibility may not be available in practice. This consists in the fact that whereas you are the only subject over whom I have a power of interference, you are only one of many over whom the state has a power of interference. Hence you cannot expect to be able to impose constraints on the state that govern its relationship with you independently of the effect on its relationship with others. You cannot expect, for example, to be able to constrain the state not to harm certain of your interests, if that constraint would be disadvantageous to others.

This dis-analogy need not be fatal, however, to the proposal. For the fact that you are born into a society with others, and the fact that others have the same interest in constraining the state, is not a condition that is imposed on you by a dominating agency; even more than the existence of the state, it is a fact about which you can have no complaint.

That being so, you cannot plausibly complain about being able to constrain the state's exercise of power in relation to you only in a manner that equally constrains its power in relation to others. To look for a special degree of constraint over the state would be to look for a dominating relationship to others of the very kind that you seek to avoid in your own relationship to the state. Thus, I assume here that whatever legitimacy requires, it requires it equally for all and that we need only be concerned with arrangements for controlling or constraining the state that assume such equality.

Suppose, then, that the state could be constrained in how it is allowed to act towards you, albeit constrained only in a manner that benefits others in the same way it benefits you. Might such constraints have the effect of removing domination from the way in which the state interferes in your life and the life of other citizens? A third dis-analogy with the original passport case appears at this point. For while you voluntarily set up the terms under which I can return your passport—you propose that I can only return it at a week's notice—you and others will not have set up constraints on the state in the same voluntary way. Given the circumstances of disagreement that characterize politics, there is no way, for example, in which you might all have unanimously agreed to the constraints to be imposed.

The response to this final dis-analogy is that, notwithstanding the considerable difficulty involved, it may be possible to identify constraints that, despite not being agreed by everyone, have at least these two characteristics. First, they are generated under a system of influence to which everyone has equal access. And second, they are constraints that everyone is ready to accept or support. Such a system of equally accessible, equally acceptable influence—such a system of equally shared control—would hold out the promise of constraining the state in a way that everyone ought to welcome, or at least everyone who is prepared to accept that they must live on equal terms with others. And such a pattern of constraint might be efficacious enough to ensure that no individual citizen was dominated by the state.[55]

5. The tough-luck test for efficacy in control

How efficacious would this system have to be in order to count as preventing domination? Any plausible system of control is bound to leave some discretion in the hands of state authorities. And so, the question is whether there is any test for when the discretion allowed is sufficiently restricted not to allow domination: any test, in effect, for when the restrictions are sufficient to make the state's exercise of power legitimate.

Being under the power or will of another is an objective condition that may obtain whether or not you are aware of its obtaining. But when you are aware that it obtains, and particularly when you are aware that the power is exercised to your detriment, that is bound to trigger resentment and indignation. These are primal, more or less universal responses to the hostile actions of another agent or agency, at least when the actions are taken to be reflections of the presence and influence of will.[56] And so, they would be entirely appropriate in response to the unwelcome interventions of a dominating subject.

Now every state is bound to establish some regulations or laws that you or others will find unwelcome. It may be an initiative that imposes a higher tax on those in your particular corner, or a zoning decision that reduces the value of houses in your neighbourhood, an immigration decision that works against those of your particular religion, or a travel restriction that you and almost everyone in the society takes to be excessively onerous. And that directs us to a test for when the state's exercise of power is un-dominating. If the state is un-dominating, then you will not have any reason to see its unwelcome decisions as actions meriting resentment or indignation. You will be able to regard the decisions, as you might regard natural accidents, as just tough

[55] Because the move to a collective system for disciplining the state is introduced on these grounds, the approach is proof against Anna Stilz's concern that it confuses protecting the citizenry as a group against domination with protecting individual citizens against that danger. See Stilz, 'The Value of Self-Determination' (n 4) 111.

[56] See PF Strawson, *Freedom and Resentment and Other Essays* (Methuen 1962); Victoria McGeer, 'Civilizing Blame' in D Justin Coates and Neal A Tognazzini (eds), *Blame: Its Nature and Norms* (Oxford University Press 2013).

luck. If the zoning decision goes against you, for example, you will be able to think of this outcome as you might think of the effects of natural chance.

The challenge before us now is to identify an equally accessible system of equally acceptable influence that might constrain the state sufficiently for it to meet the high standard required by the tough-luck test. Are there institutional designs that can support such a system? If there are, then a state that operates under those designs is going to exercise power in an un-dominating way and will count, in that sense, as legitimate. The state may occasionally allow laws to pass, or officials to be appointed, in a way that breaches the system, and in that sense, those particular laws or the appointments may be illegitimate. But insofar as it normally operates under the systemically generated constraints—insofar as breaches are incidental, isolated, and ideally remediable—the state itself will enjoy legitimacy as a body; it will exercise power in a way that respects the wills of its citizens.

This is not the place to explore the sorts of institutional designs that would support a suitable form of civic control over the state. But it may be useful to explain in sketchy outline how suitable institutions might give us a system of equally accessible, equally acceptable, and suitably efficacious influence over the state.

6. Institutions for controlling the state

In order to introduce the explanation, it is first necessary to distinguish two ways in which a group of representatives—say, a small committee delegated to make some decisions on behalf of a larger population—may go about its decision-making. The two models differ in the motives they allow members to act on, as they seek to push the group in one or another direction. Under each, the members are allowed to do the best they can by the interests and opinions they represent. But under the first, this permission is unqualified, so that they can bargain as hard as they wish for their own point of view, whereas under the second, it is significantly constrained. Members are required in this model to argue in favour of their respective proposals for how the group should go, on the basis of considerations that purport to be equally relevant, if not equally weighty, from everyone's point of view.[57] The constraint is effective to the extent that if someone fails to adduce such considerations in deliberative support of a proposal they make—if all they can say, for example, is that it would advantage their particular constituents—then they will be exposed to disesteem, even ridicule.[58]

The committee members will have to discharge three tasks in any decision. They will have to settle the menu of options among which to choose; determine the mode of decision-making to be followed in choosing; and make and vote for their preferred option. At each level, the first model would allow them to bargain, seeking

[57] Rainer Forst, *The Right to Justification: Elements of a Constructivist Theory of Justice* (Columbia University Press 2012).

[58] This model, associated in particular with Jürgen Habermas, is nicely described in Jon Elster, 'The Market and the Forum: Three Varieties of Political Theory' in Jon Elster and Aanund Hyland (eds), *Foundations of Social Choice Theory* (Cambridge University Press 1986).

to get concessions from others at least cost to themselves. The second model, by contrast, would require them at each level to make a deliberative case—a case based in purportedly shared or shareable considerations—for whatever process or policy they prefer. It would restrict each to defending one of those alternatives—and no doubt there will be a number on any issue—that are supported by some such considerations and cannot be knocked out by others.[59]

Suppose, to invoke an other-worldly possibility, that the state were governed by a committee that operated under the second model. Assume that there is no question about the universal relevance of the considerations that the members of the committee valorize. And assume that there is also no question about the fact that in every case of political decision-making the menu of options considered, the mode of voting adopted, and the actual option favoured is indeed defensible by such considerations. Under these assumptions, the decisions of the state, however unwelcome to some, are going to be acceptable to each under the abstract guise of being decisions that are supported in terms that all take to be relevant. And everyone who accepts that no one can be especially favoured by the state must find this abstract acceptability enough to silence a complaint about the content of what is decided in any case.

While this possibility is other-worldly in other respects, the idea that the citizens of a state might recognize the common relevance of certain process-related and policy-related considerations is not outlandish. When any officials or citizens of a state argue with one another about rival proposals on matters of process or policy, they are certainly likely to disagree about the proposal to realize. But if they are to argue with one another about the proposals, they must find considerations in support of their favoured candidate that are presumptively relevant for all, although perhaps not weighted equally by all.

Suppose that members of the community argue about policies like medical insurance or legal assistance, for example, the minimum wage or national defence, same-sex marriage or prosecutorial discretion. If any such argument is not to descend into brute conflict, it must proceed on the basis of commonly valorized, although hardly commonly weighted, considerations like those of equality and efficiency, privacy and protection, autonomy and fairness. While the argument generates divergence in the different proposals people defend, then, that very divergence will presuppose that the members converge on certain values and will have the effect of marking the values as accepted community standards. Those standards may be quite indeterminate in their individual demands and relative weights, at least as between familiar proposals. But at any moment they will surely outlaw an endless number of policies, rendering them more or less unthinkable. And they will be capable of becoming

[59] The approach clearly connects with the tradition of deliberative democracy: see Joshua Cohen, 'Deliberation and Democratic Legitimacy' in Alan Hamlin and Philip Pettit (eds), *The Good Polity: Normative Analysis of the State* (Blackwell 1989); Amy Gutmann and Dennis Thompson, *Democracy and Disagreement* (Harvard University Press 1996). It connects in particular, as will be clear, with the tradition in which this is taken to involve different interconnected sites of deliberation. See Jane Mansbridge and John Parkinson, *Deliberative Systems* (Cambridge University Press 2012).

more determinate over time: think of how the significance of equality has shifted in the United States with the rejection of the separate-but-equal doctrine.

We said that members of the other-worldly community we have been imagining will hardly have a complaint about the criteria on the basis of which decisions are reached by the ruling committee. But they will still have a complaint, of course, about the power of the committee. However sensitive the committee may be to community standards, it still must count as a dominating presence in their lives. While it reaches decisions that are acceptable to all in the sense explained, it is not forced to meet this constraint; it exercises its own will—by earlier argument, its own corporate will—in reaching those decisions. And so, it holds sway over the several and collective citizens for whom it decides.

But now suppose that institutions are introduced whereby others can make it more and more difficult for the committee to do anything other than select in each decision a menu of options, a mode of decision-making and a particular candidate that fit with what, from all perspectives, are universally relevant considerations. And suppose that everyone has equal access to the system that imposes this discipline on the committee. In that case, we would have an equally accessible system of influence over the state that imposed constraints that, by the earlier argument, were acceptable to all. And in that case, it would surely be plausible that each could think about any suitably formed decision, however unwelcome, that it was just tough luck that it went against them.

How might the committee with which we began be forced to make its decisions under the constraint of universal acceptability? Abstractly, it would seem to be a good idea to constrain those representatives by open, periodic, competitive election; to introduce safeguards against an elite of any kind, especially a moneyed or cultural elite, gaining special influence over elected representatives; to establish other committees for making decisions, say in deciding district boundaries or in publishing economic data, where electoral incentives are likely to be perverse; to set up independent auditing and review procedures for vetting all such bodies; to expose every level in this structure of government to public contestation, whether in courts or commissions, in the media or on the streets; to impose constraints of universal acceptability on every committee decision and on every process of contestation; and to frame such requirements under a constitution that ideally enjoys popular support and is entrenched against being amended too easily or too quickly.

These gestures at the sorts of institutions required indicate, as the republican tradition has it, that something like a mixed constitution is likely to be required. But there is nothing more that can be done here in outlining such a constitution.[60] The aim is merely to direct attention to a means whereby the control requirement on legitimacy might possibly be realized: a means that is approximated, however partially and imperfectly, in familiar democratic regimes. The satisfaction of that

[60] For a more detailed sketch, see Pettit, *On the People's Terms* (n 2) chs 4–5.

requirement not only promises to be enough to justify how a state exercises power, then; it also constitutes a condition that can feasibly be fulfilled.

While there are regimes in existence that have many features of the institutional template highlighted in this discussion, it should be noted finally that this is not a reason for complacency. The different constraints envisaged are not individually beyond our institutional reach, and are illustrated in a number of extant constitutions, but they are rarely realized as a coherent package. And when they are realized, they are usually realized only in a half-satisfactory measure. The theory of legitimacy whose feasibility they are designed to vindicate directs us to a regulative ideal, not an ideal that we can expect to be routinely satisfied.

7. Conclusion

In the first section of this chapter, we saw that the obligation owed by citizens to a legitimate state is that of opposing its laws, if they oppose them, within the system: this, as distinct from looking for regime change and starting again from scratch. That view of political obligation fits nicely with the control theory of legitimacy. For if the state were truly constrained by an equally accessible system of equally acceptable influence, it is hard to see any basis on which citizens could reasonably look for regime change. Or better, to register the fact that legitimacy comes in degrees: to the extent that a state was constrained in that way, its citizens would be obliged to contest its laws and procedures only within the system.

Suppose that the state did not perform well on this or that front; suppose, for example, that it failed to prevent a serious economic recession. If its claim to legitimacy rested only on the benefits it claimed to produce, or on the virtues it ascribed to its rulers, then we can see why citizens might well think of looking for regime change. If its claim to legitimacy rested on its operating under effective and equal democratic control, however, then things would surely be very different. The state that operated under such a constraint might fail to meet the natural expectation that it should provide various benefits. But a failure to do so would hardly offer any reason for citizens to renounce control over the state and to look for some other mode of political organization. At most, it would prompt a rethink of policy, a rejection of the elected government, a resort to constitutional amendment or, at the limit, a temporary recourse to emergency rule. The lesson, as John Dewey put it, is that 'the cure for the ailments of democracy is more democracy'.[61] But democracy, as understood in this principle, is democracy in the image of the mixed constitution: a democracy that is characterized not just by periodic electoral arrangements, but by the constraints imposed on elected government by constitutional counter-powers and an engaged, contestatory citizenry.

[61] John Dewey, *The Public and its Problems* (Ohio University Press 1991) 146.

II

Legitimate Political Authority and Expertise

Fabienne Peter

A. Introduction

Can legitimate political authority be based on expertise? Or should the justification of political authority be based on other considerations? David Estlund, for one, warns of the 'expert-boss fallacy': '[political] authority does not simply follow from expertise ... You may be correct, but what makes you boss?'[1] Relatedly, Stephen Darwall has objected to the influential Razian account of legitimate political authority in that it fails to draw a sufficiently clear distinction between expertise and legitimate political authority. Darwall claims that while the validity of an expert's claims is based on third-personal reasons, the justification of political authority requires its own mode of justification based on second-personal reasons. The latter is exemplified by public reason approaches, for example, according to which a political authority's decisions or directives are justified on the basis of reasons that are, at least in principle, acceptable to all.

My aim in this chapter is to shed light on the relationship between expertise and legitimate political authority. I will start with a brief overview of the important recent debate between Darwall and Joseph Raz on this issue (section B). This debate provides a good backdrop for distinguishing between different versions of the alleged expert-boss fallacy (section C). On the basis of this clarification of what is at stake, I will then, in section D, defend the possibility of grounding legitimate political authority in expertise—against Darwall's claims. But I will also argue that Darwall is right to draw our attention to the importance of mutual accountability as a ground for the justification of political authority. In the final section, I will offer a contingent argument for mutual accountability as a ground for the justification of political authority. I will argue that the second-personal mode of justification is important in the typical epistemic circumstances of politics, where the complexity of the decisions to be made is such that claims to expertise are often validly contested.

[1] David Estlund, *Democratic Authority* (Princeton University Press 2008) 3.

B. The Debate between Darwall and Raz on Legitimate Political Authority

In recent political philosophy it has become standard, following Raz,[2] to define legitimate political authority as the capacity to make claims that give others pre-emptive reasons for action. A pre-emptive reason for action is a second-order normative reason for action that replaces the first-order reasons for action that addressees may have.[3] While the claims (or directives, as Raz calls them) of a legitimate political authority are justified, a merely de facto authority purports to make justified claims even though they are not. But it does so successfully, such that the addressees take those claims to be giving them pre-emptive reasons for actions.

The question of whether this characterization of political authority is adequate, especially when it comes to the characterization of democratic authority, is important and has received a lot of attention.[4] In addition, there is the distinct question of how political authority is justified. What grounds the capacity of a legitimate authority to issue pre-emptive reasons for action? The debate between Raz and Darwall has focused on this second question. Darwall accepts the characterization of legitimate political authority as the capacity to issue pre-emptive reasons for action.[5] But he rejects Raz's account of how this capacity is justified. The following quote gives support to this way of interpreting the controversy:

> Although I agree with Raz that the capacity to create preemptive reasons ... is a mark of practical authority, I believe that this capacity itself requires the second-personal relation of accountability. In a slogan: No preemptive reasons without the standing to hold accountable.[6]

Using this interpretation of the controversy as my starting-point, I shall bracket the question of how practical authority is best conceptualized and focus exclusively on the question of what grounds the capacity of a political body—a representative of government, a political agency, or even the democratic collective—to issue pre-emptive reasons for action.[7]

The influential Razian conception of legitimate political authority, developed in Raz, is a 'service conception'—a legitimate political authority necessarily serves those subject to it, not its own purposes.[8] It performs this service if it enables the addressees to better comply with the reasons that apply to them anyway, independently of the directives of the authority. This is the famous Normal Justification Thesis.[9]

[2] See Joseph Raz, *The Morality of Freedom* (Oxford University Press 1986). [3] ibid 42.

[4] See, for example, Scott Hershovitz, 'Legitimacy, Democracy, and Razian Authority' (2003) 9 Legal Theory 201; Scott Hershovitz, 'The Role of Authority' (2011) 11 Philosopher's Imprint 1.

[5] See Stephen Darwall, 'Authority and Reasons. Exclusionary and Second-Personal' (2010) 120 Ethics 257.

[6] ibid 261.

[7] By focusing directly on the question of what justifies the capacity to issue pre-emptive reasons, I shall also bracket the question of the relationship between the concept of authority and obligation that is the focus of Hershovitz, 'The Role of Authority' (n 4).

[8] See Raz, *The Morality of Freedom* (n 2) 56. [9] See ibid 53.

It is based on the so-called Dependence Thesis, which states that the justification of political authority depends on reasons that obtain independently of the authority relation.[10]

The service conception takes the legitimacy of a political authority's directives to depend on whether it can correctly respond to reasons for action that apply to those under its rule. On my interpretation, shared also by Darwall, this implies that a legitimate political authority must have, or be prepared to defer to, expertise about what those reasons are. Because it might be objected that this is a misinterpretation, let me dwell on this issue briefly.[11] It might be argued that holding or being prepared to defer to expertise is not necessary on the service conception. It is sufficient for legitimacy that the authority succeeds in getting the addressees to comply with the reasons that apply to them; it does not matter how the authority does that. This objection cannot be upheld, however. To see what is at stake, consider the following example.[12] Suppose there is an emergency on a plane. A flight attendant issues directives that instruct the passengers how to efficiently evacuate the aircraft. Is it sufficient for the legitimacy of the flight attendant's authority that the directives are such that, if followed, they enable the efficient evacuation of the aircraft? Or is it necessary that the flight attendant knows what he is doing? I do not think that merely chancing upon the right set of directives is sufficient for legitimate practical authority. If the flight attendant, in panic, yells a random set of instructions that happen to achieve the right thing, what we get is merely a case of de facto practical authority that happens to work well. Legitimate practical authority is more demanding. A legitimate authority does not merely purport to issue pre-emptive reasons for action—successfully or not—it makes claims that do issue such reasons. This requires an ability to correctly identify the reasons that apply to the addressees of the directives and to issue directives accordingly; in other words, it presupposes expertise or at least a readiness to defer to expertise on this matter.

While the service conception thus grounds legitimate political authority on expertise, Darwall argues that expertise is the wrong starting-point for legitimate practical authority, in general, and for political authority, in particular. The key feature of legitimate political authority, Darwall argues, is the capacity to make valid claims on the conduct of others, claims to which they are accountable. This is what the preemptiveness thesis captures and this feature requires an account of what grounds one's standing to make claims on others. According to Darwall, the justification of political authority originates from within a relationship of mutual accountability. The claims (or directives) of a political authority are justified as long as the authority has the standing to make such claims and the addressees are accountable to the authority in this regard. Only then do these claims give the addressee a normative reason to act accordingly. In short, the accountability conception entails that a claim that a purported political authority makes towards someone is legitimate if the addressee is accountable to the authority for claims of this sort, as justified

[10] See ibid 47.
[11] I am very grateful to David Enoch for pressing me on this point.
[12] Adapted from Estlund, *Democratic Authority* (n 1) 124–25.

from within a second-personal standpoint of mutual accountability. If the authority does not have the standing to make a claim of this sort, the claim is not legitimate. This explains the 'slogan' I have quoted above: 'No preemptive reasons without the standing to hold accountable'.[13] It thus seems fitting to call Darwall's conception of legitimate practical authority an *accountability conception*.

Because it emphasizes the kind of claims that authority and addressee can mutually hold themselves accountable to, the accountability conception embodies some egalitarian commitments. But it would be wrong to think that this conception is incapable of supporting the justification of hierarchical authority relationships, such as the ones we find in the political or legal spheres. Darwall originally developed the accountability conception in *The Second-Person Standpoint*, focusing on the moral case. In subsequent writings, he has broadened the account to cover not just moral authority, but other cases of practical authority as well, including political authority. Mutual accountability, according to Darwall, is the foundation for a justificatory process that may generate reasons to support hierarchical authority relationships. On his view, the claims of a political authority are legitimate if they are either directly supported by relationships of mutual accountability or if the hierarchical structure in which they are embedded is thus supported. For example, the accountability conception is compatible with a government having the capacity to issue pre-emptive reasons for actions to its citizens as long as that government is democratically elected. The thought here is that the democratic process institutionalizes a form of mutual accountability between citizens that can justify a hierarchical form of government.[14]

To further clarify the accountability conception of legitimate political authority, let me note that the accountability conception underpins the well-known public reason conceptions of political legitimacy.[15] Public reason conceptions take the justification of political authority to depend on the reasons that are shared or that no reasonable person can reject. The accountability conception sheds light on the origin of those reasons. What determines the legitimacy of an authority's claim or directive is not that it tracks the normative reasons that apply to the addressees anyway, independently of anyone's judgement, contrary to what the service conception claims. Instead, the accountability conception maintains that political legitimacy depends on whether the addressees can accept the authority's claim as the sort of claim the authority can validly make on them.

[13] Darwall, 'Authority and Reasons' (n 5) 261.

[14] As Darwall puts it (ibid, 277–78): '[W]hat then can justify differential authority relations, as in legal and political authority? The lesson to draw from the failure of the [normal justification thesis], I believe, is that the only justification that can succeed is one that proceeds from within the second-person standpoint, beginning with the assumption that we all share a common basic authority to make claims and demands of one another at all, and proceeding from there to consider what differential claims to authority anyone could sensibly accept or no one could reasonably reject on that basis. The basic premise underlying any successful justification of differential authority, in other words, is that we share a common basic authority to make claims of each other just by virtue of being persons. Or, as Rawls put the point, to be a person is to be a "self-originating source of valid claims."'

[15] See John Rawls, *Political Liberalism* (Columbia University Press 1993); for an explication of Rawls's view, see Fabienne Peter, *Democratic Legitimacy* (Routledge 2009).

C. Interpreting the Expert-Boss Fallacy

This brief summary of the debate between Raz and Darwall reveals that the key point of contention is the role of expertise in a conception of legitimate political authority. Can legitimate political authority be grounded in expertise? This is the question I will seek to answer in the rest of this chapter. In order to make progress in answering this question, it will help to clarify what Estlund has called the expert-boss fallacy first. In this section, I will distinguish between different versions of the expert-boss fallacy and then use this distinction to make clear the positions that Darwall and Raz take on this issue.

A good way of approaching the expert-boss fallacy is via the claim that it denies. The expert-boss fallacy draws our attention to the fact that expertise is not sufficient for legitimate political authority. So, the key claim under consideration is this:

(i) Expertise is sufficient for legitimate political authority.

But to deny (i)—that expertise is sufficient for legitimate political authority—is compatible with the following two views of the relationship between expertise and political legitimacy.

(ii) Expertise is necessary but not sufficient for legitimate political authority.

(iii) Expertise is neither necessary nor sufficient for legitimate political authority.

According to the first view (ii), the expert-boss fallacy warns of a failure to recognize that, although expertise is a ground for legitimate political authority, it is not, by itself, sufficient. Additional conditions must be met for legitimate practical authority. According to the second view (iii), it warns of a failure to recognize that political authority is justified on grounds other than expertise.

With this distinction in mind, let us now consider Darwall's objection to the service conception. Darwall gives the following example to illustrate where the service conception goes wrong. Suppose you have prudential reasons to provide for your retirement and a financial expert tells you how best to do so. Darwall argues that it does not follow from the fact that you would best comply with those reasons if you were to follow her directives that she actually holds legitimate practical authority over you. Moreover, the expert does not have legitimate practical authority even if you would best comply with those reasons if you treated her as somebody with practical authority over you, not just as somebody who is in a position to give advice. Darwall uses this example to argue that legitimate practical authority presupposes the standing to hold accountable. Because the say-so of an expert does not entail the standing to hold accountable, there is a difference between expertise and legitimate practical authority that hinges on accountability. While the example is not specifically about political authority, the same point can be made in this context. Someone with expertise on a certain policy matter will not, on this basis, have legitimate political authority to issue a directive.

Surely, Darwall is right about this. Advice is different from legitimate political authority. Having expertise on what the reasons for action are that apply to an addressee and making a claim that would allow an addressee to comply with those reasons is not sufficient to generate a pre-emptive reason for action for the addressee. Raz, in his reply to Darwall, acknowledges the point and grants that expertise is not sufficient for legitimate practical authority. Raz writes:

> This leads me to think that the explanation of Darwall's example is that the [Normal Justification Thesis] is not met when the only reason to think that an authoritative instruction is correct is that it represents an expert view about what is good to do, a view which is not based on the fact that the expert will so instruct, or has so instructed.[16]

But Raz also emphasizes that Darwall's objection does not show that expertise is not necessary. As Raz puts it:

> It does not follow that expertise is not relevant to practical authorities. It is, but only when it is mixed with other considerations, such as need for co-ordination, for concretising indeterminate boundaries, and the like.[17]

Raz thus accepts that expertise is not sufficient for legitimate political authority. Like Darwall, he also rejects (i). But Raz does not conclude from the falsity of (i) that expertise is the wrong ground for legitimate political authority. His claim is, instead, that expertise needs to be supplemented with additional conditions and this explains the difference between advice and legitimate practical authority. The main issue in the debate between Darwall and Raz is, therefore, not whether expertise is sufficient, but whether expertise is necessary for legitimate political authority. Darwall disputes this. His accountability conception is committed to (iii), the claim that expertise is the wrong ground for legitimate political authority altogether and should thus be seen as neither necessary nor sufficient for legitimate political authority.

D. The Role of Expertise

Having clarified the different positions in the debate, my aim in this section is to argue, against Darwall, that expertise can be a ground of legitimate political authority. Note that this is a weaker claim than the claim that expertise is necessary for political legitimacy. My aim in this section is not to defend the claim that expertise is necessary for legitimate political authority. As I will explain in the final section, while my reason for resisting the claim that expertise is necessary for legitimate political authority is different from Darwall's, I agree with Darwall that expertise is not necessary for legitimate political authority. In addition, note that my aim in this section is not to defend Raz's service conception. I will only defend the narrower claim that expertise can be a ground of legitimate political authority. To emphasize this difference, I will, from now on, call the alternative to the accountability conception an expertise-based conception.

[16] Joseph Raz, 'On Respect, Authority, and Neutrality: A Response' (2010) 120 Ethics 279, 301.
[17] ibid.

As we saw, Darwall claims that expertise is the wrong ground for legitimate political authority because we are not accountable to experts. It might be rational for us to take on board the advice of experts, but no more. We are, however, accountable to the claims of a legitimate political authority. For Darwall, this distinction plays a central role in his argument that expertise is the wrong ground for legitimate political authority. The key claim in Darwall's argument is that legitimate authority is only possible with regard to claims we can hold ourselves accountable to. Darwall calls this Pufendorf's point,[18] drawing on Pufendorf's argument that God's commands can only exercise authority over us if we can hold ourselves rationally accountable to his commands. If we cannot hold ourselves accountable, then fear of God may lead us to comply with his commands, but acting from fear is not the same thing as acting in response to an authoritative command. I have argued elsewhere that this point, even if it is granted, does not support the accountability conception.[19] The problem has its origin in the overly sharp distinction that Darwall draws between epistemic justification and practical justification, specifically with regard to accountability. Darwall seems to think that we can only hold ourselves accountable for our actions, not for our beliefs, but that is not obvious. To hold myself accountable for my actions means that I can distinguish between actions I should do and actions that I should not do and to see myself as an appropriate target of blame if I do something I should not do. It seems to me that I can hold myself accountable for my beliefs in the same way. To hold myself accountable for my beliefs means that I can distinguish between beliefs I should hold and beliefs I should not hold and to see myself as an appropriate target of blame if I believe something I should not believe. If I believe something I should not believe given the evidence that is at my fingertips, for example, I can accept that I am an appropriate target of blame. And it is because I hold myself accountable to truth that I hold myself accountable for many of my beliefs.[20]

In light of this parallel between accountability in the practical realm and accountability in the epistemic realm, we can show how accountability to truth might be a ground for holding ourselves accountable for our actions. To see this fully, we must recognize that the truths we might hold ourselves accountable to may not just be theoretical truths, they may be practical truths—truths about what we have reason to do. If we can hold ourselves accountable to such practical truths, then there can be epistemic grounds for holding myself accountable for my actions: it is possible that the distinction between what I should do and what I should not do derives from what I should believe about what I should do and if I am an appropriate target of blame if I do something I should not do in light of what I should believe about what I should do. If we can hold ourselves accountable for actions on epistemic grounds in this way, however, then Darwall's objection that expertise cannot be a ground of legitimate practical authority fails. It is at least conceivable that I am accountable to

[18] See Stephen Darwall, *The Second-Person Standpoint* (Harvard University Press 2006) 23.

[19] See Fabienne Peter, 'The Grounds of Political Legitimacy' (manuscript).

[20] For the notion of accountability to truth, see Peter Railton, *Facts, Values, and Norms: Essays Toward a Morality of Consequence* (Cambridge University Press 2003) 298f.

true claims about what I have reason to do. And this argument shows that it is at least possible that expertise can be a ground for legitimate political authority.

The argument for the claim that expertise can be a ground of legitimate political authority is not yet complete, however. Darwall rightly highlights that there is a distinction between advice and legitimate authority. While it might be foolish of me to disregard the advice of an expert, in disregarding the claim of a legitimate political authority I do more than violate a standard of theoretical rationality. I act against what I have normative reason to do. A defence of the claim that expertise can be a ground for legitimate political authority must thus be able to accommodate the difference between advice and authority.

What I take from Darwall's point, as explained in the previous section, is that it is not sufficient for legitimate political authority that the authority holds or defers to expertise about the reasons that apply and issues a directive that allows the addressees to better comply with these reasons than if they acted on their own judgement. At least one additional condition must be met in order that the directive or claim is indeed authoritative and not just a bit of advice. I think we can explain this additional condition by borrowing from David Enoch's work on triggering reason-giving.[21] Triggering reason-giving is distinguished from epistemic reason-giving. Epistemic reason-giving merely highlights what you had reason to do all along, independently of the interaction. For example, if you point out to me that it is my grandmother's birthday today, this gives me a reason to call her. Advice is an important form of epistemic reason-giving. Triggering reason-giving occurs if the interaction with others manipulates the non-normative circumstances such that a previously latent reason becomes active. Enoch gives the example of someone setting a foot on the road, thus activating the reason for drivers 'to-stop-should-a-pedestrian-start-crossing'.[22] Again, the reason is there all along; it is not created by the interaction. But in triggering reason-giving, the interaction makes a difference. In Enoch's example, the driver does not have a reason to stop at the crossing unless a pedestrian signals that she wants to cross.

The notion of triggering reason-giving can help us see how a directive, if issued under the right conditions, triggers a reason for action for the addressees and this is how it can generate a pre-emptive reason for action. In the retirement case, no such reason is triggered. The case is based on the assumption that you have prudential reason to follow the advice of the expert. But this does not entail that the advice triggers a reason for action for you: you do not have a generic reason to follow the advice of experts, which is triggered whenever you get expert advice. In the retirement case, the advice from the expert is thus not a pre-emptive reason of the kind that a legitimate practical authority would issue. It is a case of epistemic reason-giving. You should, of course, take the advice into account in your deliberation. But beyond that, nothing of normative interest happens. This does not change if the expert acts like a practical authority in the sense that she casts her advice explicitly as a directive.

[21] See David Enoch, 'Giving Practical Reasons' (2011) 11 Philosopher's Imprint 1; David Enoch, 'Authority and Reason-Giving' (2014) 89 Philosophy and Phenomenological Research 296.

[22] See Enoch, 'Giving Practical Reasons' (n 21) 4.

She can at best achieve the status of a de facto practical authority. Her claim will not give you a pre-emptive reason for action, so she cannot gain legitimacy in this way.

Things are different in the following scenario. Suppose there is a coordination problem, say relating to road use. If drivers can choose whether they drive on the right or on the left, driving will be very dangerous. The drivers thus have an independent reason to coordinate—either by both driving on their right or by both driving on their left—but they may fail to do so if they independently try to decide which side of the road they should use. A de facto authority, issuing claims about which side of the road they should drive on, can solve this coordination problem for them. The directive of the political authority, in this case, triggers an independent practical reason to coordinate as instructed and it is legitimate because of that independently existing reason. The addressees are now accountable to obey the directives of the authority. But they are so, not because of the say-so of the authority as such. What makes the political authority's directive legitimate is the independent reason to coordinate that the directives trigger. To capture the idea in a slogan: no expertise-based legitimate authority without triggering of (independent) practical reasons. This shows that expertise can be a ground for legitimate political authority in conditions where an expert's claim triggers a pre-emptive reason to comply.

E. Legitimate Authority between Expertise and Accountability

I have just argued that we can save the claim that expertise can be a ground of legitimate political authority from Darwall's objection if we (a) understand that we can hold ourselves accountable to true claims about what we should do and (b) if we add a reason-triggering condition to distinguish between cases of mere advice and cases of legitimate political authority. If there is genuine expertise, and if the claims of a purported political authority that either has the relevant expertise or is prepared to defer to it trigger corresponding reasons for action, then this is sufficient for legitimate political authority. But that is only part of the story. The main problem with the attempt to ground legitimate political authority in expertise is that expertise tends to run out rather quickly in many political contexts. My main aim in this section is to argue that expertise is not necessary for legitimate political authority and that there is another possible ground for legitimate political authority—accountability.

Political decisions are complex and wide-ranging. Policy issues such as abortion, climate change, or social services all involve hard-to-track empirical and normative facts. We should thus expect both significant uncertainty about what we have reason to do and how best to comply with them. As a result, expertise on what directives an authority should issue is often not available and there is potential for reasonable disagreement on what the right directive is. If the experts' claims are validly contested, then the expertise-based route to establishing legitimate practical authority is blocked.

Moreover, it is clear that this happens not just in marginal cases in politics. The epistemic circumstances of politics are such that relying on expertise will often be blocked. What should we say about cases in which expertise is unavailable as a basis for legitimate political authority? If we were to insist that expertise was a necessary condition for legitimate political authority, this would imply that whenever expertise has run out, any directives of a political authority would be illegitimate. But that cannot be right. It must be possible to distinguish between legitimate and illegitimate directives even in circumstances where expertise has run out. Expertise can thus not be necessary for legitimate political authority. And indeed, this is not how many political institutions operate. A variety of political institutions, and democratic institutions, in particular, can be seen as being responses to the problems of uncertainty and disagreement about what the right directives are.[23] Their aim is to ensure the possibility of legitimate political authority even in the absence of reliable expertise on what the right directive is.

What we thus need to account for is the possibility of legitimate decisions or directives even when the conditions for expertise-based legitimate political authority are not met. A plausible theory of legitimate political authority cannot neglect the cases in which expertise is unavailable. Such a theory must appeal to an alternative source of political legitimacy, one that can establish legitimate practical authority on grounds other than expertise about the reasons that apply and how addresses can best comply with them.

When expertise is unavailable, the accountability conception of legitimate political authority can fill the gap. In the previous section, I argued that Darwall's argument against an expertise-based conception fails because we can hold ourselves accountable to true claims about what should be done. But this is not to say that we can only hold ourselves accountable to true claims about what should be done. Consider this example. In a conflict with another person and without knowing who, if either, is right in this matter, we can still agree on a particular solution and hold ourselves accountable to this solution without believing that the solution picks out who is right. The solution in question may be either a compromise or a procedural solution, as when we appoint an arbitrator. This argument shows that mutual accountability can make demands on us even in the absence of true claims about what we should do. While Darwall makes a stronger claim, I follow him up to this point.

In the political context, the possibility of holding ourselves mutually accountable to a set of decisions or institutionalized decision-making procedures is key for the possibility of legitimate political authority when the available expertise is not sufficient to identify the right course of action. In the epistemic circumstances of politics, mutual accountability will often be the only ground we have for distinguishing between unjustified attempts to exercise power over others and justified exercises of political authority. This is not, of course, an argument for democracy or for any particular set of political institutions. But it highlights the importance of agreeing on some set of political institutions that can generate legitimate directives in the absence of expertise-based guidance.

[23] See Jeremy Waldron, *Law and Disagreement* (Oxford University Press 1999); Fabienne Peter, 'The Epistemic Circumstances of Democracy' in Miranda Fricker and Michael Brady (eds), *The Epistemic Life of Groups* (Oxford University Press 2016).

In sum, I have argued that if expertise is accessible and a purported authority either has or is prepared to defer to legitimate epistemic authority with respect to what the addressees ought to do and if its directives trigger a reason for action for them, then it is legitimate. Vice versa, a purported authority that consistently fails to issue the right directives in such circumstances will not be legitimate. When the conditions are met, expertise is a ground for legitimate practical authority and disregarding available expertise will be a source of illegitimacy.

When the conditions for expertise-based legitimate political authority are not met, however, there is still scope for legitimate political authority. There is a second potential source of legitimacy—accountability to others—and claims that pass the mutual accountability test can take the place of the claims made by experts. When, for example, there is no expert, we can turn to directives about how to correctly solve a particular coordination or cooperation problem and we can still agree to follow the directives of an authority we together appoint. In this example, the reason we have to follow the directive of the authority is no longer grounded in the reasons that apply to us independently of the authority relationship and in the authority's expertise with respect to those reasons. Instead, that reason stems from our relationship of mutual accountability. If the authority is justified, it is not because the directive triggers an independent reason that applies to us, but because of our acceptance of our mutual accountability to that authority.

Which combination of accountability to expertise and accountability to others prevails in the justification of political authority depends on the epistemic circumstances that obtain, and much could and needs to be said about the scope for expertise-based and accountability-based political legitimacy. This issue is important because directives invalidly based on expertise will be illegitimate, just as attempts to justify authority on the basis of accountability will when they ignore or undermine available expertise. What we need is a hybrid theory of political justification that can explain the appropriate scope for both expertise and mutual accountability as grounds for political legitimacy, but that will have to be done elsewhere.

III

Another Voluntarism

John Rawls on Political Legitimacy

*Paul Weithman**

John Rawls barely mentioned the topic of political legitimacy in the work he published before the 1990s. This must have encouraged some readers to conclude that he thought legitimacy could play at best a minor, supporting role in theorizing about distributive justice. To those who reached this conclusion, Rawls's introduction of the liberal principle of legitimacy in *Political Liberalism*[1] would have seemed a stunning reversal. For, it might have seemed, he would not have introduced a concept he had so pointedly relegated to the periphery of *A Theory of Justice*[2] unless he was going to assign it a role in *Political Liberalism* which matched its importance elsewhere in political studies.[3] Indeed, some readers of that book interpreted him as assigning it a *central* role. A few doubled down on this interpretation, claiming that legitimacy is what *Political Liberalism* is really about.[4] Moreover, the fact that Rawls introduced the concept of legitimacy in the book in which he re-presented justice as fairness as political suggested an explanation of its introduction which promised to confirm its importance: the principle of legitimacy would be important, in a way that it had not been before, because it was needed to solve the philosophical problems that led Rawls to recast his theory.[5]

I have argued elsewhere that these commentators have mistaken Rawls's reasons for introducing the principle of legitimacy and have overstated its centrality to the

* My thinking about the subject of this chapter has benefited enormously from Arthur Ripstein, 'Private Order and Public Justice: Kant and Rawls' (2006) 92 Virginia Law Review 1391. I am grateful to Professor Ripstein and to Fred Rush for helpful comments on an earlier draft.

1 John Rawls, *Political Liberalism* (Columbia University Press 1993).

2 John Rawls, *A Theory of Justice* (rev edn, Oxford University Press 1999).

3 Thus, in his 'The Meaning and Measure of State Legitimacy: Results for 72 Countries' (2006) 45 European Journal of Political Research 499, 499, Bruce Gilley says '[t]he concept of political legitimacy is central to virtually all of political science'.

4 See David Estlund, 'The Survival of Egalitarian Justice in John Rawls's *Political Liberalism*' (1996) 4 Journal of Political Philosophy 68; also Burton Dreben, 'On Rawls and Political Liberalism' in Samuel Freeman (ed), *The Cambridge Companion to Rawls* (Cambridge University Press 2003) 316.

5 See Simone Chambers, 'The Politics of Equality: John Rawls on the Barricades' (2006) 4 Perspectives on Politics 81, 81.

Legitimacy: The State and Beyond. First Edition. Edited by Wojciech Sadurski, Michael Sevel, and Kevin Walton. Published 2019 by Oxford University Press.

project of *Political Liberalism*.[6] But even after we appreciate how the principle fits into the reconstructive project Rawls undertook in that book, much of his treatment of legitimacy remains obscure. One reason for the obscurity is that the novelty of the principle of legitimacy blinded some readers to continuities between what Rawls said about legitimacy in *Political Liberalism* and what he implied about it in *A Theory of Justice*. Another is that Rawls's presentation of the principle of legitimacy raises a number of exegetical and philosophical questions which his texts leave unresolved. I shall try to answer some of the most pressing of those questions and to recover Rawls's account of political legitimacy. I shall do so because I believe Rawls provides an interesting alternative to views of legitimacy currently on offer. Appreciating its distinctiveness is the first step towards appreciating its appeal.

In section A, I shall lay out some questions raised by Rawls's discussion of legitimacy in *Political Liberalism*. I believe the key to their solution lies in a claim made by Rawls about the character of political power. As we shall see, Rawls uses language familiar from social contract theory to describe that power, saying that it is the power of the public as a corporate body. But that description should not be taken as Rawls's wording—or his wording interpreted in light of Locke's theory—suggests. To confirm that it should not, I review Locke's treatment of the incorporation of the body politic in section B, considering but ultimately rejecting the suggestion that Rawls's treatment of legitimacy is Lockean. Rather, Rawls follows Kant in thinking that talk of a contractual incorporation is best understood as a way of expressing fundamental moral claims about the object of a constitution, about citizens' standing, and about legislators' duties. These are the claims that do the real work in Rawls's account of legitimacy. And so in section C, I lay out Kant's conception of the social contract and in section D, I argue that we can draw on that conception to understand Rawls's account of political legitimacy. Section E spells out the philosophical pay-offs of the reading offered here by showing how it solves some textual puzzles and by showing how Rawls's account differs from others that have recently been defended in political philosophy. I conclude by briefly mentioning some lingering questions about Rawlsian legitimacy.

A. Some Textual and Philosophical Puzzles

Rawls introduces the liberal principle of legitimacy early in *Political Liberalism*'s version of 'The Idea of an Overlapping Consensus'. The principle says:

> [O]ur exercise of political power is fully proper only when it is exercised in accordance with a constitution the essentials of which all citizens as free and equal may reasonably be expected to endorse in light of principles and ideals acceptable to their common human reason.[7]

[6] Paul Weithman, 'Legitimacy and the Project of *Political Liberalism*' in Thom Brooks and Martha Nussbaum (eds), *Rawls's Political Liberalism* (Columbia University Press 2015).

[7] Rawls, *Political Liberalism* (n 1) 137.

What is most immediately vexing about Rawls's introduction of the principle is that he does not appear to offer any argument for it. Instead, he seems simply to postulate the principle as the answer to the question of when political power is 'appropriately exercised'[8] or 'justifiable'.[9] And so the first and most pressing question raised by Rawls's principle of legitimacy is whether he offers a line of reasoning to support it, appearances to the contrary notwithstanding.

The way in which Rawls broaches the question the principle of legitimacy is supposed to answer is also puzzling. In the paragraph before he introduces the principle, Rawls poses 'the question of the legitimacy of the general structure of authority', a structure he equates with a society's constitution.[10] But having—in effect—raised the question of what makes a constitution legitimate, Rawls then raises and answers the question of what makes particular exercises of power legitimate. We are left to wonder what connection there is, if any, between the question about legitimate constitutions that Rawls first poses and the question he eventually answers.

Another puzzle concerns the way in which Rawls understands the latter question, for he equates the concise question of when political power is appropriately exercised with a question whose surface grammar is much more complex:

> [I]n light of what principles and ideals must we, as free and equal citizens, be able to view ourselves as exercising power if our exercise is to be justifiable to other citizens and to respect their being reasonable and rational?[11]

Recovering Rawls's treatment of legitimacy will require us to make sense of the equation.

The questions Rawls equates are raised, he says, by the fact that political power 'is ultimately the power of the public, that is, the power of free and equal citizens as a collective body'.[12] This description of political power is also puzzling. It is a staple of liberal democratic thought, elaborated in detail by some thinkers in the tradition, but it is not at all clear why Rawls chooses to describe political power that way or how he thinks the collective body of citizens was or could have been formed.

In 'The Domain of the Political and Overlapping Consensus', Rawls reiterates that description, but adds that political power is power of which each citizen has 'an equal share'.[13] This claim raises the question of just what it means for each to *have* an equal *share* of collective power—as opposed, perhaps, to each *making* an equal *contribution* to the total power at government's disposal. It raises the further question of whether this equality of shares is part of what raises the question of legitimacy and, if so, why. Is Rawls's idea that when political power is exercised, each finds herself subject to power which is partially her own and that that raises special justificatory questions which do not arise in other domains? Or does the equality of shares mean that answers to justificatory questions—which might be asked about any exercises of power—must assume a certain form in virtue of citizens' equality?

[8] ibid. [9] ibid 217. [10] ibid 136. [11] ibid 137. [12] ibid 136.

[13] John Rawls, 'The Domain of the Political and Overlapping Consensus' in Samuel Freeman (ed), *Collected Papers* (Harvard University Press 1999) 483.

Political power is, of course, immediately exercised by government: as Rawls says, it 'is always … backed by government's use of sanctions'.[14] This suggests that to show an exercise of political power legitimate is to justify government action. To show that a government action is justified would seem tantamount to showing that government was within its rights in acting as it did. And so another question raised by Rawls's text is what kind of right the government has acted within. It might be a justification right or a permission right. Rawls's implication that a showing of legitimacy is a showing of justifiability or propriety would seem to support this reading. But legitimacy is generally said to be 'the right to rule' and is often thought to be correlated with citizens' obligation to obey. This raises the possibility that the legitimation of government action shows that government has a claim-right to citizens' obedience.

One of Rawls's references to legitimacy in 'The Idea of Public Reason Revisited' suggests that he thinks this is so. There, the features of the political relationship that are said in 'Overlapping Consensus' to bear on the question of legitimacy are said in 'The Idea of Public Reason Revisited' to raise 'the question of how, when constitutional essentials and matters of basic justice are at stake, citizens so related can be *bound* to honor the structure of their constitutional democratic regime and abide by the statutes and laws enacted under it'.[15] Rawls then argues that law is 'binding' on citizens when it is legitimate. But he seems to draw back from the conclusion that defenders of political obligation want to reach by saying that legitimate law is 'politically (morally) binding' rather than that it is unqualifiedly morally binding.[16] Rawls's argument therefore raises the question of how a legitimate law's justifiability or propriety is related to its bindingness. It also raises the question of how, if at all, 'politically (morally) binding' differs from 'morally binding'. Finally, it raises the question of why puzzles about law's bindingness—like those about its legitimacy—are pressed by features of citizens' political relation with one another rather than by, say, features of their transactional histories with their governments.

I said at the outset that the key to Rawls's account of legitimacy is his claim that political power is the power of the people. I shall therefore begin to answer these questions by asking whether that feature should be understood in a Lockean fashion.

B. 'The Political Relationship in a Constitutional Regime'

One of Rawls's predecessors in the social contract tradition—John Locke—discussed the formation of a body politic in considerable detail. It may be thought that Rawls's reference to political power as 'the power of … a collective body' is indebted to him and that we can look to his work to see what Rawls means. I believe, on the contrary,

[14] Rawls, *Political Liberalism* (n 1) 136.

[15] John Rawls, 'The Idea of Public Reason Revisited' in *The Law of Peoples, with 'The Idea of Public Reason Revisited'* (Harvard University Press 1999) 136 (emphasis added); see also Rawls, *Political Liberalism* (n 1) xlv.

[16] Rawls, 'The Idea of Public Reason Revisited' (n 15) 137.

that Rawls's thought about the body politic is more deeply indebted to another strain of the contract tradition, and that examining what looks like a relevant appropriation of Locke provides an illuminating contrast with Rawls's own view.

Locke opens the chapter of 'The Second Treatise' devoted to 'the Beginning of Political Societies' by saying how a body politic is formed. It is formed, he says, '[w]hen any number of Men' in the state of nature '*consent*[] *to make one Community* or Government'.[17] Locke says in the following paragraph that when they do that 'they have thereby made that *Community* one Body, with a Power to Act as one Body'.[18] The question of how Locke thinks it possible for people to establish a body politic is therefore, at bottom, the question Hobbes had previously taken up in *Leviathan*, chapter XVI:[19] the question of how it is possible for a multitude to form a single entity capable of performing unified or coherent action that can be imputed to it. Locke answers that question by saying that those who consent to form a community thereby consent to be bound by the outcome of a certain decision procedure, namely, majority rule.[20]

If a multitude in the state of nature is to form a community, Locke says, each has to '[divest] himself of his Natural Liberty'.[21] Since Locke thinks that each person is equally free in the state of nature, he must think that all pay the same cost of entry into the community. If equal costs purchase equal portions, then he might say that each has an equal share of the corporate body's power because each has purchased an equal share of the corporation. If *that* is right, and if Rawls thinks of a body politic's incorporation in roughly the same way Locke does, then we can get some idea of what Rawls means by claiming that each has an equal share of the body politic's power and of how he would support that claim: he would mean by the claim what Locke does and would offer a Lockean argument for it.

For Rawls, the fact that each has an equal share in that power is part of what raises 'the question of the legitimacy of the general structure of authority'.[22] I said in section A that that is a question which Rawls seems to put aside without connecting it to the question of how particular exercises of power are legitimated. Locke seems to provide the concepts Rawls could use to frame and connect those questions. For three chapters after saying how people can unite into a body politic, Locke says how the body politic can establish what he regards as the most important part of a society's 'structure of authority': what he calls 'the legislative'.[23] Rawls cites that chapter of 'The Treatise' as the source of a distinction between two kinds of political power: 'the ordinary power of officers of government and the electorate exercised in day-to-day politics' and the power to 'set[] up a framework'—or a 'general structure'—'to regulate ordinary power'.[24] The puzzle about how, if at all, the legitimacy

[17] John Locke, 'The Second Treatise' in Peter Laslett (ed), *Two Treatises of Government* (2nd edn, Cambridge University Press 1967) ch VIII, §95 (emphasis in the original).

[18] ibid ch VIII, §96 (emphasis in the original).

[19] See Thomas Hobbes, *Leviathan* (Richard Tuck ed, Cambridge University Press 1991) ch XVI.

[20] Locke, 'The Second Treatise' (n 17) ch VIII, §96.

[21] ibid ch VIII, §95.

[22] Rawls, *Political Liberalism* (n 1) 136.

[23] See Locke, 'The Second Treatise' (n 17) ch XI.

[24] Rawls, *Political Liberalism* (n 1) 231.

of the general structure of authority bears on the legitimacy of particular exercises of power can therefore be rephrased as a puzzle about how the legitimacy of constituent power bears on the legitimacy of ordinary power.

As we saw, a society's 'general structure of authority' is its constitution. Understood broadly, it is the way in which society's 'framework' allocates authority among officials of all levels of government. The 'question of the legitimacy of [this] general structure' will then come up whenever the legitimacy of a particular exercise of ordinary power is in question. For to show that an exercise of ordinary power is legitimate, it is not enough to show that the person who exercised that power had the authority to do so under the governing framework that is in place. That framework must itself satisfy the standards which apply to constituent power. And so there is a connection between the question Rawls seems to raise and drop, about the legitimacy of a constitution, and the question about particular exercises of ordinary power that he tries to answer. Although he does not draw the connection as explicitly as we might like, he is aware of it. For his liberal principle of legitimacy ties the justifiability of particular exercises of power to the standard a constitution must satisfy.

Thus, Locke might seem to have provided an account of the body politic's incorporation and power on which Rawls built and to which we can appeal to fill in the gaps in his texts. But although Rawls may draw somewhat on Locke, it would be a mistake to read him as having a fundamentally Lockean view of a people's incorporation, and an even greater mistake to read him as endorsing a Lockean view of legitimacy.

One difference between Locke and Rawls comes to light when we ask what standards an exercise of ordinary power or a constitution must satisfy to be legitimate. In the section in which he distinguishes constituent from ordinary power, Locke states clearly that those standards are instrumental. He says that the 'great end' for which people incorporate into a body politic is 'the enjoyment of their Properties in Peace and Safety' and that laws are 'the great instrument and means of that'.[25] He also views the establishment of the governing framework instrumentally, saying that 'the *first and fundamental natural Law*, which is to govern even the Legislative itself, *is the preservation of the Society*, and (as far as will consist with the publick [sic] good) of every person in it'.[26]

Rawls says that 'the question of the legitimacy of the general structure of authority' is 'intimately connected' with the idea of public reason. What I take it he has in mind is that exercises of power, both ordinary and constituent, are—in his view—shown to be legitimate by appeal to public reasons. Some of these reasons will be instrumental, but some will not. For Rawls, our appraisal of a scheme of cooperation goes hand-in-hand with how we appraise the activity of upholding it, and the values that are realized in the course of upholding the scheme tell in favour of the scheme itself.

Rawls thinks the activity of upholding a just scheme is to be valued for its own sake, because only in such activity can we express our nature as free and equal

[25] Locke, 'The Second Treatise' (n 17) ch XI, §134.

[26] ibid (emphasis in the original).

rational beings—or, for the Rawls of *Political Liberalism*, as free and equal citizens.[27] Arrangements which satisfy principles of justice are not means to relationships which express our nature, still less means to a life that it would be at least logically possible for us to attain in their absence. Rather, it is by—and Rawls thinks only by—collectively supporting those institutions that we can relate to others in ways that realize what we are. And so he thinks a just scheme is also to be valued for its own sake, and not merely as an instrument for attaining ends such as self-preservation and the preservation of property. That is why Rawls rejects Locke's instrumentalism and says in *A Theory of Justice* that 'the successful carrying out of justice institutions is the shared final end of all the members of society, and these institutional forms are prized as good in themselves'.[28]

In fact, I think Locke's claim about the instrumental justification of laws and the legislative is one member of a set of views which hang together in a tidy package. Locke appears to have a thoroughly instrumental view of politics. For he says that before the establishment of a legislative for the protection of property, free and equal persons in a state of nature would leave that condition and form a body politic for the same end.[29] If we take Locke to be engaged in ideal theorizing, then the ideal he offers is of an ideally crafted instrument whose defining features are arrived at by asking what institutional arrangements will best satisfy the desire to preserve property as Locke understands it. A constitutional form such as limited monarchy is justified insofar as it serves that end.

Locke tells his readers how to construct their instrument—by mutual consent, in the case of a body politic, and by majority rule, in the case of a constitution or a legislative. These instructions outline possible historical processes: they are instructions people could actually follow were they in a state of nature. Because the processes are ones in which it would be possible for a group of people to engage, and because Locke famously thought that those who do not belong to the founding generation of a body politic could remain in it by tacit consent, he seems committed to the possibility that political authority could be legitimate because political society is a truly voluntary scheme. The fact that members of a body politic consent famously accounts for their obligation to obey.

Earlier, I suggested that Locke thinks exercises of political power must be justifiable to everyone because all have paid the same price to enter political society. On this reading, their purchase of equal shares gives them equal authority over those who exercise that power. But some scholars think that Locke grounds citizens'

[27] I cannot discuss in any detail what Rawls means by the expression of our nature, nor can I trace the development of that idea through his turn to political liberalism. For now, suffice it to say that for Rawls, the phrase 'express our nature' describes something we can do in action—or better, it describes a way in which we can conduct ourselves. The description can be taken for a close relative of the phrase 'express ourselves', and so might seem to signal a commitment to authenticity or to the individualism for which liberalism is often criticized. To read the phrase as betraying a deep individualism is a mistake, for Rawls's view—like Aristotle's—is profoundly relational. He thinks that when we regulate our conduct by principles 'that would be chosen if [our] nature were the decisive determining element' of the choice, we relate to others as free, equal, reasonable, and rational. In so relating to one another, our conduct shows us to be—or expresses our nature as—such beings. See Rawls, *A Theory of Justice* (n 2) 222.

[28] ibid 462.

[29] Locke, 'The Second Treatise' (n 17) ch IX, §124.

authority differently. They read him as endorsing a general principle according to which craftsmen have authority over what they make. As God has authority to legislate for human beings because He made them, so the human beings who craft a polity for the protection of their property have ultimate authority over the disposition of their instrument.[30] Officials who actually exercise ordinary power are therefore accountable to citizens for its use. On this reading, it is citizens' status as makers rather than as shareholders which gives them that authority and which implies that exercises of ordinary power must be justified to them.

I have already said why I think Rawls would reject what I called Locke's instrumental view of politics. I actually believe he would reject every element in the Lockean package. Rawls's rejection of the instrumental view depends on the claim that the principles on which our relations are founded are those that would be chosen were our nature 'the decisive determining element' of the choice.[31] Since he thinks no historical choice situation could make our nature decisive, the identification of political principles must be 'hypothetical and non-historical'.[32] Once the constitution of the body politic is thought of hypothetically and non-historically, it is natural to reject both the 'buyer-in' and the 'maker' accounts of citizens' authority. And so I do not think that the way to recover Rawls's account of legitimacy, or to solve the exegetical puzzles in his texts, is to locate him in the Lockean strand of social contract theory. It is much more useful to locate him in the Kantian strand instead, and to see what ideas he teased out of that strand and wove into his own view.

C. Kant and the Social Contract

To see the differences between the Lockean and Kantian strands of the contract tradition, it is useful to begin with Kant's essay on 'Theory and Practice'.[33] In that essay, Kant clearly and firmly rejects the instrumental view of agreement on a constitution, for he says that the contract for establishing a constitution differs from other contracts people might make. People within society contract into groups in order to secure ends that they naturally have, by which Kant means ends which are productive of their happiness. Although he does not give examples, he no doubt has in mind ends as different as amusement, marriage, and mutually beneficial economic exchange. By contrast, the contract which establishes a constitution is one which is

[30] For a clear statement of this reading, see Ian Shapiro, 'PLSC-118: The Moral Foundations of Politics: Lecture 13—Appropriating Locke Today (February 22, 2010)' <http://oyc.yale.edu/political-science/plsc-118/lecture-13> accessed 26 October 2018. Others read Locke as endorsing the weaker principle that craftsmen have authority over what they create *ex nihilo*. This principle, though general in form, has implications only for divine authority since only God can create *ex nihilo*.

[31] See Rawls, 'The Idea of Public Reason Revisited' (n 15) 137.

[32] Rawls, *Political Liberalism* (n 1) 271.

[33] Immanuel Kant, 'On the Common Saying: That may be Correct in Theory, But it is of No Use in Practice' in Mary J Gregor (ed), *Practical Philosophy* (Cambridge University Press, 1996) (hereafter Kant, 'Theory and Practice'). All pinpoint references are to the volume and pages of the Academy Edition of Kant's works, which this edition provides.

made to secure an end that is not given by the natural desire for happiness, but is instead an end that all the contracting parties ought to have.[34]

That end, and the purpose for which political society is constituted, is what Kant calls a 'civil condition'. When that condition obtains, all are subject to a 'basic law'[35] under which they all have equal freedom and under which rights are determined and secured.[36] Kant argues that such a law can only be adopted by an act of 'public will'.[37] The public will, he says, is the will of 'the entire people'.[38] Achievement of the end for which Kant says a constitution is established therefore raises the question of how citizens are able to constitute a single body politic capable of volition and action.

So far, Kant's view of agreement on political incorporation and the constitution might sound like quite like Locke's. For although some of the ends that Locke says people enter political society to secure are ends Kant would say they naturally have, he also says that they form political society so that everyone's enjoyment of rights will be secure. That, like Kant's civil condition, seems to be an end everyone ought to have.[39] The question of how Kant thinks it is possible to form a public will therefore seems to be just the question I said Locke raises about how it is possible to form a body politic capable of volition. And since Kant thinks the public will which is expressed in the constitution is the will of all, he might seem to share the view that each is a maker of the constitution with a maker's authority over it, or perhaps the authority of someone who buys into the civil condition by surrendering some of her pre-political rights.

But these similarities are illusory, for there are a number of deep and significant differences between Locke's view and Kant's.

For one thing, Kant denies that there are any conclusive pre-political rights, for he says that the 'right of human beings under public coercive laws' is the '*conditio sine qua non* of all other duties'.[40] He differs from Locke in thinking that the object of writing a constitution is the ongoing realization of a state of affairs—the civil condition—in which citizens have rights, not just a state of affairs in which they enjoy their pre-existing rights more securely. Kant therefore thinks it a conceptual truth that the civil condition is one in which citizens stand in a relationship that would not be available to them outside it.

This first difference gives rise to a second one. For the question of how Locke thinks it is possible to form a body politic capable of unified action is subtly but importantly different from the question about the condition of Kant's public will. We might rephrase the question about Locke by asking how Locke thinks it possible that members of a multitude, each of whom wills his own interest, can converge on a single outcome. Once we rephrase the question this way, we can see why Locke

[34] See ibid vol 8, 289–90. [35] ibid vol 8, 295. [36] ibid vol 8, 290.

[37] ibid vol 8, 294. [38] ibid.

[39] In his very illuminating 'Reason and Agreement in Social Contract Views' (1990) 19 Philosophy and Public Affairs 122; Samuel Freeman stresses this affinity between Lockean and Kantian contractualism: see 124.

[40] I exempt the right to independence. On this right, see Arthur Ripstein, *Force and Freedom: Kant's Legal and Political Philosophy* (Harvard University Press 2009) 30–56.

answers by providing his readers with a kind of 'maker's knowledge' of a polity—more specifically, by showing his readers how they could make a polity which serves the interests they would have were they in a state of nature. The question raised by Kant's account of incorporation cannot be rephrased in the way that Locke's can. For while Kant thinks that 'each [decides] about himself' in the exercise of the public will, he also thinks that the decision of each for each must be the result of 'all decid[ing] about all'.[41]

Kant's argument for this claim is highly compressed and not easy to make out, but I believe he has in mind roughly the following. People in a state of nature would all need at least some property. Moreover, they would all need some right to property. More precisely, they would need to stand in moral relations with their property and with other people. For they would need it to be the case that their possession of property changed the moral status of others, so that other people could rightfully be excluded from that property's expropriation and use. But in a state of nature, there is no way to establish those relations. Possession and control would depend on differences in strength.[42] To establish those moral relations, people would need some authoritative procedure for assigning rights, one that abstracts from or adjudicates among those differences in strength if the outcome is to be just to all.

Even without saying what that authoritative procedure is, we can label it. So, call the procedure, whatever it turns out to be, 'all decid[ing] about all'—or 'public willing' for short. The object of public willing is the civil condition, and that condition is one of freedom and equality. If a willing public is to realize that object, there will have to be constraints on how public willing operates. One constraint is that public willing must result in 'each [deciding] about himself'. So, the question raised by Kant's account is: how must the basic law and other legislation be chosen so that that constraint is satisfied? It is not at all obvious that the best answer to *that* question is given by an account of how people in a natural condition would make a polity. Instead, it might be given—as it will be in Rawls's work—by reference to a highly idealized choice procedure which members of the willing public would have no idea how to make.

This second difference leads to a third. In chapter VIII of 'The Treatise', Locke says that some social contracts of the sort he describes were actually entered into. That chapter conveys the impression that, whether or not they were, Locke thinks it important that the agreement by which a people incorporates and writes a constitution is at least a *possible* historical process. This is just what we would expect if Locke was indeed trying to convey the kind of practical knowledge I called 'maker's knowledge'. In 'Theory and Practice', Kant insists that it is not necessary that there ever was such a contract, and he adds immediately that the contract establishing a constitution is 'only an idea of reason'.[43] He is somewhat more expansive in the *Metaphysics*

[41] Kant, 'Theory and Practice' (n 33) vol 8, 294.

[42] See Ripstein, *Force and Freedom* (n 40) 168ff; also Wolfgang Kersting, 'Politics, Freedom and Order: Kant's Political Philosophy' in Paul Guyer (ed), *Cambridge Companion to Kant* (Cambridge University Press 1992) 352.

[43] Kant, 'Theory and Practice' (n 33) vol 8, 297.

of Morals, saying of the contract that it 'is only the idea of [the] act in terms of which alone we can think of the legitimacy of the state'.[44] If it turns out that public willing is best depicted by a choice procedure that could not actually take place—because of the way in which it idealizes the conditions of choice—the idea of a contract establishing the constitution can still serve its purpose in a Kantian account.

As I said earlier, Locke grounds his account of political obligation on the voluntary character of political society. If it is voluntary, it is something one can freely choose to enter from a state of nature. And so on Locke's view, those in a pre-political condition enjoy a kind of freedom which is robust enough that its exercise can give rise to obligations. Kant seems to allow for the conceptual possibility of a kind of pre-political freedom. But in 'Doctrine of Right', he calls that kind of freedom 'wild [and] lawless',[45] by which I take it he means at least that someone who exercised that kind of freedom would not act from maxims that had the form of a law. Although I cannot argue the point here, I do not think that Kant believes one could incur political obligations by exercising that kind of freedom. In his view, the grounds of such obligations lie elsewhere.

Finally, because Kant thinks that persons in a pre-political condition enjoy only 'wild, lawless freedom', comparison with that condition does not show that those who constitute a body politic give up something of value to enter it, something whose value can be measured against the gains of entry.[46] The description of entrants to political society as buyers-in is mistaken. It would therefore be a mistake to say that Kant thinks citizens have the kind of authority over political society that 'buyers-in' would have. It would also be a mistake to think that he granted them maker's authority over it, as we saw that some scholars think Locke did. For as we have seen, Kant does not seem to attach any importance to the possibility that citizens actually did or could make political society. But actual making would seem to be what is required to ground maker's authority.

So, while Kant may have been willing to grant that the description of citizens as makers or contractors is useful for some purposes, its connection to citizens' authority is indirect. To see the connection, it will help to look briefly at the kind of authority Kant thinks citizens *do* have.

Immediately after Kant says in 'Theory and Practice' that the contract is an idea of reason, he says that the idea can still have what he calls 'practical reality':

> [N]amely to bind every legislator to give his laws in such a way that they could have arisen from the united will of a whole people and to regard each subject, insofar as he wants to be a citizen, as if he has joined in voting for such a will.[47]

[44] Immanuel Kant, 'The Metaphysics of Morals' in Mary J Gregor (ed), *Practical Philosophy*, vol 6 (Cambridge University Press 1996) 315. Again, the pinpoint reference is to the Academy Edition. The German of this difficult passage is 'eigentlich aber nur die Idee desselben, nach der die Rechtmäßigkeit desselben allein gedacht werden kann'.

[45] ibid vol 6, 316.

[46] At ibid, Kant says: 'And one cannot say: the human being in a state has sacrificed a part of his innate outer freedom for the sake of an end; but rather, he has relinquished entirely his wild lawless freedom in order to find his freedom as such undiminished, in a dependence upon laws, that is, in a rightful condition.'

[47] Kant, 'Theory and Practice' (n 33) vol 8, 297.

When Kant says that the idea of a social contract has 'practical reality', I take him to mean that it has 'practical import'—import for how we live our lives. Given his aims in 'Theory and Practice', this is a point he quite clearly wishes to establish. The import it has is of a particular kind: it has *moral* import or *moral* significance. I take the import of the contract to be that there are two moral requirements of realizing the civil condition: legislators are to give only laws that they sincerely think could have been chosen by an act of public willing and they are to treat each person who is subject to the law as someone who '[decided] about himself'. If that is correct, then it follows that legislators are required to accord citizens an important kind of standing: the standing to have their interests—as they see them or would see them if suitably informed and rational—taken into account when laws are made.

That implication would be a natural one for Kant to draw. For in the civil condition everyone has standing as an equal bearer of rights and each relates to everyone else as a person with that standing. It stands to reason that that condition can obtain over time only if legislators treat citizens as having that standing when they make the laws. So, citizens have authority in this sense: legislation must be consistent with the standing of all citizens as free and equal. The test of consistency is whether the law 'could have arisen from the united will of a whole people'—that is, whether the law could be publicly willed.

But citizens do not enjoy their authority or standing because they are makers. Instead, crudely put, citizens can be represented as makers because they have standing. For I take the idea of citizens as makers of a constitution which renders them free and equal to be a 'mode of representing' the claim that living as free equals is the object or the *raison d'être* of a constitution.[48] A constitution which realizes its object is one which makes available a new mode of life, one that would not be available in the absence of a constitution that could be publicly willed. That is why Kant—like Rawls under his influence—so vigorously rejects the instrumentalism of Locke and Hobbes. I take the idea of citizens who make a constitution by public willing to be a mode of representing the claim that a constitution can achieve its object only if it is such that each could affirm it were she deciding for all and for herself. And I take the idea of citizens as makers of a constitution which empowers 'the legislative' to be a mode of representing the requirements I have said Kant thinks legislators are under.

I said at the end of the previous section that Rawls rejects all of the elements of what I called 'the Lockean package' of views about incorporation and the social contract. It should be clear that Kant does so as well, and that he offers a very different package instead. Kant arrives at the content of that package by reflecting on what must be in place if citizens are to have property. Rawls reaches his conclusions from a different starting point, but the views he ends up with, and many of the steps by which he arrives at them, bear striking similarities to Kant's. And so I now want to draw on the Kantian package of views on those topics to address the puzzles in Rawls's discussion of the liberal principle of legitimacy.

[48] This phrase is taken from William Hastie's (philosophically laden) translation of the passage from 'The Metaphysics of Morals' quoted at n 44; see <http://www.marxists.org/reference/subject/ethics/kant/morals/ch04.htm> accessed 23 August 2017.

D. Rawls on Political Legitimacy

At the end of section A, I said that the key to Rawls's treatment of legitimacy is his claim that political power is the power of the people as a collective body of which everyone has an equal share. One of the puzzles about that claim, I said, is that Rawls does not say how the collective body is formed. Another is that it is not clear what it means to say that everyone has an equal share of its power. These are questions to which Locke seems to have given a clear answer. But if we take Rawls to have a Kantian rather than a Lockean view of incorporation, we can understand what he means by these claims in a way that shows why he does not feel compelled to say as much about how the corporate body is formed as they did.

In the previous section, we saw that for Kant, the original act of incorporation would have to be an act of public willing—more specifically, it would have to be the public willing of a constitution which makes all free and equal. We also saw that he thinks incorporation by public willing is a mode of representing 'the idea by which the rightfulness of the process of organizing the constitution may be made conceivable'. At the end of the last section, I said how it represents what makes that process rightful. I take Rawls to agree with Kant about how we have to understand the formation of a collective body. I also take him to agree with Kant in thinking that the idea of formation-by-public-willing is a way of conveying more fundamental moral claims about the object of a constitution, about how to test the 'rightful[ness]' of a constitution, and about the constraints that legislators are under. And I take the claims he uses the idea to convey to be those Kant used it to convey.

If we read Rawls this way, then we can see why he does not think he needs to discuss how the body politic is incorporated. For what does the work in Rawls's argument for the principle of legitimacy are those more fundamental claims. We can also see what he means to represent by saying that 'citizens have an equal share' in the coercive power of the body politic. He does not mean, as Locke might have, that citizens are equal because each contributes equally to society's power of enforcement or that each purchases an equal share when she gives up her pre-political freedom. Rather, I take it he means to stake a claim about citizens' equal standing. Rawls does not make those claims explicit or say how he would defend them, but perhaps he would reason as follows.

The point of a constitution is to enable people to live together justly as free and equal citizens. A minimal condition on legislation, which is passed in accordance with the constitution, is that it be consistent with realizing that object. Since laws must be coercively enforced, the power to legislate and the power to coerce are inseparable.[49]

[49] The way in which Rawls puts this point suggests that he thinks law is inseparable from coercion because it requires forcible, and perhaps violent, enforcement. I believe what he should say is that a body of law which places all on a footing of freedom and equality will inevitably limit citizens' freedom. And he should follow Kant in equating coercion with such limitations, leaving aside any suggestion about how the limits are enforced. He could move from there to the conclusion he wants without leaving himself open to criticisms like that of Helga Varden, 'Kant's Non-Voluntarist Conception of Political Obligations: Why Justice is Impossible in the State of Nature' (2008) 13 Kantian Review 1, 3.

So the enforcement of law must also be consistent with citizens' freedom and equality. I believe Rawls thinks that the way to determine whether enforcement meets that condition is to determine whether the citizens could publicly will the law's enforcement. And so when Rawls says that everyone has an equal share of coercive power, I believe what he has in mind is that because everyone is to be included among those who are to live on a footing of freedom and equality, everyone is to be considered a participant in the public's legislative and—hence—coercive will.

This conclusion is rather abstract, but it has what Kant called a 'practical reality'. For according to Kant's constraint on public willing, which I take Rawls to accept, the implication of something's being publicly willed is that each person who is reckoned a participant in the public willing could will it for himself, as a free and equal citizen. So, the 'practical reality' of everyone's having an equal share of coercive power is that each has the standing to demand that laws be ones that she could will. The demand that is generated by citizens' standing is not one that can be turned aside by pointing to their choice to enter political society or by their right of exit. For while Kant entertained a limited comparison with pre- or extra-political condition, Rawls entertains no comparison at all. He simply says the political relationship is one that we enter by birth and exit by death.[50]

Rawls implies that *the* question which the liberal principle of legitimacy is supposed to answer is conditioned by the two distinguishing features of a political relationship. Those two features are that the power which is regularly imposed on parties to that relationship is 'the power of free and equal citizens as a collective body'[51] and that that power is inescapable. We can now see how these features give rise to *a* question about any exercise of political power. Any exercise of power must be consistent with citizens' freedom and equality. Some exercises of power have more far-reaching implications for citizens' freedom and equality than others. And so that question will be most pressing when the most fundamental political matters are at stake.

In section A, we saw that one of the textual questions raised by Rawls's treatment of legitimacy is what connection he sees between a question about 'the general structure of authority' and one about particular exercises of authority. In section B, when I considered whether Rawls is a Lockean about legitimacy, we saw how questions about the justifiability of particular exercises of authority lead to questions about authority's 'general structure'. For as I said then, to show that an exercise of ordinary power is justifiable, it is not enough to show that the person who exercised it had the authority to do so under the governing framework that is in place. That framework must itself satisfy the standards which apply to constituent power. By reading Rawls as a Kantian instead of a Lockean, we can make the connection between the justifiability of constituent and ordinary power more precise.

Constituent power is the power to form a constitution. I have said that Rawls follows Kant in thinking that the constitution must establish citizens' freedom and equality. That is what a constitution is for. To fulfil its purpose, a constitution must provide certain guarantees that put citizens on a footing of freedom and equality,

[50] Rawls, *Political Liberalism* (n 1) 136. [51] ibid.

and assure them adequate protections from government. It must also establish legislative, executive, and judicial procedures. So, any time ordinary power is exercised, the nature and inescapability of that power raise the question of whether power was exercised within the constraints and according to the procedures laid down by the constitution *and* they raise the question of whether the constitution itself realizes its object. Only if the answer to both questions is 'yes' is that exercise consistent with citizens' freedom and equality. And Rawls thinks if exercises of ordinary power are consistent with citizens' freedom and equality—and only if they are consistent—then they are 'fully proper' and hence legitimate.

Call the question of whether exercises of power satisfy this standard 'the consistency question'. Justificatory concepts are defensive, used to turn back objections or complaints.[52] Since Rawls thinks that showing an exercise of power to be legitimate justifies it, his discussion of legitimacy raises the question of what objection to or complaint about exercises of political power a demonstration of their legitimacy is supposed to rebut or pre-empt. The consistency question shows what that worry is: a worry about the consistency of an exercise of the public's coercive power with citizens' freedom and equality.

The consistency question may not seem to be a question about legitimacy as that notion is ordinarily understood, since it is not obviously connected with political obligation, for example, or with territorial sovereignty. In the next section, I shall address this challenge. But if we grant for now that that challenge can be met—and so grant that the question of whether an exercise of political power is legitimate is equivalent to the consistency question—then we can see why Rawls equates the former question with the complicated one I quoted in section A, above. And we can see how he would defend his principle.

Recall that the question with which Rawls equates that of when the exercise of political power is justifiable is:

> [I]n light of what principles and ideals must we, as free and equal citizens, be able to view ourselves as exercising power if our exercise is to be justifiable to other citizens and to respect their being reasonable and rational?[53]

While Rawls says later in *Political Liberalism* that ordinary citizens exercise power by voting, that is not what he is talking about here when he speaks of 'our exercise' of political power. Rather, context makes clear that he is talking about exercises of ordinary power by public officials. And so when Rawls uses the phrase 'view ourselves as exercising power', I take him to mean that we can adopt a certain point of view on the exercises of that power. We think of ourselves as free and equal citizens who are in the position of deciding how power is to be exercised and we can think of the exercises of power by public officials as executions of our decisions. And I take him to mean that the laws enacted by public officials, the executive orders they issue, and the administrative and enforcement actions they undertake, are justifiable or legitimate only if, once we think of ourselves this way, we can also view those

[52] See A John Simmons, 'Justification and Legitimacy' (1999) 109 Ethics 739, 740.
[53] Rawls, *Political Liberalism* (n 1) 137.

exercises of power as having been willed or chosen on the basis of certain principles and ideals. Rawls's question is what those principles and ideals are.

The nature of political power and of those over whom it is exercised constrain the answer. Those over whom power is exercised are reasonable and rational. Political power is to be thought of as the power of free and equal citizens. We have seen that for Rawls, the 'practical reality' of this latter claim is that exercises of power have to be such that they could be publicly willed. Rawls's treatment of public willing implies that the imaginative exercise of the last paragraph—the exercise of imagining ourselves as political decision-makers—will have to be considerably more abstract and complicated than it first appeared if it is to issue only in legitimate law. But what matters for present purposes is this: the principles and ideals which answer Rawls's question will have to guide that exercise so that the results are consistent with the freedom and equality of citizens who are reasonable and rational. That is why I take what I called 'the consistency question' to express the question the liberal principle of legitimacy is supposed to answer.

If we take Rawls's principle to be an answer to the consistency question, we can also see how he would defend it. According to that principle,

> our exercise of political power is fully proper only when it is exercised in accordance with a constitution the essentials of which all citizens as free and equal may reasonably be expected to endorse in light of principles and ideals acceptable to their common human reason.[54]

I take the 'principles and ideals' to which Rawls refers here to be or to include those that would be endorsed in a choice situation, such as the original position, in which citizens are represented as free, equal, reasonable, and rational. Since the principles and ideals would be endorsed by citizens represented as reasonable and rational, those principles and ideals are 'acceptable to their common human reason'. And since they would be endorsed by citizens when represented as free and equal, a constitution whose essentials reflect those principles is one whose essentials 'all citizens as free and equal may reasonably be expected to endorse'.

A constitution would be endorsed just in case it does what I have said constitutions are supposed to do: establish relations among citizens on a footing of freedom and equality—by, among other things, requiring equal liberty and an adequate social minimum.[55] Rawls does not say what he means by 'in accordance with', but I do not think he means only that power must be exercised according to the procedures laid out in the constitution. He must also think that exercises of power are in accordance with a constitution only if they are consonant with its aims. If that is right, then exercises of power will be 'in accordance with a constitution the essentials of which all citizens as free and equal may reasonably be expected to endorse in light of principles and ideals acceptable to their common human reason' just in case they are consistent with citizens' freedom and equality. So, I believe Rawls would defend his liberal principle of legitimacy on the grounds that it singles out just the conditions under which the consistency question receives an affirmative answer.

[54] ibid. [55] See ibid 227–29.

An exercise of power that satisfies the liberal principle of legitimacy also satisfies the Kantian requirement that I said is represented by Rawls's claim that citizens have an equal share of political power: the requirement that exercises of power be such that each could will them for himself. For in Rawls's hands, that requirement says that exercises of power must be such that each could will them for himself as a free and equal citizen. And it seems that each *could* will an exercise of power as free and equal provided that the exercise can be shown consistent with her status as such.

Why does everyone have the standing ascribed to them by the argument? What is the source of this status that every citizen is said to have and why is everyone said to have it? Because Rawls makes the working assumption that citizens are born into political society, he, like Kant, would deny that they should be thought of as buyers-in.[56] And, like Kant, Rawls denies that citizens must actually enter into an agreement on a constitution. Indeed, because Rawls's mode of representing 'the idea by which the rightfulness of the process of organizing the constitution may be made conceivable' includes the veil of ignorance,[57] it does not represent even a possible historical process. And so Rawls would also deny that citizens' standing is due to their having made political society.

Rather, I think the Rawls of *Political Liberalism* would have said that citizens' status or standing is one of the 'basic intuitive ideas' he finds in and appropriates from democratic culture. That idea does not just express an abstract belief about citizenship. Rawls says in 'Reply to Habermas' that '[i]t is part of citizens' sense of themselves, not only collectively but also individually, to recognize political authority as deriving from them'.[58] I read this remark as extending the 'mode of representation' Rawls began by claiming that everyone has an equal share of political power. For I read it saying not just that everyone has the relevant standing, but that members of democracies have and prize a sense of themselves as citizens with that standing.

E. Some Textual and Philosophical Pay-Offs

I have tried to interpret Rawls's introduction of the liberal principle of legitimacy in a way that addresses many of the textual puzzles I identified in section A, above, including the question of how he would defend that principle. I believe these interpretive efforts provide a philosophical as well as an exegetical pay-off, for I think we find in Rawls a way of thinking about legitimacy that is interestingly different from other ways of thinking about the subject that have some currency in political philosophy. To bring out what is interesting and different about it, it will help to see how Rawls would respond to some critical discussions of his treatment of legitimacy.

[56] See ibid 276. [57] See Rawls, *A Theory of Justice* (n 2) 172–74.
[58] Rawls, *Political Liberalism* (n 1) 431.

1. Justification and legitimacy

I observed earlier that the consistency question might not seem to capture a concern about legitimacy as that notion is often understood. One way of understanding it is expressed by John Simmons. Simmons thinks that legitimacy attaches in the first instance to states. He describes a state's legitimacy as 'the complex moral right it possesses to be the exclusive imposer of binding duties on its subjects, to have its subjects comply with these duties, and to use coercion to enforce the duties'.[59] He distinguishes state legitimacy from the justification of the state. To show a state is justified, he says, 'involves showing that the ... state is morally acceptable and a good bargain'.[60] The meaning of 'legitimacy' is not clearly fixed in ordinary political discourse or in the contemporary philosophical and political theoretic literature. It seems to me that the property Simmons calls 'justifiability' is sometimes called 'legitimacy'. And I think Simmons himself would grant as much. For he is much less concerned to argue that he has correctly identified the meaning of the term than he is to distinguish two separate forms of political evaluation and to contend that Rawls ignores the importance of the distinction. Some of the interest of Rawls's treatment of legitimacy can be brought out by looking at why Simmons says Rawls ignores it.

Simmons thinks that philosophers in the Kantian strand of contractualism glide over the distinction between justification and legitimacy because they blur the distinction between actual and hypothetical consent. Thus, he says of Nagel:

> [His] suggestion ... seems to be that the ideal of a fully voluntary society should of course guide us, but the (regrettable) facts of political life force us to accept instead non-voluntarist standards of legitimacy which appeal only to (what Nagel calls) 'quasi-voluntariness' ... In fact it seems clear that contemporary Kantian and hypothetical contractarian political philosophies [including Rawls] have illicitly appropriated the justificatory force of voluntarism while being (like Kant) in no real way motivated by it.[61]

Whatever may be true of Nagel, Rawls would deny that we should be guided by the ideal of a society in which membership is voluntary in the sense of the term Simmons has in mind, for the voluntarist ideal which motivates him is a society which is fully voluntary in a very different sense. It is the ideal of a society in which all will together, as a collective body, but in which each at the same time wills for herself. A society in which membership is actually freely chosen—that people actually join voluntarily—might not realize that ideal. Indeed, it might not even approximate it. The question for Rawls is how we are to understand the ideal that he thinks *should* guide us. That question is difficult. But its difficulty is not due to 'the (regrettable) facts of political life'. The difficulty is philosophical, and Rawls thinks the only way the question can be answered is by appeal to hypothetical consent.

That, and not as an expression of wistful yearning after a society in which membership is voluntary, is the way to take his claim that 'a society satisfying the principles of justice as fairness comes as close as a society can to being a voluntary scheme, for

[59] Simmons, 'Justification and Legitimacy' (n 52) 746. [60] ibid 758.
[61] ibid 761.

it meets the principles which free and equal persons would assent to under circumstances that are fair'.[62] Rawls may be wrong to imply that his well-ordered society 'comes as close as a [political] society can' *possibly* come to being voluntary. Whether or not he is is a matter for further argument. But at the very least, Rawls's claim provides us with a salutary reminder that there is an 'ideal of a fully voluntary society'—and a voluntarist strain of theorizing about political legitimacy—that does not appeal to actual acts of the will.

Once we take that reminder to heart, we may be much less worried about Rawls's alleged conflation of legitimacy and justification. Simmons thinks that because Rawls fails to distinguish them, he holds—mistakenly, in Simmons's view—that a state whose constitution does what a constitution is supposed to do is not only a good bargain, but is also legitimate in Simmons's sense of the term. But I have said that it is a mistake to think of Rawlsian citizens as 'buyers-in' to political society. That suggests that 'a good bargain' is at least an inapt metaphor for what Rawls thinks of a state with a justifiable constitution. I also think Simmons is mistaken to imply that Rawls simply overlooks the question of what is required for states to impose duties on their citizens. For although I cannot adduce textual support for my reading here, I conjecture that the Rawls of *Political Liberalism* held a somewhat modified version of the natural duty account he espoused in *A Theory of Justice*. According to the modified account, we have a *pro tanto* natural duty to uphold institutions which make it possible for us to live as free equals. Since upholding such institutions normally requires complying with legitimate law, those who live under such institutions therefore have a *pro tanto* duty to obey the law.[63]

This reading is not only more charitable to Rawls, it also shows some of what distinguishes his treatment of legitimacy from Lockean views like Simmons's. For it shows that while Rawls departs from many philosophers in denying a conceptual connection between legitimacy and political duty or obligation, he does argue that there can be a connection of a different sort. That connection goes by way of a natural duty. It is because of that natural duty that states with justifiable constitutions have a claim-right to their citizens' compliance with legitimate law. If we grant that Rawls's account of legitimacy merits the label 'voluntarist',[64] then we can read him as exploring the possibility of a voluntarist account of citizens' duty to comply that

[62] Rawls, *A Theory of Justice* (n 2) 12.

[63] I describe the duty as '*pro tanto*' for what I suspect is the same reason Rawls describes it as 'politically (morally) binding': an account of our duties all-things-considered would require Rawls to go beyond the bounds of his political liberalism.

[64] The question of whether the label is appropriate for Rawls's view, or for other Kantian views, raises issues I cannot adequately address here. There is a body of literature arguing that Kant is not a voluntarist because he did not think that the bindingness of the categorical imperative requires an actual act of will; see, for example, Karl Ameriks, 'On Two Non-Realist Interpretations of Kant's Ethics' in *Interpreting Kant's Critiques* (Oxford University Press 2003). But Ameriks's position is compatible with the view that Kant, or Kantians such as Rawls, are meta-ethical voluntarists because they think, as Robert Adams puts it, that 'moral properties have their seat, not in the objects, states or actions to which they are ascribed, but in the valuing faculties of an intelligent being or beings ... in the sense that they are constituted by some attitude or action of those faculties'. See Robert Merrihew Adams, 'Voluntarism and the Shape of a History' (2004) 16 Utilitas 124, 130; also Patrick Kain, 'Self-Legislation in Kant's Moral Philosophy' (2004) 86 Archiv für Geschichte der Philosophie 257, 301.

does not depend on their actual consent. That possibility seems to me to be worthy of further study. For despite the difficulties with actual consent theories, voluntarism of some kind is perennially attractive. Its attractions do not seem to me to be captured, nor its difficulties avoided, by views which connect legitimacy with political obligation via versions of consent that are highly strained.

2. Coercion and legitimacy

One philosopher whose views of legitimacy and obligation *do* resemble Rawls's is Christopher Wellman. Wellman thinks that legitimacy 'is necessary but not sufficient for political obligation'.[65] Like Rawls, he connects the two via a natural duty—in Wellman's case, the natural duty of good samaritanism. We can appreciate the distinctiveness—and, I think, the more compelling character—of Rawls's treatment by contrasting Rawls's and Wellman's views of the doubt that showings of legitimacy are supposed to dispel.

Wellman writes that:

> Political states coerce those within their territorial borders; if you are in country X, X threatens to punish you if you disobey its legal commands. An account of political legitimacy explains why this coercion is permissible.[66]

Thus, Wellman thinks that questions about the legitimacy of state action arise simply because state action is coercive and the permissibility of its coercion needs to be shown. And he says liberals think that state coercion raises the question of political legitimacy because they are committed to allowing each person control over her own affairs.[67] But any coercion—by an association, an employer, or a criminal—threatens people's control over their own lives. What Wellman says, therefore, suggests that he thinks the state's power to coerce, while no doubt much greater than the power available to these other agents, is not of a fundamentally different character. Coercion by the state would not, therefore, seem to raise a different problem from coercion by any other agent.

Rawls thinks that political power differs from other kinds of power because of its ultimacy and inescapability, because the various agents which exercise it—at least in a democratic society—routinely claim that it is the power of the people, and because the regularity and publicity with which they do so encourages citizens to think of themselves as its source. Citizens who are coerced are thus encouraged, in effect, to believe that their own power is being used against them. And so, to paraphrase Wellman, the Rawlsian view is that an 'account of political legitimacy explains what is meant by these claims about political power and it explains why coercion by political power so understood is permissible'. Thus, whatever the other similarities in their views, Wellman differs from Rawls about how questions of legitimacy arise and

[65] Christopher H Wellman, 'Liberalism, Samaritanism and Political Legitimacy' (1996) 25 Philosophy and Public Affairs 211, 212.
[66] ibid 211–12. [67] ibid 212.

about what doubt showings of legitimacy are supposed to dispel. I take that difference to be significant and interesting.

Charles Larmore agrees with Rawls in recognizing the importance of the first feature of the political power: its inescapability.[68] But he thinks that Rawls does not go far enough in showing why the state's exercise of inescapable power is justified, for he thinks that Rawls fails to make explicit the basis on which he accepts his own principle of legitimacy.[69]

The basis of that principle, Larmore contends, is the moral imperative to show respect for persons.[70] Respect for persons supports the principle of legitimacy because respecting persons enjoins us 'to look for common ground, to seek the principles of our political life in the area of reasonable agreement'.[71] I believe that Larmore intends the phrase 'principles of our political life' to include constitutional principles or constitutional essentials. So, respect enjoins us to establish a constitution—to use Rawls's phrase—'the essentials of which all citizens as free and equal may reasonably be expected to endorse in light of principles and ideals acceptable to their common human reason'. The establishment of such a constitution is a legitimate or justified exercise of constituent power. And if Larmore assumes that ordinary power is justifiably exercised when it is exercised in accordance with a justified constitution, then he can infer Rawls's liberal principle of legitimacy. He can claim to have provided the argument for that principle that Rawls himself omitted by appealing to respect for persons.

While Larmore puts forward his argument for Rawls's principle as an elucidation of what Rawls should have said, he appears to defend the principle without appeal to the second feature of political power identified by Rawls. That feature is that political authority is the authority of citizens as a collective body. Thus Larmore differs from Wellman in appealing to one distinguishing feature of political relations, but he seems to differ from Rawls in appealing to *only* one. At this point, I think Rawls would insist that it is Larmore who has not laid out his argument as explicitly as is desirable. For on the reading of Rawls that I have presented here, the second feature of the political relation is a way of representing the claim that the exercise of political power must be publicly willed, on the basis of reasons which all can recognize as good ones. It is this feature, which Larmore fails to mention, that Larmore needs to move from the first step of his argument to the second.

Larmore *does* appeal to the collective will at one point, but as I read him, he appeals to it in a different argument. That argument is not intended to establish the liberal principle of legitimacy. It is instead supposed to show that principles which are the object of reasonable agreement are authoritative. In the relevant passage, Larmore says:

> [T]he norm of respect does not have the same sort of standing as the constitutional principles worked out on its basis. Those principles are legitimate in virtue of being able to be the object

[68] Charles Larmore, 'Political Liberalism: Its Motivation and Goals' in David Sobel, Peter Vallentyne, and Steven Wall (eds), *Oxford Studies in Political Philosophy*, vol 1 (Oxford University Press 2015) 77; also Charles Larmore, 'What is Political Philosophy?' (2012) 10 Journal of Moral Philosophy 1, 10.

[69] Larmore, 'Political Liberalism' (n 68) 75. [70] ibid 79–80. [71] ibid 80.

of reasonable agreement and their political authority can accordingly be said to derive from the collective will of the citizens.[72]

But whether the argument to which Larmore gestures in this passage is Rawlsian depends on what he means by 'can accordingly be said to derive from'. If he means 'therefore derive from', then he thinks that the collective will of the people is the real source of the constitution's authority, and that we know the constitution enjoys that authority because its essentials could be 'the object of reasonable agreement'. On the reading of Rawls offered in this chapter, talk of an original contract is a 'mode of representing'. For Larmore's view to comport with what I take Rawls's to be, his phrase 'can accordingly be said to derive from' would have to mean 'can be represented as deriving from'. The fundamental moral claims that are represented are those identified earlier. The fact that a constitution's essentials could be agreed to show that the constitution does what constitutions are supposed to do. The principles of the constitution have authority because they establish the conditions under which we can live as free equals. If this is not what Larmore means, then while his view is nominally or verbally similar to Rawls's, it—like the views of many others now writing about legitimacy—is at bottom quite different.

F. Some Lingering Questions

Even if the interpretation of Rawlsian legitimacy that I have sketched here answers the textual and philosophical puzzles I identified at the outset, a number of questions remain.

I said that Rawls thinks that constitutional principles are authoritative because they enable us to live as free equals. And I conjectured that Rawls endorses an account of political obligation according to which we have a duty to support a constitution which enables us to live that way. These elements of my interpretation suggest that Rawls thinks we are subject to an imperative to live as free equals. If that suggestion is right, then it raises a number of questions about what grounds the imperative, whether it expresses a duty to others or to self, and why that imperative can be satisfied only by living with others under a justifiable constitution and a body of legitimate law, rather than under institutional arrangements of some other sort. It may be, as the Rawls of *A Theory of Justice* believed, that we realize an important part of ourselves only by living in political relations ordered by principles of justice.[73] But while that would show that we can enjoy a very great good by living as Rawlsian free equals, as the Rawls of *A Theory of Justice* also believed, it would not show that there is an imperative to live that way.[74]

Another set of questions concerns societies whose constitutions fail fully to establish conditions of freedom and equality. Stipulate for the sake of argument that all the essentials written into the US Constitution are such that they can be endorsed on the basis of our 'common human reason'. That stipulation does

[72] ibid 81.

[73] See Rawls, *A Theory of Justice* (n 2) 501.

[74] See ibid 503.

not imply that all the essentials that could be so endorsed are written into the Constitution. Indeed, some obviously are not—such as a decent minimum and guaranteed health care.[75] Moreover, some of the written essentials have arguably been interpreted unreasonably, as when the Supreme Court held that corporations may make unlimited contributions to political campaigns under colour of free speech.[76] So, there seem to be at least two ways in which the US Constitution, as interpreted, might be said to fall short of being 'a constitution the essentials of which all citizens as free and equal may reasonably be expected to endorse in light of principles and ideals acceptable to their common human reason'.

Rawls's principle states the conditions under which exercises of power are '*fully* proper'. The principle may not, therefore, express a necessary condition on the legitimate or proper exercise of power. But even if not, it—when conjoined with the shortcomings of the US Constitution—does seem to imply that none of the exercises of power by the US government is fully proper. Since that seems to be too strong and sweeping a conclusion, it raises the question of whether the principle of legitimacy is not in need of significant qualifications, qualifications which would enable us to distinguish exercises which are fully proper from exercises which are somewhat less so. Alternatively, Rawls may intend the principle's condition on constitutions to be permissive enough that the US Constitution satisfies it. In that case, if the principle is to guide our judgements of legitimacy under non-ideal conditions, we will have to know just how permissive it is.

[75] See Rawls, *Political Liberalism* (n 1) 228–29.

[76] *Citizens United v Federal Election Commission* 558 US 310 (2010).

PART II

LEGITIMACY OF THE STATE

IV

The Future of State Sovereignty

*Joseph Raz**

A. Introduction

This chapter is a speculative reflection on the theoretical implications, or some of them, of contemporary developments in the international scene.

There is a widespread view that the international sphere has undergone, and is undergoing, radical and swift changes. Naturally, there is no agreement on the main sources or features of the changes: the end of the Second World War, the end of the Cold War, the rise of American supremacy, the end of American supremacy, economic globalization, and so on.

To the more legally minded: the explosive development of international law, and related phenomena such as the emergence of the World Trade Organization, the rise of international human rights, and the emergence of international administrative law may seem to be the decisive factors.

From my point of view, one can be ecumenical and take all of these and others as features of the changes.

It is far from clear whether the changes, whatever they are, call for a theoretical rethink. Should not theories of law, for example, be robust in the sense of being true of law in all places, all times?

Yes and no: a successful general theory of law would (i) identify the important essential features of the law and (ii) explain why the law is or was central to the self-consciousness and political organization of some societies. The two desiderata may point in different directions: think of Sharia law, or of rabbinical law, or canon law. All are law and a good theory of law will confirm that. But in many countries when these laws were dominant features of their political societies the best theories of the essential structures of these societies may well not have identified them as law, in our sense. Their mingling of law, morality, and theocracy are missed when we think of them as law, that is, as instances of the type of social practice or social organization

* This chapter was written as a talk and retains its character as a talk.

Legitimacy: The State and Beyond. First Edition. Edited by Wojciech Sadurski, Michael Sevel, and Kevin Walton. Published 2019 by Oxford University Press.

many instances of which do not allow for the kind of mingling of law and morality that Sharia law exemplifies.

So, good theorists of these societies may well have had a different analysis of their normative structures, different from that of modern political societies, in which law dominates.

By the same token, a time may come, may have come, when the fact that there are and are likely to remain state legal systems in contemporary political societies is consistent with a need for new theory that will show—if this is indeed the case—that nowadays, a state legal system is no longer the or one of the most important normative structures in our societies.

I am not, however, going to make that possibility the core of my speculation—not quite.

What has attracted calls for a new theory was the so-called 'death of the state'—perhaps mostly expressed these days in less extravagant terms as the rise of legal pluralism or transnational law. I will not discuss these theoretical developments themselves. Rather, my aim is to examine the general case for rethinking legal theory in light of the erosion of the post-Westphalian doctrine of state sovereignty.

For a long time, legal theory has been focused on state law as the paradigm of a legal system. The recognition of the principle of state sovereignty in Article 2(7) of the UN charter seemed to promise that that focus would remain justified for a long time to come. But the subsequent erosion of state sovereignty raises doubts, some of which I will discuss.

1. A note on method

To repeat: this is a speculation about some aspects of possible directions in which international relations may proceed. I focus on the future of sovereignty, for it seems plausible to think that the way in which state sovereignty seems to be changing, or at least the way in which it is subjected to pressure to change, encapsulates some central trends in the development of international relations.

I will be slow to judge the desirability or undesirability of different options and trends, although some thoughts about it will come to the fore later on. Even before that, the analysis is impregnated by normative considerations. Most prominent among those will be:

First, judgements that certain features are important, and that's why the analysis is based on them, or highlights them, their importance being in their relevance to whether institutions, trends, and so on are more or less desirable.

Second, that certain features are 'healthy', that is, conducive to the well-functioning of the institutions concerned.

Both are not ordinary normative properties, as health can contribute to the institutions being bad as well as to their being good, and importance may mark undesirable as well as desirable features.

B. A Prospect of World Government?

Some people discern a trend that may lead to the eventual emergence of a world government. Why think that that may be our actual direction of movement? Here is one very speculative suggestion: over the last sixty years or so, and at an accelerating pace, more and more aspects of international relations (that is, relations among states, among international institutions, and between states and institutions) have been legalized, as I shall say. That is, standards of international law governing them have emerged, and matters that until then were decided by negotiation, or actions leading to more or less coercive outcomes, are now settled in processes that involve reference to these international standards. I am trying to be realistic. The difference is not that now these matters are determined by the international standards. Often, they are not, but even then, the existence of the standards has an impact on the outcome. The outcome is tilted towards these standards. Perhaps we can say that the standards provide a default position, although one can negotiate one's way, more or less coercively, away from their straightforward application.

Does the growing legalization of international affairs constitute an improvement? Not necessarily. After all, laws can be good, bad, or indifferent, and their impact in different circumstances may be bad even if the law is otherwise good. But perhaps there is at least one feature of legalization that tends to give it some value in many, if not most, situations. In as much as an international standard has an impact on the outcome of disputes and disagreements, it distances the outcome from one that reflects the balance of power between the competing sides at the time the dispute arises or is being dealt with. In that sense, it tends to make the outcome more impartial, and often that may be an advantage. It may tend to make the settlements of disputes more equitable, but quite apart from that it may make the outcome more stable as, where the way the outcome is reached is thought to be impartial, or relatively impartial, it may be more willingly accepted and more faithfully implemented.

As I keep repeating, these observations are empirical speculations, whose truth may vary depending on circumstances. Sometimes a treaty applies to predictable circumstances, and that enables it to enshrine a bias favouring one party. In such circumstances, a treaty may make things worse rather than better.

The points relevant to our reflections on world government are, first, that legalization encourages the emergence of dispute-resolution bodies and procedures that will adjudicate disputes and disagreements by applying the international standards. And, second, that these bodies generate pressure towards harmonization, towards shaping the emerging international standards in ways that make them express a more or less coherent outlook manifested in the way they govern international relations.

All of this may happen and leave us a long way from world government. But it represents a trend that may culminate in arrangements that are or are close to the existence of a world government.

The sensibly sceptical will say that mine is nothing but a 'Just So' story. And taken literally and independently, that is what it is. It should be taken as pointing to trends that, given appropriate circumstances, would exert pressure towards the emergence of something like a world government. Among other things, a lot depends on whether people would welcome or dread such a development.

C. Analytic Framework

1. Defining sovereignty

But what is a world government? And what kind of systems of international relations are inconsistent with it? At this point, speculation about the future invites a degree of conceptual clarity. The two—conceptual clarity and speculation about the future—are not as distinct as may be thought. Concepts die or get transformed, and in speculating about the future, we should also speculate about the concepts that will become dominant in people's understanding of their own political organizations.

I'll focus on one alternative to world government: the existence of many sovereign political systems. I discuss it not because it is the most likely or most desirable alternative, but because it is where we are now. It is the state of international relations that we are moving away from.

Sovereignty is used in multiple ways and in many diverse contexts. So, there is inevitably a stipulative element in my clarification of it. I do not mean to deny the propriety of other uses or meanings—merely to clarify how it is used by me. I am of course talking of sovereignty of political societies, like states. But I get there by defining the sovereignty of authorities.

Absolute sovereignty, I will suggest, consists of a double immunity. An authority is sovereign if both internal authorities and external authorities *acknowledge* that they do not have the power to rescind or modify its decisions and rulings.

Weaker sovereignties can be defined by relativizing this definition to particular subject matters, or in other ways, or by having a comparative scale, even a crude one, of degrees of sovereignty. Such weaker concepts will not be useful unless they cover major aspects of the powers to take decisions.

Absolute world government will exist when there will be only one authority such that there are no authorities outside it, and all internal authorities acknowledge that its decisions are immune to change by them.

2. Authority and political societies

The question is what are those internal and external authorities? The reference is to those that are inside and those that are outside the relevant political society. That is, we define sovereignty as a property of a political authority that marks its standing both inside and outside a political society of which it is a part.

The connection between sovereignty and political society complicates matters.

We are concerned with one, broadly conceived, yet only one type of political society. Think about authorities in the sense in which an essential feature of authority is that it possesses *a general normative power*. A normative power is an ability to change someone's practical reasons (which includes changing their property or other rights and their normative status) by one's say-so, provided that the reason for having that ability is the value or desirability of that person having it.

As well as authorities so understood, there can be proclaimed or believed authorities, that is, people or institutions that claim that they have authority or who are believed by some people to have authority of the kind we are considering. Some such proclaimed or believed authorities do in fact function as (justified) authorities would function had those subject to them been willing to put up with the exercise of their authority. These are de facto authorities.

To clarify: a de facto authority may or may not be a justified, legitimate authority. It is one that claims or is believed to have legitimate authority, acts as one would were one to have that legitimate authority (although not necessarily in the sense of acting as justly, for example, as a good legitimate authority would), and whose actions are put up with, not generally resisted by, those whom they affect. From now on, when referring to authorities, I will be referring to de facto authorities, unless the contrary is indicated. Sometimes authorities of this kind are part of the definition of a political society. This can take various forms. For example, there may be a political society consisting of all, or a certain subgroup, of those subject to that authority, or of all or a subgroup of those who can control the constitution of the authority (by election, or otherwise). States are an example of such political societies, but there are others.

It is not assumed that members of political societies regard their relations to the authorities, or the existence of those authorities, as the primary justification of the existence of the political society. They may regard common ethnicity, geographical distinctness, common interests, and so on as the justification, or they may doubt or deny that there is any justification. What matters here is that the boundaries of the society are determined in a way that is essentially related to the relevant authorities. That gives us a necessary condition for the existence of a political society: an essential relationship to one or more authorities.

What would be a sufficient condition for the existence of a political society? Perhaps one additional condition, which moves us closer to having a sufficient condition, is that a political society is an authority-defined society, where the relevant authorities constitute *a harmonious authority group*.

In talking of a harmonious authority group, I am trying to distance myself from any association with the Kelsenian framework, whereby a political system is defined by reference to relations of constitution and authorization: one political system consisting of all the authorities that derive their powers from one norm, a norm that Hans Kelsen thought has additional features that make it a basic norm (in his meaning of the term) and that HLA Hart thought has other features that make it the ultimate rule of recognition (in his meaning of the term).[1] Hart, even though he remained wedded to the idea of a single organizing rule, pointed the way towards an alternative approach that dispenses with it. He suggested that what keeps a legal

[1] See, for example, Hans Kelsen, *General Theory of Law and State* (Anders Wedberg tr, Harvard University Press 1945) ch X; Hans Kelsen, *Pure Theory of Law* (2nd edn, Max Knight tr, University of California Press 1967) ch V; HLA Hart, *The Concept of Law* (3rd edn, Oxford University Press 2012) ch VI.

system together, what makes it one, is the attitude of the population, or sections of it, to the authority of institutions; that is, the acceptance of that authority by those subject to it. My suggestion is that we come closer to a sufficient condition for the existence of a distinct political society if it is an authority-defined society, whose members, by and large, accept the authority of those defining institutions over them, and so do the various institutions. In other words, it is a society of people who are subject to institutions that are de facto authorities, and where, for example, if A regards itself as an authority over another authority, B, then harmony prevails if B accepts the authority of A, and so on.

Note: the test of de facto authority is one of attitude, willingness to put up with the other. It does not depend on any reason for the attitude. There may be various reasons, real or imagined, or none.

A political society of this kind is sovereign if no authority outside it claims to have normative power to rescind decisions of its authorities.

There is one more point to make before returning to international trends: one of the most important features of political societies is the degree to which they are healthy. Their health consists in a measure of solidarity among the people in that society, which manifests itself most importantly in the degree to which they are willing to make sacrifices, or to suffer disadvantages for the sake of other members of their society, and the degree to which they take their society to be, with all its shortcomings, basically decent and morally satisfactory. The health of a society assures its internal stability. Its absence subjects the society to inner tensions and disintegrative tendencies.

This provides us with an idealized picture of an international society of sovereign states: they are subject to law in their inter-relations, that is, moral law and customs. There are also treaties, binding by the agreement of the contracting states, but no super-national authorities.

D. A Clarification regarding International Customary Law

My remarks expressed a conventional and traditional view of the nature of customary international law. One may doubt whether it was ever true to the reality of international law. I will not express a view on that. But I want to put to one side two challenges to this view. First, for a long time, some international lawyers felt challenged and unappreciated by other lawyers who doubted that international law was law at all. Not that it was not state-law. That is obvious, but that it is not law. Some in their anxiety to rehabilitate it as law devised interpretations of customary law as the enactments of communities and such like. These were unnecessary fictions. More serious is the second, contemporary challenge that regards much customary law today as the product of multilateral treaties (given some additional conditions). Much has been written about the changing faces of customary international law today, and it is fascinating stuff. I avoid it because I am referring here to the older kind of customary international law.

E. The Eroding Trends and their Outcome

Now back to the growing legalization of international relations: in itself, the subjection of states to norms not of their making does not affect their sovereignty. Most people know that they are subject to moral norms, and many either identify those with social practices or, at any rate, know that states are subject to social practices, local or global, with no loss of sovereignty. (We can think that all such norms, including international ones, while binding on states, require some form of incorporation to be reflected in their law.)

The legalization of international relations leads to a reduction of sovereignty because de facto it brings in its wake international authorities that claim superiority over state authorities, in at least some of the matters within their jurisdiction. This can take the form of claiming that state institutions lost their power in certain domains, so that matters within these domains must be handled directly by those international bodies. More commonly, and I will refer only to this kind of limitation of authority, the jurisdiction of state authorities remains unaffected (or largely unaffected), but their decisions can be overturned on appeal or via some other process by international authorities. Alternatively, the international authority can impose a duty on state authorities to refrain from acting on their own rulings that conflict with its.

Claims to such powers by international authorities limit the sovereignty of states, and if the trend continues, they will do so more and more.

1. Sovereignty: survival and decay

As things stand, the erosion of sovereignty does not threaten its survival. No alternative to sovereignty appears on the horizon. The European Union is perhaps the clearest potential exception: an ever-greater union may be taken to have, as its ultimate goal, an end to the sovereignty of the member states and their absorption into one federal entity. But political trends indicate that that is not a realistic prospect today. They manifest a strong preference for separate sovereignty and against transfer of power to the Union. To mention but one example: the German Federal Constitutional Court in its decision about the Lisbon Treaty has established that Germany's Basic Law limits in an unamendable way the degree to which European integration can erode the sovereignty of Germany.[2] Similar trends are visible in other parts of the world.

There are exceptions. But they are largely confined to countries recently emerging from being subject to oppressive regimes or to foreign domination, for whom adoption of international standards and joining international organizations are desirable as signs of being admitted into the 'international community' and becoming

[2] Judgment of the Second Senate of the Federal Constitutional Court of 30 June 2009, 2 BvE 2/08.

respectable. Recent developments in the former Eastern Bloc show how superficial such tendencies often are.

Resistance to loss of sovereignty is everywhere powered by a desire to retain local identity.

2. The emerging shape

Which way are we going? What is the shape of things to come? Needless to say, I offer no answers, merely some observations. Developments like the ones we noted need not erode the jurisdiction of internal authorities, nor need they erode their sovereignty. They can be confined to merely adding to the norms that bind sovereign authorities.

But they are very likely to lead to erosion of sovereignty, though in a fragmented way, and towards fragmented institutions. Again, there may be exceptions and the EU could be one of them. These exceptions apart, what we see and are likely to see more of are the strengthening of international institutions, and the emergence of new ones, which erode sovereignty without replacing it, simply because each one of them has limited jurisdiction and their proliferation leads to an erosion of state sovereignty in favour of a fragmented array of international organizations.

F. Institutional Fragmentation may be Welcome

I hope that you will bear with me while I briefly survey some points for and against fragmentation, suggesting that, on balance, it may not be unwelcome.

- (i) It will reduce the resistance to a big world government.
- (ii) It may generate a desirable balance of power capable of correcting policy faux pas through negotiations and bargaining among institutions.
- (iii) It may generate conditions that favour diversity and sensitivity to local needs, perhaps through endorsing principles of subsidiarity.

Needless to say, fragmentation means that the hankering for world government will remain unassuaged, but then *it is based on a series of mistakes*:

- (i) Mistakes about obedience to rules: I suspect that adherents to the ideal of world government believe that, if only there could be a common authority issuing rules addressed to everyone, with the kind of enforcement institutions we are used to in sovereign states operating on a global level, peace and order would prevail. But levels of compliance with law are enormously varied and depend on many factors, which vary across the globe.
- (ii) Mistakes about the likelihood that there will be more justice or welfare under a world government, rather than that it will lead to more injustices and to greatly entrenched pockets of poverty. I know of no reason to believe that.

(iii) More specifically, I suspect that the dream of a world government is nourished by awareness of the limitations that territorial sovereignty involves and of the impotence of governments to cope with various problems because their jurisdiction is limited. Criminals can escape, for example. These limitations are, of course, real. But there is every reason to think that a world government will have its own limits, even though they will take different forms.

In brief, much more than law is needed to cope with the injustices and other undesirable aspects of life today. Needless to say, how much good a world government may bring will depend on its shape—*but why assume that it will have, or that it will for ever keep, the preferred shape?*

I should add that some objections to world government may also be ill-founded. For example—a matter particularly close to my heart—it is sometimes complained that governmental authority is legitimate only if it is a form of self-government by its subjects, and that world government is too big, remote, and anonymous to meet this condition. True, but so are state governments, and indeed all governments except those of very small and cohesive communities.

To be taken more seriously is the worry that a world government would impose uniformities that do not respect the diversity of cultures and ways of life, and the interest in autonomy (communal self-rule) needed to protect them. It is not that world government must disregard these concerns. It is merely that it is very likely to violate them.

G. A Normative Framework

Even those who would agree with my observations so far will find them unsatisfactory. They are a scatter of remarks, which may indeed hang together in some way, but which do not arise out of a general normative framework guiding the assessment of international bodies and the laws that govern them and that they apply to those subject to them.

Embracing subsidiarity principles provides an important step towards such a framework. A subsidiarity principle specifies that 'a central authority should have a subsidiary function, performing only those tasks that cannot be performed effectively at a more immediate or local level'.[3] That is, a subsidiarity principle specifies that, regarding a certain domain, institutions have legitimate powers only if they pursue worthwhile ends that can be better secured by them than without any institutional intervention or by less centralized institutions. Much more is needed to clarify the idea. I will just add that the principle is to be understood to include a comparative measure: their ends are worthwhile if achieving them does not have undesirable consequences that are too severe, for instance. For the rest I rely on our familiarity

[3] *Oxford English Dictionary* (3rd edn, Oxford University Press 2012).

with the concept, which derives from Catholic social doctrine and is familiar in the European Union.[4]

Principles of subsidiarity introduce the question that is crucial for judging the case for more centralized authority: would it be more secure in realizing desirable ends than the way in which things would work out when relying on no authority or on less centralized authorities only?

By a straightforward and common understanding, subsidiarity principles work like this: there is a good that people would benefit from, or that they are entitled to have, such as educational opportunities, protection from violence, or health care. Under some circumstances, it is possible to have it with or without institutional intervention; however, it may be that the state, or the city, is better or would be better at securing it than any less central authority. In which case, the subsidiarity condition of legitimacy is satisfied. So understood, the subsidiarity condition does not exhaust the conditions for legitimacy of institutional authorities. I will conclude by examining two further considerations.[5]

There may be a value in the existence of a political institution that cannot be realized independently of such institutions. Any institution functions through the activities of individuals involved in it, as officials, voters, and so on. Thus, the existence of political institutions provides opportunities for people and some of them cannot exist except in such contexts. One paradigmatic example is the opportunity to be a citizen of a democratic country, that is, a citizen who has a right to participate in the public life of the institution, as a voter, a candidate, or merely someone who can publicly express his views on public affairs. This opportunity adds the possibility of a rich and potentially very rewarding dimension to people's lives, which some will take advantage of, while others will ignore.

There can be, therefore, a case for political institutions that says: even though achieving some worthwhile goals would be jeopardized by the institution, its existence is justified because, by its very existence, it secures other, more important, ends that cannot be reached without it, such as democratic citizenship.

It would be interesting to explore whether the existence of super-state organizations realizes such ends. It is not difficult to sketch an argument that membership of a neighbourhood swimming pool and local park committee, while providing opportunities for social and political involvement with neighbours, does not involve all the desirable opportunities that citizenship of a state provides. But is there more value secured by the very existence of super-national organizations than is secured by state citizenship? If not, then the legitimacy of super-national institutions depends,

[4] Pope Pius XI, *Reconstructing the Social Order: Encyclical Letter Quadragesimo Anno* (Australian Catholic Truth Society 1955) para 79: 'It is a fundamental principle of social philosophy, fixed and unchangeable, that one should not withdraw from individuals and commit to the community what they can accomplish by their own enterprise and industry. So, too, it is an injustice and at the same time a grave evil and a disturbance of right order, to transfer to the larger and higher collectivity functions which can be performed and provided for by lesser and subordinate bodies. Inasmuch as every social activity should, by its very nature, prove a help to members of the body social, it should never destroy or absorb them.'

[5] As intimated, subsidiarity principles can be given a more comprehensive, if less natural, reading that subsumes under them the two conditions I will discuss and others.

broadly speaking, on instrumental considerations. That is not the way in which most people understand the case for state sovereignty. States have emotional and symbolic significance for people, which goes beyond their success in securing services and opportunities.

H. The Super-National Dilemma

Now we have arrived at the heart of our predicament. It is not whether fragmentary erosion of sovereignty is inferior to world government. It is likely to be better than world government. It is whether super-national organizations can succeed simply by being more efficient ways of securing common services and opportunities without their existence having intrinsic, non-instrumental values. That is the dilemma because, arguably, sovereign countries can succeed instrumentally, can succeed by meeting the subsidiarity condition, only because they are perceived by so many of their members as having additional value, and in particular, citizenship in such states is taken by many to be intrinsically valuable.

The case for that conclusion is simple enough: the effectiveness of governments in securing services and opportunities depends on those subject to their rule being loyal to them and having a strong sense of solidarity with each other. Without loyalty and solidarity, the ability of governments to require restraint and cooperation from people, including restraint and cooperation that people perceive to adversely affect their personal interests, is severely undermined. Official measures would meet resistance and persistent attempts to avoid compliance. Trying to overcome such resistance would call for interference with people's privacy and restrictions on their freedom. The more limited the loyalty and solidarity, the more likely is the government to resort to repressive measures that undermine its moral legitimacy.

But in our world, loyalty and solidarity, the willingness to forego personal advantages for the sake of anonymous others, that is, others who are not family or friends, are not commercial commodities. They depend on valuing common citizenship for its meaning, for its symbolic value.

Can it be different with international super-state organizations? Can they thrive because of their instrumental value only? There is strong evidence that often the answer is affirmative. The coordination rules for international aviation, radio and internet communications, international postal services, and many others show the value of international organizations that succeed and whose success is essential for life in advanced societies. Yet in all such cases, the instrumental case for coordinated regulation is sufficient to secure it.

The evidence also strongly suggests that this kind of success is limited. It is tempting to find principles that explain the limits. Perhaps success is confined to areas where coordination does not involve significant self-restraint and, therefore, where people do not feel that they are making 'sacrifices'. Such explanations have some value. But it is also the case that controversy and resistance can arise accidentally and that they can be manipulated. Is opposition to various international trade agreements currently being negotiated, or to genetic manipulation of crops, or the like, due to genuine interests of the objectors, or is it manipulated by interested parties? For our purposes, what matters is that, without loyalty and solidarity, important, perhaps the most important, super-state organizations meet growing difficulties. State sovereignty may be eroding, but there are few, if any, super-state organizations that are perceived as having more than merely instrumental value. Therefore, few, if any, attract loyalty and solidarity. And therefore, even their instrumental success is in jeopardy. The problem affects all regional organizations, like the European Union, the African Union, and the United Nations. It also affects all human rights organizations. A revival of—not very attractive—nationalism embracing extensive state sovereignty is a real possibility.

I. Misleading Arguments

Some arguments against super-state organizations enjoy great popularity in Britain and elsewhere in spite of being confused or based on false premises. One is an argument against super-state bodies because they are not democratically governed. The argument is misguided for it is not based on a cogent understanding of the nature of democracy and its uses. Another is the argument that says that we want to govern ourselves rather than be governed by, say, the bureaucrats in Brussels. To the extent that this argument presupposes that one is more free when one's ability to successfully form and pursue goals is limited by market forces or naked threats and coercion than when one's options are limited by institutionally adopted and enforced standards, it is confused.

The valid concern that sometimes motivates adopting these arguments is a worry that super-national organizations are likely to be blind to the diversity of different cultures and to different legitimate ways of allocating opportunities and processing disputes. Absent sensitive acknowledgement of legitimate diversity, institutions will not enjoy loyalty and will not be underpinned by solidarity among those subject to them, and they will fail to acquire positive symbolic meaning for their subjects.

J. What are the Perceived Advantages of Sovereign Nations?

It appears, to me at any rate, that the legitimacy of super-national institutions depends on their recognition of value-pluralism and their ability to adjust their structures of government and their aims and modes of activity to value-pluralism. That is necessary for them to be responsive to local needs and interests, to diversity in tastes and preferences, and to local traditions, ways of life, and ways of doing things (including business).

Perhaps value-pluralism indicates a case for limiting the growth of super-national organizations. Perhaps sovereign states, negotiating international agreements when they are useful, are the best protectors of legitimate value-pluralism. One great advantage of trusting the task to sovereign states is that they can respect value-pluralism without recognizing it. Each state may respect the values that are recognized by its inhabitants, while denying the legitimacy of other ways of life enjoyed by the peoples of other states, which luckily it cannot do much to affect. If super-national organizations are to be trusted with that task, they will need to recognize the legitimacy of plural values, and will encounter mistrust and hostility from people who deny value-pluralism.

If a culture of respect for value-pluralism can spread around the world, then perhaps international organizations can adjust to respecting value-pluralism. Subsidiarity principles, when applied much more aggressively than is the case in the European Union at the moment, are themselves important instruments for protecting pluralism. Fragmentation leading to checks and balances can also serve a useful role, when motivated to protect value-pluralism.

But they are not enough. What is needed is an interpretation of universal standards, such as the basic principles of human rights, in a way that allows for diverse correct interpretations of their requirements and applications in different circumstances. Call this *simultaneous interpretive pluralism*, namely, a method of, or approach to, interpretation allowing that incompatible interpretations can all be valid at the same time and in the hands of the same court.

To a degree, the European Court of Human Rights, in interpreting the European Convention of Human Rights, allows for such interpretive pluralism through its doctrine of a margin of appreciation. But the pluralism I point to is not to be confused with a band of toleration of mistaken judgements due to the different conditions and traditions of different national courts. Nor is it to be confused with exceptions like those in Article 10(2) of the Convention, which provides that the right to freedom of expression may be

> subject to such formalities, conditions, restrictions or penalties as are prescribed by law and are necessary in a democratic society, in the interests of national security, territorial integrity or public safety, for the prevention of disorder or crime, for the protection of health or morals, for the protection of the reputation or rights of others, for preventing the disclosure of information received in confidence, or for maintaining the authority and impartiality of the judiciary.[6]

Here, the matter in hand is conflict between different values. Interpretive pluralism allows for a plurality of incompatible interpretations of one value.

In brief, the legitimacy and success of super-national institutions and their ability to replace some of the functions of states, thus eroding states' sovereignty, depend on their ability to develop loyalty and broaden people's sense of solidarity. And these depend on the people of the world coming to recognize the validity of value-pluralism, and on super-national institutions proving able to embody in their constitutions and activities recognition of legitimate value-pluralism.

[6] Convention for the Protection of Human Rights and Fundamental Freedoms (opened for signature 4 November 1950, entered into force 3 September 1953) 213 UNTS 221.

V

The Legitimacy of Whom?

Nicole Roughan[*]

A. Introduction

This chapter argues that legitimacy (or illegitimacy) attaches not to a state as such, but to its component powers, institutions, and agents, so that an evaluation of state legitimacy must include a breakdown of these objects of evaluation. The chapter then concentrates on what I call 'micro-legitimacy', which assesses not the state as a whole, nor any or all of its specific powers (potential or as exercised), nor even the institutions of which it is comprised, but the officials who claim and wield the powers that are in need of justification.[1] Micro-legitimacy opens up the prospect and necessity of analysing directly the roles, standing, and conduct of those who speak for, act for, are accountable to, and represent the state.

* This chapter was prepared with research assistance from Bryan Ching and Ryan Hong, supported by a Start-up Grant from the National University of Singapore. I am grateful to audiences at the University of Melbourne's Legal Theory Workshop, the Network on Transnational Legal Theory meeting in Edinburgh, the University of Sydney Julius Stone Institute's conference on 'Legitimacy and the State', and the NUS Law Research Design Seminar. Particular thanks are due for comments and/or challenges offered by Triantafyllos Gouvas, Cormac Mac Amhlaigh, Shaun McVeigh, David Lefkowitz, Joseph Raz, Arie Rosen, Kristen Rundle, Wojciech Sadurski, Dale Smith, and Kevin Walton; and from my colleagues Damian Chalmers, Michael Dowdle, David Frydrych, Andrew Halpin, Swati Jhaveri, James Penner, Alec Stone Sweet, Kevin Tan, and KarLuis Quek.

[1] Other discussions of 'micro-legitimacy' of states have used the term to connote the legitimacy of particular rules, practices, or political acts, in contrast to the legitimacy of its structures, institutions, and general patterns of norms/practices. See, for example, Alexander Guerrero, 'Political Functionalism and the Importance of Social Facts' in Michael Weber and Kevin Vallier (eds), *Political Utopias* (Oxford University Press 2017) 5–6. As is made clear in section C, my discussion of micro-legitimacy does not aim at the same distinction, but denotes both a level and a kind of object of analysis of legitimacy (namely, the level of agents and actors, not systems and structures), rather than a distinction of scale or particular versus general objects. On this usage of the micro in social theory, and the resulting meta-theoretical issue of the 'micro-macro' problem, see Joseph Berger, Dana Eyre, and Morris Zelditch Jr, 'Theoretical Structures and the Micro-Macro Problem' in Joseph Berger and Morris Zelditch Jr (eds), *Status, Power and Legitimacy* (Transaction Books 1998) 55–70. My approach here may be consistent with, but does not adopt, the distinctions offered up by New Institutionalism in the social sciences, between macro-, meso-, and micro-analyses. Although such distinctions may (controversially) be descriptively useful, my project is a normative project—and I will argue for a view of micro-legitimacy which makes it impossible to hold on to a tight distinction between the evaluative objects.

Legitimacy: The State and Beyond. First Edition. Edited by Wojciech Sadurski, Michael Sevel, and Kevin Walton. Published 2019 by Oxford University Press.

Micro-legitimacy analyses permeate the state's institutional structure to look at the official roles inside it and the agents who fill them. It turns away from evaluating an institution's constitutive rules, which generate powers and set their limits, to evaluate the standing and conduct of agents who, qua moral agents, remain both capable of practical reasoning, and subject to moral duties. As agents of institutions, officials have special roles complete with powers and duties that would not attach to their private agency, but they also remain moral agents subject to inter-personal duties that may at times conflict with their institutional roles. Micro-legitimacy evaluations capture the importance of this dual view of officials, which also preserves the possibility of officials' autonomous action, notwithstanding the institutional constraints they face. It also recognizes that officials shape institutions, not the other way around.

In a full analysis of the legitimacy of the state, however, it remains important that the evaluation of such micro-legitimacy need not and should not come at the expense of attention to the other objects of legitimacy—including structural evaluation of institutions and the application of conditions under which certain powers are legitimate. Only the evaluation of institutional rules, and the powers they entail, will reveal whether there are fundamental defects in the institutional structuring of legitimate authority or coercive power, even before an official has had the chance to use her discretion in applying the rules or exercising the powers. Micro-legitimacy analyses will thus require close attention to more familiar objects of evaluation, including rules, organizations, and other institutions through which the state's powers of authority and coercion are typically exercised. This effectively adds officials to a chain of evaluation, so that, in the final analysis, an evaluation of a state's legitimacy must also examine how these are actioned by agents and consider whether those agents act with legitimate standing.

Section B offers a sketch of three potential objects of evaluation—powers, institutions, and agents—exploring the distinctions between them and their disjunctive or conjunctive relationships. Section C then makes the case for concentrating on official agents of the state as key objects of legitimacy. Such micro-legitimacy entails attention to both the standing of those who claim or wield the state's powers and control its institutions, and the manner in which they do so. Motivated by this argument, section D then sets out a conception of officials, to whom standards of legitimacy can be applied. The standards require that officials use their agency to pursue, in good faith, the conditions that would legitimate both their powers and their institutions.[2] Section E then revisits the overall evaluation of state legitimacy, suggesting the need for an account which integrates micro-legitimacy with a pluralist dimension of 'macro-legitimacy', in which the state is one among many claimants of authority, one among many principals with official agents. This integration will, in turn, have important implications for the complex tasks of officials who seek to realize both macro- and micro-legitimacy.

[2] This chapter does not address the potential interaction of this standard of legitimacy with the possible duties of justice owed by officials. That question, and its relationship to the matter of legitimacy, is explored elsewhere in my project on officials.

B. Breaking Down the Objects of Evaluation: Powers, Institutions, and Agents

Without foreclosing other ways of breaking down state legitimacy into component parts, this chapter highlights three potential objects to which a standard of legitimacy may apply: powers, institutions, and agents.[3] The first two are the most familiar referents of inquiries into the legitimacy of the state, although there is at times slippage between them or a lack of clarity about which, in any given account, is under evaluation.[4] Each of these objects is an important component of an evaluation of the state's legitimacy, but, in a full evaluation, they must be complemented by the third object, which targets both the standing and conduct of those who fill the roles of the state's officials.

Before breaking down the objects of legitimacy, the project faces a preliminary and important objection: why break down the objects of legitimacy at all? One possibility, for instance, is that, when we are concerned to evaluate the state in general, or any particular manifestation of its power over subjects, we simply look at what has happened or is about to happen and evaluate whether it is justified?[5] In other words, if we are simply talking about the (*ex post* or *ex ante*) evaluation of decisions, actions, or outcomes, it may not make a difference whether our concerns fixate on a specific component of that decision, action, or outcome. We might simply want to know whether a specific action is consistent with a particular normative standard—whether, for instance, it is legitimate for a president to ban all immigration from certain countries or for the executive to require teachers to report behaviour considered indicative of a child's susceptibility to terrorist influence.[6]

There is something to be said for the directness of the wider-lens approach, and in particular, it cuts to the chase in a way that may be helpful for some subjects of state power faced with a choice between conformity and mounting a challenge. A subject challenging a decision may not need to know the precise aspect of the decision that is most problematic; it may be enough simply to reject it, arguing some general illegitimacy which is salient, if not precisely located.

[3] This does not purport to exhaust the possible objects of legitimacy. Others have made similar attempts to clarify the objects of legitimacy, including analyses which distinguish between actions, norms, actors, and systems, and others which extend the range of objects to include ideas and ideologies. For analysis of the distinctions used in literature on legitimacy in international legal theory, see Christopher Thomas, 'The Uses and Abuses of Legitimacy in International Law' (2014) 34 Oxford Journal of Legal Studies 729.

[4] For instance, Buchanan suggests that institutions are the primary objects of evaluation, but his account of institutional legitimacy combines agents, institutions, and their powers. See Allen Buchanan, 'The Legitimacy of International Law' in Samantha Besson and John Tasioulas (eds), *The Philosophy of International Law* (Oxford University Press 2010) 79–80.

[5] At this point, the debate over the content of the standard, and whether or not it tracks an objective justification or subjective acceptance, is not important. See text to n 33.

[6] My thanks to Joseph Raz both for pressing me on this point, and for offering the example of the United Kingdom's 'Prevent' strategy.

Yet this simplicity is both illusory and potentially unhelpful. The broad-brush analysis would fail to capture debates over whether a decision, policy, or rule is illegitimate because it is not made by a proper decision-maker, and thus fails to have procedurally legitimate authority, or whether it fails to have substantively legitimate authority. It also obscures the possibility that a particular decision may be illegitimate because, while it is made by a generally legitimate authority, its obvious substantive incorrectness or deviation undermines any general authoritative status.[7] These distinctions go to the very heart of what theorists of authority and legitimacy argue about, and it makes little sense to avoid the clarity of options that these debates might bring, not only to theoretical analyses of state legitimacy, but also to subjects' strategic responses to the state's manifestations of power. Perhaps more often than not, a subject will need to know which part of a decision goes wrong, before she can mount a successful or even credible challenge against it.[8] The location of the illegitimacy may also make a difference to the ways in which it can be challenged, for instance by mounting legal challenges if the failure is justiciable or by rejecting the outcome through political or disobedient action if it is not. For instance, if one can pinpoint the failure on the conduct of certain officials who are acting in violation of legal or constitutional requirements, or ultra vires, it may be easier to mount an effective resistance against those particular agents wielding power, rather than against an amorphous system or institution.

Questions about legitimacy are also, importantly, about more than just exercises of legitimate authority, so that, even armed with the fine distinctions of authority theory, an evaluation of the legitimate authority of decisions would still obscure too much. Decision-focused assessments of legitimacy contain something of a bias towards decisions, moments of action, conflict, and change, which may obscure either non-decisional (or pre-decisional and post-decisional) spaces and the manifestations of power they embody, as well as institutionalized normalities which are not the result of conscious decisions.[9] This worry cannot be circumvented by admitting 'non-decisions' or even indecision as kinds of quasi-decisions which could still be the objects of legitimacy analyses, for these would still fail to identify the locations of illegitimacy. In that failure, there is a risk of missing illegitimacies that are either obscured or defended by reference to a 'basically ok' outcome. Perhaps most importantly for present purposes, generic outcome-focused assessments of legitimacy risk eliding the potential for a decision to go wrong at different points along a chain containing elements of both action and normative ordering. A decision may have been made by an unauthorized or illegitimate agent, or it may amount to an

[7] As many theorists of authority have maintained, there is a fundamental difference between these evaluations. The framing here is intended to leave open the possibility of either/both substantive and procedural conditions for legitimacy, so that the argument holds whichever is favoured, alone or in combination.

[8] This is most obviously true of legal challenges to state power, which must be organized in forms that the law makes possible and which often require clarity over whether failings are procedural or substantive (eg judicial review of administrative decisions, tortious claims against wrongdoing officials, claims that a particular law or policy is inconsistent with protected rights).

[9] I am grateful to Kristen Rundle for discussions of her ongoing work on these points.

illegitimate use of her legitimate powers. It may be substantively unjustified despite being authorized and/or procedurally legitimate; or it may be legitimate as a formal rule or policy, yet be carried out in ways that detract from that legitimacy. Simply looking at decisions and outcomes may also mask differences between institutional rules and structures that are not legitimate, and decisions which may be, because of their departure from those rules. These distinctions, I argue below, are not only important to capture, but can be better captured by introducing a micro focus on officials, rather than an undifferentiated evaluation of decisions and outcomes.

Finally, the position of this chapter is that it is also insufficient to refer questions of legitimacy solely to standards of legality and validity.[10] Even setting aside general jurisprudential arguments about the relationship between law and morality, and their implications for the legitimacy of the state's legal authority, inquiries into the legitimacy of the state cannot hide behind consistency with legal standards and the powers and duties they confer. Although the state often acts through legal forms and institutions, the many uses of its public powers do not always occupy a straightforwardly legal domain or contain legal avenues for constraint or challenge. The public powers to which standards of legitimacy are to be applied are therefore often underdetermined by legal forms and their content, instead reflecting degrees of continuity with moral authority (and its legitimacy) and/or political argument, in both cases defying limitation by strictly formal legal authorizations. On this view, even where a strictly formalist legal authorization might be thought to confer validity and thus create a standard for evaluation, this would not be sufficient to confer authority for the purposes of a full evaluation of legitimacy. Such a 'moral continuity' view holds that the authorization is only legitimately authoritative if, because, and insofar as, the authorization process is itself justified as a means of conferring authority. That view posits moral authority as the foundations from which law's claims to authority are to be judged.

To put these points about the objects and standards of legitimacy together is to argue for both a tighter focus on objects of evaluation, such that we can identify points along a chain of potentially legitimate objects (and spot any weak links), as well as a less formalist sense of the standards to be applied to those objects. Moving through a chain of evaluations, from systems and institutions through to powers and the agents who wield them, opens the prospect of multiple standards and important puzzles about how they fit together. Each object seems to prioritize different focal questions about legitimacy. If we are interested in the legitimacy of powers, for instance, we might ask whether the state has legitimate authority to bind subjects or whether it can legitimately enforce its laws or borders with coercive measures. To evaluate those powers, we might refer to objective values or to subjective recognition and acceptance, or we might pick some set of institutionalized normative

[10] I have defended this position against contending accounts of the relationship between authority and legality in Nicole Roughan, 'Normativity and the Sources of International Law' in Jean d'Aspremont and Samantha Besson (eds), *The Oxford Handbook of the Sources of International Law* (Oxford University Press 2017).

constraints with which to evaluate the state's specific powers.[11] If we are theorists of institutions, we might ask whether the institutions of the state have been created through processes conferring subjective acceptance or carrying objective virtues of reasonable acceptability, and/or whether they are consistent with the rule of law, or contain mechanisms for accountability, oversight, transparency, and revision.[12] We might also apply to institutions such substantive standards as are thought to render those institutions just. Finally, if we are theorists of agents, we may ask whether those who in fact wield the state's powers, and who design, control, and manage its institutions, occupy valuable or justifiable roles and act legitimately in carrying out those roles. While the standards used to evaluate powers, institutions, and agents may be pieced together into coherent puzzles depicting subjective or objective legitimacy, each piece will offer a part of the picture that the others will not.

The metaphor of the puzzle thus reveals an important caveat to the micro-legitimacy analysis. Although the objects of legitimacy may reveal different focal questions which may be (and often are) treated separately, the details of their content and the standards for their evaluation reveal that it makes little sense to explore one without the others. Breaking down the objects of legitimacy may make it easier to reveal defects and/or strengths in the legitimacy of particular links or components, but the components are obviously interdependent and intricately entwined. In the context of the state, powers tend to be housed in institutions and are wielded by official agents; institutions consist in the organization of powers and are created and represented or manifested by official agents; and official agents only take on their official role because of their institutional empowerments. Ultimately, the work done here to break down the objects of legitimacy into component parts may be of most utility for the purpose of rethinking how they should be put back together.

1. Evaluating powers

The first object is the set of normative and/or de facto powers held by the state, manifested in its institutions and executed by its agents. The familiar list of these powers includes powers of authority and coercion, powers associated with territory/property, and powers of sovereignty (which is itself often conceived as some combination

[11] For instance, are its actions constitutional or permitted by international law or in conformity with some other set of internal or external normative constraints? This form of evaluation implicates the macro element of legitimate authority. For instance, normative constraints that are extra-constitutional may include not only constraints imposed by relative international or supra-national authorities, but also constraints imposed by cooperative arrangements with other non-national authorities, such as indigenous, religious, or other non-state authorities.

[12] See, for example, the set of questions explored by those who have generated the field of Global Administrative Law, notably in its seminal article. See Benedict Kingsbury, Nico Krisch, and Richard B Stewart, 'The Emergence of Global Administrative Law' (2005) 68 Law and Contemporary Problems 15. See also the work of scholars embracing the public-institutionalist approach to international legal authority, for example, Armin von Bogdandy, Rudiger Wolfrum, Jochen von Bernstorff, Philipp Dann, and Matthias Goldmann (eds), *The Exercise of Public Authority by International Institutions: Advancing International Institutional Law* (Springer 2010). For discussion of the relations between these approaches, see Megan Donaldson and Benedict Kingsbury, 'The Global Governance of Public Law' in Cormac Mac Amhlaigh, Claudio Michelon, and Neil Walker (eds), *After Public Law* (Oxford University Press 2013).

of the others). There is, then, an important question: are these separate powers to be assessed independently, or do they (and the conditions of their legitimacy) travel together, so that legitimate authority must be paired with legitimate coercive and other powers if a state's power is, overall, to be legitimate?[13] If that is the case, then a full assessment of the legitimacy of the state would need to be attuned not only to the state's legitimate authority, or not only to its political legitimacy understood as a justification for coercive enforcement of its rules, but also to all these other powers, collectively and relatedly.[14] The combined approach also adds the important possibility of differentiated and unevenly legitimate powers, in which a state may be lacking in legitimate authority, but still exercise legitimate coercive powers or engage in legitimate defence of its territory, and so on.[15] For present purposes, however, I will concentrate on the authority object, leaving open the possibility that very different accounts might be needed to explore the legitimacy of other powers of coercion, property, and sovereignty.

Orthodox debates over the legitimacy of authority tend to divide between treating authority as a social power—a capacity to get other people to do what the authority demands, dependent on de facto obedience or recognition and constituted by facts of salience, compliance, or acceptance by subjects—or a normative power—a capacity to impose duties and change the reasons that apply to a subject, dependent on and constituted by rules and reasons.[16] Yet these two approaches become entangled if we understand authority to involve both an element of normativity (authority's reason-giving and reason-dependent character) and sociality (authority's dependence upon the fact of people accepting, trusting, or at least recognizing actual authorities).[17] That entanglement, in turn, makes salient the differences between objective and subjective conditions for legitimate authority, and while there may be

[13] Buchanan, for instance, suggests that the dominant philosophical view of state legitimacy treats the right to rule as a collection of exclusively justified coercive and authoritative powers, in addition to a right to attempt to govern. See Buchanan, 'The Legitimacy of International Law' (n 4) 81–83. In addition to the powers noted by Buchanan, other powers for assessment could include sovereign powers of international representation, foreign policy-making and agency, and (controversially) underlying title to property.

[14] On political legitimacy as legitimate coercive enforcement, see, for example, Phillip Pettit, 'Legitimacy and Justice in Republican Perspective' (2012) 65 Current Legal Problems 59; Arthur Ripstein, 'Authority and Coercion' (2004) 21 Philosophy and Public Affairs 2; and Ronald Dworkin, *Law's Empire* (Hart Publishing 1986).

[15] Joseph Raz, 'Authority and Justification' in Joseph Raz (ed), *Authority* (New York University Press 1990) 115–17.

[16] These distinctions are explored in full in Nicole Roughan, *Authorities: Conflicts, Cooperation, and Transnational Legal Theory* (Oxford University Press 2013) ch 2; and see Scott Shapiro, 'Authority' in Jules Coleman and Scott Shapiro (eds), *The Oxford Handbook of Jurisprudence and Philosophy of Law* (Oxford University Press 2002). Note that these distinctions also play into the manner in which the accounts differentiate authority from other forms of power: distinctions which lie in either the authorities' own claims to legitimacy or subjects' belief in the same. For instance, Weber's classical sociological account treats legitimate domination as domination that is believed (by its subjects) to be morally legitimate, as distinct from power that is merely backed up by coercion, while Raz treats a de facto authority's claim to legitimacy as distinctive of its authority.

[17] Nicole Roughan, 'From Authority to Authorities: Bridging the Social/Normative Divide' in Roger Cotterrell and Maksymilian Del Mar (eds) *Authority in Transnational Legal Theory: Theorising across Disciplines* (Edward Elgar 2016).

some room for integration or conjunction of such conditions, there remain important divisions over their precise content.[18]

The present project does not require intervention in those debates about the content of the standard; rather, it concentrates on being precise about the object (authority) that they seek to evaluate. Evaluating the authority of the state against any type of standard is not an abstract inquiry into the powers a state might hold, but an evaluation of activities in which those powers are used. On the normative conception of authority, for instance, to ask whether the state has legitimate authority is to ask whether its uses of its de facto authority are indeed legitimate, so as to give rise to normative consequences for its subjects. It is to consider whether the instances in which a state brings its authority to bear on its subjects (through making, applying, and enforcing rules which purport to change the reasons that apply to subjects) actually do have such a normative effect. This approach concretizes the powers and, indeed, any account of the conditions of their legitimacy. In turn, it suggests that to fully understand the conditions for legitimate authority and, indeed, the legitimate use of that power, we must not simply engage in abstract evaluations, but also understand where powers are housed and manifested in institutions.

2. Evaluating institutions

The second group of potential objects of legitimacy are the institutions, and the institutional structures, within which the relevant powers are constituted and contained. The evaluation of legitimate institutions unites concerns in political and legal theory, at times sharing this object with theories of justice and indeed with theories that combine or blur legitimacy and justice.[19] Regardless of the structure or content of such evaluations (and whether legitimacy and justice are standards to be separately applied), their objects are institutions, understood as organizations, clusters of rules, or (sometimes) as atomized rules. This is true of both ideal and non-ideal political theories: some accounts of 'political legitimacy' are closely attuned to questions of institutional design and what, in reality, legitimacy requires, while

[18] For instance, subjective consent, by itself, is widely thought to be insufficient. Some of the most well-known objections appear in John Simmons, *Moral Principles and Political Obligations* (Princeton University Press 1979) chs 3–4; Joseph Raz, *The Authority of Law: Essays on Law and Morality* (2nd edn, Oxford University Press 1979). Compare many recent variants, such as David Estlund's 'normative consent' in David Estlund, *Democratic Authority: A Philosophical Framework* (Princeton University Press 2008) and Margaret Gilbert's hybrid associative/consent theory of 'joint-commitments' in Margaret Gilbert, *Joint Commitment: How We Make the Social World* (Oxford University Press 2013). These hybrids only rescue a role for consent by tying it to some non-voluntary normative ground, which then subsumes any independent value for consent.

[19] On the importance of a distinction between the virtues of justice and legitimacy, and for a theory of legitimacy that detaches legitimacy from institutions and instead attaches it to their coercive enforcement, see Philip Pettit, *Legitimacy and Justice in Republican Perspective* (Princeton University Press 2012).

others focus on defending an ideal or non-ideal standard of legitimacy to which an institution will be held.[20]

Such institutions are also the bedrock of much contemporary work in legal theory, where the influence of MacCormick's institutional theory of law continues[21] and where the more general notion that law is an institutionalized normative practice generates as near to universal agreement as jurisprudence is ever likely to generate.[22] There remain disagreements about what sorts of institutions characterize law and/or might 'count as legal institutions', but regardless of how or whether some institutions are delineated with the characteristics of legality, they are then held up as objects for evaluation against standards of legitimacy.

Legitimacy is not the only measure of an institution's value; rather, it bears a complex and controversial relationship with other values. Justice is one, but there are others, including procedural qualities such as those associated with the formal rule of law, virtues such as transparency, or other markers of 'good governance' which require some form of supervision over the exercise of institutional powers. Among the evaluative questions, therefore, and continuing the theme of the interdependence of these objects of evaluation, are questions about whether institutional structures are best suited to the realization of their legitimate powers, and/or whether institutions place appropriate empowerments and constraints upon the agents who act on their behalf.

3. Evaluating agents

The final object, or set of objects, in a full inquiry into legitimacy are the agents who act, with institutional empowerment, to wield the authority of the state over its subjects. Mostly, although with some interesting exceptions, these agents are the state's officials—those who occupy offices—who have both the standing and the responsibility to act either on behalf of the state or as manifestations of the state.[23]

[20] For a revised call for more attention in political theory to questions of institutional design, rather than abstract political ideals, see Jeremy Waldron, *Political Political Theory* (Harvard University Press 2016).

[21] In legal theory, the most sustained attention to institutions and institutionalization starts with Neil MacCormick. See most notably, Neil MacCormick, *Institutions of Law: An Essay in Legal Theory* (Oxford University Press 2007); and see essays in Maksymilian Del Mar and Zenon Bankowski (eds), *Law as Institutional Normative Order* (Ashgate 2009). Some of these influences are taken in new pluralist directions which challenge the formality of law's institutionalisation: see, for example, Keith Culver and Michael Giudice, *Legality's Borders: An Essay in General Jurisprudence* (Oxford University Press 2010).

[22] See Raz, *The Authority of Law* (n 18). And recently see Raz's lecture, 'Why the State?' in Nicole Roughan and Andrew Halpin (eds), *In Pursuit of Pluralist Jurisprudence* (Cambridge University Press 2017), recommitting to that view of the importance of institutions. Compare Gerald Postema on normative social practices: for example, Gerald J Postema, 'Custom, Normative Practice and the Law' (2012) 62 Duke Law Journal 707. There is clearly some distance between these views, but they are views on a spectrum, where the institutionalization of the normative practice makes a difference to, without displacing, law's social character.

[23] Non-official agents of the state include those who are tasked with particular functions on behalf of the state without holding an office. Without the standing institutional structure of powers and responsibilities that constitute the roles of officials, however, the powers and duties of non-official agents are conferred on an ad hoc basis, relying on institutional forms such as contracts and treaties. Examples range from contractors who carry out public functions inside or outside the state, including some that

In the present context of an analysis of state legitimacy, a familiar and non-exhaustive list of such officials would include: clear cases of 'high-officials', including members of the executive, judiciary, and legislature; enforcement officers (including police and immigration officials); and lower-level bureaucrats. Distinctions between these categories typically sound in the amount of discretion allocated to the official or the type or amount of powers entailed in their role, as well as their characterization as straightforward employees of the state or agents. The higher the official, the more likely it is that there will be some special procedure required for entry to the office, such as processes of statutory appointment, democratic election, or even coronation, which differ from ordinary practices of employment in the standing they purport to carry.[24] These processes tend to render those who pass through them as agents rather than mere employees of the state.[25]

Regardless of the details of who counts as an official, it might seem puzzling to treat these officials (whether agents or employees) as a third category of evaluation. Couldn't officials be treated simply as institutions or, at least, subsumed within the category of institutional objects of legitimacy? Alternatively, isn't the conduct of officials, in exercising the powers associated with their offices, simply an instance of the exercise of powers, without any need for special consideration of the agents who wield them? The slight awkwardness of asking 'is an official legitimate?' and the worry about whether it should matter who exercises a power, suggest that the case for evaluating the micro-legitimacy of officials requires a separate and sustained defence.

are controversial such as the running of prisons or other security functions. A large body of work in public law and international law now explores the questions over the outsourcing of state/official functions and the chains of liability or responsibility that result. See, for example, Laura T Dickinson, 'Public Law Values in a Privatised World' (2006) 31 Yale Journal of International Law 383; Michael P Vandenbergh, 'The Private Life of Public Law' (2005) 105 Columbia Law Review 2029; Jody Freeman, 'Extending Public Law Norms through Privatisation' (2003) 116 Harvard Law Review 1285. For an extended critique, see Avihay Dorfman and Alon Harel, 'The Case against Privatisation' (2013) 41 Philosophy & Public Affairs 67.

[24] Take the tricky example of judges, who are often, in the strict sense, employees of executive ministries of justice, but whom we conceive as having an independent standing that is separate from their status as employees. Although the present part of the project does not offer a comparative analysis, it is important that the precise content of official roles varies from country to country. For instance, on matters of judicial independence (from the executive), the extent to which there is formal administrative independence differs. See, for example, Martin Shapiro, *Courts: A Comparative and Political Analysis* (University of Chicago Press 1986). Some countries have created formally independent judiciaries, others harbour judges within civil service terms of employment (eg cf Italy, with its independence, and France's civil servant model). See ibid 151–53.

[25] The exact contours of agency are significantly more complex than this. The agency of officials resides not only in the processes which formally confer the powers of agents of state institutions, but also in a role as quasi-agents of collectives or polities or *demoi* served by those institutions. While the fiduciary conception of officials does not directly correspond to my account, the work done to explore the fiduciary characteristics of some official agents raises similar complex questions surrounding the 'mapping' of obligations and empowerments owed between officials, institutions, and subjects. See Ethan J Lieb and Stephen R Galoob, 'Fiduciary Political Theory: A Critique' (2016) 125 Yale Law Journal 1820; David L Ponet, Ethan J Leib, and Michael Serota, 'Translating Fiduciary Principles into Public Law' (2013) 126 Harvard Law Review Forum 91.

C. The Case for Micro-Legitimacy

The case for a separate inquiry into the micro-legitimacy of officials rests upon at least three key claims. The first is a foundational claim that officials are distinctive objects who are best conceived as *both* personal agents and institutional agents, and who are thus distinct from both the institutions they represent and the powers they wield. The second is that important aspects of legitimacy (or illegitimacy) will be missed if officials are not part of a legitimacy analysis. The third claim is that it matters who exercises powers and who controls institutions because these 'who' questions are not simply descriptive, but are laden with normative content and implications.

1. Officials as dual agents

The standard idea of an official is of a person who occupies an office and who is both empowered and constrained by that office. I argue, however, that institutional constraints and empowerments are only part of the story.[26] An official, unlike an office, is not an institution, and an official's institutional powers and duties are not the only powers and duties an official will hold. An official, unlike an institution, remains a moral agent qua person, subject to reasons and duties, charged with moral powers and duties, and capable of independent judgement and action.[27] Officials are thus agents in a dual sense: agents qua representatives of institutions and agents with the powers and duties their human or personal moral agency entails.[28] This foundational claim, put to use, raises a potential tension between the institutional and personal moral duties. It may mean that officials who operate institutional norms and powers can (and sometimes may or should) make unauthorized departures from or changes to those norms when that is required by their personal moral duties.[29]

Contrast this with the standard, institutional accounts of an official, which equate an official with his or her office, understood as a role entailing some separation

[26] The full defence of my dual account of officials appears in my book-in-progress, *Officials*.

[27] Compare this to Raz's discussions of judges being 'humans, too', and therefore subject to morality. The question here asks whether judges, as judges, are subject to morality. See Joseph Raz, 'Incorporation by Law' (2004) 10 Legal Theory 1.

[28] The simplest sense of moral agency entails the ability to make moral judgements. The more complex notion is the subject of a rich literature, exploring, most pertinently, the relationship between moral agency, moral subjection, and moral responsibility. For present purposes, I mean to simply use 'moral agency' to capture these three aspects of being a moral agent qua person. The first is the ability to make moral judgements (these can of course be mistaken, and may be difficult); the second is to be subject to moral reasons (which include reasons that apply also to others, and reasons that are subject-specific); and the third is to be morally responsible (to be appropriately ascribed responsibility for the evaluations of reasons entailed in moral agency). The full account is to appear in *Officials* ch 2.

[29] The exact relationship to be struck between the institutional and personal moral duties cannot be part of a general account of officials' duties. It differs not only among different official roles, but also among different normative systems in which officials play their roles. The normative practices establishing such systems will differ in their evaluation of the official who acts out of personal rather than institutional duty, and vice versa.

between personal and institutional capacities/statuses.[30] Such a separation supposedly captures the difference between a role that is official and a role that is not. Relatedly, an office is normally conceived as a role that is constituted and constrained by duties, in which occupants are required to conform to rules that are generated externally to any particular instance of the office, and independently of the identity, beliefs, or preferences of its holder. An office also seems to require some conferral of status upon a person, not self-appointment, and the office holder's acceptance of that status.[31] This is significant, for it suggests that for someone to hold an office, they must willingly enter that office through some process, in accordance with some normative practice in which that process is justified.[32]

Perhaps most importantly, there is a very clear association of an office with a particular specialized function that the office-holder is supposed to perform and a set of powers enabling its fulfilment. Thus, in addition to having special duties, officials have special powers that only they can exercise and special restrictions on what they can do. These powers are often, though not always, powers to make or change rules and policies and/or to apply those rules and policies to non-officials and/or other officials, as subjects. In addition, officials might have special immunities or other privileges that protect their ability to do things that non-officials cannot. The powers and immunities entailed by the office, moreover, are justified by their furtherance of the justified institutional function.[33]

[30] This separation of personal and official roles is found throughout the literature, including the literature on private offices and their occupants. Recent versions of this idea of an office include work in property theory: Larissa Katz, 'Governance through Owners: How and Why Formal Property Rights Enhance State Power' (2012) 160 University of Pennsylvania Law Review 2029; and Christopher Essert, 'The Office of Ownership' (2013) 63 University of Toronto Law Journal 418 (although cf Avihay Dorfman, 'Private Ownership and the Standing to Say So' (2014) 64 University of Toronto Law Journal 402). This is broadly consistent with and borrows ideas from earlier work in public law theory, as well as jurisprudential attention, such as Leslie Green, 'Law and the Role of a Judge' (2014) Oxford Legal Studies Research Paper no 47/2014 <https://ssrn.com/abstract=2495953> accessed 3 April 2018. The role of parent, for instance, is an unofficial role, in that there is no separation between the personal and institutional statuses. It would be awkward to consider the parent as occupying an official role, and a parent cannot 'step out' of the role in any meaningful sense.

[31] Exceptionally, a person who currently occupies some office might, by that office, be empowered to appoint herself to another office. Often, this would be a temporary appointment, with a requisite process by which approval of other officials would be required.

[32] The need for justification is a feature of all roles: see, for example, Scott Hershovitz, 'The Role of Authority' (2011) 11 Philosophers' Imprint 1, arguing (in the case of the moral role of authority) that the justification of the role of authority is dependent upon the justification of the practice which assigns the roles of authority and subject. The kind of process that will be justified will then depend upon the kind of office at stake, the qualities it requires of its holder, and the purposes it serves. Thus, an office requiring specialized expertise and/or impartiality of its holder (for instance, a referee or a judge) could (justifiably) be conferred neither by a vote among people who could not adequately evaluate expertise nor a partisan appointment process that could not (demonstrably) point to the office-holder's impartiality.

[33] See, for example, John Finnis, *Natural Law and Natural Rights* (2nd edn, Oxford University Press 2011) ch 9. Finnis argues that the existence of officials with authority is necessary for the institutionalized pursuit of the human goods, but that duties upon judges and legislators are not simply duties established by convention, but duties to employ their capacities of practical reasonableness, understood as duties grounded upon both natural justice and institutional justification. See also John Finnis, 'Natural Law: The Classical Tradition' in Jules Coleman and Scott Shapiro (eds), *The Oxford Handbook of Jurisprudence and Philosophy of Law* (Oxford University Press 2002) 10–15.

Many of these features of officials in the standard picture continue into my account, in which the institutional element of the idea of officials survives. Yet the account is a dual one, which also makes a turn away from a focus on institutions and the rules they use to allocate the functions, powers, and duties of offices, towards powers and duties that are earned or owed by virtue of the moral agency of officials. Of these, the most significant for present purposes are the relational duties owed by officials as agents in their relations with other (non-official and official) agents. Importantly, this view recognizes that some kind of relationship exists between an official and the persons to whom the official applies or administers rules and policies.[34]

The relationship between officials and subjects is characterized by several features that will go on to make a difference to my account of the legitimacy of officials. First, officials conceived as moral agents in relations with others retain the capacities and burdens of their moral agency vis-à-vis those others. Officials, as moral agents, can choose, they can act for reasons as well as make choices that are simply exercises of will, they can face moral conflicts, they can make mistakes (both excusable and inexcusable), and so on. This renders officials' dealings with subjects of their powers to be matters of relational morality, not just institutional application.[35]

Second, and equally importantly, there is at least a degree of vulnerability on the part of subjects to the activities of the officials. Subjects might depend on an official doing what she is supposed to do or they might be vulnerable to an official not only doing her job, but doing it fairly, expertly, or reasonably, or doing it well in some other respect. The official–subject relationship is a relationship of power and vulnerability in both normative and de facto senses.[36] That relationship may, though will not always, include some mechanism of supervision and accountability of officials, in which the subjects may have a chance to participate. When this is sufficiently robust and participatory, it may partly offset the vulnerability of subjects or even bestow powers upon the subjects to which the officials themselves are vulnerable. Thus, not all relationships are straightforwardly hierarchical with the official on the top, but they are nevertheless relationships of power.

Bringing these strands together into an account of officials as dual agents reveals that the role of an official relates its occupant to other people through a set of powers and duties that can affect the rights, powers, and duties of these others.[37] The role of an official thus combines institutional rules and inter-personal relationships, such

[34] In addition, there are secondary relationships among official agents, whose secondary character does not diminish their importance, particularly for exploring the ways in which their roles and conduct may achieve or detract from legitimacy.

[35] Raz's point in 'Incorporation by Law' (n 27), that judges are humans too, is different from my own. His account about the subjection of judges to morality (offered in argument against inclusive legal positivism) does not set up a distinction between the content of moral duties owed by judges qua judges, and judges qua humans subject to morality.

[36] Note that the official-subject relationship is not best understood as a legal relationship with legal correlatives; in particular, note the unavailability of Hohfeldian conceptions of rights, which detail relations between persons (not officials).

[37] The asymmetry here is deliberate. In *Officials*, I go on to argue that officials, qua officials, do not have rights. The persons occupying those offices will have the ordinary rights of employees and whatever general and particular rights apply to them as persons.

that the official cannot be reduced to the technical constitutive rules of an institution or an institutionalized system; nor are officials simply people owing inter-personal duties. They owe the duties of their office and their person. Their relational capacities and responsibilities are thus mediated by their offices, and vice versa, so that their actions are not entirely free; rather, they are constrained by both institutional and personal duties and realities.[38]

Because of this duality, neither set of constraints and empowerments is absolute. The office's institutional constraints may operate to immunize its occupant, at least partially, against certain inter-personal moral demands that might otherwise be made upon that occupant as an individual. (This is the core idea of 'role morality' to which I return below.) However, the institutional constraints upon officials' actions do not determine those actions outright; rather, there remains space for the personal agency of the official to act contrary to or even in direct challenge to the institutional rules surrounding her office. In this sense, the duties of officials can be explained as instances in which responsibilities ('role obligations') are owed by officials to those for whom they hold office and who are made vulnerable by the powers of the officials. Some of these will be defined by the institutions the officials represent, but others arise out of the fact that officials remain moral persons, even as they wield their institutional powers.

This raises a final point which is critical for an inquiry into micro-legitimacy, and which concerns the difference between conceptions of the official as either a dual or a hybrid agent. A true hybrid would somehow integrate the powers and duties from the personal and institutional elements.[39] Yet in the case of officials, there is obvious potential for the two elements to generate constraints and empowerments that are in tension with one another. An official's institutional duties may conflict with her personal duties; or her institutional empowerments might be in tension with her powers of personal agency. Such practical conflicts within a role are often explained and explored through the notion of role morality, which is sometimes taken to license the occupant of a role with special permissions or justifications for acting contrary to general morality. The force of such a case then rests on the extent to which the institution itself is justified and whether the action is necessary to furthering its purposes.[40] In the case of officials, such an account would suggest that only a strongly justified institution could ground a case for its officials' departures from the relational duties they bear as moral agents.

[38] The counter-example of a parent might again be illustrative. It would misrepresent the character of the relationship of the parent and child to consider them as official and subject, not because of a lack of rights, duties, and powers, but because the rights, duties, and powers implicated in the relationship are not the central feature of the relationship.

[39] The argument thus far is agnostic about whether it is preferable for the duties to be merged into a true hybrid. Arguably, some kinds of offices are created in which personal relational duties are to be integrated with the official role itself. An example might be some offices in the family court, where an ethic of care is in effect institutionalized in the role of child advocates. If that argument were successful, it would pertain only to some offices and leave others where the separation is preserved as an institutional priority.

[40] On role morality in general, see Michael Hardimon, 'Role Obligations' (1994) 91 The Journal of Philosophy 333. These arguments are controversial, particularly when they are used to defend the conduct of generally unpopular actors in society, such as those who wield public power.

An alternative view, however, would conceive of the official's institutional moral duties and her personal moral duties as a straightforward case of moral conflict, wherein the official should act in accordance with the weightier duty, but he or she is not, in a strong sense, morally permitted to do so.[41] This 'moral conflicts' position seems to offer no special protection to institutional justifications, unlike the role morality accounts. Instead, any conflicts are straightforward moral conflicts, in which the weight of the institutional moral duty and the weight of the personal moral duty simply contend with each another.

The account of officials here does not prefer or protect either the institutional or the personal duties, as a category, over the other. Nor does it resolve whether potential conflicts between these categories are best analysed through an account of role morality (which distinguishes personal from role obligations) or simply as personal practical conflicts. For present purposes, the point is to suggest that the presence of these duties, and even their potential conflicts, motivate a distinct assessment of the legitimacy of officials to see and evaluate how the duality and conflicts play out.

2. Consider the alternatives

The second set of reasons to treat officials as a separate object of evaluation is tied up with what the alternatives tend to leave out. If the dual conception of officials reveals that there is indeed a distinctive object at the end of a chain of legitimacy evaluations, then it makes no sense to stop part-way through that chain. While it may be quicker or simpler to ask about the legitimacy of a decision or a norm that underpins it, that simplicity will not be defensible if it turns out to miss important details.

Some of these details are implicit in what has already been set out. For instance, the institutional alternative categorization—'officials as institutions'—would miss the importance of the dual senses of agency and its reminder that agents are capable of action, and thus capable of acting for reasons or in spite of reasons in important ways that institutions are not. Legal officials, in particular, are often treated as institutions personified, and their agency is relied upon to give literal and metaphorical voice to the claims of law over its subjects—claims which an institution cannot make until an agent comes along.[42] This point, though seemingly trivial, entails something important, namely the complete dependence of institutions (including legal as well as other institutions of the state) upon their agents.[43]

[41] See, for example, Matthew Kramer, 'Moral Conflicts, the "Ought"-Implies-"Can" Principle, and Moral Demandingness' in Marcel van Ackeren and Michael Kühler (eds), *The Limits of Moral Obligation: Moral Demandingness and Ought Implies Can* (Routledge 2016).

[42] See Joseph Raz, *Ethics in the Public Domain* (Oxford University Press 1995) 217.

[43] The point has been well-treated in the literature on law's claims to authority. See, for example, the original challenge from Ronald Dworkin in 'Thirty Years On' (2002) 115 Harvard Law Review 1655, extended by Kenneth Himma, 'Law's Claim of Legitimate Authority' in Jules Coleman (ed), *Hart's Postscript: Essays on the Postscript to* The Concept of Law (Oxford University Press 2001), and further developed by Matthew Kramer, *Where Law and Morality Meet* (Oxford University Press 2004). See persuasive replies from John Gardner, 'How Law Claims, What Law Claims' in *Law as a Leap of Faith: Essays on Law in General* (Oxford University Press 2012). My full response to that literature is developed in Nicole Roughan, 'The Official Point of View and the Official Claim to Authority' (2018) 38 Oxford Journal of Legal Studies 191.

If we just treat officials as representatives of their institutions, giving their voice and action to bring norms and decisions to bear upon subjects, we might miss noticing that it is the officials who are in control. This point is particularly salient when evaluating institutions in which officials have high degrees of discretion as to whether or how an institution's powers are exercised or applied. But it is not just about discretion. Institutions cannot apply their own norms, nor make decisions about their own reform or replacement. An institution cannot be born except through agency, nor can it be improved or damaged except through the work of those agents who have some degree of capacity to make such changes. This has implications for how we should think about legitimacy.

A focus on the micro-legitimacy of officials, not just their institutional location, takes seriously the inability of institutions to act for themselves or in respect of others, as well as the potential for the agents of an institution to act in ways that can count as effective or ineffective ways of exercising the institution's powers. An official, who might act *intra vires* or *ultra vires*, and who brings her agency to bear on the application of an institution and the exercise of its authority, should be a central object of evaluation because only her conduct determines whether an institution will manifest legitimate authority. In other words, an institution may have the potential to be legitimately authoritative—for example, it might have the potential to serve its subjects in the right kind of way and with the right kind of accountability—but unless that potential is brought to fruition by its officials in a legitimate way, it will not have legitimacy. Both powers and burdens thus stand and fall upon the officials of those institutions, who both claim authority and hold the only hope of realizing its legitimacy.

In this regard, a micro-legitimacy analysis also avoids eliding the officials themselves with the powers they wield. A conception of officials as (mere) power-wielders would insist that we learn all we need to know about legitimacy by evaluating the powers themselves (either *ex ante* or *ex post* their exercise). Yet focusing on powers risks missing an important difference, and relation, between the power (eg 'authority') and the role of the one who exercises that power. The role is not simply a vacant or contingent part of the legitimacy analysis. Rather the role (eg of 'an authority') is a position of standing from which the power ('authority') is claimed and exercised.

To ask whether a holder of a power is legitimate is, in part, to ask whether she has legitimate standing. A private person might have particular standing because of a private role he fulfils, such as a parent, teacher, or employer, while an official or appointed agent of the state will have standing attached to the public role, such as judge, diplomat, or legislator. The legitimacy of that standing can then be scrutinized—does it satisfy certain procedural requirements or is it accepted by those who are its subjects? Offering a focus on state officials' legitimacy, for instance, entails a requirement that those who wield authority in the name of the state do so as a result of normatively or sociologically legitimate processes of appointment, election, or other means of entering the official role.

It is possible and may be desirable to consider these requirements of standing and their evaluation as conditions for the legitimacy of the authority power itself, in which case the focus on officials' legitimacy would not be separate on this point.[44] Yet often they are not—in particular, the importance of standing can get lost in the hum of debate over the respective merits of procedural and substantive conditions.

The insight of a focus on officials, distinct from procedure versus substance debates, is that the particular roles within which standing is conferred must themselves be justified if the standing is to have normative significance. The justification for the role of a state official (whether the role is administrative, legislative, or adjudicative) acts as a precursor to the legitimacy of that official as an authority, as well as to the legitimacy of the authority she wields. This echoes the manner in which some theorists of authority have argued for a two-stage set of conditions for its legitimacy: first, there must be a justification for having authority in the first place, rather than independent decision-making, then there must be a particular substantive or procedural or conjunctive condition determining whether a candidate for such authority actually has legitimate authority.[45] In the echo, however, the intervening step of justifying a role for officials is subtly different from the justification of authority itself. It requires a justification of a special role of an official as an agent of the state's authority, a justification which rests upon the value of public institutionalized authority and its capacities to issue binding norms, determinations, and decisions over a community of subjects.[46] This, unlike the justification for authority per se, is a justification of a public, official role that is to rule, not a justification of a generic right to rule.

The second insight secured by a focus on officials, not just their powers, arises even if the condition of standing for officials' legitimacy is subsumed within the conditions of legitimate authority. The remaining standard concerns the importance of the manner in which powers are exercised. Officials not only manifest an institution's powers over subjects, so that their conduct determines effective and ineffective uses of those powers; officials also determine *how* they are manifest—in good or bad ways.[47] Ways of wielding authority might be evaluated by reference to values that,

[44] See, for example, Hershovitz, 'The Role of Authority' (n 32); and Roughan, *Authorities* (n 16) 127–29. Even if the matter of standing can be subsumed among procedural conditions for legitimacy, it bears separate emphasis here to deflect objections from any wholly substantive theory of legitimate authority. I have argued elsewhere for a conjunctive account in which both standing and standards (procedure and substance) are included in the conditions for legitimate authority. A defence of this conjunctive view against objections from Arie Rosen appears in Nicole Roughan, 'Relativity under Review: A Response to Commentators on *Authorities*' (2015) 40 Australian Journal of Legal Philosophy 212. cf other hybrid accounts, including Thomas Christiano, *The Constitution of Equality: Democratic Authority and its Limits* (Oxford University Press 2011); Allen Buchanan and Robert Keohane, 'Legitimacy and Global Governance Institutions' (2004) 20 Ethics and International Affairs 405.

[45] Even Raz's substantive account, however, leaves some room for standing, in the form of the 'independence condition', which in determining the jurisdiction of an authority contra an independent decision, suggests a kind of precursive role for standing. See Joseph Raz, 'The Problem of Authority: Revisiting the Service Conception' (2006) 90 Minnesota Law Review 1003. See also an analysis of the idea of jurisdiction in Dimitrios Kyritsis, *Shared Authority: Courts and Legislatures in Legal Theory* (Hart Publishing 2015); Hershovitz, 'The Role of Authority' (n 32); and Jeremy Waldron, 'Authority for Officials' in Lukas H Meyer, Stanley L Paulson, and Thomas W Pogge (eds), *Rights, Culture and the Law: Themes from the Legal and Political Philosophy of Joseph Raz* (Oxford University Press 2003).

[46] See Hershovitz, 'The Role of Authority' (n 32).

[47] There are parallels here with Avishai Margalit's work in *The Decent Society* (Harvard University Press 1998), which emphasizes the importance of the manner in which institutions and bureaucracy

while not among the conditions determining the legitimacy of authority itself, are nevertheless requirements for the legitimacy of those administering such authority. For instance, in some official roles, social virtues, such as basic courtesy, decency, and inter-personal respect, might demand of officials that their engagements with subjects of institutional powers be conducted so as to minimize the insult of subjection itself. Or there may be institutional virtues—an official might be required to give subjects the full suite of respects entailed in the idea of 'natural justice', including opportunities to be heard, offering reasons and reviews of decisions, even where these fall outside of the conditions for the exercise of legitimate authority. They might also, in addition or alternatively, require that official actions conform to the formal requirements of the rule of law or substantive and reflective ideals along the lines of public reason. Even if these ideals are not among the conditions for legitimate authority, strictly conceived, they may yet feature in the assessment of the legitimacy of those who claim and wield that power. The importance of the manner in which institutional powers are applied may be missed if agents are simply treated as the wielders of authority.

3. Why should it matter who exercises a power or who controls an institution?

Quite aside from what would otherwise be missed, there are important positive reasons to pursue the evaluation of officials' micro-legitimacy. To focus upon officials is to see that it matters who is acting, not just what is done. Micro-legitimacy asks us to think about the occupant of an office, not just the existence of an office or its activities.

This matters because officials not only are, descriptively, the agents who operate institutions and their powers, but also, as the bearers of moral burdens, are responsible for what they do. Some of these burdens are clear, such as the self-generated duties of an official who takes an oath of office and thus binds herself to what she has agreed to do. But others are more opaque. For instance, officials, qua agents of state institutions, claim the authority of those institutions over their subjects. This, I have argued elsewhere, is not an empty claim; rather, it entails burdens upon the one doing the claiming.

To claim authority is to commit oneself to the good faith pursuit of whatever would make that authority legitimate for its subjects.[48] The claim is not to truth, but to justification; not a claim that one already has legitimate authority, but that one is justified in claiming it.[49] On this understanding, the claim to law's authority

itself operate. I am grateful to Alessandro Ferrara for pointing out this connection, which also echoes Tom Tyler's work on the felt character of legitimacy (detailing the impact of the quality of subjects' treatment on their perceptions of legitimacy). See also Martin Krygier, 'The Rule of Law and State Legitimacy' in this volume.

[48] See Roughan, *Authorities* (n 16) 153–54. I take this to be a different and stronger claim than Raz's argument that authorities 'publicly claim that they attempt to function' as legitimate authorities. See Joseph Raz, *The Morality of Freedom* (Oxford University Press 1986) 47.

[49] Roughan, 'The Official Point of View and the Official Claim to Authority' (n 43).

is a claim that law is due authority. So understood, it includes a commitment and is imbued with a distinct normative character for the agent who makes the claim. If an official claims legitimate authority, she owes *to subjects* a duty to use her best efforts to realize the conditions under which that claim could be true.[50] The official who claims authority in her role as agent or representative of the state (or indeed the law), by virtue of that claim, bears the burden of the pursuit of legitimate authority and thus is central to its realization. To focus on officials as objects of evaluation, then, is to lay the responsibility for the pursuit of legitimacy in someone's hands, instead of leaving it at the gate of an institution.

D. The Standard of Officials' Legitimacy

Even if the possibility and the value of isolating officials among the objects of legitimacy can be shown, and even if we know what an official is and who counts as an official, what does it mean for an official to be legitimate? To hold officials out as objects of such evaluation and to know what officials are supposed to pursue will require a candidate set of standards for legitimacy. How, if at all, do those standards differ from those applicable to institutions and powers, in assessments of their legitimacy? How, if at all, are the standards related or integrated?

There are several layers to the legitimacy of officials. The first is a foundational justification for the value of having officials (and not just any old agent with authority) in respect of that activity or domain. The second layer adds a justification for the particular roles of officials—both in relation to one another and in relation to subjects, in light of the foundational base layer. The third layer requires that those who enter official roles do so through proper processes, whatever these may be. Finally, the fourth layer demands that those who have successfully and appropriately taken on official roles act in pursuit of that which would render their powers and institutions legitimate, mindful of both their institutional and relational moral duties. I will argue below that these four aspects are laid in the manner of brickwork, so that a defect in part of one layer will weaken the structure, but need not bring the whole edifice down.

In more detail, the foundational layer of official legitimacy lies in the value of the official role itself. For state officials, this turns on the value of some actors being charged with making (and being entitled to make) claims on behalf of the state over subjects. Such value may include the necessity of having human agents involved in schemes of governance aimed at public coordination, dispute settlement, policy administration, public defence, and, ultimately, decision-making. It seems a straightforward case to say that human agents are necessary to the governance of human affairs.[51] Yet the case is not only based on necessity and effectiveness. Human

[50] In addition to exercising her institutional powers and complying with her institutional duties, the official may then have additional burdens to seek to remedy defects in legitimacy that she notices in the course of her official role.

[51] See, for example, Finnis, *Natural Law and Natural Rights* (n 33) 3 and ch 9. Finnis argues that the existence of officials with authority is necessary for the institutionalized pursuit of the human goods.

agency comes with the potential to not only act, but to act on the basis of reasons, including making decisions based on the particular prioritization of reasons (and values) that is either demanded by a subject population or is determined for them by some subset of their number. Agency also entails the capacity to make decisions and choices when reasons run out or are incommensurable. Thinking optimistically, then, the role of officials is what makes governance not only possible and effective, but also potentially just. While the dark side of agency is also present—agents of the state cannot only make mistakes, they can and sometimes do abuse or misuse the powers they wield and the institutions they control—there are often institutional supervisions, remedies, and punishments (themselves designed and controlled by other agents) to deal with such cases when they occur.

Beyond the base justification for having officials at all, however, are pressing questions about what makes particular official roles (and particular kinds of official roles) legitimate. If there is value in having some agents in positions of power, then it is crucial to ask what sorts of constraints and supervisions should attach to roles in which power is exercised, in order for the value to be pursued. This set of questions forces attention to the roles of officials in precise contexts, which may differ from one another. The legitimate role of a judge, for instance, while contested and differentiated between systems, still differs in obvious ways from the legitimate role of, for example, a legislator, police officer, diplomat, ombudsman, or policy adviser in a government department. The inquiry into particular roles reveals two important features. The first is that the requirements of legitimacy for particular official roles turn out to be parasitic on, but not subsumed by, accounts of the legitimacy of their institutions and powers. To give a specific account of the legitimate role of a judge, for instance, requires a consideration of how the role relates to both the judicial institution and its authority *in relation to* other institutions and other powers.[52]

If the particular roles of officials are justified, the focus then turns to those who occupy the roles themselves. To be a legitimate official, an agent must enter the official role in the appropriate manner for that role. In the case of state officials, entry is typically by appointment, election, coronation, or some other process. These processes are, invariably, bilateral—they involve the conferral of power (either by other officials or subjects) and its acceptance (often in the form of oaths/affirmations of office and/or written contracts).[53] Officials' legitimacy can be hindered at this stage

Even if the most enthusiastic proponents of artificial intelligence had their way, humans' roles in determining inputs, standards, and values to be worked into artificial-intelligence systems and their choices to carry out the outcomes of algorithmic decision-making would still be determinative (to say nothing of the ability to hit the off switch or physically take charge of machines and their data).

[52] These are controversial, and theories of adjudication—as well as theories of law they support or entail—offer distinct arguments over the character and extent of the judicial role. We can then tease out and test the logical and normative connections between the legitimacy of institutions, powers, and officials.

[53] Oath-taking is sometimes thought to carry special significance in thinking about the idea of officials, invoking divine sanction for as well as public commitment to officials' duties, and often committing officials to exercise their duties in virtuous ways. Yet there are officials who do not take oaths (especially those of lower rank) and non-officials who do (such as witnesses giving testimony before a court). The ideas of oaths and oath-taking, including their role in supporting and contouring official duties and the very idea of officials, are explored at length in Nicholas Aroney, 'Faith in Public

by improper means of entering an office. A presidential election which is rigged, tampered with, or beset by interference renders defective the legitimacy of its victor by justifying doubt that he is a legitimate occupant of his office. An appointment made on grounds other than merit and qualification does the same for the judge or civil servant emerging from an appointment process. The absence of any actual appointment, in which a person is treated as an official when she has not passed through the proper process to be an official, is still more suspect, as is the coronation of a monarch who has ousted her predecessor in unnatural or unjustified ways.

After entry into office, the legitimacy of officials turns upon what they do once they get there—how they use their role, with its associated powers, to further whatever values justify the existence of the office, but mindful of the officials' ongoing relational duties.[54] This is where abuses of power or the shirking of duties cause defects in the legitimacy of an official. It is also where any divergence between official roles and private beliefs, attitudes, or dispositions can become most obvious. Many high-profile controversies about officials have this structure—including concerns over racist dispositions and their implications for law enforcement, clerks refusing to issue marriage licences to gay couples in defiance of legal rules permitting such marriages and prohibiting such discrimination, and preferential treatment being given by administrative officials to friends and family. These are condemned or defended depending on the views we adopt of the official role and its separation from personal agency.[55] In legal-academic contexts, perhaps the most prominent debates involve intense reactions whenever judges render the law with their views of what, morally, should be done, enraging those who see the judicial duty to apply the law as a formal and exclusively institutional duty, and giving hope to those who see the institutional duty itself as leaving room for moral reasoning by judges as moral agents.

Office: The Meaning, Persistence and Importance of Oaths' (*ABC Religion and Ethics*, 23 November 2015) <http://www.abc.net.au/religion/articles/2015/11/23/4358054.htm> accessed 3 April 2018, and further in Mark R Rutgers, 'The Oath of Office as Public Value Guardian' (2010) 40 American Review of Public Administration 428.

[54] One potential objection to all of this is that what I am calling relational duties might be alternatively explained as virtues. An aretaic account of the official role would indeed include some of the same elements listed here as duties, but that approach can be resisted for two reasons specific to the idea of officials (setting aside for now any general or more foundational debates between duty-based and virtue-based accounts, or between morality and ethics, distinctly conceived). The first reason lies in the relational reading of the official role, in which officials wield powers over subjects. The fact of such powers, and the position of dependence in which subjects are placed, renders officials' good faith, impartiality, etc as matters of official duty, owed to subjects, not simply virtuous qualities. Arguably, wherever there are roles to which authority is attached, and where there is both normative and de facto subjection of some persons to others, there are relational duties upon those with the authority, not simply virtuous ways of exercising their powers. The second, related, reason places the conformity with duties, including the good faith pursuit of legitimacy, as part of what it means to be an official. My point is not that all officials do in fact act in good faith, but that by virtue of their roles as officials (which, recall, are voluntarily assumed), they are committed to doing so, as a matter of duty.

[55] Not all of these conflicts are as serious or as politically charged, and sometimes the official-personal contest plays out in more positive ways. Few would object to the near-daily media stories in which some official (often a lower official such as a police/traffic officer) does something heart-warming and personal (eg a police officer buying a child restraint instead of ticketing a father for driving with his child unrestrained) even when it contravenes his official duties.

The exact standards and the balance to be struck between the institutional and the personal will vary according to particular roles in their social context, as established by normative social practices. Among legislative offices, there are different expectations of fidelity to constituents' preferences across different types of political systems; among judicial offices, there are different approaches to fidelity to law in different jurisdictions, and so forth. At the very least, however, (and despite these variations across official roles and different theories of those roles, the different processes of entry, and the different expectations of conduct) officials have in common the (shared) burdens set out in the previous section. In claiming the state's authority (in various forms and through various means), they are committed to using their offices in ways that pursue its legitimacy. In holding and exercising the state's authority over subjects, whether directly or indirectly, they owe it to those subjects to use their powers in a legitimate way or, at least, to try to do so.

The standard of legitimacy for officials corresponds to those burdens. As institutional agents, officials must exercise their institutional powers and duties in good faith, seeking to improve the legitimacy of both their institutions and powers, and to conduct their relations with subjects in ways that respect those subjects despite their subordination. Conformity with duties is thus not a matter of strict adherence to formal institutional requirements, not of conduct being merely *intra vires*. An institutional duty might be outweighed by a relational duty that requires nonconformity with the institutional duty; conduct could be *intra vires* but not legitimate (for instance, conduct that is in bad faith, is disrespectful of subjects, or exploits a loophole in formal powers).

The vagaries and variances here render the standard of legitimacy something of an ideal—rather than a matter of binary conditions for achievement.[56] Legitimacy need not require the perfect conformity of officials with both the institutional and the personal duties of their role, partly due to their potential conflicts, but also because human agency itself renders perfection improbable if not impossible. Still, there are likely to be threshold markers of illegitimacy. One of the differences in exploring the legitimacy of officials, rather than institutions or powers, is that it applies standards to human agents, albeit d ones in institutional roles. Institutionalization does not imbue officials with superhuman judgement, wisdom, or infallibility. In contrast, institutions can be designed to be the best they can possibly be, given what we know about the way in which the world works and what is valuable. Human agents representing and operating those institutions, however, cannot be designed to a plan nor remodelled to fix any defects. Bad faith or lack of attempts to realize legitimacy are clearly illegitimate. Trying hard and falling short, however, are acceptable and, indeed, to be expected.

[56] In this respect, it parallels Raz's explanation of legitimate authority 'through describing the ideal exercise of authority'. See Raz, *The Morality of Freedom* (n 48) 47.

E. Conclusion: A Speculative Starting Point for Micro- and Macro-Legitimacy

All of this micro-level breaking down of legitimacy analyses does not change a fundamental interdependence among official roles, as well as among the powers and institutions they operate. Official roles, and their legitimacy, exist in complex networks where there are lines of hierarchy, cross-checking, supervision, review, and appeal. Their relatedness, and the ways in which they share in or even compete over claiming the authority of the state, mean the legitimacy of the specific roles of officials needs to be considered interdependently. This interdependence and sharing in the burdens of legitimacy not only includes official agents of the state itself, but also, arguably, includes all those with whom legitimate powers are shared.

I have argued elsewhere for an account of 'relative authority' which characterizes the state's authority, coerciveness, and other powers among a broader set of practices, both within and beyond the state, in which the state is one claimant purporting to be legitimate for subjects it shares with other claimants.[57] My account argued that such overlap and interaction renders the authority itself relative, such that the legitimacy of the powers depends on the relationships the claimants form with one another. The full implications of that account for the present project on the legitimacy of officials cannot be explored here, but there are several obvious starting points for exploring the relationship between what I have called here micro-legitimacy and what might be called 'macro-legitimacy'. The most important is that if, as I have argued, officials are committed to pursuing the legitimacy of their powers and their institutional homes, then the macro-legitimacy lens alters what that pursuit will entail. It will require that officials cultivate practices and possibly new institutional forms to bring about the relationships that are required to realize relative legitimate authority.

The full implications of the combined micro-macro lens thus include a shift in the content of the roles of officials themselves. Rather than technicians operating to give effect to state institutions, officials' roles (and their constituent duties) may—particularly for senior officials—include engagements with other officials not located in the same institutional structures and not always sharing a common goal. In the macro lens, these can include officials outside of the state apparatus, including international legal officials, officials of other states, officials of religious or ethnic orders within the state, and officials of transnational regulatory bodies. Each of these

[57] This was the central idea of Roughan, *Authorities* (n 16). The argument for conceiving and evaluating what I called 'relative authority', rather than independent authority, is that any evaluation of authority is driven by, and serves the purpose of, exploring the limits of what the authority can legitimately require of its subjects. If there are multiple claimants of authority over the same subjects or over distinct subjects whose interactions require the involvement of 'their' authorities, then the question of the extent to which any of those authorities can be legitimate (and thus generative of binding obligations upon subjects) is a question that needs to be asked in respect of all purportedly legitimate authorities, not independently, but in light of their plurality. Although the emphasis in that work was on 'relative authority', it leaves open the prospect of relativity of other powers, including coercion, so that the justification for the state's use of coercion must include an evaluation of its relations with other potentially justified coercers.

relationships has the power to support or detract from the officials' legitimacy in what they do as agents of the state's institutions.

Finally, and perhaps most expansively, the integration of micro and macro concerns raises the possibility that, not only can powers be overlapping and interacting in the way explored by the relative authority theory, but so too may be the officials and institutions themselves. A full analysis would thus need to explore all dimensions of the potentially *interdependent* legitimacy of the state's officials, institutions, and powers with various non-state, supra-state, or inter-state officials, institutions, and powers. This full view of macro-legitimacy, then, has the potential to de-emphasize the state in the determination of officials' duties and the assessment of their legitimacy, although whether this will be the case will depend on a full working-out of the integration of the micro and macro accounts.

The challenge of uniting an account of micro-legitimacy with the full analysis of macro-legitimacy is going to take more care than this initial work. The present chapter has focused instead on the key insight that to think about legitimacy *and* the state is not (or not only) to think about the legitimacy *of* the state. Rather, there are matters of legitimacy that manifest not only in and around the state's powers and institutions, but at the micro level, in the roles, standing, and conduct of officials.

VI

The Rule of Law and State Legitimacy

*Martin Krygier**

The rule of law is today lauded as good for so many things—economic development, democracy, human rights, and much more—that it was only a matter of time before someone asked: what has it ever done for state legitimacy? I will consider that question. My answer is that it depends how you think about the rule of law.

The first three sections of the chapter set out three elements of a particular way of approaching the rule of law that I have advocated in many places: drawing on its traditional resonances (section A), looking first to the point for which one seeks the rule of law, rather than to the anatomy of legal structures (section B), and finding that point in hostility to arbitrary power, a hostility I share (section C), though would extend beyond the state to other forms and sources of arbitrary power. To the extent that the rule of law really does diminish arbitrary exercise of significant power in a society, I believe it contributes to state legitimacy. Section D reminds us that not everyone agrees, by drawing attention to some prominent arguments, from the right and the left of the political spectrum, that question whether state legitimacy is enhanced by the rule of law.

In section E, I turn to lawyers and legal philosophers, among whom one might imagine the expertise lies. However, I find questionable their common assumption that it all is to be sought and found in the places they work, or work on: the official legal institutions, rules and practices of states. I question that assumption for its lack of sociological sensibility and imagination, a lack that is particularly telling in a discussion of legitimacy, which needs to concern itself with how the state looks in the eye of the legitimacy-bestowing beholder.

I pursue the implications of that lack in sections F to H, focusing in particular on a failure to reach what are likely to be concerns of those 'ordinary people' whom Jeremy Waldron rightly castigates his colleagues for ignoring and claims to have taken into account. In section F, I accept his diagnosis but not his cure, which shares precisely the assumptions that I question among those he criticizes. In section G, I suggest that the rule of law is better viewed as an 'insofar as' social reality, achieved insofar as power is not exercised in arbitrary ways, rather than as an assortment of

* I am grateful to the participants in the 'Legitimacy and the State' conference, and particularly to Arie Rosen, discussant of this chapter, for their insightful comments.

Legitimacy: The State and Beyond. First Edition. Edited by Wojciech Sadurski, Michael Sevel, and Kevin Walton. Published 2019 by Oxford University Press.

legal institutions, or formal or procedural aspects of rules, which may or may not contribute, in different times, places, and circumstances, to that end. Whether or not that is right about the concept of the rule of law, I suggest it must be right about state legitimacy. For this is unlikely simply to flow from formal or procedural features of legal institutions and/or rules, on their own, but rather from how they work, how they are *perceived* to work, and how other things work, in the world. In section H, I draw on a large body of social-psychological findings on what people most value from state agencies that deal with them, in particular the central importance of procedural justice, and explore some implications of these findings for our understanding of links between the rule of law and state legitimacy, both as we actually perceive those links and as we should.

In section I, I raise two issues about state and society interactions, one to do with the many and diverse social variables that influence the functioning of law and the state in society; the other with non-state, social, sources of arbitrariness. In both cases, a solipsistic concentration on state legal forms and procedures is unhelpful. On the one hand, a focus on legal rules, forms, and procedures is unreliable as a guide to law's actual social functioning, notwithstanding that that should be our primary concern. On the other hand, the rule of law needs to deal with more than *state* arbitrariness, and unless it does so may contribute little to state legitimacy, however well formed the state's laws might be. Function is likely to be more important than form for both the rule of law and state legitimacy. However, regnant accounts of the rule of law tend to concentrate on form, more than they explore socially contingent and variable function.

In section J, I concede deontological significance to state compliance with several conventionally identified rule of law conditions, irrespective of how they work in the world. However, I conclude in section K, by recalling the Hobbesian condition for state legitimacy: effectiveness. Without that, citizens are unlikely to, and nor should they, consider a state legitimate, however many rule of law 'laundry lists' its law satisfies.

A. Concepts and Traditions

My brief is more complicated than might appear, since its fundamental terms are so variably understood and continuously contested. To simplify, I will try to avoid conceptual controversies about state and legitimacy, which other contributors to this volume are more competent to explore, and confine myself to what I imagine to be safe, relatively capacious—orienting rather than defining—conceptions of the two concepts. I have more to say about rule of law, variations in understanding of which are multiple and central to my story.

I start with the state. To locate the terrain, I draw upon Gianfranco Poggi's expression of the modern distinction between, on the one hand, its domain—'the structures and events directly connected with public authority, with the constitution and management of the polity'—and on the other, that of 'society'—'the structures and events which individuals generate as they pursue their private interests, express their emotions, acquire and exercise their capacity for judgment, establish and manage relationships with one another'.[1] Nothing in what follows hangs on the details of this distinction; I use it merely as a rough marker of where you might find, and what you might find to be, some of the central and distinctive activities and concerns of the state, as it has come to develop and be thought about over the past couple of centuries.[2]

As for legitimacy, a simple way to think of it is as normative (rather than merely prudential or consequential) justification for support. Holders of state power find it useful to buttress their positions and the exercise of powers that goes with them with claims that these positions are rightly held, those powers justifiably, legitimately, exercised.

All states claim to be legitimate. The claim is borne out *sociologically* to the extent it is accepted as normatively justified by those to whom it is addressed. A state is *morally* legitimate if there are persuasive reasons of political morality that justify the claim. Of course, these two sorts of legitimacy overlap, but they can come apart; often are destined to. Since states need sociological legitimacy, they will seek it, whether or not they deserve it. If they are successful they will have (sociologically) *legitimized* or *legitimated* their rule, but we may well deny that they are (morally) legitimate.

One more distinction: legitimacy is not the same as justice. Sociologically, judgements of legitimacy might flow from many sources other than the justice of the state: pedigree—divine, old, or both; charisma; legality; and so on. As a matter of political morality, I follow Wojciech Sadurski's suggestion that legitimacy 'is a standard located halfway between the benchmarks of validity and justice'.[3] Considerations relevant to the (sociological and moral) legitimacy of a state in exercising power—whether it is democratically elected, uncorrupt, acting according to law, etc—might well differ from those that have to do with whether it acts justly. There might be overlaps and there might be tensions: sociologically, legitimacy of a government might lessen appreciation of injustices it commits[4] and, both sociologically and morally, sufficient injustice might well erode a claim of legitimacy. But if they overlap, they are still distinct.

A great deal more than that can be said, but in relation to state and legitimacy, I think that is enough for my purposes. I will have to say more about the rule of law, however, for two reasons. First, law arguably has a special relationship to state and legitimacy in modern times, and second, *the rule of law* is a notoriously complex, polysemous, and much contested concept. What conception of the concept one

[1] Gianfranco Poggi, 'State and Society: Modern Trends of a Problematic Relationship' in *Varieties of Political Experience* (ECPR Press 2014) 43.

[2] For more on the concept of the state, see Quentin Skinner, 'The Genealogy of the Modern State' (2009) 167 Proceedings of the British Academy 325.

[3] Wojciech Sadurski, 'Conceptions of Public Reason in the Supranational Sphere and Legitimacy beyond Borders', Chapter VIII, 165, in this volume.

[4] Charles W Mueller and Miriam J Landsman, 'Legitimacy and Justice Perceptions (2004) 67 Social Psychology Quarterly 189, 198.

chooses will significantly affect how one appraises the contribution, if any, of the rule of law to the legitimacy of the state.

First, as Max Weber emphasized, state, legitimacy, and law are peculiarly intertwined in modernity, since law is a distinctively central element in the legitimacy claims of modern states. In terms of his three ideal types of legitimacy, the staple/stable type of legitimacy claims by governments all over the world for most of human history was based on tradition, 'the authority of the eternal yesterday',[5] interspersed from time to time with charismatic eruptions, where a would-be leader claimed, often quite without support from tradition or office, to be in the position to say 'it is written ... but I say unto you'.[6] Tradition is a more stable and enduring source of legitimacy than charisma, since an individual's claim to the latter is commonly difficult to make plausible and, even when successfully made, is difficult to transmit once the personally anointed figure fails or dies. The 'routinization of charisma' is a complicated matter of institutionalization of what was once purely personal; many apply, but few are chosen. The Roman Catholic Church has managed it for a very long time; the Thousand Year Reich vanished after twelve years, with the failure *and* death of its charismatic founder.

According to Weber, modernity does things differently. Traditional legitimacy has weakened, while charisma, as always, remains unpredictable and episodic. Key to the claim of modern states is law, and law of an unprecedentedly *depersonalized* and *positivized* sort, within a system of impersonal secular rules, not personal or divine fiat. The rules are posited by humans, not given by God, but who the particular human is doesn't matter once she occupies a legally authorized office. So long as she comes to occupy a legally created and recognized position by legally authorized means, she can exercise powers made available and legitimized by the law. So, law today has a special centrality, or so Weber argued, at least to the sociological legitimacy of the modern state.

But if law is distinctively significant as a legitimator in modern times, what of 'the rule of law'? Does it add anything to law, sociologically or normatively? Well, to repeat, it depends. The concept has had a long career in various forms of verbal expression, even in English let alone other languages, and even the meanings given to the English phrase, launched for this purpose but not invented by Albert Venn Dicey late in the nineteenth century, are hugely, some say 'essentially', contested.[7] So parsing the specific words and phrase popularized by Dicey will not on its own reveal the problematic of concerns, threats, and responses to which discourses about the rule of law have long been addressed, and for which this phrase and others like it have come to be shorthand indicators.[8]

[5] Max Weber, 'Politics as a Vocation' in HH Gerth and C Wright Mills (eds), *From Max Weber: Essays in Sociology* (Routledge 2009) 78.

[6] Max Weber, *Economy and Society: An Outline of Interpretive Sociology*, vol 3 (Bedminster Press 1968) 978.

[7] Jeremy Waldron, 'Is the Rule of Law an Essentially Contested Concept (in Florida)?' (2002) 21 Law and Philosophy 137.

[8] See Julian Sempill, 'Ruler's Sword, Citizen's Shield: The Rule of Law and the Constitution of Power' (2016) 31 Journal of Law and Politics 333, 338–40; Jeremy Waldron, *The Rule of Law and the Measure of Property* (Cambridge University Press 2012) 8.

All that was true even before the apotheosis of the phrase in the past thirty years.[9] With its contemporary all-purpose omnipresence, choices must be made. We must specify *which* rule of law. Is it Dicey's? Fuller's? Raz's? Shklar's? Dworkin's? Selznick's? Is it what international rule of law promoters' checklists mandate and chequebooks subsidize? Or what rule of law indices measure? If so, which indices? The World Justice Project's 'Rule of Law Index'? The World Bank's 'Governance Indicators'? The Heritage Foundation's neoliberally inflected index? That deployed by Freedom House, focusing on civil and political rights? Each differs from the others.[10] Are we to prefer rule of law 'thin' or 'thick', 'formal' or 'substantive'?[11] Or is it something altogether richer and deeper than contemporary, in some circumstances mandatory, deployments of a fashionable logo allow us to glean?

No one is in a position to legislate on these matters. Any proposal is precisely that, to be judged on its ability to capture, illuminate, maybe clarify, maybe improve upon, common understandings and uses of the concept; its helpfulness in approaching problems to which the concept is addressed; but also, if the concept has figured in traditions of serious concerns with important matters over long periods, its capacity to capture the problems, reflections, apprehensions, and concerns that generated it, and that were borne by those traditions. Concerns with these issues are millennia old, after all, at least in Western legal traditions. None of us invented the concept or the problems, nor the generations of thought about one and the other. Conceptions of the rule of law have been transmitted and contested within traditions of legal and political thought that often compete with each other. Within the traditions, there are continuing arguments as well. As a result, debate about the rule of law is part of an ongoing conversation, not a mere pointer to easily and uncontroversially identifiable pieces of the conceptual and normative landscape.

So, instead of picking some impoverished and flattened conception of the rule of law, reduced by fashion and interest to the ephemeral concerns of the moment, we would do well to 'pursue the intimations'[12] of significant traditions of thinking about it. Those intimations may lead in different directions and not get you where, or all the way, you want to go; they might disappoint, or no longer resonate, and there is likely a lot of work left to do. But it would be foolish, hubristic, to imagine—as many now do imagine[13]—that it all starts now, with us.

[9] See Martin Krygier, 'The Rule of Law after the Short Twentieth Century: Launching a Global Career' in Richard Nobles and David Schiff (eds), *Law, Society and Community: Socio-Legal Essays in Honour of Roger Cotterrell* (Ashgate 2014).

[10] See Mila Versteeg and Tom Ginsburg, 'Measuring the Rule of Law: A Comparison of Indicators' (2017) 42 Law & Social Inquiry 100.

[11] See Randall Peerenboom, 'Varieties of Rule of Law: An Introduction and Provisional Conclusion' in Randall Peerenboom (ed), *Asian Discourses of Rule of Law* (Routledge 2004).

[12] Michael Oakeshott, 'Political Education' in *Rationalism in Politics and Other Essays* (expanded edn, Liberty Press 1991).

[13] For an argument that leads in this direction, see Deval Desai, 'In Search of "Hire" Knowledge: Donor Hiring Practices and the Organization of the Rule of Law Reform Field' in David Marshall (ed), *The International Rule of Law Movement: A Crisis of Legitimacy and the Way Forward* (Harvard University Press 2014) 45.

Although I am not a philosopher, the approach I advocate conforms to a suggestion Joseph Raz has made in relation to the concept of authority, of which he writes:

> The philosophical explanation of authority is not an attempt to state the meaning of a word. It is a discussion of a concept which is deeply embedded in the philosophical and political traditions of our culture ... There is not, nor has there ever been, complete agreement on all aspects of the concept's place and connections with other concepts. But there is, as part of our common culture, a good measure of agreement between any two people on many, though frequently not the same, points. Accounts of 'authority' ... are partisan accounts furthering the cause of certain strands in the common tradition, by developing and producing new or newly recast arguments in their favour. The very activity is also an expression of faith in the tradition, of a willingness to understand oneself and the world in its terms.[14]

This is an exemplary way to approach culturally significant, enduring, much invoked, derided, and contested concepts that one considers important, although it does not seem to me (or to Julian Sempill, who introduced me to this passage and to this doubt[15]) a strategy that Raz himself follows in his writings on the rule of law.[16] I have tried to commend and pursue something like that approach elsewhere in relation to the rule of law,[17] and I will try, more briefly, to follow it here. For like authority, the rule of law is 'a concept which is deeply embedded in the philosophical and political traditions of our [but not every[18]] culture'. It speaks to important and enduring issues of politics and law that can be forgotten or ignored by contemporary rule of law enthusiasts. Trying to get some sense of its role and significance in such traditions will not rule out controversy, but it might give any conception chosen a grounding in common, lasting, and arguably important concerns.

B. Teleology before Anatomy

If we are to connect in the ways Raz suggests, with traditions of any longevity and large influence, we are unlikely to do so by starting at the level of detailed institutional prescription. For one thing, institutions change over time and differ from

[14] Joseph Raz, *The Morality of Freedom* (Oxford University Press 1986) 63.

[15] See Sempill, 'Ruler's Sword, Citizen's Shield' (n 8) 342–43n16.

[16] See particularly Joseph Raz, 'The Rule of Law and its Virtue' in *The Authority of Law: Essays on Law and Morality* (2nd edn, Oxford University Press 2009); and Sempill's critique on this point in Sempill, 'Ruler's Sword, Citizen's Shield' (n 8).

[17] Martin Krygier, 'The Rule of Law: Pasts, Presents, and Two Possible Futures' (2016) 12 Annual Review of Law and Social Science 199.

[18] See Heinz Popitz, *Phenomena of Power* (Gianfranco Poggi tr, Columbia University Press 2017) 42: 'Only rarely, in the history of societies, has a chance presented itself to even just pose in a planned and purposive manner the question of the limitation of institutionalized violence. Basically, this happened only in the Greek polis, in republican Rome, in a few other city-states, and in the history of the modern constitutional state. The answers to that question have been surprisingly similar: the postulate of the supremacy of the law and of the equality of all before the law ("isonomia"), the principle of limitations to all legislation (basic rights), norms regarding competences (division of powers, federalism), procedural norms (decisions taken by established organs, the public nature of their operations or of the operations of those, the possibility of appeal to higher organs), norms of occupancy (rotation, elections), norms regarding the public sphere (freedom of opinion, freedom of assembly).'

place to place. The institutions that occurred to Aristotle to distinguish 'the rule of law' from 'that of any individual' were not those specified in Magna Carta; those had little in common with those that drew on Montesquieu; what he lit upon was different from Dicey's homegrown selection; these from Hayek's; those from Oakeshott's; his from Fuller's; his (though not so much) from Raz's; any of theirs from Shklar's; hers from those chosen by rule of law indexers; theirs from each other.

Not only *do* such institutions and practices differ; they are *bound to* since the circumstances in which they operate, the problems they are called upon to deal with, their capacities, differ hugely over time and place, both quantitatively and qualitatively.[19] They are affected, too, by vast differences and changes—cultural, religious, demographic, economic, and technological. The modern state thinks differently from other states, does different things and in different ways, both because different things are thinkable and because much is doable and done by states, for better and worse, that has never been done or doable before. So, a search for the identity of institutions and practices will not take us far, or far back.

However, if instead of starting with particular institutions, one seeks to understand the rule of law from the perspective of 'the philosophical and political traditions of our culture', one might be alerted to underlying and overlapping concerns, perennial problems, cumulatively pondered and debated responses to them, and functions or ends valued within such traditions over time, and perhaps still to be valued. Here too there is no unanimity, but there are often 'strands in the common tradition' to be found, which 'partisans' might draw upon in 'developing and producing new or newly recast arguments in their favour'.

So, I suggest we do well to follow a different way into the rule of law than is today common: one that begins with problems and purposes, rather than practices, and with teleological questions, rather than anatomical or morphological ones. Not first off, '*what* is the rule of law?', but '*why* care?'; more specifically, not 'what's the solution?', but 'what is the problem, for which we should seek a solution?' Teleological accounts of an ideal like the rule of law begin by seeking to identify the predicament or circumstances thought to require attention and the value or end that any solution is hoped to serve, its point or telos, in relation to that predicament or those circumstances. Anatomical accounts, by contrast, nominate particular features of official state legal institutional arrangements, practices, and/or rules, as amounting together to the rule of law, and often only then ask what these features are for.[20]

We seek the rule of law for purposes, enjoy it for reasons. Unless we seek first to clarify those purposes and reasons and, in their light, explore what would be needed and assess what is offered to approach them, we are bound to be flying blind, even in deciding what of the myriad institutions of a legal order should be included as 'the rule of law'. My contention, then, is that we should start with those purposes and reasons. Even if we do not come to agree on a particular set of problems, values, and

[19] See Nicola Lacey, 'Philosophy, Political Morality, and History: Explaining the Enduring Resonance of the Hart-Fuller Debate' (2008) 83 New York University Law Review 1059, 1072–78.

[20] See Martin Krygier, 'The Rule of Law. Legality, Teleology, Sociology' in Gianluigi Palombella and Neil Walker (eds), *Relocating the Rule of Law* (Hart Publishing 2009).

ends in answer to the first question, and consequently are led to different ways of achieving the ends we postulate, we will at least know why we differ.

C. Tempering Power

Many problems have been identified for the rule of law to solve, these days too many.[21] However, one set of questions that has generated reflection over centuries has to do with power and its pathologies. Political and legal traditions have long expressed and borne long-familiar concerns over predictable abuses and perversions of power: What do we have reason to hope for/fear from holders of significant power? How might power be rendered at least safe and then, more positively, helpful for those subject to it, rather than loom as a perennial source of threat and fear? How might its exercise be channelled towards useful ends and away from recurrent objectionable forms and tendencies?

Rule of law traditions have particularly worried about *arbitrary* exercise of power, often using precisely that word, as the anti-hero in the rule of law story.[22] A common thought has been that, left to their own devices, wielders of power will frequently face temptations, incentives, and opportunities to act in their own, rather than the public's, interest (however that is defined) and cannot be relied on to avoid exercising it arbitrarily. Some rulers might confound such pessimistic expectations, but we should not have to rely on their beneficence alone. For the possibility of arbitrary exercise of power is a perennial concern. If we are left merely to the 'will', 'pleasure', or 'caprice' of the power-holder (to use traditional terms of apprehension), arbitrariness will be a constant possibility and, if so, a constant worry. That is because, to put briefly what many writers have argued in many places, even the potential of its arbitrary exercise diminishes subjects' freedom;[23] causes their lives to be fearful;[24] denies them respect, dignity,[25] and moral equality;[26] and destroys possibilities of

[21] This section distils and develops a section, 'The Problem', of my 'The Rule of Law: Pasts, Presents, and Two Possible Futures' (n 17). The specific choice of 'tempering', as distinct from the more common qualifiers of rule of law discussion, such as 'limiting', 'curbing', 'restraining', 'taming', is defended in Martin Krygier, 'Tempering Power' in Maurice Adams, Anne Meuwese, and Ernst Hirsch Ballin (eds), *Constitutionalism and Rule of Law: Bridging Idealism and Realism* (Cambridge University Press 2017).

[22] See John Philip Reid, *The Rule of Law: The Jurisprudence of Liberty in the Seventeenth and Eighteenth Centuries* (Northern Illinois University Press 2004).

[23] Philip Pettit, *Republicanism: A Theory of Freedom and Government* (Cambridge University Press 2012).

[24] Judith N Shklar, 'Political Theory and the Rule of Law' in Stanley Hoffmann (ed), *Political Thought and Political Thinkers* (University of Chicago Press 1998).

[25] Lon L Fuller, *The Morality of Law* (2nd edn, Yale University Press 1969); Raz, 'The Rule of Law and its Virtue' (n 16) 221; Jeremy Waldron, 'Thoughtfulness and the Rule of Law' (2011) 18 British Academy Review 1; Jeremy Waldron, 'The Rule of Law and the Importance of Procedure' in James E Fleming (ed), *Getting to the Rule of Law* (New York University Press 2011).

[26] Paul Gowder, *The Rule of Law in the Real World* (Cambridge University Press 2016); Sempill, 'Ruler's Sword, Citizen's Shield' (n 8); Nick Cheesman, *Opposing the Rule of Law: How Myanmar's Courts Make Law and Order* (Cambridge University Press 2015).

fruitful cooperation among citizens and between citizens and states.[27] So it is worth thinking about how it might be avoided.

The thought has often recurred that law might offer key resources for tempering power and the dangers that typically flow from its arbitrary exercise. That pairing of feared pathology and hoped-for cure has frequently recurred in many writings concerned with tempering state power, and remains at least a central, if not *the* central, element in what we call the rule of law. Concern with such problems goes a long way back. There is nothing in our traditions, long traditions, that renders concern about arbitrary power exotic; nothing original about the choice. And that should be reassuring, not a source of disappointment. Thinkers might want the rule of law for many other reasons, but hostility to arbitrary power is a good and comfortably traditional reason.

The concept of 'arbitrariness' is notoriously under-theorized.[28] Recently,[29] I have sought to clarify it somewhat, in an ostensive way, by drawing attention to three forms of it or, perhaps better, three modes of exercising power that make people vulnerable to arbitrary treatment, and that have been central matters of concern in rule of law traditions. They are different ways in which power is liable to be exercised without the power-wielder being required to take into account the legitimate interests, expectations, and opinions of those subject to the power; that is, being free to act arbitrarily. Often, they are not distinguished, and there may be others, but these have each figured as targets of rule of law thought and writings. There may be some reason to deny that the concept of arbitrariness captures all three, although I can't see it. But if so, I am happy to retreat to my three examples of objectionable exercise of power and give up the unifying label. In the meantime, I will stick with 'arbitrary'. I expand on them in the sources cited and will only mention them here: power is arbitrary when it is *uncontrolled, unpredictable, and/or unrespectful.*

Different thinkers and different traditions have been more or less concerned with one or other of the above forms; often they have been elided. They can be distinguished, however, at least analytically, and what one does about each might need to be different. Each deserves to be opposed. A regime is not home free because it scores well (low) on one but not another dimension of arbitrariness. It should do well on all three. There are all sorts of benefits that might accrue to a regime that applies stable and understandable rules, for example, but if rulers are free to act purely by exercising sovereign will, even if they choose not to, and even more if the rules shut those affected out from consideration, subjects—more accurately objects[30]—of power are vulnerable to its arbitrary exercise.

Over generations, indeed millennia, thought about the rule of law has been haunted by the spectre of arbitrary exercise of state power, in one or other of these senses. Where arbitrariness is available, many classical authors feared, despotism is

[27] Friedrich A Hayek, *The Constitution of Liberty* (Routledge & Kegan Paul 1960).
[28] Timothy Endicott, 'Arbitrariness' (2014) 27 Canadian Journal of Law and Jurisprudence 49.
[29] Krygier, 'The Rule of Law: Pasts, Presents, and Two Possible Futures' (n 17).
[30] See Martin Krygier, 'The Grammar of Colonial Legality: Subjects, Objects, and the Australian Rule of Law' in Geoffrey Brennan and Francis G Castles (eds), *Australia Reshaped: 200 Years of Institutional Transformation* (Cambridge University Press 2002).

not likely to be far away; indeed, a standard contrast classically made and repeated has been between arbitrary despotism, or tyranny, and government according to the rule of law. An arrangement of forces and resources, so that power is routinely not available for arbitrary exercise, particularly when the power of some over others is considerable, is not a simple or natural state of affairs. Unless something is done to prevent it, arbitrariness is often available where power is concentrated, as it so often is, in the big hands of small numbers.

That is why much of liberal thought has been given to institutions intended to separate, distribute, balance, and temper the exercise of power. If any configuration of state power is considered illegitimate in the liberal tradition, it is precisely the sort that enables or allows arbitrary exercise of power. Liberals did not invent but inherited this distaste from long pre-liberal legal traditions, in England notably, and in many other countries as well.

Certainly, commitment to tempering power is not an absolute, all-or-nothing affair. It is more urgent as arbitrariness is more gross and, since taming arbitrary power is never the only thing we want, devotion to it might well need to be balanced against, tempered by, other goals that we deem valuable.[31] Still, on a liberal assessment, or indeed the assessment of most partisans of the rule of law that I can think of, a state that exercises power in ways that are typically not arbitrary in the three ways noted, and perhaps in others, has come a considerable way towards legitimacy. Not all the way, since the content of the law might still be repugnant, but some considerable way. Certainly, if the reverse is true, if power is exercised in ways that are grossly or routinely uncontrolled, unpredictable, unrespectful, this would delegitimate exercise of power by any persons or institutions that act that way. Non-arbitrariness is unlikely ever to be a sufficient condition for state legitimacy, but it is arguably a necessary one, and a centrally important one too, since states typically have a lot of power, and abuse of it can do a lot of harm. Even where the state avoids these three 'u's, other aspects of its behaviour might delegitimate it, but on these views, at least in relation to the ways in which the state exercises power, a state that is uncontrolled, unpredictable, and unrespectful is to that extent illegitimate.

D. Enemies

For what it's worth, that is my view. It would be nice were it everyone's, but it is not self-evident and not everyone agrees, some because they are not hostile to arbitrary state power; others because they do not think the nature of *state* power is a central concern.

Just taking the last century, for example, Carl Schmitt, the conservative and, when given the opportunity Nazi, legal theorist, insisted that the liberal *Rechtsstaat*, with its 'strong guarantees of moderation and an adequately secure protection of freedom and property against arbitrariness and misuse of the legal form',[32] its 'entire

[31] See Raz, 'The Rule of Law and its Virtue' (n 16) 228–29.

[32] Carl Schmitt, *Legality and Legitimacy* (Jeffrey Seizer tr, Duke University Press 2004) 20.

system of demilitarized and depoliticalized concepts',[33] could deliver only an apolitical, anti-political, and mediocre *legality*, ungrounded in any deeper substantive value,[34] fit perhaps for shopkeepers playing for low stakes but unable to match the demands of *politics*, least of all when the stakes are high. There, and then, a state depends upon the wilful *decision* of an unbound and in principle legally unbindable sovereign political decision-maker, prepared and able to identify and define the fundamental political distinction between friend and enemy, and act at the revelatory moment of exception in which 'the power of real life breaks through the crust of a mechanism that has become torpid by repetition'.[35]

One might have thought that the twentieth century, and the works of Schmitt's one-time boss, would have killed for all time the charm of his notion of legitimacy. I like to think that it has killed the possibility of persuading anyone at the normative level that arbitrary power is to be welcomed, although the frequent resuscitations of and occasional apologies for Schmitt by those one would have thought totally opposed to his principles appear to show that, if an idea is bad enough, it never really dies. Certainly, empirically, Schmitt's line of thought, and practice in line with thought, has not died at all or, if it did seem dead for moments after 1945 and 1989, has been revived over the past few years. Think contemporary Hungary and Poland, and it does not get better as you travel further East and South. One interesting thing about contemporary revivals is how easily they seem to combine with many of the superficial forms of democracy. Less so with the rule of law in the sense discussed above, which is always an early target.

It is not only the right, however, that has suspicions of the rule of law as a source of legitimacy. From the other end of politics to Schmitt's, but with a remarkably similar understanding of politics, Lenin explained in the first months of Soviet rule that the 'dictatorship' of his Bolshevik Party 'is rule based directly upon force, and unrestricted by any laws. The revolutionary dictatorship of the proletariat is rule won and maintained by the use of violence by the proletariat against the bourgeoisie, rule that is unrestricted by any laws.'[36] This was a statement of fact and a boast, not an apology.

Of course, many despots have acted similarly without a thought, but neither Schmitt nor Lenin lacked arguments, and even those not disposed to dictatorship, nor very close to the proletariat (academics, for example), have been influenced by such arguments. Take Marxism, for example, liberalism's 'other' through much of the 'short twentieth century'[37]between the First World War and the collapse of European communism. Classical Marxism had no natural theoretical or moral space

[33] Carl Schmitt, *The Concept of the Political* (George Schwab tr, University of Chicago Press 1996) 71.

[34] See Gianfranco Poggi, 'Juridical Aspects of European State-Making: A Retrospect' in *Varieties of Political Experience* (ECPR Press 2014) 132.

[35] Carl Schmitt, *Political Theology: Four Chapters on the Concept of Sovereignty* (George Schwab tr, University of Chicago Press 1985) 15.

[36] VI Lenin, 'The Proletarian Revolution and Renegade Kautsky' in *Selected Works*, vol II (Foreign Languages Publishing House 1951) 41.

[37] See Eric Hobsbawm, *The Age of Extremes: The Short Twentieth Century, 1914–1991* (Michael Joseph 1994).

for the rule of law and generally ('Bonapartism'[38] apart), until increasingly troubled sophistications after the 1970s, not too much concern with the character of state power; these were essentially secondary things.[39] Thus, many 'left' critiques of states that claimed to embody the rule of law did not so much bother to deny the truth of the claim, or even the legitimizing intent of those who made it, as they denied the legitimating virtues attributed to it. Up to at least the early 1980s, for example, it was common on the left to treat the rule of law, not as a characterization of how power was truly exercised or relevant to its appraisal, but rather, at best, as part of the ideology that rulers chose to propagate in the aim of (sociologically) legitimating their power. The orthodox response was not so much to deny that the state manifested this pretended virtue, but to deny that it mattered or, in more nuanced accounts, could matter much.

Marxism combined political distaste for law with theoretical conviction that the legitimating pretensions of the rule of law were *necessarily*, not just contingently, exaggerated. The distaste stemmed from a belief, shared by many on the left, whether Marxist or not: in class-divided societies, state and law necessarily, at least 'in the last analysis', serves the interests of ruling classes and, in one way or another, aids in their exploitation of those they rule. They might serve ruling class power by repression, by ideological mystification (legitimation in the non-normative sense, often through generating 'false consciousness'), or by setting out and enforcing rules of a rigged game, that ensures the haves come out ahead and the have-nots do not. In the latter years of the short century, everything 'Marxist' became complicated, not to say convoluted ('relative autonomy' versus 'the last analysis', etc), but for a long time, it was believed that to view the rule of law as an equal opportunity constrainer of significant power is simply to buy a marketing pitch, the task of which is to misrepresent the character of the market.

Distaste for state and law did not just float in mid-air. It resulted from a combination of a distinctive social theory and a partly theoretically, partly eschatologically derived prophecy. In existing class-divided societies, Marx claimed, the rule of law *cannot* do what is claimed for it, in particular normatively legitimate the exercise of power, since not only does it serve the haves in their exploitation of the have-nots, but also because it is concerned with a secondary, subaltern, domain of life—the state, not the economy, where the real action is. In the grand scheme of things, again at least in the last analysis, as Marxists used to add when appearances might seem unsettlingly otherwise, the economy, not the state, calls the shots, even if the state orders them to be fired. So the notion that state power could be rendered morally legitimate by the rule of law, while class exploitation continued to dominate 'material' life, could not make sense. As for the radiant future, when class divisions will be overcome, there will be no place for law and no need for the rule of law. In conditions of classlessness, state and law will 'wither away', as Engels put it, with nothing

[38] Karl Marx, 'The Ancient Brumaire of Louis Bonaparte' in Karl Marx and Friedrich Engels, *Selected Works*, vol I (Progress Publishers 1951).

[39] See Martin Krygier, 'Marxism and Bureaucracy: A Paradox Resolved' (1985) 20 Politics 58.

left to do.[40] Such fantasies[41] were used to 'legitimate' many polities with huge and voracious states, much arbitrariness and much law, but little rule of law, for much of the last century.

But although the rule of law was nothing much to boast about, Marxists complained, liberals kept doing so, and not without effect. For those in charge of liberal states could deploy the term as part of a 'legitimation story'[42] by which they sought to make their positions of power and position acceptable—sociologically legitimate—to subjects of state power, although there was nothing to them morally. Insidiously, to the extent that the story was believed by those for whom it was fabricated and to whom it was communicated, it could serve to legitimate the illegitimate, by mystifying and celebrating ways of organizing affairs which it misrepresented. And so, as one sympathetic expositor of Marxist understandings of law put it: 'The principal aim of Marxist jurisprudence is to criticize the centrepiece of liberal political philosophy, the ideal called the Rule of Law.'[43]

Over the span of the short century, confidence in this theoretical/prophetic package ebbed and, towards its end, Marxists and others on the left, such as the Critical Legal Studies (CLS) movement, came to devote more attention to state and law, which increasingly were conceded to have 'relative autonomy' from economic power, and might even have some uses now and perhaps in the future. However, one could go too far, and in 1975, the eminent and veteran Marxist historian EP Thompson, in a notorious eleven-page conclusion to a rich and highly orthodox Marxisant analysis of eighteenth-century criminal law, did just that.

Interestingly for our purposes, Thompson tied up Marxism, sociological, and moral legitimacy in one complex bundle. Sure, eighteenth-century England was ruled by a ruthless, self-interested ruling class; most of the book was devoted to showing that and exploring its particular implications for the case he was investigating. Sure, too, law was a means of serving and (sociologically) legitimizing the power of the ruling class, especially since in the eighteenth century, as distinct from earlier centuries where tradition and religion were the major sources of claims to legitimacy, law was becoming key. But that very fact was pregnant with normative implications. The very ideological use of law involved not cheating all of the people all of the time, for the ideology must be believed, and

> [t]he essential condition for the effectiveness of law, in its function as ideology, is that it should display an independence from gross manipulation and actually seem to be just. It

[40] I have discussed these matters, in relation to state and law, at greater length in Krygier, 'Marxism and Bureaucracy: A Paradox Resolved' (n 39); Martin Krygier, 'Marxism and the Rule of Law: Reflections after the Collapse of Communism' (1990) 15 Law and Social Inquiry 633; Martin Krygier, 'Marxism, Communism, and Narcissism' (1990) 15 Law and Social Inquiry 709.

[41] On Marxism as 'the greatest fantasy of the century', see Leszek Kołakowski, *Main Currents of Marxism*, vol III (Oxford University Press 1978) 523.

[42] See Bernard Williams (not a Marxist) in 'From Freedom to Liberty: The Construction of a Political Value' (2001) 30 Philosophy & Public Affairs 3, 25: 'For there to be legitimate government, there must be a legitimation story, which explains why state power can be used to coerce some people rather than others and to allow people to restrict other people's freedom in some ways rather than others.'

[43] Hugh Collins, *Marxism and Law* (Oxford University Press 1982) 1.

cannot do so without obeying its own logic and criteria of equity; indeed, on occasion, actually *being* just.

Not only couldn't all the people be fooled all the time, but neither could all the rulers, for

it is not often the case that a ruling ideology can be dismissed as a mere hypocrisy; even rulers find a need to legitimize their power, to moralize their functions, to feel themselves to be useful and just. In the case of an ancient historical formation like the law, a discipline which requires years of exacting study to master, there will always be some men who believe in their own procedures and in the logic of justice. The law may be rhetoric, but it need not be empty rhetoric.

As these last sentences suggest, Thompson believed the fact that it was *law* being used as ideology had its own consequences, '[f]or class relations were expressed, not in any way one likes, but *through the forms of law*; and the law . . . has its own characteristics, its own independent history and logic of evolution'.[44]

All those heresies might have been overlooked, were it not for the crescendo to which they built. For Thompson went on to insist

upon the obvious point, which some modern Marxists have overlooked, that that there is a difference between arbitrary power and the rule of law. We ought to expose the shams and inequities which may be concealed beneath the law. But the rule of law itself, the imposing of effective inhibitions upon power and the defence of the citizen from power's all-intrusive claims, seems to me an unqualified human good. To deny or belittle this good is, in this dangerous century when the resources and pretentions of power continue to enlarge, a desperate error of intellectual abstraction.[45]

For this paean to the rule of law, Thompson was excoriated by former comrades and, indeed, excommunicated by a former colleague of mine: 'The nub seems to be that Thompson is not a Marxist historian.'[46] A harsher condemnation from within the tribe is hard to conceive.

By then, however, the state-led catastrophes of that century had taught many people (but not my colleague) that state power with the rule of law might sometimes be better than without it. However, even Morton Horwitz, a more nuanced CLS critic who felt the weight of the century, could not bring himself to applaud the rule of law with Thompson. Such modest virtues as it might have were decidedly mixed, Horwitz insisted:

Unless we are prepared to succumb to Hobbesian pessimism 'in this dangerous century,' I do not see how a Man of the Left can describe the rule of law as 'an unqualified human good'! It undoubtedly restrains power, but it also prevents power's benevolent exercise. It creates formal equality—a not inconsiderable virtue—but it promotes substantive inequality by creating a consciousness that radically separates law from politics, means from ends, processes

[44] All passages quoted are from EP Thompson, *Whigs and Hunters: Origins of the Black Act* (Penguin 1975) 262–63 (emphases in the original).

[45] ibid 266.

[46] Adrian Merritt, 'The Nature and Function of Law: A Criticism of E.P. Thompson's "Whigs and Hunters"' (1980) 7 British Journal of Law and Society 194, 210.

from outcomes. By promoting procedural justice it enables the shrewd, the calculating, and the wealthy to manipulate its forms to their own advantage. And it ratifies and legitimates an adversarial, competitive, and atomistic conception of human relations.[47]

More generally, the rule of law 'is a conservative doctrine', Horwitz insisted, and acceptance of 'the Hobbesian vision of the state and human nature on which our present conceptions of the rule of law ultimately rest' could only be explained, but still not acclaimed, if 'Hitler, Stalin, and all of the other horrors of this century' showed it was the best we could get. This was not a conclusion Horwitz was inclined to embrace. He put Thompson's strange enthusiasm down to a bad century, and the old man's age (he was 50).

The balance of fashion has shifted considerably since then, and fewer people concern themselves with Marxist social theory or prophecy. In general, I think that is no tragedy, but it is not what Thompson would call 'an unqualified human good' either. For if we ignore the social contexts of legal forms, we will be ignoring a lot, both about the rule of law and about what it might contribute to state legitimacy. I will return to this qualification throughout the second half of this chapter.

E. Friends Like These

As a social formation, lawyers are less likely to be swayed or daunted than are Marxists—even ex-lawyer Marxists such as Marx and Lenin—by sociological, still less eschatological, doubts about the importance of law. For lawyers and legal philosophers, law is properly a central focus of concern, it is important in the affairs of mankind, likely to stay around, and its character matters. But if we are interested in the rule of law and the extent to which it can legitimate the state, how would we explore that?

The typical way of lawyers and legal philosophers with this question, unless they are pretty morally 'thick' about the rule of law, is to focus all their attention on the nature and behaviour of official legal artefacts: institutions, practices, and rules. Certainly, Dicey did so when, in emphasizing the particular character of English law and legal institutions, he sold their virtues—in the form and under the name of the rule of law—to the English-speaking world, worryingly threatened by Anglophone social reformers (and the example of Francophone public lawyers).

For Dicey, the rule of law was 'peculiar to England, or those countries, like the United States of America, which have inherited English traditions'.[48] At one point, he mixes his national pride with epistemological humility, faced with 'the extreme vagueness of a trait of national character which is as noticeable as it is hard to portray'.[49] As is notorious, however, he then goes straight on to portray it, in highly specific, precise, and nationalistic-legalistic terms. It stems, he argued, from

[47] Morton Horwitz, 'The Rule of Law: An Unqualified Human Good?' (1977) 86 Yale Law Journal 561, 566.

[48] AV Dicey, *Introduction to the Study of the Law of the Constitution* (8th edn, Liberty Press 1982) 110.

[49] ibid 109.

the existence of three distinctive elements of the common law institutional fabric: inability of authorities to exercise 'wide, arbitrary, or discretionary powers of constraint'; subjection of all citizens, whatever their 'rank or condition', to the same, ordinary, law administered by the same ordinary courts; and constitutional principles that flowed up from court judgments in particular cases, rather than down from general written constitutional documents. The rule of law in England (technically a tautology) rested on just these three foundations. It was contrasted with 'every system of government based on the exercise by persons in authority of wide, arbitrary, or discretionary powers of constraint', and such were to be found not very far away. Like most who use the word, he doesn't tell us what he means by 'arbitrariness', but he makes it clear that, unlike the despotisms of early modern Europe, England had peculiarly avoided it and the despotism that goes with it. Unlike Voltaire, for example, Englishmen did not face 'a whole life [as] a series of contests with arbitrary power' under 'the wayward arbitrariness of the French Government ... inherent in the royal system of administration'.[50] Lest, chastened by Dicey's descriptions, you think to go anywhere else on the Continent, don't bother; the French were far from the worst.

Judith Shklar rightly lamented Dicey's 'unfortunate outburst of Anglo-Saxon parochialism ... The Rule of Law was thus both trivialised as the peculiar patrimony of one and only one national order, and formalised, by the insistence that only one set of inherited procedures and court practices could sustain it'.[51] Yet Dicey is not the only patriot in rule of law promotion. Lawyers and rule of law promoters often follow this element of his example, whether influenced by him or not, and identify the rule of law with what they like about their own legal orders. More globally, his predilection for the way we do things here is generalized by vast numbers of rule of law promoters who are perhaps less nationalistic and more optimistic than he would have been about the prospects of successfully 'transplanting' favoured institutions to benighted societies, but start from a similar, if geographically slightly larger, place. Moreover, if these ventures are less *nationally* parochial than Dicey, they share his *institutional* parochialism without much thought, and to a fault. For there is the assumption that underlies all of Dicey's specifications and that most of Dicey's legal critics share: the rule of law is identified with central state legal institutions, their rules, and their practices. If these exist and are of the right kind, you have the rule of law; if not, then not. As Hadfield and Weingast observe, 'the great majority of academic and policy work takes the concept [of the rule of law] for granted, generally equating it with the institutions and practices in those (relatively few) parts of the world where the rule of law has been largely achieved'.[52]

Analytical legal philosophers, as befits people who plumb the depths and rise to the heights, do not limit themselves, consciously at least, to detailed specification of any particular country's or region's legal order. After all, theirs, as Chaim Perelman

[50] ibid 112. [51] Shklar, 'Political Theory and the Rule of Law' (n 24) 26.

[52] Gillian K Hadfield and Barry R Weingast, 'Microfoundations of the Rule of Law' (2014) 17 Annual Review of Political Science 21, 22.

used to insist,[53] is the universal audience. Their rule of law is a matter of rather generally characterized formal characteristics of legal rules, as in Lon Fuller's and Joseph Raz's 'laundry lists', as Waldron calls them,[54] to which he adds another list in recent work, this time of legal procedures.

Thus, and famously, Lon Fuller lauded the 'inner morality of law' as consisting of more generic features of legal rules, institutions, and practices than Dicey mentioned, the existence of which communicated 'reciprocity' between state and citizen, and gave citizens grounds for 'fidelity to law'. This list has frequently been adopted or adapted to constitute the conditions of the rule of law. Briefly, these conditions are that there must be: (1) general rules; (2) made public; (3) non-retroactive; (4) comprehensible; (5) non-contradictory; (6) possible to perform; (7) relatively stable; (8) administered in ways congruent with the rules as announced.[55] In principle, you could find the inner morality of law anywhere legal rules exemplified these features, even in France.

Many analytic legal philosophers have substantially followed or developed Fuller's list of formal features of rules, although not all of them endorse the moral evaluation Fuller gave to them. No one appears embarrassed to find that they weren't really part of the specification of the rule of law in the common law, for example, until about the eighteenth century,[56] even though many people, Dicey above all, have believed that the common law was about as close to the rule of law as European history had then ever yet got, and for a very long time. This might not be an example of the *national* parochialism of which Shklar accused Dicey, but it might be one of temporal parochialism, and even more so of legal-institutional parochialism.

For what all these conceptions—legal and legal-philosophical—have in common is: (1) the unargued, because apparently self-evident, assumption that the central ingredients of the rule of law emanate from state legal institutions; and (2) the equally confident assumption that we are in a position to stipulate in both precise and general terms what aspects and elements of these institutions and rules add up to the rule of law. These assumptions are so common, indeed, that they largely go without saying in discussions of the rule of law, whether among philosophers, lawyers, or the swarms of international rule of law promoters who have so contributed to the unprecedented public prominence of the concept. Where else, after all, could the rule of *law* be than in official institutions, practices, and rules *of* law?

Now this focus by lawyers, and their philosophical onlookers and analysts, on the institutions and practices of their trade is not surprising. It accords with the familiar tendency of technical professionals to view what they do, where they do it, and what they do it with, as uncontroversially the main activities, the main arenas, and the main equipment of the main game. But it may not always be helpful.

[53] See Chaïm Perelman and L Olbrechts-Tyteca, *The New Rhetoric: A Treatise on Argumentation* (John Wilkinson and Purcell Weaver trs, University of Notre Dame Press 1991).

[54] Waldron, 'The Rule of Law and the Importance of Procedure' (n 25) 5–6.

[55] Fuller, *The Morality of Law* (n 25) 39. For a good discussion and development of ideas in this spirit, see Raz, 'The Rule of Law and its Virtue' (n 16).

[56] See Reid, *The Rule of Law* (n 22).

F. Ordinary People

Recently, Jeremy Waldron has criticized conventional analytic philosophers' accounts of the rule of law on several grounds. One of these[57] is that

> [w]hen I pay attention to the calls that are made for the Rule of Law around the world, I am struck by the fact that the features that people call attention to are not necessarily the features that legal philosophers have emphasized in their academic conceptions of this ideal ... this formal conception is not what ordinary people have in the forefront of their minds when they clamor for the extension of the Rule of Law into settings or modes of governance where it has not been present before.[58]

Waldron purports to capture such features, what 'ordinary people are urging', by supplementing Fuller-style *formal* features with 'elements of legal *procedure* and the institutions like courts that embody them'.[59] He commends a list of ten such features, mainly to do with the fair, impartial, open, and appealable conduct of legal hearings before 'a legally trained judicial officer' and with a 'right to representation by counsel'. The point is to ensure that 'no one should have any penalty, stigma, or serious loss imposed upon him by government'[60] in the absence of such legal procedures. This is an important supplement, with a morally well-motivated core—respect for human dignity—that arguably has no geographical, ethnic, or religious boundaries. It might be noticed, however, that it all happens (or, to the detriment of the Rule of Law, fails to happen) in the procedures adopted by the central legal institutions of state, and ones familiar—to us—at that. The big shift in institutional focus between Fuller and Waldron is from official legislatures to official courts, primarily criminal courts. That is not an enormous distance to travel, even from the point of view of a domestic lawyer who doesn't get out much. In comparative or sociological perspective, such procedures move barely an inch from the formalities they supplement.

What of keeping faith with 'what ordinary people are urging'? The rule of law is not an arcane treasure to be hoarded and contemplated merely by Western jurists. It is a common English term, with analogies (though rarely exact equivalents) in a variety of languages.[61] Rule of law values are called in aid in many parts of the world. Lawyers might seek to explain its workings and philosophers might elucidate some of the term's presuppositions, but it is not obvious why their stipulations should override common understandings of a term in common use, and values in common demand. Indeed, elsewhere Waldron makes precisely this point: 'For this ideal is not the property of the analytic philosophers and it is certainly not our job to go round

[57] I discuss other suggestions of Waldron's in Martin Krygier, 'Legal Pluralism and Value of the Rule of Law' in Nicole Roughan and Andrew Halpin (eds), *In Pursuit of Pluralist Jurisprudence* (Cambridge University Press 2017), from which this section is largely drawn.

[58] Waldron, 'The Rule of Law and the Importance of Procedure' (n 25) 4.

[59] ibid 5 (emphasis added).

[60] ibid 6.

[61] See Martin Krygier, 'Rule of Law (and *Rechtsstaat*)' in James D Wright (ed), *International Encyclopedia of the Social & Behavioral Sciences*, vol 20 (2nd edn, Elsevier 2015).

reproaching laymen for not using the term in the way that (for example) Joseph Raz uses it.'[62]

Yet it is not clear that Waldron's salutary supplement to traditional understandings goes anywhere near far enough. As he would doubtless agree, the vulnerabilities, aspirations, and values that lead people to clamour for the rule of law are not primarily to be judged by what it does for or how much it appeals to lawyers, still less legal philosophers. If the rule of law is a good, it is a social good, and it is challenged, inter alia, by social bads. Not all of these have much to do with what goes on before judicial tribunals. If Afghan citizens, for example, or Syrians or Iraqis or South Africans or ... (the list is long), lament the absence of the rule of law in their societies, is it obvious that they are talking only about receiving unclear legal messages from the government (Fuller), or having a hard day in court (Waldron)? Perhaps the irrelevance of the law or any other institutional constraints, to the ways power is experienced in their everyday lives, might matter to them more immediately, and even more, than their (likely rare) appearances before judicial tribunals (where they exist). Such problems do not only infest exotic climes.

In pursuing Waldron's agenda, then, we should be open to expanding the social and institutional range of our 'conceptual geography',[63] to use a phrase from another context. We need at least to consider whether the values that animate concern with the rule of law, and when realized, help it contribute to the legitimacy of the state, might need and draw support from other than the usual suspects, as well as whether there might be other conditions for, and alternatives to, effective state-law contributions to that putatively charmed state of affairs. In seeing these contributions, conditions, and challenges more clearly, we might have to reconsider the role and contributions of state law to the rule of law, more than anyone I have mentioned hitherto appears to have done, or even thought to do.

G. An 'Insofar As' Reality

Let us recall Thompson.[64] One salutary aspect of his analysis is where he starts: with a valued achievement, not a bunch of hallowed institutions. Perhaps fortunately, Thompson was not a lawyer, a legal philosopher, or a rule of law promoter. Unlike most who write about or seek to promote the rule of law today, he didn't identify it with any particular checklist, recipe book, or template of legal and institutional hardware. Rather, he began with the 'obvious point' that 'there is a difference between arbitrary power and the rule of law', the latter identified by a valued achievement—'the imposing of effective inhibitions upon power and the defence of the citizen from power's all-intrusive claims'. It was only to the extent such defences operated that so did the rule of law. This order of proceeding is not the same as, and makes much

[62] Waldron, *The Rule of Law and the Measure of Property* (n 8) 16.

[63] Tony Judt, 'The Rediscovery of Central Europe' (1990) 119 Daedalus 23, 25.

[64] I develop these remarks about Thompson further in Martin Krygier, 'The Rule of Law between England and Sudan: Hay, Thompson and Massoud' (2016) 41 Law & Social Inquiry 480.

more sense than, beginning with some particular box of legal tricks and identifying it as the rule of law, wherever it happens to be planted or transplanted.

Second, where did Thompson look for evidence of the existence of the rule of law? Again, not in particular legal forms and institutions which, he noted, were constantly being 'created ... and bent' by 'a Whig oligarchy ... in order to legitimize its own property and status'.[65] Still, that oligarchy could not do as it wished; its hands were often tied by the law it sought to exploit. How did Thompson show this? He called in aid facts such as that:

> What was often at issue was not property, supported by law, against no-property; it was alternative definitions of property-rights ... law was a definition of actual agrarian *practice*, as it has been pursued 'time out of mind' ... 'law' was deeply imbricated within the very basis of productive relations, which would have been inoperable without this law. And ... this law, as definition or as rules (imperfectly enforceable through institutional forms) was endorsed by norms, tenaciously transmitted through the community.[66]

Thompson was right to begin where he did—with a valued end rather than some contingent set of legal means—and he was also right to seek his evidence where he did, in social facts rather than merely in institutional artefacts. By contrast, most lawyers and legal philosophers identify the rule of law with a particular set of legal institutions, or the formal or procedural character of legal rules. And rule of law promoters so often imagine they are building the rule of law, or bringing it to benighted countries whose deepest problems might have little to do with any particular list of legal *bric-à-brac* for export and installation, but more with social and political realities of which lawyers are often ignorant.

I have been making this argument for some time, seeking to persuade someone, anyone, that the ideal of the rule of law, and 'what ordinary people have in the forefront of their minds when they clamour for the extension of the Rule of Law', is likely to express an aspiration for a complex social, political, and legal achievement—the reduction of the possibilities of arbitrary exercise of power—to which acts of state and the forms of law might contribute, in varying degrees, but never on their own. What we take to be its elements are supposed to add up to something, to be good for generating or securing that state of affairs; they aren't of much value if that state remains unreached. I have drawn on a phrase used in another context by Gianfranco Poggi. He characterizes Durkheim's concept of society—what distinguishes it from a mere mass of people—as a contingent, 'insofar as reality', 'real *insofar as* certain things go on':[67] in that case, socially patterned behaviours, shared and internalized norms, and so on.

I think of the rule of law that way. It is a relative and variable achievement, not all or nothing. But one can say it exists in good shape or repair insofar as a certain sort of valued state of affairs, to which law contributes in particular and variable ways, exists. On the conception advanced here, the rule of law is in relatively good order insofar as the exercise of political, social, and economic power in a society is

[65] Thompson, *Whigs and Hunters* (n 44) 260. [66] ibid 261 (emphasis in the original).

[67] See Gianfranco Poggi, *Durkheim* (Oxford University Press 2000) 85 (emphasis in the original).

effectively tempered, constrained, and channelled to a significant extent by and in accordance with law, so that non-arbitrary exercises of such powers are relatively routine, while other sorts, such as lawless, capricious, and wilful exercises of power, routinely occur less.

If we were engaged in a conceptual inquiry into the question 'what is the rule of law?', then a plausible rejoinder to my argument might be that the rule of law *is* a matter of features of legal institutions and/or rules, even though their *effectiveness* might depend on external, among them social, supports.[68] A wheel is round, even if it is not good for every terrain. I am not convinced that such a sharp distinction can be made between the institution and its conditions of effectiveness when we talk of ideals. In what sense do we have the rule of law if the laws are as Dicey or Fuller or Raz or Waldron describe them, but no one is listening, or significant parts of the society are in thrall to Mafiosi, clans, or just unofficial but normative networks with their own ways of working, as a result of which the state's laws have little purchase, and/or non-legally channelled power is exercised as the power-holder wishes, as unpredictably as she wishes, with as much or little respect for the voice, perspective, or dignity of those affected by their power, and without reference to the state and law. But for the purposes of this chapter and volume, I can afford to lose that argument. For we are here discussing the *legitimacy* of the state, and the state's legitimacy cannot depend upon the formal (or procedural) character of state institutions and rules alone. For in questions of legitimacy—even the legitimacy of the state—the vantage point *of* the state cannot be primary. It might be interesting to find out whether bureaucrats or politicians consider the state to be legitimate, which, at least when they are in government, they typically do, but when we ask whether a state is legitimate, we must look further afield. It is the legitimacy of the state in relation to its *citizens* which is of central importance—obviously sociologically, but also morally—and to find out about that we will have to think about them and how they find and believe it relates to them. As Wojciech Sadurski puts it in his chapter in this volume, legitimacy 'is in the eyes of the beholder'.[69] Not much conventional discussion of the rule of law, however, takes much account of the non-legal-philosophical beholder at all.

H. The Eye of the Beholder

Empirically, we know quite a bit about 'the beholder' of state activity. While economists and public choice theorists might suggest that people would obey rules primarily for instrumental or prudential reasons, there is a large literature in social psychology that suggests, on the contrary, that legitimacy is key, and that in turn is primarily dependent on citizens' perceptions of the ways in which authorities behave. Of particular significance, as numerous studies have shown, is the extent to which institutions and organizations are thought to deliver procedural justice and

[68] See Joseph Raz, 'The Politics of the Rule of Law' (1990) 3 Ratio Juris 331.

[69] Wojciech Sadurski, 'Conceptions of Public Reason in the Supranational Sphere and Legitimacy beyond Borders', Chapter VIII in this volume 167.

be motivated by trustworthy motives—judgements that are, in turn, intertwined.[70] This literature, which began with a book by Thibaut and Walker[71] and has been greatly influenced by the work of Tom Tyler[72] and his colleagues, distinguishes these considerations of procedural justice and trustworthiness from judgements both of whether outcomes produced are distributively fair and even whether they favour those asked. A repeated finding is that 'procedural justice is the aspect of personal experience that most strongly influences legitimacy'.[73] Indeed, procedural justice and trustworthiness are so salient that: 'Even when people lose, they feel better about that loss when they experience procedural fairness; conversely, when they win, they do not feel as good about that outcome absent procedural fairness.'[74]

Two elements of procedural justice are commonly emphasized in this literature: quality of decision-making and quality of interpersonal treatment. Elements taken to make up quality decision-making include

> making decisions in neutral and unbiased ways using objective information, and not personal biases and prejudices. In neutral decision making, authorities make decisions based upon rules consistently applied across people and situations. Because neutrality involves the use of objective information about the situation, people are more likely to view procedures as neutral when they are given an opportunity to present evidence and explain their situation.[75]

Interpersonal treatment, second,

> includes treatment with dignity and respect, acknowledgment of one's rights and concerns, and a general awareness of the importance of recognizing people's personal status and identity and treating those with respect, even while raising questions about particular conduct. As with neutrality, one factor that accords respect is allowing people to voice their concerns. In addition, people value having the reasons for the actions of authorities justified and explained, and having their right to appeal unfair decisions affirmed.[76]

How authorities deal with people, particularly how trustworthily, fairly, and respectfully they are thought to have made decisions is, then, a crucial source of beliefs in the legitimacy of state (and other) authorities, of the durability of such beliefs,[77] and of people's willingness to obey social rules. These findings make sense of and within hostility to arbitrary treatment in any of the three senses mentioned earlier—uncontrolled, unpredictable, unrespectful—although, so far as I can see,

[70] Tom R Tyler, 'Procedural Justice, Legitimacy, and the Effective Rule of Law' (2003) 30 Crime and Justice 283, 299.

[71] John W Thibaut and Laurens Walker, *Procedural Justice: A Psychological Analysis* (Erlbaum 1975).

[72] Apart from articles cited here, see Tom R Tyler, *Why People Obey the Law* (Yale University Press 1990); Tom R Tyler and Yen J Huo, *Trust in the Law: Encouraging Public Cooperation with the Police and the Courts* (Russell Sage Foundation 2002). See also John J Jost and Brenda Major, *The Psychology of Legitimacy: Emerging Perspectives on Ideology, Justice, and Intergroup Relations* (Cambridge University Press 2001). Most recently, see the exchanges between Tom R Tyler, Daniel S Hagan, and Cody W Telep in (2017) 13 Annual Review of Law and Social Science.

[73] Tyler, 'Procedural Justice, Legitimacy, and the Effective Rule of Law' (n 70) 313.

[74] Rebecca Hollander-Blumoff and Tom R Tyler, 'Procedural Justice and the Rule of Law: Fostering Legitimacy in Alternative Dispute Resolution' [2011] Journal of Dispute Resolution 1.

[75] Tyler, 'Procedural Justice, Legitimacy, and the Effective Rule of Law' (n 70) 350.

[76] ibid 350. [77] ibid 296.

the experiments don't really examine whether the institutions concerned are controlled. They are more concerned with how people experience and/or perceive the way in which existing official (and organizational) agencies make decisions and treat those whom their decisions affect (my second and third forms of arbitrariness).

There is overlap between these empirical findings and some of the lawyers' and legal philosophers' characterizations of the rule of law that I have discussed. But there are differences as well. More important for our purposes, these results do not hang on the specific formal or procedural characteristics of institutions and rules per se, but on people's perceptions of how they are actually treated by agencies of state. Whether there are links between particular forms and experience of treatment is a separate question. Legal philosophers often make that link by intuitive leaps from particular institution, form, or procedure to putative social impact; untutored beholders, however, do not always seem to register the same connections.

First, these findings have been replicated in many parts of the world, so you don't have to be English. Second, they are not identified with the specific institutions that Dicey or, for that matter, Waldron, take to be paradigmatic. The procedures involved vary greatly within systems and cross-culturally, and informal modes of dispute-resolution, including arbitration, mediation, negotiation, restorative justice conferences,[78] and plea-bargaining[79]—without the trappings of court procedure that Waldron takes to be central, are commonly preferred to formal ones. More generally, findings 'do not suggest that there is some type of universal fair procedure that is appropriate in all situations. On the contrary, the same studies suggest that people view different procedural elements as being key to defining procedural fairness within particular situations'.[80]

Again, the *style* with which people are treated is often key for real 'beholders'. Allowing for the difference in context of discussion—he was discussing decency and distributive justice, we are discussing legitimacy and procedural justice—this accords with Avishai Margalit's observation that '[t]he requirement that a just society should also be a decent one means that it is not enough for goods to be distributed justly and efficiently—the style of their distribution must also be taken into account ... a distribution may be procedurally humiliating in spite of being inherently just'.[81] Similarly, one might say, the rule of law—certainly in the sense Waldron has in mind—cannot be merely a matter of forms and procedures; it also extends to matters of style, and this in turn can be significant in relation to legitimacy. But there's little style in discussions of the rule of law.

A larger and more overarching point is that citizens' concerns are less likely to be with forms than with effective performance of functions that citizens value. And this is not simply a matter of sociological significance, but is morally significant as well. Not only is it unlikely that citizens will be taken in by forms that don't function as

[78] Tom R Tyler, 'Psychological Perspectives on Legitimacy and Legitimation' (2006) 57 Annual Review of Psychology 375, 380.

[79] Tom R Tyler, 'Social Justice: Outcome and Procedure' (2000) 35 International Journal of Psychology 117, 121.

[80] ibid 121.

[81] Avishai Margalit, *The Decent Society* (Harvard University Press 1996) 281.

they are purported to; as a normative matter, they should not be taken in by them. To the extent that institutions' functioning the way they should would lend them legitimacy, when they do not, it should not. However, effective performance is only partly, contingently, and variably a matter of those forms; it is a matter of what the anthropologist Sally Falk Moore explores as 'social causality', which can and does surprise in many ways and depends on many causes. Moore points out that 'legislation is based on folk notions of social causality, on ideas of how to make things happen through the use of the power of government';[82] what she says of legislation is no less true of jurisprudes' accounts of the rule of law. And yet, as she notes elsewhere, official activities 'have all been shown to exist only in the presence of officially unacknowledged or parallel societal realities'.[83] Should this matter? I think so, for reasons both empirical and normative.

I. State and Society

What if we find that our state and its laws have the forms or procedures stipulated in accounts of the rule of law, but these laws do not function in the society at large as they are assumed by lawyers to perform? That is likely to be a common situation in any society, because of the myriad intervening factors, which vary from society to society, between 'law in the books' and *action*, which is not simply 'law in action'. 'Law in action' is still a product of what the state does, and closer to the books than the many activities of individuals surrounded and at times ruled, but in any event variably and often strongly affected, by numerous social forces of varying character, power, and level of synchronization with official law.[84] That is a repeatedly confirmed finding of the literature of legal pluralism even in the most legally well-appointed countries in the world.[85] It emerges in parodic form when rule of law promoters take forms and procedures travelling to many countries, and produce not the rule of law, but 'isomorphic mimicry ... adopting the camouflage of *organizational* forms that are *successful elsewhere to hide their actual dysfunction*'.[86] Institutions, forms, rules, and procedures are shipped or copied, but the outcomes expected do not eventuate.

[82] Sally Falk Moore, 'Introduction' in *Law as Process: An Anthropological Approach* (2nd edn, James Currey 2001) 6.

[83] Sally Falk Moore, 'An Unusual Career: Considering Political/Legal Orders and Unofficial Parallel Realities' (2015) 11 Annual Review of Law and Social Science 1, 13.

[84] See David Nelken, 'Law in Action or Living Law? Back to the Beginning in Sociology of Law' (1984) 4 Legal Studies 157.

[85] See Marc Galanter, 'Justice in Many Rooms: Courts, Private Ordering, and Indigenous Law' (1981) 9 Journal of Legal Pluralism 1; Martin Krygier, 'Good, Bad, and "Irritant" Laws in New Democracies' in Jan Zielonka (ed), *Media and Politics in New Democracies. Europe in Comparative Perspective* (Oxford University Press 2015); Krygier, 'Legal Pluralism and Value of the Rule of Law' (n 57).

[86] Lant Pritchett, Michael Woolcock, and Matt Andrews, 'Capability Traps? The Mechanisms of Persistent Implementation Failure' (2010) Center for Global Development Working Paper 234 <https://www.cgdev.org/publication/capability-traps-mechanisms-persistent-implementation-failure-working-paper-234> accessed 3 April 2018 (emphasis in the original).

Does one then have the rule of law because the institutions and rules appear to be in place, or lack it because nothing works as it should?

Conversely, what if one gets the function, but with forms that should not, according to one's legal intuitions, produce them? One a priori hypothesis, for example, extremely common among lawyers and legal theorists, is that whatever contributes to making legal rules less vague, ambiguous, and open-ended, and renders them more formally precise, tightly specified, and univocal, contributes to making law more certain and, therefore, reliable.[87] It seems to stand to reason, after all, that, if a legal rule is minted sharper, more precise, and less open to interpretation, it will be easier to understand, predict, and follow. Indeed, Max Weber built a theory of the relationship between the formal-rational qualities of the *Rechtsstaat* and the birth of capitalism that has greatly influenced later initiatives in rule of law promotion and in law and development. He argued that modern capitalism depended on high predictability and that, since formal rational civil law as perfected on the European Continent promoted the greatest degree of legal generality, clarity, and formal certainty, it must be the most predictable. Therefore, maximum formal rationality of law, as found in Continental Europe, was indispensable for the rise of modern capitalism. Except where it was not, as in the great capitalist nations of the nineteenth and early twentieth centuries, England and America, whose common law

> all in all … presents a picture of an administration of justice which in the most fundamental formal features of both substantive law and procedure differs from the structure of Continental law as much as is possible within a secular system of justice, that is, a system that is free form theocratic and patrimonial powers … Nor is there any visible tendency towards a transformation of the English legal system in the direction of the Continental under the impetus of the capitalist economy. On the contrary, wherever the two kinds of administration of justice and of legal training have had the opportunity to compete with one another, as for instance in Canada, the Common Law way has come out on top and has overcome the Continental alternative rather quickly.[88]

Given that these common law countries were the foremost exemplars of modernity and capitalism in the nineteenth century, and *rechtsstaatlich* Germany was relatively backward in these domains, this—Weber's so-called 'England problem'—was not a small embarrassment for the theory. Blurring form with function, and driven by the logic of 'the more the better', but chastened by facts that he was too observant and too honest to deny, he was led to a series of ad hoc explanations of how Great Britain managed to do capitalism better than anywhere else with a highly 'irrational' legal system, compared, say, to the rationality of German law, which accompanied a less

[87] See Joseph Raz, 'Legal Principles and the Limits of Law' (1972) 81 Yale Law Journal 823, 841, where Raz argues that one 'fairly obvious' reason for preferring rules to principles in the direct regulation of behaviour is that '[p]rinciples, because they prescribe highly unspecific acts, tend to be more vague and less certain than rules' and '[s]ince the law should strive to balance certainty and reliability against flexibility, it is on the whole wise legal policy to use rules as much as possible for regulating human behaviour because they are more certain than principles and lend themselves more easily to uniform and predictable application'.

[88] Max Weber, *Economy and Society: An Outline of Interpretive Sociology*, vol 2 (Bedminster Press 1968) 891–92.

developed economy. These concessions were a tribute to his character and powers of observation, but not to this aspect of his social theory.

For, as his contemporary Eugen Ehrlich[89] emphasized, so much that tells for the arbitrariness or reliability of the law is not the doing of formal legal institutions, but of what Ehrlich identified as the 'living law' that regulates the lives of communities for so much of the time. The interrelationships between official 'rules for decision', as Ehrlich called them, and 'living law' are complex and variable, but there is no reason to believe that formal rationality of the former will produce its direct and faithful reflection in the latter.

And if one does not like (as Kelsen very much did not like) to talk of 'living law', just think how the exercise of power by non-state forces, whether domestic—social networks, prominent (dominant?) families, clans, religious leaders, Mafia bosses, or assorted fellowships of 'dirty togetherness'[90]—or the increasingly pervasive ramifications of globalization, 'a process that transgresses and perforates national or state borders, undermining familiar roots of legitimacy',[91] might mess with legal intuitions about the socially causative consequences of the forms and procedures of state laws. If, whatever the state's law says, such outfits are free to act arbitrarily, capriciously, wildly, does it make sense to insist that nevertheless the rule of law exists because purported institutional underpinnings of a legal order are present or standard practices are observed by the state and its lawyers? And, even if one decides that where the legal institutions work according to whichever list one prefers, even if ineffectively and with their effects bent, refracted, transmuted by forces unlisted, this really is the rule of law, is it likely that 'rule of law' of this sort is likely to, or should, add a dime's worth to the legitimacy of the state?

That leads to one more sociological point to be made about state, society, law, legitimacy, and arbitrary power. I have made it elsewhere at length, so I will be brief here. It is less concerned with social sources of state effectiveness or ineffectiveness than with the need to attend to non-state sources of arbitrariness in their own right; less with state institutions as the sole carriers of the rule of law than as its sole targets. I have argued that, whatever its source, if arbitrary power is as bad as many people have believed, then it is bad wherever it is powerful enough and arbitrary enough to do harm, whatever its source. In the contemporary world, sources of arbitrary power are multiple and many do not emanate from the state, either within domestic society or internationally. If the state cannot control them, then however well *it* acts, on this view, it has not contributed to securing the rule of law in society. To the extent that citizens rightly hope that it can do that, that failure deserves to undermine its legitimacy. In many countries in the world, that is just what happens. It speaks directly both to the adequacy of our conceptions of the rule of law, and to their connection with state legitimacy. Robin West puts it well, speaking immediately of Waldron,

[89] See Eugen Ehrlich, *Fundamental Principles of the Sociology of Law* (Transaction Publishers 2001).

[90] Adam Podgórecki, *Polish Society* (Praeger 1994) 51, 115, 131–32.

[91] See, for example, Antje Wiener, Anthony F Lang Jr, James Tully, Miguel Poiares Maduro, and Mattias Kumm, 'Global Constitutionalism: Human Rights, Democracy and the Rule of Law' (2012) 1 Global Constitutionalism 1, 11.

but more generally of contemporary accounts of the rule of law. All these accounts presuppose

> that the problem of power to which law is the solution is that of the beleaguered individual pressing up against an overbearing sovereign state. But this is not the only problem of power to which law is or ought to be the solution. Rather, law is, and I would suggest the Rule of Law is, perhaps quintessentially, the solution to the problem of private power. Without a state that monopolizes the weapons of force, any individual is vulnerable to the private violent power of any other, as Hobbes witnessed …
>
> But there is nothing of this function of law and nothing of this in the articulation of law's ideals in most Rule of Law scholarship, including Jeremy Waldron's latest intervention. This is, I think, mightily odd. This is, after all, the Rule of *Law* we're talking about, and a lot of our laws are about protecting individuals against the undue aggressions of other individuals or corporations, not only through the criminal law but through much of private law as well. This purpose, in other words, is right at the heart of law's point. But this understanding of law's point is somehow invisible in contemporary Rule of Law scholarship.[92]

J. A Partial Deontological Caveat

West is right. It's all mightily odd. The successful attainment of the rule of law is a *social* outcome (broadly understood: it is obviously political and other things as well), not a merely legal one. What matters, here as everywhere with the rule of law and with legitimacy, is how the law affects the lives of citizens. But since the distance between law in books and action is often long, the space full of many other things and, in different places full of different things, it is a matter of comparative social investigation and theorization what might best, in particular circumstances, in particular societies, further that goal. A docket of the *rechtsstaatlich* features of legal instruments, even buttressed by citations to Fuller, Hayek, Raz, or even Weber, will not do the trick.

The grounds I have presented for scepticism about the tradition's privileging of the state and its laws, as both threat and promise, are purely instrumental. I reject accounts of the rule of law, not because it is instrumental, but because its instrumentalism is only partly baked: if the telos is curbing arbitrary power, we should look to where we find good ways to do that, and lawyers' defaults may well be inadequate to guide us. Thus, we must contemplate having to look beyond the usual suspects and also beyond the usual legal repertoires devised to catch them; significant sources of arbitrariness might often come from elsewhere and so too significant responses to them.

But I can't quite end here, since I have been troubled by a murmuring anxiety that the trajectory of my argument might lead to neglect of a feature of the rule of law's contribution to legitimacy that was central to Lon Fuller's understanding of the rule of law, and is typically ignored by Fuller's critics. Until recently, I have found

[92] Robin West, 'The Limits of Process' in James E Fleming (ed), *Getting to the Rule of Law* (New York University Press 2011) 45–46 (emphasis in the original).

it elusive, but it is important. Fuller first stirred this apprehension in me and it was re-stirred by Arie Rosen, who commented on this chapter when it was first delivered, and then again by Alon Harel, in his book *Why Law Matters*.[93]

Kristen Rundle insists that it is

> crucial not to understand Fuller's eight principles as a simple checklist for the features which law must possess. The principles instead speak to an idea that is broader, and more fundamental, than the sum of eight parts: namely, the distinctive kind of relationship between power and those subject to it that law constitutes, and which is brought into being, regulated and served by the principles of the internal morality of law.[94]

I am sure that is right about Fuller and I think that is a key question to ask about the rule of law, although the bridge that supposedly connects formal features of the law with any *actual* relationships 'between power and those subject to it that law constitutes' seems to me to be assumed to exist, without any visible (social) means of support. All we have from him as sources of this salutary relationship between power and subjects are those formal features of legal rules. There must be more to be said here, but, unfortunately, like so many lawyers and legal philosophers, he rests with the law.

However, Fuller's conjectures were smarter than most, as when in his arguments with Hart over Nazi law, he observed that '[t]hroughout his discussion Professor Hart seems to assume that the only difference between Nazi law and, say, English law is that the Nazis used their laws to achieve ends that are odious to an Englishman'.[95] Fuller details several of the many ways in which the Nazis had undermined the character and role that an Englishman might expect law and legal institutions to play. They had corrupted the instrument, not merely wielded it for unsalutary purposes, so that what was called law was frequently not merely perverse in its effects, but deformed and perverse at its core and in its character.

Still, there are limits on the extent to which even uncorrupted legal forms could trump Nazism, and that is not the only, nor necessarily the most important, sort of argument that Fuller deploys, although it is the one pounced upon by his critics. For, effects aside, Fuller had other concerns which arguably went deeper with him and have more to do with the intrinsic character of the law than with its contingent effects. The moral character of the relationship between a state and its citizens lies, for Fuller, not merely in its social consequences. It expresses something we should be able to demand from our public representatives, more than we do from everyone, maybe anyone, else. On this account, it is not conjectures about contingent relationships between 'inner' morality and external achievements, but rather concerns

[93] Alon Harel, *Why Law Matters* (Oxford University Press 2014). This section and the first paragraph of the next draw on my response to this book, Martin Krygier, 'Why the Rule of Law Matters' (2017) 9 Jurisprudence 146.

[94] Kristen Rundle, *Forms Liberate: Reclaiming the Jurisprudence of Lon L. Fuller* (Hart Publishing 2012) 10.

[95] Lon L Fuller, 'Positivism and Fidelity to Law: A Reply to Professor Hart' (1958) 71 Harvard Law Review 630, 650. See Jeremy Waldron, 'Positivism and Legality: Hart's Equivocal Response to Fuller' (2008) 83 New York University Law Review 1135.

about the moral character of those relationships *as such*. On this account, the deeper importance of the inner morality is that

> [e]very departure from the principles of the law's inner morality is an affront to man's dignity as a responsible agent. To judge his actions by unpublished or retrospective laws, or to order him to do an act that is impossible, is to convey to him your indifference to his powers of self-determination. Conversely, when the view is accepted that man is incapable of responsible action, legal morality loses its reason for being. To judge his actions by unpublished or retrospective laws is no longer an affront, for there is nothing left to affront indeed, even the verb 'to judge' becomes itself incongruous in this context; we no longer judge a man, we act on him.[96]

The issue here is not one of instrumental effectiveness, as Hart and other critics so easily assumed, but of intrinsically moral requirements, peculiarly incumbent on states, to act in ways that show respect for the persons on whose behalf they, and sometimes they alone, have rights, responsibilities, and duties to act. True, Fuller spoke of his 'inner morality' as encompassing 'principles of craftsmanship', but he also emphasized that its laws are not to be measured simply by their 'efficacy'; for they 'express'[97] moral attributes even when they don't effect morally or other desirable outcomes. Fuller spoke of 'trusteeship',[98] others have written of a distinctive 'fiduciary' responsibility of states.[99] And, as Paul Gowder has remarked, 'the moral evaluation of a given socially determined expressive meaning does not itself depend on social facts. Once we determine that some law expresses the inferiority of some members of the community, that law is to be condemned on rule of law grounds whether or not anyone (or, indeed, everyone) in that community endorses this message'.[100]

The state, particularly a democratic state, *does* have a special role in contemporary societies, and arguably it has deontological obligations and responsibilities of special kinds, that not everyone shares, or at least, not for the same reasons and not to the same extent. Even if we rest with my focus on arbitrariness and its three configurations—uncontrol, unpredictability, and unrespect—there are good Kant-like reasons to insist that the state incorporate, say, some tempering internal legal balance for control,[101] rules whose character is intended to allow predictability[102] and rules intended to accord a hearing that gives voice and respects the dignity[103] of people being judged by the law. One might need considerably to tweak and revise

96 Fuller, *The Morality of Law* (n 25) 162–63.

97 Gowder, *The Rule of Law in the Real World* (n 26).

98 See the discussion in Rundle, *Forms Liberate* (n 94) 107.

99 Evan Fox-Decent, 'The Fiduciary Nature of State Legal Authority' (2005) 31 Queens Law Journal 259.

100 Gowder, *The Rule of Law in the Real World* (n 26) 40.

101 See Gianluigi Palombella, 'The Rule of Law as Institutional Ideal' in Leonardo Morlino and Gianluigi Palombella (eds), *Rule of Law and Democracy: Inquiries into Internal and External Issues* (Brill 2010).

102 See Friedrich A Hayek, *Law, Legislation and Liberty*, vol 3: *The Political Order of a Free People* (University of Chicago Press 1979) 41; and see Hayek, *The Constitution of Liberty* (n 27) 215, 221.

103 See Harel, *Why Law Matters* (n 93); Waldron, 'The Rule of Law and the Importance of Procedure' (n 25).

the specifications in various ways, to adapt to changes in law and society,[104] but this intrinsic dimension is, I now believe, morally significant, independent of how things work out with power in the world. This would accord somewhat with prescriptions of rule of law orthodoxy, but for very different reasons than are usually asserted to support them. It leaves consequences to the side.

K. The Hobbesian Condition

OK. That's law, but what about life? There is still all that power in the world, wielded by all sorts of actors, state and non-state, and much of it is exercised arbitrarily. The stakes are high, because its effects can be terrible. That is what was recognized by those long traditions seeking to temper and moderate the ways in which power is exercised in the world, that have expressed hope that law might be enlisted in that perennial struggle. Should they be satisfied to learn that, even if it might make little consequential difference, their state behaves in conformity to conditions of rule of law morality? Is *that* the only reason people have fought to protect the rule of law from despots, terrorists, and torturers, legal and illegal? Is a state that fails to perform some of the basic functions of a good state, although its own operations might be clean as a whistle, as much entitled to claim legitimacy as one that is effective in serving its citizens by tempering the ways in which both its own power and that of others are exercised throughout a society?

To repeat, the successful attainment of the rule of law is a *social* outcome (broadly understood: it is obviously political and other things as well), not a merely legal one. What matters, here as everywhere with the rule of law and with legitimacy, is how the law affects the lives of citizens.

To speak sensibly of the rule of law as a significant element in the life of a society and thus a source of legitimacy for the state, the law's norms must be socially *normative* and, to some considerable degree at least, effective. If people know nothing of the law, or knowing something think nothing of it, or think of it but don't take it seriously, or even, taking it seriously don't know what to do about it or can't do anything about it, then their lives will not be enriched by the rule of law and they might not think well of the state that purports to provide it.

This is a matter that goes to the heart of relationships between the rule of law and state legitimacy. The reason is simple, and it has long been known. For the rule of law to contribute to state legitimacy, it must pass Hobbes's test—effectiveness. Unless it does that, Hobbes insisted, its otherwise unbreakable claim to legitimacy and to citizens' obedience is, well, broken; they are entitled to do what they like. Partisans of the rule of law are unlikely to go that far and, as Locke showed admirably, they would certainly not endorse Hobbes's pared-down understanding of effectiveness. However, even if there are rules, forms, and procedures in abundance, and even if

[104] See Edward Rubin, 'Law and Legislation in the Administrative State' (1989) 89 Columbia Law Review 369.

the state honours them, but it cannot get its messages across, or the messages that get across are not its, or it cannot or will not curb the arbitrary acts of powerful others, my guess is that the ordinary beholder, like Hobbes, will say the rule of law is not in great shape in that society and, therefore, neither is the state's legitimacy. And they would be right.

VII

The Nation State's Legitimation in Post-National Society

A Social Systems Perspective of Values in Legality and Power

Jiří Přibáň

A. Introductory Remarks

In September 2015, the anti-corruption boss of the Chinese communist leadership Wang Quishan stated that 'the legitimacy of the ruling party' also depended on 'the mandate of the people'. According to the media, this was 'the first public use of the word legitimacy by a Chinese leader in connection with the party's rule'.[1] What does this particular moment of the communist party's self-reflection mean in the general context of modern politics and statehood? How relevant is it for our globalized post-national polity?

The question of legitimacy is a general question of the right to rule. Legitimacy's opposite is illegitimacy, which invites the right to protest and rebel against illegitimate rule. In modern polities without direct access to divine will, legitimacy thus turns into a permanent process of legitimation of political decisions and the values behind them.[2] It connects normativity of reason with volitional acts of power and examines social conditions of their acceptance. General distinctions between reason and will, norm and fact, and enforcement and recognition are translated into particular political conditions and processed through specific organizations such as the state. The question of legitimacy thus connects three very different academic disciplines: moral and political philosophy, legal theory, and general sociology.

The modern state is a specific political organization legitimately processing decisions, yet equally relying on transcendental values and 'self-evident truths'.[3] Unlike the American and any other revolutionaries or the Chinese officials, social and legal scientists have to examine a simple fact that these truths, held as self-evident and universally valid, are often severely contested within the same polity and ignored or

[1] See 'A Crisis of Faith' *The Economist* (London, 16 January 2016) 21, 23.
[2] See, for instance, David Beetham, *The Legitimation of Power* (Macmillan 1991) 16–17.
[3] Michael Zuckert, *The Natural Rights Republic* (Notre Dame University Press 1997).

Legitimacy: The State and Beyond. First Edition. Edited by Wojciech Sadurski, Michael Sevel, and Kevin Walton. Published 2019 by Oxford University Press.

suppressed by other polities.[4] Modernity may be defined as the permanent struggle between different sets of self-evident truths and the state is expected to fulfil the paradoxical double role of the guardian of these universal truths and the selector enforcing some truths and values against other truths and values. Legitimacy gets stabilized by legality generated by the state, yet equally becomes contested in the process of transvaluation of values claiming to guarantee the right to the rule of law.

The problem of legitimacy needs to be reformulated as the distinction between legitimacy and illegitimacies selected and eliminated in the legitimation process. The nation state evolving in modern society used to be a central organization using the medium of legality to process these distinctions between political legitimacy and illegitimacies. Nevertheless, recent shifts in power generated by economic, political, legal, and other societal forms of globalization require new distinctions between legitimacy and illegitimacies evolving within and beyond the nation state. For instance, one can find many examples of illegitimate economic power intruding and destroying democratically legitimate institutions, including the state and its rule of law. It is, therefore, important to ask what constitutes the legitimacy of the state and other organizations emerging at supranational and transnational levels of global society.

In the European context, the problem of statehood and its legitimacy has, since the 1950s, been reformulated as the problem of European supranational and transnational integration. The nation state was held responsible for the worst political and societal extremities of nationalism and totalitarianism and its sovereignty was diluted and power limited by supranational European institutions.[5] Nevertheless, the final dream of European federalists was another form of statehood: a federalized union with democratic legitimacy and constitutional settlement beyond the modern framework of nation states. Its opponents considered it a nightmare of illegitimate social engineering destroying the established democratic institutions and traditions of member states. The institutional framework, societal limitations, and legitimacy of the modern state became a battlefield of political arguments, normative expectations, and symbolic imaginations regarding the nature and functions of the democratic state and supranational integration in post-1945 Europe.

These expectations, arguments, and imaginations were also profoundly affected by the collapse of communist states in Central and Eastern Europe in 1989 and European Union enlargements in 2004, 2007, and 2013.[6] This unification of Europe significantly affected the common market, due to the accelerated movement of capital and labour, and politics, including external diplomacy and internal power shifts within the Union. One example of these arguments and legitimacy battlefields was the Brexit referendum in the United Kingdom in June 2016, in which the anti-EU campaigners successfully claimed that, because of the Union, the United

[4] Jeremy Waldron, 'A Right-Based Critique of Constitutional Rights' (1993) 13 Oxford Journal of Legal Studies 18, 28.

[5] Neil MacCormick, *Questioning Sovereignty: Law, State, and Nation in the European Commonwealth* (Oxford University Press 1999).

[6] Wojciech Sadurski, *Constitutionalism and the Enlargement of Europe* (Oxford University Press 2012).

Kingdom could not control immigration and social welfare policies and economically suffered under EU market regulations. The Brexit supporters argued that they wanted 'their country back'[7] and used the symbolic image of alleged threats to parliamentary democracy and sovereignty from unaccountable bureaucrats in Brussels and other member states, most notably, Germany and France, exploiting EU institutions to promote their national interests.

Finally, EU discussions of the legitimacy of the state have been increasingly affected by sub-state nationalisms and separatist tendencies illuminated, for instance, by the Scottish 'legal' and Catalan 'illegal' referenda in 2014 and 2017.[8] The EU antinomy of nation states and transnational regions formulated in the slogan and policy of 'Europe of regions' did not weaken political and international aspirations of nations without statehood, such as the Basques, the Catalans, the Flemish, and the Scots, which demand national independence and the right to self-determination maturing in state sovereignty. This paradox of regional nationalist movements emboldened by the supranational and transnational politics of European integration and demanding both state sovereignty and EU membership clearly indicates the continuing legitimation force of statehood even in the post-sovereign and post-national European and global political condition.

For whatever reasons, ideological constructs, and symbolic political landscapes, the nation state remains the basic institution of democratic legitimacy, despite ever-growing supranational and transnational politics with their specific forms of legitimation. Therefore, it would be intellectually reckless to discard recent backlashes against globalization and Europeanization as mere manifestations of regressive and reactionary nationalism, racism, nativism, xenophobia, and so on. This superficial criticism only obscures persistent political aspirations and legitimate expectations of the nation state in globalized society, especially its capacity to democratically confront societal risks and crises caused by economic and political globalization.

In this chapter, therefore, I do not want to open yet another debate about the relationship between the nation, its state, and its legitimacy, considered as a set of values, and their transformation vis-à-vis the process of globalization. Instead, I engage in a more general socio-legal inquiry separating, first of all, the general and classic problem of legitimacy from the specific and modern problem of statehood. Second, I emphasize the difference between the philosophical and sociological conceptualization of legitimacy and the impact of social and sociological theories on the concept of legitimacy by legality. I especially focus on the problem of values and their ambiguity in legitimation of the nation state. Finally, I address the problem of legitimacy beyond statehood and normative expectations in post-sovereign and post-national globalized society. In this society, the state's legitimacy by efficiency is diminished because of its limited capacity to deal with global social problems, such

[7] See, for instance, Colin Crouch, 'Globalization, Nationalism and the Changing Axes of Political Identity' in William Outhwaite (ed), *Brexit: Sociological Responses* (Anthem Press 2017).

[8] For the social context and mobilization, see especially Donatella Della Porta, Francis O'Connor, Martin Portos, and Anna Subirats Ribas, *Social Movements and Referendums from Below: Direct Democracy in the Neoliberal Crisis* (Policy Press 2017) 92–103.

as tax avoidance, security, health, and environmental risks. At the same time, supranational and transnational organizations and their normative regimes addressing these problems are already constituted with legitimacy deficits because they cannot emulate the state's strong legitimation by democratic procedures or civil rights and liberties. Analysing the concepts of legitimacy and the state in their supranational and transnational context therefore involves revisiting the classic sociological understanding of law as one of many normative systems in society and the state as one of many societal organizations. Moving beyond national symbolic imaginations and nationally constituted value foundations, I come to the conclusion that legitimation procedures are constituted by systemic communication between politics and law within the nation state as much as beyond its organizational framework. Apart from procedural efficiency, this communication involves internalization of external values by the systems of positive law and politics. However, these values are not transcendental foundations normatively constituting the totality of society from its outside. They are internally generated expectations defining the difference between social systems and their environment and, therefore, the difference between legitimacy and illegitimacies in both politics and law.

B. Transcendental Expectations, Immanent Responses: On the Socio-Legal Perspective of Legality and Legitimacy of the State

Despite the specific modern context linking legitimacy of the constitutional state to its constituent nation, the question of legitimacy represents a general problem of turning *power* into *authority*.[9] The process of legitimation of power is not limited to political or public life and can be identified in many different forms in any social environment. It can be detected in all social structures, including criminal gangs and organizations. The general character of the question of legitimacy is illustrated, for instance, by the world of art and fiction when Michael Corleone, the main character of Mario Puzo and Francis Ford Coppola's *Godfather* Mafia trilogy, promises his wife that he will make their family, so deeply entrenched in the organized crime business, legitimate in five years.[10]

Since ancient Roman times, lawyers and politicians associated public authority with its legality. *Legitimus* derived from *lex* and originally meant something fixed and begotten by law or in line with the law. The same meaning was preserved for *legitimatus* in Medieval Latin.[11] For over 2,000 years, politics and law thus treated the problem of legitimacy as legal authorization and limitation of political power.

[9] For this classic distinction, see, for instance, Norman Uphoff, 'Distinguishing Power, Authority & Legitimacy: Taking Max Weber at His Word by Using Resources-Exchange Analysis' (1989) 22 Polity 295, 299–301.

[10] Alessandro Camon, '*The Godfather* and the Mythology of Mafia' in Nick Browne (ed), *Francis Ford Coppola's The Godfather Trilogy* (Cambridge University Press 2000) 66.

[11] Michael Wilks, *The Problem of Sovereignty in the Later Middle Ages: The Papal Monarchy with Augustinus Triumphus and the Publicists* (Cambridge University Press 1963) 444.

The rule of law, so much treasured and invoked by the moderns as the ultimate basis of modern constitutionalism, was actually familiar to the ancients.[12] A long time before modern peoples started politically integrating themselves into democratic and constitutional nation states protecting their rights and liberties, the ancients had been fully aware of the difference between the rule of law and the rule of men by elevating the former to the first political principle and virtue and warning against the latter as a source of arbitrariness and tyranny.

Nevertheless, modern society also offers evidence that laws equally can provide an effective tool to dignify and legitimize the will of a particular type of tyranny which pretends to be acting within the framework of an efficient and generally applicable legal system. In these systems, tyrants are considered simple officials of the law which, nevertheless, is used as a repressive tool against the totality of society. Instead of the classical Aristotelian distinction between the rule of law and men, modernity confronts us with the paradoxical situation of the rule of men significantly expanded and legitimized by legality. It is not the absence of laws but their presence that unbounds political power and turns citizens into slaves. The problem of legitimacy by law subsequently transforms into the problem of legitimacy of law and its rule.[13]

Legitimacy is associated with transcendental principles and values, yet depends on the power to enforce collectively binding decisions and steer the polity. It signifies the political system's capacity to deliver policy goals by normatively framed decision-making processes. Turning the prescriptive distinction between the rule of law and the rule of men to the sociological description of the relationship between the systems of positive law and politics, it is then possible to see structural coupling in which public and politically organized power requires a secondary coding by the medium of legality and thus becomes subject to the system of positive law. Power can change the existing law only through legal procedures and, because of this secondary coding by legality, can be described as the rule of law.[14]

The general secondary coding of power through legality conditions its legitimacy in both the success/failure distinction of efficiency and the compliance/non-compliance distinction of normativity. Organizing power within the political system means avoiding the permanent and immediate threat of physical force and violence in society. The function of power is to eliminate the destructive effects of violence.[15] Paradoxically, this can be done only by granting power to the monopoly of violence which, nevertheless, is defined by the capacity to eliminate these initial conditions and operate as a system of legitimate rules. This elimination of violence through violence in the political system is achieved by the transformation of

[12] Edward M Harris, *Democracy and the Rule of Law in Classical Athens: Essays on Law, Society, and Politics* (Cambridge University Press 2006).

[13] For these dilemmas and difference between legal formalism and the substantive concept of the rule of law in modern history, see Martin Krygier and Adam Czarnota (eds), *The Rule of Law after Communism: Problems and Prospects in East-Central Europe* (Ashgate 1999); Ruti Teitel, *Transitional Justice* (Oxford University Press 2000).

[14] Niklas Luhmann, *Trust and Power* (John Raffan, Howard Davies, and Kathryn Rooney trs, Christian Morgner and Michael King eds, Polity Press 2017) 161.

[15] ibid 174–75.

effective power through legal norms. Politically productive power gets reproduced as the rule of law, and realistic goals of politics get reformulated as the idealistic values and principles of law's generality, impartiality, equality, and impersonality, which match their capacity to protect personal autonomy, democratic public order, and international relations.[16]

The secondary coding of power by legality gave rise to the specifically modern organization of the constitutional state in which political constitutions facilitate legitimacy themselves.[17] In the constitutional state's legitimacy, there is nevertheless an intrinsic tension between transcendental normative expectations and the fact that the state is an immanent social institution with historical origins and evolution. The state may be historical, yet its values and foundations providing it with legitimacy are expected to have universal validity.

The temporality of the state is matched by the eternity of its legitimacy. This paradox manifests itself in specific constitutional provisions, such as the German Basic Law's *Ewigkeitsklausel*—the eternity clause of Article 79(3), stating that some fundamental principles of the German constitutional democratic state can never be changed, even by Parliament. Similar clauses can be found in the constitutions of other contemporary constitutional democratic states, for instance in Article 9(2) of the Czech Republic's Constitution, which states that 'any changes in the essential requirements for a democratic state governed by the rule of law are impermissible', and in Article 139 of the Constitution of the Republic of Italy, which declares that the republican form of government shall not be a matter for constitutional amendment.[18]

The state as political institution originating in early modern Europe gradually has spread all around the world and still significantly affects contemporary globalized politics, from secessionist movements within the supranational European Union to the recent constitutional developments and state formations and transformations in Europe, the Middle East, Africa, and Latin America. The political and legal semantics of the legitimacy of the democratic constitutional state persist in post-national and post-sovereign global society.[19] The tension between de jure authority and de facto power, which defines the problem of the nation state's legitimacy and gets reformulated as the tension between transcendental expectations of political power and its immanent social function, is also typical of supranational and transnational globalized law and politics beyond the state. Any theory of legitimacy of the state in global society, therefore, needs to consider supranational and transnational networks and regimes of power and their normative frameworks.[20]

[16] Judith N Shklar, *Legalism: Law, Morals, and Political Trials* (Harvard University Press 1964) 15–20.

[17] For this societal function of constitutions and variety of political and societal goals to be constitutionally legitimized, see especially Kelly L Grotke and Markus J Prutsch (eds), *Constitutionalism, Legitimacy, and Power: Nineteenth-Century Experiences* (Oxford University Press 2014).

[18] For the constitutional and comparative context of these 'eternity clauses', see Yaniv Roznai, *Unconstitutional Constitutional Amendments: The Limits of Amendment Powers* (Oxford University Press 2017) ch 2.

[19] John W Meyer, John Boli, George M Thomas, and Francisco O Ramirez, 'World Society and the Nation-State' (1997) 103 American Journal of Sociology 144.

[20] Saskia Sassen, 'Spatialities and Temporalities of the Global: Elements for a Theorization' (2000) 12 Public Culture 215, 215.

Studying the legitimacy of the state in global society thus cannot be reduced to analysing nation-state institutions and their functions and limitations in supranational and transnational organizations. This study has to focus on the general process of transformation of multiple power networks into legitimate forms of authority and rules governing post-national and post-sovereign society. In particular, values, their ambivalence, fluidity, role, and limitations in the process of legitimation of both nation states and supranational and transnational legal and political institutions must be subject of a socio-legal analysis to address the complexity of the legitimacy of the state in globalized society.

C. From the Philosophy of Legitimate Politics to the Sociology of State Legitimation

The general problem of legitimacy demonstrates a typically modern split between philosophy and the social sciences. Political philosophy defines normative conditions of legitimacy through different models of political association and cooperation, such as the social contract, class conflict, and civil society ethics. Moral and political philosophers always have been focusing on the initial transition of humankind from its state of nature to the political state with decision-making power on a particular territory which has the capacity to protect the rights and interests of those living on it. Normative theories of legitimacy mainly analyse the entitlement of de facto power to de jure authority over the whole polity.[21] Legitimacy, therefore, is considered a *normative externality* constituting the general validity of both the system of politics, operating through the medium of power, and the system of positive law, operating through the medium of legality.

On the other hand, modern social sciences focus on the performance and operations of these social subsystems and the procedures through which authority and its decisions are manifested in society. Different social systems—economy, politics, law, science, religion, and so on—make different validity claims in modern society. This social differentiation and particularization of validity claims effectively disputes any appeal to universal validity made by moral and political philosophy or theology.

According to this view, the possibility of universal validity binding all these systems with particular societal power regimes and networks has been lost in modern society. Normative hierarchies are replaced by horizontally connected heterarchies in functionally differentiated modern society which has no direct access to its basic norm and cannot be integrated from one centre of political, moral, economic, or religious authority. The state's legitimacy is considered the question of efficiency, functioning governability, and acceptability of decisions, so far as they are made by a recognized authority. Any legitimation crisis of the modern state is then perceived

[21] See, for instance, Robert Nozick, *Anarchy, State, and Utopia* (Basic Books 1974) 114.

as a lack of its governing capacities and responsiveness to societal demands and expectations.[22]

Incommensurability between philosophical and social-theoretical views of politics, power, and its legitimacy was succinctly summarized by Hannah Arendt, who even warned against the risk of the public realm, with its virtues, being taken over by the social realm, defined merely by needs and interests, in the following words:

Excellence itself, *arête* as the Greeks, *virtus* as the Romans would have called it, has always been assigned to the public realm where one could excel, could distinguish oneself from all others ... While we have become excellent in the laboring we perform in public, our capacity for action and speech has lost much of its former quality since the rise of the social realm banished these into the sphere of the intimate and the private.[23]

Arendt distinguished between the public realm of political freedom and the social realm of mutual dependence in which the sheer survival of humans assumes the ultimate significance. According to her view, the private and intimate realm as well as the public realm are being colonized by the constantly growing social realm.[24] The state has become the welfare state and the general principle of justice has been transformed by specific calls for social justice.

For Arendt, the sociological perspective of politics, with its focus on functions, operations, and performance, is a symptom of modern political crisis. Her critical philosophy of politics and modern culture[25] is shared by other philosophers, such as Alasdair MacIntyre, who talk about the loss of civic virtues and the exhaustion of political traditions within our culture, which is heading for 'the coming ages of barbarism and darkness'.[26] For MacIntyre and others, power without virtue and a metaphysical grounding is plain illegitimacy.

According to this general philosophical view, so heavily criticized by Friedrich Nietzsche and his most original disciple, Max Weber, the legitimacy of a political order depends on the notion of justice as a virtue drawing on the moral unity of a human life and the metaphysical concept of good as an end towards which human beings are naturally directed by reason. In other words, the primacy of philosophy over social sciences has to be reaffirmed because the common good of a polity cannot be constructed by the immanent public discourse and different social needs and interests.[27]

[22] For a classic summary, see especially Seymour Martin Lipset, 'The Social Requisites of Democracy Revisited: 1993 Presidential Address' (1994) 59 American Sociological Review 1, 7.

[23] Hannah Arendt, *The Human Condition* (University of Chicago Press 1958) 48–49.

[24] ibid 28–33.

[25] Hannah Arendt, *Between Past and Future: Eight Exercises in Political Thought* (Faber & Faber 1968) ch 6.

[26] Alasdair MacIntyre, *After Virtue* (Duckworth 1981) 263.

[27] In this respect, Jürgen Habermas's philosophy of discourse ethics and communicative reason represents a special attempt at reconciling the philosophical and social theoretical perspectives of legitimacy. See especially Jürgen Habermas, *Legitimation Crisis* (Thomas McCarthy tr, Beacon Press 1975) 68–75; Jürgen Habermas, *Between Facts and Norms: Contributions to a Discourse Theory of Law and Democracy* (William Rehg tr, Polity Press 1996) 42–81.

These philosophical criticisms of social sciences are specific responses to the general tendency in modern thinking described by Sheldon Wolin as the turn from politics to social science and engineering. It involves the most general and categorical shift from *polity* to *society*, which has serious consequences for the concepts of the state, power, and its legitimacy.[28]

While Aristotle considered it evident that the state as a whole is necessarily prior to each individual,[29] modern conceptualizations of politics, rather, consider it constituted through the will of humans to associate, maintain, and cultivate mutual bonds and live in this social symbiosis guaranteed by the sovereign power. The liberty of citizens became a condition of the state's legitimacy. Before the state's sovereign power can be executed, it needs to be legitimized through values and interests evolving in society and formulated as civil rights and liberties and legally constituted as the first principle of the rule of law. The state does not precede society. Rather, it is formed by individuals and society as an outcome of many different forms of social interaction, such as conquest, contract, and consensus.[30]

D. The State and Law in the Social System

It was not until the Middle Ages and jurists such as Bartolo di Sassoferrato that the relationship between *lex* and *rex* was established as the theory of sovereignty authorizing without authorization and unbound by laws.[31] This was the first step towards reformulation of the political theory of the state as part of the general theory of power.[32] Blaise Pascal's later comment that it is power of the people which the sovereign should fear most made it clear that the political world consisted of power struggles and contestations, not divine authority and entitlements.[33] Human fear and fragility constituted a political order which was therefore dependent on the natural order of human society. With Hobbes, political power became the right to use force on a specific territory, and this view, together with Machiavelli's concept of power, still informed Max Weber's sociological definition of the state through the monopoly of the legitimate use of physical force within a given territory.[34] In this context, Jeremy Bentham's definition of sovereignty as an exercise of commands depending on the general habit of obedience already belonged to the social and not the political realm.[35]

[28] Sheldon Wolin, *Politics and Vision: Continuity and Innovation in Western Political Thought* (Princeton University Press 1960) 4.

[29] Aristotle, *Politics* (Ernest Barker tr, Oxford University Press 2009) book I, 1253a, 20, 25.

[30] Lawrence Krader, *Formation of the State* (Prentice-Hall 1968).

[31] For further historical contextualization, see JG Merquior, *Rousseau and Weber: Two Studies in the Theory of Legitimacy* (Routledge 1980) 2.

[32] Norberto Bobbio, *Democracy and Dictatorship* (Polity Press 1989) 65, 70.

[33] Blaise Pascal, *Pensée* (WF Trotter tr, EP Dutton 1958) 85.

[34] Gottfried Eisermann, 'Max Weber und Carl Schmitt' (1994) 33 Der Staat 76.

[35] Leonard J Hume, *Bentham and Bureaucracy* (Cambridge University Press 1981) 209–37.

Similarly, the problem of modern statehood and its legitimacy demonstrates profound differences between social and legal sciences. The distinction between sociological and legal methodologies studying the modern state was already clear in Georg Jellinek's *General Theory of the State*, originally published in 1900.[36] Jellinek's study evidences the rise of the concept and doctrine of the *Rechtsstaat* characterizing the state as a legal person and translatable to English as 'the rule of law' only with strong reservations. The state is primarily perceived as a legally constituted organization fully defined by techniques and procedures of public law. However, this legal structure of statehood is also a social organization impossible to juridically isolate from society and specific social relations.[37]

The difference between legal and sociological perspectives on the modern state is defined by the difference between the normativity (*ought*) and the facticity (*is*) of statehood. Jellinek's difference between the state as a social organization with its historical existence and legal organization of norms independently manifesting themselves in that existence was profoundly influenced by Weber's distinction between the ideal validity of the legal point of view and the empirical validity of the sociological view of the state and any other legally regulated social organization. It was exactly this difference that was later adopted by Hans Kelsen as a starting point of his pure theory of law and critique of dualist theories of the state and law.[38]

Political *will*, legal *norm*, and social *facts* outline crossroads of political, legal, and sociological perspectives on the state and its legitimacy. However, what has completely changed in modern legal, political, and social sciences is the relationship between the state and society. As Norberto Bobbio comments:

> For centuries the political organization was the object *par excellence* of all reflection on the social life of humankind, on man as a social animal, as *politikon zoon* where *politikon* includes without differentiation the two contemporary meanings of 'social' and 'political' ... Today political sociology is a part of general sociology, and political science is one of the social sciences. The state as political system is now a sub-system in relation to the social system.[39]

A sociologist of law might add that the modern state therefore has to be studied as a specific organizational subsystem *connecting* two different systems in society, namely politics and law, because, apart from being a political organization of power, the state is also defined as a legal person by public law.

The classic question of whether *might* is *right*, which has led the finest philosophical minds to contemplate the legitimate constitution and conditionality of political power, is reformulated by modern sociology as two distinct questions—efficiency of power and its normative legal justification. The question of legitimacy then typically stretches in both directions. It is a matter of the efficient use of force delivering expected outcomes and running the state as Hobbes's *machina machinarum*

[36] Georg Jellinek, *Allgemeine Staatslehre* (Häring Verlag 1900).

[37] For tensions between the state's unity and social or political pluralism, see, for instance, David Runciman, *Pluralism and the Personality of the State* (Cambridge University Press 1997) 64–86.

[38] For Kelsen's critique of Jellinek, see Massimo La Torre, *Law as Institution* (Springer Verlag 2010) 26.

[39] Bobbio, *Democracy and Dictatorship* (n 32) 52, 54.

(artificial society). At the same time, it legally defines conditions of the justified use of force and normative expectations of the sovereign state's right to command and its citizens' duty to obey its commands.[40]

E. Legitimacy *by* Legality or Legitimacy *of* Legality?

Every power calls for legitimacy. In democratic society, however, legitimation of power cannot be limited to the power-holders and needs to be extended to the rest of society. The modern state, therefore, is to be considered a political organization permanently selecting between matters to be governed through its power and those that should be left for other societal sectors and their regimes of governance.[41]

For instance, the crisis of the totalitarian state was caused by its ambition to absorb the totality of society and regulate it according to the basic norm of ideology.[42] Totalitarianism pursued the goal of creating a state with one official opinion—something impossible to achieve in modern functionally differentiated society, the political system of which uses the private/public dichotomy and generates its legitimacy from different sectors and the normative expectations of what philosophers and theorists of politics and law commonly call civil society.[43]

As anti-political science, sociology turns political problems into the matter of different modes of social normativity and discipline.[44] Nevertheless, the shift from polity to society also includes a profound critique of those philosophical and theoretical views which take the problem of legitimacy as the normative externality of social and/or political order. For sociologists, validity claims are generated from within society, such as the systems of positive law and politics. They cannot be formulated outside society by pure or communicative reason, *volonté générale*, universal values, transcendental virtues, or commandments imposed on humans by deities.

According to the sociological and socio-legal views, the state is a social organization of coercive techniques which require further justification beyond the efficient use of force. The modern *Rechtsstaat*—the law-governed state—formulates normative expectations and limitations of the state by legality. This notorious definition of legitimacy by legality, however, extends the problem of legitimation from the political system now legitimized by legality, to the legal system itself. The problem of legitimacy *by* legality thus becomes the problem of legitimacy *of* legality, which hardly can be reduced to the legal system's efficiency, but equally cannot be made subject to the higher-legitimacy test of universal ethics, natural law, or such like.

[40] Murray Forsyth, 'Thomas Hobbes and the Constituent Power of the People' (1981) 29 Political Studies 191.

[41] Rodney Barker, *Political Legitimacy and the State* (Oxford University Press 1990) 20.

[42] Adam Podgorecki and Vittorio Olgiati (eds), *Totalitarian and Post-Totalitarian Law: A Sociolegal Analysis* (Ashgate 1996).

[43] Andrew Arato and Jean Cohen, *Civil Society and Political Theory* (MIT Press 1992).

[44] Michel Foucault, *On the Punitive Society: Lectures at the Collège de France, 1972–1973* (Bernard E Harcourt ed, Graham Burchell tr, Palgrave Macmillan 2015) 240.

The rule of positive law has its internal structure and principles which, nevertheless, have an external function and value in eliminating arbitrariness, not only of the state, but any other form of societal power coming from the systems of economy, religion, education, and so on. The concept of formal legality paradoxically includes substantive conditions of political power, and limitation is just one of them. Furthermore, the political tradition of the rule of law recursively leads to the self-limitation of legality itself and thus minimizes potential risks of injustices produced by the system of positive law.

The rule of law is not just control of power by its limitation, because it equally introduces values such as clarity, consistency, congruence, coherence, and non-contradiction into the public and social reality. It is both the first political principle and common societal practice. It is an intrinsic part of the political system, which contradicts legitimation by universal principles of natural law as much as the arbitrary will of the stronger. This is what makes legality both an efficient tool legitimizing power and the primary public good legitimized by its intrinsic values and their external effect on other social systems.[45]

The internal paradox of legitimacy by legality, which cannot be reduced to the systems' functionality and the harshness of legal/illegal binary coding,[46] yet equally cannot be subject to the code of universal morality, was well demonstrated in the Luhmann-Habermas debates which started in the 1970s.[47] Two decades later, Niklas Luhmann significantly radicalized his position when he stated that legitimacy by external values considered moral foundations of the positive rule of law was important only for those who considered it important. He commented:

> Nowadays, people look for moral rules or values to found the legal system in nonlegal norms—the famous Jellinek-Weber-Habermas line of 'legitimation', or the American discussion of moral aspiration versus original intent as a guideline for an interpretation of the constitution. My advice would be to unask such questions—or to 'deconstruct' them—and to replace them with the question of how the system organizes its own closure, its own social autonomy, and its own immunity in fulfilling its function.[48]

In this robust statement, Luhmann effectively banned the topic of legitimacy from social theory because of its deontological nature. In response to this challenge, it is, however, necessary to ask if 'immunity' is possible to achieve without irritations of the legal system's environment and its exposure to the viral dissenting voices beyond the conflicts between legal normativity and political power.[49]

[45] Lon L Fuller, *The Morality of Law* (2nd edn, Yale University Press 1969) 91–94.

[46] N Luhmann, *Law as a Social System* (Klaus A Ziegert tr, Fatima Kastner, Richard Nobles, David Schiff, and Rosamund Ziegert eds, Oxford University Press 2004) 190–91.

[47] Loet Leydesdorff, 'Luhmann, Habermas, and the Theory of Communication' (2000) 17 Systems Research and Behavioral Science 273.

[48] Niklas Luhmann, 'Operational Closure and Structural Coupling: The Differentiation of the Legal System' (1992) 13 Cardozo Law Review 1419, 1426.

[49] I was exploring these possibilities in, for instance, Jiří Přibáň, *Dissidents of Law: On the 1989 Velvet Revolutions, Legitimations, Fictions of Legality and Contemporary Versions of the Social Contract* (Ashgate 2002).

Furthermore, the capacity of the intrinsic values of legality, most notably the generality, clarity, coherence, stability, and non-contradiction of rules, to externally guarantee the legitimacy of power makes its secondary legal coding much more than just a technique of structural coupling between law and politics. Externalizing its internal characteristics and functional preconditions as political and societal values, legality recursively transforms itself into the legitimate rule of law, while its values are sufficiently generalized to operate as legitimation formulas beyond the systems of law and politics.[50]

Responding to Luhmann's advice to study the systemic organization of closure, I argue, therefore, that it must involve studying the process of internalization of societal externalities by the system of positive law and their reformulation as legality's intrinsic values. This process of legitimation of legality is as important as legitimation of power by the secondary code of legality. Understanding these complex operations and transformations of efficient techniques to normatively shared values and vice versa requires the elaboration of the concept of externality which, rather than philosophically defining the transcendental foundations of society, sociologically analyses the capacity of different social systems to internalize and operationalize externalities as the distinction between legitimacy and illegitimacies.

F. Legality and Legitimacy by Ultimate Values: Necessary, Yet Impossible

Unlike law, politics is not deontological and organizes society according to the medium of power into matters of ruling and being ruled. As Weber already pointed out, the state is one possible form of organizing people ruling over other people.[51] Nevertheless, the ultimate point of the legitimation of state power is neither its efficiency nor its exercise within the constraints of general rules of legality: it is the meaning of politics formulated in the language of values.

However, this philosophical element in Weber's sociological analysis of legitimacy is immediately disputed by Weber himself when he concludes that there is no chance that values would be generally shared and accepted as universally valid in modern political society. This society is morally pluralistic and 'polytheistic',[52] with different people endorsing different, conflicting, and incommensurable values.

While expected to facilitate universal validity, objectivity, and social stability, values in modern society actually suffer from instability, changeability, contestability, and contradictions. The most important part of Weber's general definition of authority (*Herrshaft*) as

[50] Martin Krygier, 'The Rule of Law: Legality, Teleology, Sociology' in Gianluigi Palombella and Neil Walker (eds), *Relocating the Rule of Law* (Hart Publishing 2009).

[51] Max Weber, *Economy and Society*, vol 1 (Guenther Roth and Claus Wittich eds, University of California Press 1978) 56.

[52] Max Weber, 'Science as Vocation' in David Owen and Tracy B Strong (eds), *The Vocation Lectures* (Rodney Livingstone tr, Hackett Publishing 2004) 22.

the situation in which the manifested will (command) of the ruler or rules is meant to influence the conduct of one or more others (the ruled) and actually does influence it in such a way that their conduct to a socially relevant degree occurs as if the ruled had made the content of the command the maxim of their conduct for its very own sake[53]

is not the Kantian language invoking 'maxims', but their 'as if' character. The ruled obey on the basis of their *belief* in objective and generally valid values behind the manifested will and power.

The Kantian categorical imperative of 'its own sake' is confronted by the plurality of values and cannot match the modern state's capacity to govern all people living on its territory on the basis of their belief that legal rules are both their own and universally valid. Similarly, the state cannot guarantee its legitimacy internally by integrating ultimate and generally valid values into legal normativity.[54] It is, therefore, the bureaucratic order permeating all forms of domination in society which eventually guarantees the political requirement of general obedience, despite the fact that, according to Weber, the personal and conflictual concrete form of politics and the impersonal and abstract form of bureaucracy are inherently alien to each other.[55]

In modern society, all values, by definition absolute, can only be relative, while all bureaucratic rules, by definition relative and specific to official competences and social steering, are the ultimate source of the general validity of political commands. However, these general paradoxes of legitimation and the intrinsic tensions between public officials and political leaders show that impersonal and abstract bureaucratic rationality is also both systemically and normatively *external* to the otherwise persuasive, conflictual, and, after all, deeply personal and charismatic nature of politics.[56] In this sense, sociological theories of legitimacy by administrative efficiency, bureaucratic governance, regulatory reason, and so on are surprisingly close to the philosophical theories of legitimation by universally valid principles and values externally founding the systems of positive law and politics.

According to Weber, politics requires a paradoxical adherence to the ultimate existential meaning and value of political power, even in the modern disenchanted world. Like science or economy, politics is nevertheless impossible to ground in universal values binding the totality of human life and offering final solutions to the ultimate question of the meaning of life. The only meaning of politics is in the disillusionment and knowledge that neither politics, nor science, nor any other human enterprise can grant us access to universally valid principles and values. In modern society, all these enterprises are

serving this particular god and will *give offense to every other god*. For you will necessarily arrive at such-and-such ultimate, internally meaningful *conclusions* if you remain true to yourselves. We may assert this at least in principle. The discipline of philosophy and the discussion of

53 Max Weber, *Economy and Society*, vol 2 (Guenther Roth and Claus Wittich eds, University of California Press 1978) 946.

54 For this position, see especially Ronald Dworkin, *A Matter of Principle* (Oxford University Press 1985) 171–74; Ronald Dworkin, *Law's Empire* (Fontana 1986) 176–224.

55 Weber, *Economy and Society* (n 53) vol 2, 959.

56 Nikolas Rose and Mariana Valverde, 'Governed by Law?' (1998) 7 Social and Legal Studies 541.

what are ultimately the philosophical bases of the individual disciplines all attempt to achieve this. If we understand the matter correctly (something that must be assumed here) we can compel a person, or at least help him, *to render an account of the ultimate meaning of his own actions.*[57]

Every meaning and all values are internally defined by different disciplines. The only exception is philosophy, but its quest for the ultimate meaning and truth cannot simply be applied to other disciplines, enterprises, and activities. In other words, the vocation of politics, law, science, or any other intellectual discipline or social activity consists in the recognition that objective legitimacy by values is both necessary and impossible. The value of scientific knowledge is in the recognition of constant questioning of any scientific knowledge, the value of political action is in the recognition that no ultimate values can be enforced by power as both personal and generally shared by those under its rule, and so on.

G. Nations as Reservoirs of Values and National Unity as Part of Societal Differentiation

The state is a historical invention and has many different forms, from liberal, democratic, and constitutional to socialist, populist, authoritarian, and even totalitarian. However, the modern state has two typical tendencies: apart from the already discussed bureaucratization, its polity tends to be constituted as a nation which is identified with specific sets of generally shared values, ideals, historical goals, and collective destiny.[58]

All nations are the same in their self-description as unique and exceptional. The particularities of individual nations gravitate towards the general political organization of the modern state. The paradox of legitimacy by values that are impossible to enforce yet necessary for the ultimate justification of enforcing power helps to explain why the concept of the nation achieved sacred status in modern secular society and became the ultimate societal foundation of the legitimacy of the state as its political organization.[59]

Modern nationalisms precede the existence of nations by creating national myths and histories.[60] Nations thus become imagined[61] and worshipped by their individual members, the sacrifice of whose lives in conflicts with other nations it demands. National identity is based on the extraordinarily strong sense of togetherness and emotions that elevate it to the status of the real force and true existence of society. National heroes are glorified, and national history is treasured as a source of human authenticity and collective self-creation.

[57] Weber, 'Science as Vocation' (n 52) 26 (emphasis in the original).
[58] Samuel H Beer, *To Make a Nation* (Cambridge University Press 1993) 312.
[59] Edmund Morgan, *Inventing the People: The Rise of Popular Sovereignty in England and America* (Norton 1988) 83.
[60] Ernest Gellner, *Nations and Nationalism* (Blackwell 1983) ch 5.
[61] Benedict Anderson, *Imagined Communities* (Verso 1991) 7.

Nations are immanent sources of legitimation of the modern state operating as real power determining the settlement of political constitutions. However, they also constitute themselves as the ultimate foundations and reservoirs of transcendental values protected and represented by the state and its constitution. This paradox exceeds the common paradox of modern constitutionalism limiting the nation's constituent power by the state constitution because it makes the nation part of both the sacred and the profane spheres of society.[62]

This shift of the classic distinction between the sacred and the profane to the realm of national identity has profound semantic and structural effects on modern statehood, namely the structural transformation of the modern state into the nation state and its democratization as nationalization.[63] In modernity, the concept of the nation as the people becomes a political concept describing the political system as constituted from within society by the people's collective will and growing out of its shared history, culture, and folkways. Sovereign will externally imposed on the body politic by a monarch could no more be legitimized in politically self-democratized modern society. After the French Revolution, this will could only emanate from within society and thus constitute the modern democratic state with a legal constitution incorporating the nation's values in the language of liberties, rights, and democratic participation.[64]

The concept of the multinational state then typically refers to its pre-political ethnic multinational segmentations, yet even these commonwealths of different nations search for common values, identity, and overarching political nationhood, as illustrated by recent debates on Britishness in the United Kingdom and the Spanish constitutional crisis triggered by the basic question of whether Catalans can be constitutionally recognized as a nation.[65] On the other hand, federal republics, such as the United States and Germany, can survive and function only if their constitutional systems are strongly supported by the constituent power of respective nations. It looks as if it is only within the state that the people as the modern political nation can legitimize power by imposing it on itself and making it work as a vehicle for the materialization of the ultimate values shared by its members.

The inclusive capacity of nations to treat all members as equal found its constitutional expression in the principle of equality of all citizens before law. Individuals as members of the nation lost their concrete characteristics of social status and origins and, being mutually equal, started to be treated in terms of their belonging to functional social systems—politics, with its equal participation of all citizens in political power, and law, with its equality of all before the law.[66] Nevertheless, these modern

[62] Anthony D Smith, *Nationalism* (2nd edn, Polity Press 2010) 153.

[63] Istvan Hont, 'Permanent Crisis of a Divided Mankind: The Contemporary Crisis of the Nation-State in Historical Perspective' (1994) 42 Political Studies 166.

[64] Bernard Yack, 'Popular Sovereignty and Nationalism' (2001) 29 Political Theory 517, 523.

[65] See, for instance, Andrew Gamble and Anthony Wright (eds), *Britishness: Perspectives on the British Question* (Wiley-Blackwell 2009); Xavier Cuadras Morató (ed), *Catalonia: A New Independent State in Europe? A Debate on Secession Within the European Union* (Routledge 2016).

[66] Wojciech Sadurski, *Equality and Legitimacy* (Oxford University Press 2008) 25–39.

nations were typically formed in violent processes of wars, ethnic and linguistic cleansing, and concentration of political power.

The concept of the nation was a specific response to the general 'demand for the establishment of unity in a state, and to this extent the distinction between cultural nation [*Kulturstaat*] and state-nation [*Staatsnation*] was of secondary importance'.[67] This unity of the political system through self-organization of the nation into a state delegitimized earlier social segmentations and stratifications and opened the possibility of the democratic and liberal reforms of the nineteenth and early twentieth centuries that led to universal suffrage.[68] The new political value of national self-determination found its way into the language of politicians, revolutionaries, and, later, international and constitutional lawyers.

Within the nation state, society found new conceptualizations and self-descriptions of permanent criticism, improvement, and reform, including transvaluation of the nation as a value itself, for instance, by using the *ethnos/demos* distinction and condemning politics of ethno-nationalism while praising civic and republican patriotic values.[69] However, the nation's political function as a guarantor of the state's unity leads the *demos* to policies which may be openly hostile to some cultures and even to invoke the *ethnos*-based concepts such as *Leitkultur* (a leading culture).[70]

Nations and nationalisms, therefore, are historical constructs operating as quasi-theological forces which can unify modern polities by exercising the general will through state structures. Nevertheless, constitutional principles of the democratic rule of law are always confronted by ethnic, religious, and cultural heterogeneities within structures of modern nation states. Nation states are thus unities of differentiations and the ideas of democracy and basic rights, including the right to self-determination, cannot fully materialize through the semantics of national unity, due to the permanent risk of ethnic, religious, and cultural fundamentalisms and exclusions.

This unifying function of the nation as a particular reservoir of universal values is paradoxical, yet the whole period of Romanticism was driven by this attempt to reconcile universal ideals of humanism and particular national identities and political aspirations.[71] This sociological paradox explains why nationalism became such a powerful basis of modern political legitimation—it legitimized the state by fundamental values, while making them in permanent need of protection and enforcement by the same state.

67 Niklas Luhmann, *Theory of Society*, vol 2 (Rhodes Barrett tr, Stanford University Press 2013) 287.

68 Chris Thornhill, *A Sociology of Constitutions* (Cambridge University Press 2011) 275–309.

69 For this normative distinction, see, for instance, Michael Ignatieff, *Blood and Belonging* (Farrar, Strauss, and Giroux, 1993) 7–13.

70 Bassam Tibi, *Europa ohne Identität: Leitkultur oder Wertebeliebigkeit* (Siedler Verlag 1998).

71 Terry Pinkard, 'Romanticized Enlightenment? Enlightened Romanticism? Universalism and Particularlism in Hegel's Understanding of Enlightenment' (1997) 35 Bulletin of the Hegel Society of Great Britain 18.

H. Fluidity of Values and Temporality of Legitimation beyond the Nation State

The contrast between the general problem of legitimacy and the specific organization of the state shows why the question of legitimacy persists in globalized politics and law beyond the sovereign nation state. Politics communicates through the medium of power, irrespective of its organizational subsystemic differentiation into states, international and transnational organizations and networks. The self-referential juridification of power as the rule of law is not limited to the modern state and actually expands the concepts of constitutionalism, democracy, human rights, and fair trial to the supranational and transnational levels of global society, including its territorial segments, such as the European Union with its multi-layered organizations, networks, and regimes.

Social expectations of the concepts of democracy, statehood, nation, and popular sovereignty acquire new meanings in globalized modern society. The structural transformation of power to authority is an intrinsic part of the globalized systems of politics and law. The modern nation state, which represents a specific historical response to public power legitimation, becomes part of more general power configurations and societal expectations unlimited by the imagined community of a nation.

This global societal expansion of the problem of legitimacy challenges modern political hierarchies and legal validity established by the nation state. Global society shifts challenges of legitimacy from hierarchies of the state and its law to the horizontal relations between law and other social normative structures and systems.[72] It is, therefore, important to focus on what Luhmann described in the text quoted above as self-organization, closure, and autonomy of the globalized systems of positive law and politics and new configurations of state organizations in them.[73]

Modern society does not have one 'super-medium' unifying all social communication in all social subsystems. Neither moral and legal norms nor political force can unify society beyond its functional differentiation. As symbolically generalized media of the systems of law and politics, legality and power only perform specific operations and cannot fully integrate and/or found society. However, structural coupling between globalized politics and law leads to new power constellations calling for legitimation.[74]

As regards the legitimacy of the state in global society, it is increasingly limited and questioned because of nation states' lack of capacity to deal with global social problems. However, the state's growing deficit of legitimacy by efficiency is accompanied by the legitimacy deficits of newly constituted supranational and transnational

[72] Gunther Teubner, 'The King's Many Bodies: The Self-Deconstruction of the Law's Hierarchy' (1997) 31 Law and Society Review 763.

[73] Luhmann, 'Operational Closure and Structural Coupling' (n 48).

[74] Poul F Kjaer, *Constitutionalism in the Global Realm: A Sociological Approach* (Routledge 2014) 23–39.

organizations and their normative regimes, which may address European or global governance crises, yet cannot replicate the state's legitimacy by democratic values or civil rights and liberties.

Normative theories of European and global cosmopolitan society make one typical mistake by identifying polity with society and, while correctly unbounding the concept of polity from national imaginations and state structures, pursue the goal of reconstituting strong political identities and bonds, which used to define nation states, beyond their structural and semantic boundaries.[75] Nevertheless, the first goal of theories of legitimacy in post-sovereign and post-national globalized society should not be a doctrine outlining normative conditions for states and other organizations operating in globalized politics. Instead, these theories must address the problem of how legitimation procedures are produced by systemic communication between law and politics within the nation state and beyond its organizational framework at supranational and transnational levels.

Falling short of full-scale democratic settlement and procedures typical of the constitutional democratic state, supranational and transnational political organizations and their legal regulation typically look for alternatives, such as human rights and cosmopolitan values, which are easier to globalize than structures of the nation state. Unlike political procedures and legal regulations, values are relatively easy to globalize exactly because of their appeal to universal validity. This ease also explains the recent proliferation of value arguments, promises, and commitments within supranational and transnational organizations.

For instance, the German Chancellor's laudable response to the migrant crisis of 2015 was driven by both the efficiency promise of 'Wir schaffen das!' (We'll make it!)[76] and the argument that the effort was driven by European values. Nevertheless, political and societal reality immediately struck back and challenged the general status and validity of European values. First of all, it was striking to see how long these 'values' had been ignored by Germany and other EU member states before the crisis reached their borders. Until then, calls for more EU solidarity and policy coordination regularly made by Italian and Greek governments had not been addressed even when the causes and urgency of the migrant crisis had been the same.

Apart from this temporal relativity, the migrant crisis of 2015 also revealed the extent to which these values are vague, clash, and irreconcilable when the same German Chancellor sidelined EU diplomacy and her government negotiated a morally controversial deal with the Turkish autocratic government which left thousands of genuine asylum seekers stranded in Greek camps. Furthermore, it significantly weakened the Union's capacity to criticize the Turkish government's gross abuses of power and fundamental breaches of basic human rights in the wake of the military coup and President Erdogan's counter-coup in the summer of 2016.[77]

[75] See, for instance, Ulrich Beck, 'The Cosmopolitan Society and its Enemies' (2002) 19 Theory, Culture & Society 17–44.

[76] Protokoll der Bundespressekonferenz, 31 August 2015.

[77] For a critique, see, for instance, Kelly M Greenhill, 'Open Arms behind Barred Doors: Fear, Hypocrisy and Policy Schizophrenia in the European Migration Crisis' (2016) 22 European Law Journal 317.

This and many other examples clearly demonstrate that values, despite their normative claims and universal appeal, are far too unstable and conflictual to provide normative foundations for supranational and transnational organizations. These organizations can hardly secure their legitimacy by philosophical calls for politics of values and identity. These calls actually may easily become sources of legitimacy deficits and even illegitimacies themselves. Post-national legal and political organizations, therefore, require further institution-building and constitution-making to transform these values into autonomous structures and semantics, such as constitutional rights and supranational or transnational constituent polities.[78]

I. Concluding Remarks: On Procedural Legitimation by Value Waiting Lists

Instead of accepting Weber's scepticism regarding the irreconcilability between the meaning and functionality of social life and therefore between legitimacy by values and by efficiency, I want to conclude by reformulating the problem of values in state, international, and global law and politics as a problem of their temporality and fluid validity. 'All value lists are waiting lists',[79] yet this does not mean that political legitimacy is exclusively achievable by legal procedures and entirely depends on their efficiency and performativity. The systems of positive law and politics already incorporate values which are internally operationalized and reformulated as intrinsic values of legality, yet remain external to the purely technical concepts of law and politics.

Systemic closures are necessary for legitimacy as much as systemic externalities. The fact that we always wait for legal and political decisions, for instance, in the form of judgements of constitutional courts or constitutional acts enacted by parliaments means that the problem of legitimacy can never be settled. Values always can be contested, and different legal and political bodies may select and follow different values. Legitimacy subsequently needs to accommodate the permanent process of legitimation selecting between legitimate and illegitimate values in law and politics.

The systems of law and politics draw on the legitimation paradox of the counterfactual nature of values existing independently of their efficiency, yet systematically intertwined with efficiency, as guaranteed by positive procedures of the system. The legitimacy of the nation state and any political organization of post-national society relies on facticity of normative expectations formulated through the concept of values, yet this concept needs to be internalized by the systems of positive law and politics and enforced by legal or political agencies, such as courts, arbitrations, and administrations.

[78] See especially Chris Thornhill, *A Sociology of Transnational Constitutions* (Cambridge University Press 2016) 69–101.

[79] Niklas Luhmann, '*Quod Omnes Tangit*: Remarks on Jürgen Habermas's Legal Theory' (1996) 17 Cardozo Law Review 883, 886.

Value waiting lists are less important for their content than the moral hopes and values that are invested in the very act of waiting. Optimists believe that their Godot of values will come one day, pessimists do not believe in his coming, and sceptics act as if he is going to come, even when their knowledge and experience tell them that it is impossible. Moralists then pretend that they have found him and tell the rest of us how we must act to meet his expectations. Some even resort to the state's power and invoke the language of principles and heroic figures of philosopher-kings, Hercules-judges, and so on to ensure that these expectations materialize in society.

In these circumstances, it is the job of a social theory of law to study the transformation of legitimacy, initially defined as the normative foundations of a polity, to the processes of legitimation, perceived as selection between legitimate and illegitimate values internally processed by the systems of positive law and politics. Unlike philosophies of law and politics, socio-legal theory cannot define *what* makes the state and other political organizations legitimate. However, it can describe *how* these organizations achieve their legitimacy. It therefore studies the processes of internal emergence, enforcement, evolution, and evaporation of immanent normative structures described as transcendental values in state law and any form of supranational and transnational legality.

PART III

LEGITIMACY BEYOND THE STATE

VIII

Conceptions of Public Reason in the Supranational Sphere and Legitimacy beyond Borders

Wojciech Sadurski

Is a vocabulary and a conventional set of normative intuitions about legitimacy—coined as they are within the confines of nation states—exportable beyond national borders to the supranational sphere, which is marked by its own distinct and specific relations of authority and power? When we engage in a translation of a legitimacy discourse from the national to the international or supranational sphere, can such an exercise be successful and, well, legitimate? These are the themes explored in this chapter.

I begin, in section A, by reflecting upon the reasons why we consider the notion of legitimacy beyond national borders in the first place. I argue that these special reasons, which are specific to the supranational sphere—and, in particular, those which are related to the democratic deficit of supranational authorities—drive the *concept* of legitimacy which is applicable to that sphere, that is, legitimacy which is concurrently weak (ie supporting a duty to respect, but not necessarily to obey), single norm oriented (ie an attribute of a specific norm/decision rather than of an authority or regime in general), and subject-fragmented (ie the attribute of legitimacy is conferred by the subjects to which the norms are addressed). While critics may view these distinctions as arbitrary definitional fiats, I argue that they respond to the real concerns which we have about legitimacy in the supranational sphere.

In section B of this chapter, I contrast two alternative accounts of public reason within the international/supranational domain. These are Rawls's 'public reason of the Society of Peoples' and Supranational Public Reason (SPR) *sensu stricto*. I show that, even though Rawls used in 'The Law of Peoples' the concept of 'public reason', which in his broader system of political liberalism had been clearly embedded in the legitimacy discourse, 'public reason of the Society of Peoples' is not meant to, and cannot, perform the role of a legitimating device. Rather, its main role is to support and explain the conditions of *toleration* among peoples, which is normatively distinct from the question of *legitimacy*. In contrast, SPR *sensu stricto* can be properly seen as a (partial) conception of legitimacy in the supranational sphere. Whether it

Legitimacy: The State and Beyond. First Edition. Edited by Wojciech Sadurski, Michael Sevel, and Kevin Walton. Published 2019 by Oxford University Press.

is a successful conception is a different matter, but at least it can be seen as a coherent account of such a conception.

In section C of this chapter, I reflect upon the applicability of SPR *sensu stricto* in solving legitimacy dilemmas with respect to supranational authorities with the aim of finding traces of actual (even if tacit) adoption of SPR in the legitimating strategies of some leading supranational judicial authorities, such as the European Court of Human Rights (ECtHR). Accordingly, this part examines, in particular, the relationship between the supranational norms emerging from such supranational judicial authorities and legitimacy established at the *state* level. While the use of judicial authorities as exemplars of public reason may be seen as obvious, it is the *supranational* character of these authorities which offers clues as to why SPR responds to the concerns about legitimacy in the supranational sphere—the concerns outlined in the first part of this chapter.

A. The *Concept* of Legitimacy beyond Borders?

There are many *conceptions* of legitimacy that seek to explain what characteristics render an institution, a regime, or a rule legitimate. These conceptions respond to substantive issues posed by different kinds of authority in the modern world—for example, the significance of the allegiance, loyalty, respect, and compliance of those who are considered to be under the jurisdiction of that authority. But as a meta-issue, or a conceptually prior matter with regard to these substantive issues, there are also different *concepts* of legitimacy, that is, different notions concerning what legitimacy *is about*. These concepts are not entirely a matter of definitional fiat, but respond to different *concerns* that arise when we raise the issue of legitimacy. These concerns are—at least to some degree—driven by the kind or site of authority that we are reflecting upon. For example, we will have different concerns which may lead us to question the legitimacy of a military commander, the World Trade Organization (WTO), the government of the United States, or the hearsay rule. Accordingly, prior to developing conceptions of legitimacy, it is necessary to understand why we are concerned about the legitimacy of these institutions, rules, or regimes. It is likely that the answer to this question will differ in accordance with the type or site of authority.

This chapter is concerned with only one—relatively novel—site of authority, that is, the authority of supranational norm-producing organizations, institutions, and entities which transcend—by their reach and their aspiration—national boundaries. There exists a plethora of bodies and organizations within the supranational sphere. Some are adjudicatory, while others are regulatory. Some are regional, while others are universal. Some are 'public', while others are non-state-based. Some enact peremptory rules and others issue only soft law. Such bodies and organizations may be territorial or functional, autonomous or embedded in other international organizations, and so on. They exercise various forms of authority and elicit various degrees of compliance from communities across national borders.

Supranational norm-producing organizations create standards which seek to control the conduct of states and/or individuals, firms, associations, and other entities, despite the fact that supranational norm-producing organizations are not mere extensions of states. Rather, their decision-making is largely independent of states, and they are unable to rely on the authority of state-specific canons of accountability and democracy. As a result, they often establish standards which, formally speaking, may appear to be non-binding, but, as Gráinne de Búrca observes, they 'can become effectively authoritative in ways that are similar to national decision-making ...'.[1] De Búrca provides, inter alia, an example of the guidelines and norms issued by the Basel Committee on banking supervision, which was originally established with the aim of improving the quality of international banking. The standards became highly influential and have been adopted by many states. As a consequence, the International Monetary Fund and the World Bank have made compliance with these standards compulsory for indebted countries. This serves to demonstrate how 'the fragmented but complexly interwoven transnational governance domain can render decisions authoritative, even when they are originally non-binding'.[2] It is the authoritative, legal, or quasi-legal character of these entities that calls for an explanation of their *legitimacy*.

In a recent book, Liam Murphy objected to the characterization of various decisions and standards, such as those of 'the purely private International Standardization Organization (ISO)', as 'law', suggesting that 'though they can have pervasive impact both on domestic law and decisions by treaty-based international organizations, [they] surely do not have legal force'.[3] But in my view, a discussion of whether or not to characterize decisions such as those described by De Búrca or those referred to by Murphy as 'law' is not particularly interesting. If we replace the phrase 'legal force' with 'authoritative effect' in Murphy's just-quoted phrase, the proposition becomes less extravagant than he suggests it is. Murphy continues:

> It is true that ISO standards are incorporated into legal regulation, for example through the WTO ... but that fact does not make the standards themselves legally binding—no more so than regulation of banks and other financial institutions that refers to and incorporates the decisions of private ratings agencies makes Moody's a lawmaker.[4]

Again, if we replace the words 'legally binding' with 'authoritative', the idea of the ISO (as an example of a supranational authority) issuing authoritative standards becomes far more plausible, insofar as (1) the standards are issued with the intention of guiding the behaviour of various state or non-state entities, (2) the standards are received as such by the intended addressees, and (3) there are such negative consequences of disregarding those standards that non-compliance becomes an excessively costly option. Thus, the broader notion of 'authority' is better suited to transnational normative phenomena than the narrower notion of 'law' because it

[1] Gráinne de Búrca, 'Developing Democracy beyond the State' (2008) 46 Columbia Journal of Transnational Law 221, 235.

[2] ibid. [3] Liam Murphy, *What Makes Law* (Cambridge University Press 2014) 165.

[4] ibid 166.

frees us of the intuitive assumptions about law being a comprehensive and final normative order—assumptions which are unhelpful in situations of inter-dimensional conflict, competition, and overlap between normative orders in the supranational sphere.

Supranational bodies and organizations often issue binding norms or directives, even though they have no traditional, hierarchically structured means of enforcement and can rarely appeal—in supporting the authoritative character of their norms—to explicit state consent typical of classical international law. Yet they question states' claims to exclusive authority in governing all aspects of public life in their territories. These situations render the need to develop a theory of legitimacy of such authority compelling. As the authors of an important article-manifesto accompanying the launch of the *Global Constitutionalism* journal put it: '[G]lobal constitutionalism grapples with the consequences of globalization as a process that transgresses and perforates national or state borders, *undermining familiar roots of legitimacy*'.[5] Arguably, the 'familiar roots of legitimacy' to which Antje Wiener et al refer in this phrase are primarily of a *democratic* character. Hence, the most important reason why we reflect upon, search for, and wish to establish (or refute) conceptions of legitimacy in the supranational sphere is a persistent, endemic, and drastic democratic deficit of supranational authorities.

To many, this may appear such a sweeping statement that it demands further support beyond a mere assertion. But for the purposes of this chapter, I will take it for granted that supranational authorities, as we know them in the modern world, by and large lack a robust democratic character—however considered—and that various attempts to identify democratic pedigree or the democratic nature of such entities have been by and large unsuccessful. In a recent book, Philip Pettit argues that 'international rules and agencies' do not raise any major problems for democracy (at least in theory) because 'the states that set them up ought to be capable of controlling such agencies'.[6] But it is enough to cite the evidence provided by Pettit for this proposition: 'The appointed officials in international agencies and institutions are subject to the constant threat of being called to book, whether as a result of hostile media publicity, hostile NGO criticism, or internal whistleblowers',[7] to see how fragile these aspects of democratic control of international bodies are, *in comparison with their national equivalents*. Whether using various templates of democracy borrowed from the context of nation-states to judge supranational entities—an exercise which by critics will be pejoratively dubbed 'methodological nationalism'—is justified is another matter. I will assume (here, without argument) that it *is* justified. Elsewhere, I have reflected upon whether attempts at uncoupling democracy from nation states—and in the process of doing so, vindicating legitimacy at a supranational level—are successful.[8] My view is that, generally speaking, they are not.

[5] Antje Wiener, Anthony F Lang, James Tully, Miguel Poiares Maduro, and Mattias Kumm, 'Global Constitutionalism: Human Rights, Democracy and the Rule of Law' (2012) 1 Global Constitutionalism 1, 11 (emphasis added).

[6] Philip Pettit, *Just Freedom* (Norton 2014) 170.

[7] ibid 169–70.

[8] Wojciech Sadurski, 'Supranational Public Reason: On Legitimacy of Supranational Norm-Producing Authorities' (2015) 4 Global Constitutionalism 396.

However, I will assume here, again without much argument, that *democratic* legitimacy at a supranational level is, at best, embryonic and thin in comparison with any persuasive notions of democracy that we usually fashion based on the nation state (or sub-national) context, which is a proper paradigmatic site for democracy. It is *this* concern that drives most of our reflections upon the legitimacy of supranational norm-producing authorities.

The thinking about the legitimacy of such authorities has been affected and facilitated by the 'constitutional turn' in the scholarship of international law and international relations. As Anne Peters observes, the language of global constitutionalism may help emphasize the disconnection of legitimacy from the nation state: '[T]he constitutionalist reading [of international law] should clarify that the legitimacy of norms and of political rule does not depend on the structures of government or governance being exactly state-like'.[9] This is convincing insofar as the notion of legitimacy is, among other things, an important constitutional notion, in that one of the most important functions of a constitution is to confer legitimacy upon all constitutionally established institutions and upon the norms they produce. As a result, an extension of legitimacy beyond the nation state in such a constitutional perspective is natural. However, the question this raises is what *concept* of legitimacy we wish to use in that sphere, especially once we have dispensed with (as we have to) the predominantly democratic *conceptions* of legitimacy of supranational authorities—and this is the proper subject matter of this part of the chapter.

Let me begin with an unashamedly pre-theoretical, intuitive attempt at identifying 'the point' of having a standard of legitimacy. Under my semantic intuitions (admittedly, a problematic starting point, but one has to start somewhere), it is a standard located halfway between the benchmarks of validity and justice. It is stronger than validity because it confers *some* moral authority upon a norm, but is weaker than justice because reasonable people can disagree about the justness of a particular norm while agreeing upon its legitimacy. Hence, it is a typically liberal standard about the grounds for respecting a rule the merits of which we do not necessarily agree upon. Accordingly, a good test for the legitimacy of a rule is to ask ourselves whether we should respect it (deem it legitimate) despite disagreeing with its substance.[10]

Three distinctions concerning the concept of legitimacy are important and include: (1) weak and strong legitimacy; (2) the legitimacy of authority and the legitimacy of authoritative decisions; and (3) 'subject fragmented' and 'subject uniform' concepts.

First, legitimacy is sometimes taken to be equivalent to a duty to obey a legitimate rule so that once we validate an authority or a decision as legitimate, we must conclude that we (people within the authority's jurisdiction) have a duty to obey

[9] Anne Peters, 'The Merits of Global Constitutionalism' (2009) 16 Indiana Journal of Global Legal Studies 397, 410.

[10] This is, of course, a deliberately cursory formulation. For my more extensive reflections on the notion of legitimacy, see Wojciech Sadurski, *Equality and Legitimacy* (Oxford University Press 2008) esp 1–17, 237–45.

it. This is a strong meaning of legitimacy, but is by no means the only or even the dominant understanding of legitimacy in legal philosophy. There is also a weak understanding of legitimacy whereby to state that an authority is legitimate is to say that its holder has a right to issue authoritative directives, but the only categorical, correlative duty of citizens is to consider these directives with a degree of respect, although not necessarily to obey. If the authority's legitimacy is based predominantly on a certain form of *justification* of its decisions, as is arguably the case with Joseph Raz's 'service conception of authority' (if we read it in the language of legitimacy),[11] then we need some *extra* arguments to support our duty to obey. No one has a duty to obey a decision merely by virtue of the fact that it is justified: it may be prudent or even wise to do so, but no one has a duty to be prudent or wise. So, I understand legitimacy as an attribute related to the *justification* of decisions; that is, this chapter adopts a weak sense of legitimacy because it seems better suited to the supranational level, where the grounds of compliance are more contested and feebler than in a nation-state setting.

Second, legitimacy may be seen as an attribute of either authorities (regime legitimacy) or their specific decisions. At first sight, this may seem to be a pedantic distinction, and we may be tempted to admit that, by definition, legitimate authorities issue legitimate decisions, and decisions are legitimate by virtue of being issued by legitimate authorities—but it is not necessarily so. On occasion, illegitimate authorities may issue legitimate decisions, while legitimate authorities may issue illegitimate laws from time to time. Nothing of conceptual clarity is achieved by connecting these two things by definitional fiat. As stated, there may be decisions made by legitimate authorities that breach the principles of legitimacy—for instance, due to procedural defects or violation of rights which the regime otherwise respects. As Philip Pettit observes: '[T]here is ... room for claiming in the same sense of the term that while a regime is generally legitimate, certain laws or appointments ... are illegitimate: they happen to breach conditions of legitimacy that the regime generally respects'.[12] I prefer, in this chapter, to focus on the legitimacy of decisions rather than that of authorities or polities because this dimension seems better suited to supranational spheres where we *may* identify—without much uncertainty—various rules, decisions, instructions, or guidelines which are meant to be binding upon states, but where the existence of supranational 'authorities'—not to mention 'polities'—is much less certain.

Third, we may have concepts of legitimacy derived from an individual perception of how the rule is justified in the light of the addressee's own preferences and, on the other hand, we may have concepts that locate the quality of legitimacy in the character of the rules themselves. In this chapter, I adopt the former concept, that is, legitimacy is something that must be perceived as such *by* someone, and

[11] Joseph Raz, *Ethics in the Public Domain: Essays in the Morality of Law and Politics* (Oxford University Press 1994) 211–15.

[12] Philip Pettit, *On the People's Terms: A Republican Theory and Model of Democracy* (Cambridge University Press 2012) 139.

more particularly, by the addressees of norms, decisions, or rules. Again, Raz's 'service conception' is a good example: whether an authoritative directive is found legitimate under the 'normal justification' test is crucially dependent upon a person's values and preferences, and these will vary among the addressees of the same rule. In this sense, subjects *confer* the legitimacy of authorities or—to put it more mildly—legitimacy is *recognized* by subjects. Here, authorities may aspire to, or claim, legitimacy, but this legitimacy will only exist when it is recognized by those to whom the putatively legitimate directives are addressed. John Tasioulas labels this characteristic, in his discussion of the legitimacy of international law, 'subject fragmentation'. This means that certain norms may enjoy legitimacy with respect to some, but not all, of its putative subjects.[13] To put this in a slightly different way and make the point sharper, legitimacy—under this concept—is in the eyes of the beholder. Thus, it does not pertain to the rules themselves, but, rather, to an addressee's perception of the quality of the rule. This feature holds special importance in the supranational sphere, where the variety of circumstances, interests, traditions, and cultures is wider than on a national scale, and where these differences may trigger more widely divergent perceptions of the legitimacy of authoritative norms.

To sum up the conceptual argument about legitimacy so far: I adopt here a concept of legitimacy which is (1) weak, (2) about specific decisions/rules, and (3) 'subject fragmented'. In turn, my preferred *conception* of legitimacy, as applicable to supranational authorities, is an extrapolation (*mutatis mutandis*) of a familiar idea of the public-reason-based liberal principle of legitimacy. It starts from a stipulation that the legitimacy of political decisions depends upon the nature of the *reasons* provided for these decisions—and not only 'provided', but also demonstrable, as the most likely purposes pursued by a decision-maker. Accordingly, a 'public reason' conception of legitimacy claims that publicly admissible reasons which are endorsable (or non-refutable) by those to whom they apply confer legitimacy upon decisions.[14]

The idea of public reason insists on screening off the rationales for public coercive action which are factional or self-interested in a way that makes them unacceptable to some addressees of the decision. In Jürgen Neyer's good formula: 'Justifications are speech acts that aim at legitimating one's own preferences by providing evidence for their compatibility with the shared goals of the community'.[15] Correspondingly, decisions or norms issued by authorities, including by supranational ones, must match this criterion of compatibility with shared goals.

[13] John Tasioulas, 'The Legitimacy of International Law' in Samantha Besson and John Tasioulas (eds), *The Philosophy of International Law* (Oxford University Press 2010) 103.

[14] See John Rawls, *Political Liberalism* (Columbia University Press 1993) 212–54; John Rawls, 'The Idea of Public Reason Revisited' in *The Law of Peoples, with 'The Idea of Public Reason Revisited'* (Harvard University Press 1999).

[15] Jürgen Neyer, 'Justice and the Right to Justification: Conceptual Reflections' in Dimitry Kochenov, Gráinne de Búrca, and Andrew Williams (eds), *Europe's Justice Deficit?* (Hart Publishing 2015) 216.

B. Two Conceptions of Public Reason beyond Borders

In this part of the chapter, I will examine the differences between SPR, as I understand it, and the concept of 'public reason of the Society of Peoples', as outlined in John Rawls's 'The Law of Peoples' ('LP').[16] This distinction is important because the conception of public reason, as understood in contemporary political philosophy, is based primarily on Rawls's theory. Rawls mainly discusses the concept of public reason in *Political Liberalism* and in his essay 'The Idea of Public Reason Revisited'. Interestingly, this essay has been published in the same volume as LP, which may suggest that Rawls identified a degree of affinity between public reason at a state level and in 'the Society of Peoples'. One would therefore be excused for thinking that Rawls simply extrapolated his original notion of 'public reason' (constructed, as it originally was, for a territorially bounded liberal society) into an international sphere. This is further confirmed by Rawls's express statement that 'the role of public reason among free and equal peoples is analogous to its role in a constitutional democratic regime among free and equal citizens'.[17]

And yet, SPR, for the purposes of this chapter, is fundamentally different from Rawls's 'public reason of the Society of Peoples' (or, as I will occasionally call it for brevity, 'international public reason'). The main difference is that Rawls's 'international public reason' concerns a *horizontal* realm, that is, the relationship between states, or peoples, while SPR, as used in this chapter, is primarily about vertical relations, that is, between supranational authorities and states (and other entities). That Rawls's concept applies only to horizontal relations is obvious to any reader of 'LP': we are told, for instance, that the book concerns 'the ideals and principles of the *foreign policy*';[18] the 'mutual relations' of liberal peoples 'as peoples';[19] 'a foreign policy and affairs of state that involve other societies';[20] 'a particular political conception of right and justice that applies to the principles and norms of international law and practice';[21] and 'the political relations among peoples'.[22] As one can see, the privileged locus of Rawlsian international public reason is international law—traditionally conceived—as governing the relations between states (called here peoples). This 'horizontality' of Rawls's conception is bolstered by the idea of the Law of Peoples (as a conception, not just the title of the essay), which is the proper space for Rawlsian international public reason, and which is about the relationships traditionally controlled by international law and international relations between sovereign states.

Of course, the 'horizontality' of Rawls's Law of Peoples is not merely an incidental feature of his theory, but is adopted for good reasons. An investigation of these reasons is useful to put into perspective the difference between the two conceptions of public reason in the international sphere: that of Rawls and that which is affirmed

[16] John Rawls, 'The Law of Peoples' in *The Law of Peoples, with 'The Idea of Public Reason Revisited'* (Harvard University Press 1999).

[17] ibid 55. [18] ibid (emphasis added). [19] ibid. [20] ibid 56.

[21] ibid 3. [22] ibid 57.

in this chapter. In order to explain this difference, I will proceed as follows: I will first describe two 'puzzles' about Rawls's theory, which are (1) the status of illiberal (though 'decent') peoples in the Law of Peoples, and (2) the special characteristics of the social contract employed to reach the principles that make up the Law of Peoples; I will then suggest that the underlying moral value adopted by Rawls in LP is toleration understood in a specific and controversial way; finally, I will explain why the meaning of toleration adopted by Rawls for the purposes of 'LP' is deficient and, therefore, why his understanding of international public reason (underwritten, as it is, by his conception of toleration) is not helpful as a legitimacy-conferring device.

The first, perhaps most striking, puzzle in Rawls's theory is the status of 'illiberal decent peoples'. The distinction between liberal peoples and other 'well-ordered' societies that are also 'worthy of membership in a Society of Peoples' is of central importance to Rawls's theory. To be characterized as *liberal*, a state must meet certain relatively stringent requirements for liberal-democratic institutions and rights, including those described in Part III of Rawls's *Political Liberalism*. The problem begins with the characterization of societies that are not liberal and yet deserve to be recognized as 'equal participating members in good standing of the Society of Peoples'.[23] The main aim of such recognition is the ascertainment of 'how far liberal peoples are to *tolerate* non-liberal peoples'.[24] 'Toleration', in this context, goes far beyond simple non-intervention: it includes, on the part of liberal peoples, 'a duty of civility requiring that they offer other peoples public reasons appropriate to the Society of Peoples for their actions'.[25] In this way, illiberal yet decent peoples enter into the community in which public reason governs mutual relationships.

There are three main ways in which illiberal-decent peoples, in Rawls's terminology, depart from the standards of liberal peoples. First, they incorporate certain 'basic inequalities among their members';[26] second, there is *some* liberty of conscience, but not '*equal* liberty of conscience'[27]—this may include, for instance, an established state religion, as long as other religions are not persecuted;[28] third, these people lack what we would consider a normal system of political, representative democratic institutions, but instead have a 'decent consultation hierarchy'.[29] Embracing societies tainted by such important defects (from a liberal-democratic perspective) into the community of peoples raises, for a liberal, a serious dilemma. If we refuse, in our own societies, respect to those moral-political conceptions that would postulate redesigning our societies along these illiberal lines, why should we respect such societies *abroad*? The only solution to this puzzle lies in the specific notion of toleration adopted by Rawls—a point to which I will return below.

The second puzzle about LP is a redesign of the social contract, as compared to the account in *A Theory of Justice* ('*TJ*').[30] In moving from *TJ* to LP, Rawls made significant changes in the description of the conditions of the social contract. These changes are responsible for the startling thinness of the Law of Peoples as a *critical* theory of international justice. The main change was in the composition of the

[23] ibid 59. [24] ibid (emphasis added). [25] ibid. [26] ibid 70.
[27] ibid (emphasis added). [28] ibid 76. [29] ibid 71.
[30] John Rawls, *A Theory of Justice* (Harvard University Press 1971).

'participants' in the deliberative process in the original position: those operating in *TJ* as spokespersons for the *individuals* representing different social groups and strata have been replaced in LP by 'peoples' as the relevant parties to the social contract. It is important to recognize the implications of this move. If individuals were to be represented in the original contract, the confining of the rules of international justice to the eight principles articulated by Rawls would be indefensible.[31] Under the method of social contract behind the veil of ignorance, the principles of international justice would have to consist of the rules that would have been plausibly agreed upon by the representative individuals, *each unaware of the specific society to which they belong*. This type of ignorance would correspond to the *TJ*-style veil of ignorance, that is, ignorance as to (among other things) an individual's place in a real society in which one will find oneself once the social contract has been concluded. If, in contrast, it is the 'peoples' who are represented, understood as unitary corporate entities, the Law of Peoples as a fair system of international justice becomes much more convincing because it is incomparably less ambitious.

Consequently, a major change effected in the transition from *TJ* to LP in the design of the conditions of the social contract is in the selectiveness of the composition of the parties in the latter. In *TJ*, no representative position in a society, however defined, was a priori excluded from a role in contributing to the hypothetical contract. In LP, in contrast, only some peoples are included in the contract-making: namely the 'well-ordered' peoples. It should be noted that this category, in Rawls's taxonomy, occupies the two highest positions in the classifications of peoples on the planet: the liberal and non-liberal but 'decent' peoples. All the remaining peoples (which Rawls divides into 'outlaw states', 'societies burdened by unfavourable conditions', and 'benevolent absolutisms')[32] remain beyond the pale and do not participate in the contract. This, of course, is a consequence of the 'peoples-based' rather than the 'individuals-based' contract. If the rules of international justice were to be contracted by the representatives of individuals, the luckless inhabitants of the last three categories of societies would be in greatest need of the benefits derived from the critical potential of international justice, and they would correspond to the representative worst-off persons in *TJ*.

What can justify such a change? The social contract stands *for something*, and the impoverishment thereof reflects a change in the model of reasoning. In *Political Liberalism*, Rawls insisted that the 'social contract' is a device of representation of our moral reasoning on justice. It models 'restrictions on reasons in such a way that it becomes perfectly evident which agreement would be made by the parties as citizens' representatives'.[33] Accordingly, in LP, Rawls declares: 'Since the original position includes the veil of ignorance, it also models what we regard as appropriate *restrictions on reasons* for adopting a political conception of justice'.[34] By disallowing

[31] The eight principles of the Law of Peoples are: (1) freedom and independence of peoples; (2) duty to observe treaties; (3) equality of the peoples; (4) duty of non-intervention; (5) the right of self-defence as the only reason to instigate war; (6) honouring of human rights; (7) restrictions in the conduct of war; and (8) a duty to assist other peoples. Rawls, 'The Law of Peoples' (n 16) 37.

[32] ibid 62–63.

[33] Rawls, *Political Liberalism* (n 14) 26.

[34] Rawls, 'The Law of Peoples' (n 16) 30 (emphasis added).

the parties to the original position a choice from a reasonably broad menu of possible principles, and by confining their choice to those principles that can be culled only 'from the history and usages of international law and practice',[35] Rawls clearly identifies rigorous restrictions upon reasons available to the parties in the original position when the rules of international justice are to be decided. These reasons are largely confined to the already existing (although properly pruned) principles of customary law and good international practices.

These two puzzles about the status of illiberal peoples and the erosion of social-contract methodology can only be explained, in my view, by the overarching value that is responsible, in LP, for these features of the theory: the ideal of toleration. There can be very little doubt to readers of LP that whenever troubling questions concerning the bias in favour of realism in the 'realistic utopia' appear, it is the importance of toleration for non-liberal societies that is provided as an answer. Samuel Freeman accurately states that: 'Rawls's primary aim in *The Law of Peoples* is to define the limits of liberal people's *toleration* of nonliberal peoples'.[36]

In explaining why liberals should not attempt to force their ideals of good society upon non-liberal peoples, Rawls states in LP that '[i]f all societies were required to be liberal, the idea of political liberalism would fail to express *due toleration* for other acceptable ways (if such there are, as I assume) of ordering society'.[37] In the same context, Rawls urges that his use of the word 'toleration' goes beyond the precept of non-interference: '[T]o tolerate means not only to refrain from exercising political sanctions—military, economic, or diplomatic—to make a people change its ways. To tolerate also means to recognize these nonliberal societies as equal participating members in good standing of the Society of Peoples, with certain rights and obligations . . .'.[38]

However, if toleration is an answer, what was the question? Before inquiring into whether the ideal of toleration can perform such an onerous job as it is assigned in Rawls's theory (encapsulated in my argument above as accounting for two 'puzzles'), it is important to be clear about the *function* that the ideal of toleration *may* perform (if we share the assessment of its worth) in a conception of international justice such as Rawls's. To put it in negative terms, it is important to clarify what the ideal of toleration is *not* about in this context.

Toleration is not about the permissibility and the potential scope of governmental interference by one state (say, a liberal state) with the institutional and legal arrangements of another state (say, a non-liberal state). This is clear from Rawls's own declarations, as quoted above, and has also been observed by perceptive commentators on Rawls's work.[39] An initial question, preceding that of possible sanctions and interference, is whether we, as individuals, have sound reasons to try and effect change within societies that we dislike. The principle of toleration may pre-empt,

[35] ibid 41.

[36] Samuel Freeman, 'Introduction: John Rawls—An Overview' in Samuel Freeman (ed), *The Cambridge Companion to Rawls* (Cambridge University Press 2003) 46 (emphasis added).

[37] Rawls, 'The Law of Peoples' (n 16) 59 (emphasis added).

[38] ibid.

[39] See Charles R Beitz, *The Idea of Human Rights* (Oxford University Press 2009) 154.

and render improper, such an aspiration at *this* stage, even before the question of governmental interference arises. To be sure, Rawls, at times, appears to be oscillating between two orders: the order of an ideal theory containing prescriptions for individual liberal citizens and the order of pragmatic policy proposals with prescriptions for governmental action. He states, for example, in a phrase which would support the latter interpretation: 'A decent hierarchical society meets moral and legal requirements sufficient to override the political reasons we might have for *imposing sanctions* on, or *forcibly interfering* with, its people and their institutions and culture.'[40] However, the principle of toleration that is relevant to the context of international justice (in order to play the role assigned to it, ie explaining why we should embrace some non-liberal societies within the Law of Peoples) does not answer the question of the acceptability of governmental sanctions or coercive interference. It should be treated in the context of international justice as an ethical norm rather than a pragmatic policy recommendation. From this perspective, the question is whether this ethical norm is capable of supporting the inclusion of hierarchical, non-liberal but decent peoples into the Society of Peoples with the consequences described by Rawls? Or, working backwards in the chain of reasoning (and bringing in the second 'puzzle'), whether the norm is capable of persuading us to modify the rules of the social contract, with constraints on the options, the abandonment of the maximin strategy, and—most importantly—the replacement of individuals by 'peoples' in the original position?

Regardless of which conception of—and rationale for—toleration we choose, it would have to be for the asserted good of the individuals concerned (the beneficiaries of our toleration). The moral worth of the principle of toleration would stem from the alleged benefit to the individual to whom 'toleration' is due. Otherwise, the toleration would be left in a moral vacuum. It would be perverse to demand toleration for an individual's choices if we thought that there was no corresponding benefit (of high moral significance) conferred upon the individual concerned. Ultimately, toleration is based upon normative individualism. It is the good of the individual (the 'recipient' of toleration) that endows the ideal of toleration with moral worth.

However, LP fails to identify any convincing connection between the principle of toleration and the resulting good to individuals who are to be tolerated. Instead, in Rawls's book it is the peoples, rather than the individuals themselves, who are the avowed beneficiaries of the principle of toleration. But if a 'people', through its institutional design and practices, is intolerant towards some of its members, then the benefits of liberal toleration are due to those individuals rather than to the 'people'—it is *their* good that is the ultimate source of the moral worth of toleration. Rawls never tries to convince his audience, and we have no reason to believe, that individual members of the illiberal but decent peoples are the net beneficiaries of the principle of toleration as espoused in LP. The central question that would have to be asked is: What is the balance of benefits and costs for individual members of the decent hierarchical societies resulting from the international adoption of

[40] Rawls, 'The Law of Peoples' (n 16) 83 (emphases added).

the principle of toleration towards such societies? If Rawls had followed the line of reasoning suggested by this question, he would no doubt have had to give a rather complex answer: he would have had to admit that the benefits and costs divide unequally *within* hierarchical societies, and that some are net beneficiaries, while others (perhaps, a majority) are net losers. For instance, the principle of 'toleration' of gender inequality in a hierarchical society will definitely make many people worse off (compared to the outcomes of international *in*tolerance), even though it will also make some people satisfied in sustaining their ways of life based, as they are, on societal discrimination against women. But the connection between the principle of toleration and an unequal distribution of the benefits and costs produced by this principle for its alleged beneficiaries is not elucidated in LP. Rather, this consideration is simply precluded by identifying 'peoples' as the beneficiaries of the principle of toleration.

Moreover, an advocate of Rawls's principle of toleration would have to go one step further and test not only whether different members of decent hierarchical societies benefited from non-interference by liberal societies, but also whether they actually *supported* it. The exercise of 'toleration' towards someone who does not want it loses its moral value. In this sense, 'paternalistic tolerance' is a contradiction in terms. To be sure, it would be difficult to verify whether all (or even many) members of 'hierarchical but decent' societies favour the policy of non-interference in their domestic arrangements. By the very description of those societies provided by Rawls, a reliable account of the views, values, and public opinion in those societies, is not easily available. But in general, it is a plausible hypothesis that those who do support external interference find themselves on the lowest rung of the social ladder and would thus be representative of the worst-off people who—from the *TJ* perspective—would need to be considered first in designing the system of justice. Unless we adopt a deeply implausible (and alien to the overall philosophical system of Rawls as developed in *TJ* and *Political Liberalism*) collectivist ontology of 'a people', under which it constitutes a single entity with its own undifferentiated subjectivity, we have no reason to accept at face value the declarations of the leaders (and their ideologues) of 'decent hierarchical peoples' concerning the true values of those peoples.

In conclusion: in its aspiration, rationales, and effects, Rawls's 'public reason of the Society of Peoples' concerns the relationship between states, as designed by the states themselves, and the shape of international law as traditionally understood (with states being its only subjects). This construct is fundamentally different from SPR, as understood in this chapter. Moreover, the principle of toleration, which plays such a pivotal role in Rawls's theory, is highly contestable. Rawls applies it to states, not the individual members of states or peoples. This is an odd and question-begging ideal. However, even if it were meaningful and attractive, it would not perform the same function of legitimating authoritative decisions and norms as the SPR is tasked to perform. The principle of toleration is not a device of legitimating authoritative decisions, but rather one concerning mutual relationships among individuals who disapprove of one another's values. In this way, it is not a 'vertical' value, so to speak, and does not govern the limits on the use of coercion by authorities. Accordingly, to say that a state 'tolerates' an individual action is a misnomer, and to say that a state expresses 'intolerance' through a prohibition on individual action is a misleading metaphor. The prohibition may reflect a prior intolerance within the society, but such intolerance per se is not relevant to the judgement of legitimacy under a conception of public reason. Rather, it may be based on reasons which are publicly avowable, or not. Hence, there is no congruency between the value of toleration and that of public reason, including in its supranational version.

C. Supranational Public Reason and the Question of Legitimacy

Supranationalism provides a space in which there should be a degree of synchronization between national and international actors based on standards of justification of authoritative directives by appeal to public reasons. This is the key assumption behind a 'translation' of a state-based public reason conception of legitimacy into the supranational arena. When state-based parties and, in particular, individual citizens (but also associations, business entities, NGOs, etc) contest decisions taken at a national level and demand scrutiny at a supranational level of claims that are improper or for which insufficient reasons have been provided at the state level, supranational legitimacy may be fashioned even without any concern for the democratic (or otherwise) pedigree of those supranational scrutineers.

This general proposition may sound irritatingly Panglossian, so before attempting to substantiate it, two caveats must be made. First, the proposition does not apply to the entire supranational sphere—I am not making a claim that every supranational authority, as we know them, follows the pattern of public reason. It is an ideal, not an account. Second, it does not apply to *any* exercise of authority by those supranational institutions which *can* be seen as exemplars of supranational public reason. Rather, the proposition is a certain ideal model of what happens when supranational authorities are at their best. The point of this proposition is to claim that some supranational authorities may open up the space for legitimating their non-state-based authority by appeals to public reason and thus effectively fill the gap created by the absence of democratic legitimacy.

Most requirements of public reason are not specific to the supranational sphere, although at a supranational level they acquire a special urgency due to the absence of a default legitimating factor: democratic decision-making. Allen Buchanan, for one, has developed a convincing theory of international human rights based on the epistemic requirements of a credible public justification. As Buchanan observes: 'The legitimacy of an international order grounded in the commitment to human rights depends in part upon whether there is a credible public justification for human-rights norms and decisions by international human rights institutions.'[41] These requirements amount to an overall general threshold quality for legal decisions. This is what Armin von Bogdandy and Ingo Venzke call 'the legitimatory significance of justifying legal decisions in a way which lives up to the standards of the profession

[41] Allen Buchanan, 'Human Rights and the Legitimacy of the International Order' (2008) 14 Legal Theory 39, 63.

and that meets expectations of participants in legal discourse'.[42] However, other conditions are more specific to *supranational* authorities. These include epistemic access to broad comparative material and to an enlarged sample of views, and the capacity to harmonize and coordinate norms and actions on a large scale.

The most attractive exemplars of SPR (even if only present in a rudimentary and imperfect form) are provided by supranational adjudicatory bodies, such as international and regional courts and tribunals, including the ECtHR. It is the force of reasons and the persuasiveness of reason-giving that, in a situation of diverse state and non-state actors who need to solve specific problems of a global dimension, may provide proper grounds for the legitimacy of supranational standards and the decisions taken by international courts. A condition is that the nature of the reasons provided for such standards and decisions are such that 'others can be expected to acknowledge, even as they disagree about how the variety of relevant reasons add up'.[43]

A variety of transnational legitimate authorities are supported by different kinds of transnational networks, which constitute quasi-communities; no legitimate authority is likely to exist transnationally without such supporting networks. Accordingly, the *expertise* which they possess—or claim to possess—may be a source of legitimacy for some transnational authorities, such as various standard-setting bodies which regulate transnational industries, cross-border trade and finance, transnational professions, and sports authorities. Such standard-setting authorities are rarely democratically created and maintained, but rely on an acknowledgment by the addressees of their regulations—often on the basis of recognized technical expertise or, at least, upon their capacity for efficient *coordination* and identification of solutions to collective-action problems. This coordinating function of international law was stressed by Samantha Besson, who applied this conception to 'the need for international regulation on difficult matters of common concern among subjects whose diversity of views creates pervasive and persistent disagreements'.[44]

It is, of course, not surprising that judicial or quasi-judicial bodies provide the best examples of supranational public reason in action. As Alec Stone Sweet puts it: 'Courts . . . govern not through the sword or the purse, but through reason-based justification and the propagation of argumentation frameworks (doctrine), to the extent that they draw non-judicial actors into dynamic, "jurisgenerative" fields of action'.[45] Ultimately, the authority of international judicial bodies rests upon the force of the arguments they provide. This is the case even where states within their jurisdiction commit themselves to respect and abide by their rulings, as there is usually no system of enforcement other than that of a symbolic, 'naming and shaming'

[42] Armin von Bogdandy and Ingo Venzke, 'On the Democratic Legitimation of International Judicial Lawmaking' (2011) 12 German Law Journal 1341, 1344.

[43] Joshua Cohen and Charles F Sabel, 'Global Democracy?' (2004) 37 New York University Journal of International Law & Politics 763, 780.

[44] Samantha Besson, 'The Authority of International Law: Lifting the State Veil' (2009) 31 Sydney Law Review 343, 367.

[45] Alec Stone Sweet, 'A Cosmopolitan Legal Order: Constitutional Pluralism and Rights Adjudication in Europe' (2012) 1 Global Constitutionalism 53, 54–55.

character. It is rare—as is the case in EU law—that the implementation of the top court's decisions is entrusted formally to national courts. Where this occurs, it produces the effect of strong 'embeddedness', meaning that supranational decisions 'can be implemented without governments having to take actions to do so'.[46]

My main example of SPR in action is that of the ECtHR: a court that was initially set up as an extraordinary, super-appellate judicial body, but which has become (in recent decades) a quasi-constitutional court for Europe. The fundamental purpose of the ECtHR is to scrutinize the reasons provided by states to justify laws and decisions which putatively infringe the European Convention on Human Rights ('European Convention').[47] Of particular importance in this context is the Court's use of proportionality analysis. As Mattias Kumm observed:

> Since comparatively little is decided [under a proportionality analysis] by acknowledging that a measure infringes a right, the focus of rights adjudication is generally on the reasons which justify the infringement ... Assessing the justification for rights infringements is ... largely an exercise of structured practical reasoning without many of the constraining features that otherwise characterizes legal reasoning.[48]

The role of the ECtHR in conducting practical reasoning that resonates with an idea of public reason has been greatly facilitated by a combination of (1) explicit catalogues of permissible and legitimate aims, which may justify public-reason-oriented restrictions on some rights in the European Convention (namely, the non-absolute rights in Articles 8 to 11) and (2) a canonical proportionality analysis, which assigns a separate stage in argument to an assessment of legislative aims, as cited by governments in defence of the laws impugned. An important, potentially legitimating virtue of a proportionality analysis is that it has become a quasi-universal idiom of contextual and purposeful analysis of legal rights. As Michel Rosenfeld noted, writing about proportionality analysis as part of the constitutional ordering of different constitutional levels, 'using the same test within different layers and segments is likely to create parallels and greater congruity ... Proportionality and balancing ... can cement both vertical and horizontal congruencies without relying on a hierarchy or any imposed conciliation across constitutional units'.[49] After all, for the legitimacy of supranational decisions, it is not necessary that they identify a *consensus* with the addressees at the level of states—that is often impossible and, in any event, may not be useful for legitimacy. But there must be a degree of commonality in language, idiom, approach, and method of analysis. Beyond this, divergences of values and choices need not undermine supranational legitimacy. Accordingly, judgements of a supranational court, such as the ECtHR, will be read and often

[46] Robert O Keohane, Andrew Moravcsik, and Anne-Marie Slaughter, 'Legalized Dispute Resolution: Interstate and Transnational' (2000) 54 International Organization 457, 458.

[47] Convention for the Protection of Human Rights and Fundamental Freedoms (opened for signature 4 November 1950, entered into force 3 September 1953) 213 UNTS 221.

[48] Mattias Kumm, 'Institutionalising Socratic Contestation: The Rationalist Human Rights Paradigm, Legitimate Authority and the Point of Judicial Review' (2007) 1 European Journal of Legal Studies 1, 11–12 <http://cadmus.eui.eu/handle/1814/7708> accessed 2 November 2018.

[49] Michel Rosenfeld, 'Rethinking Constitutional Ordering in an Era of Legal and Constitutional Pluralism' (2008) 6 International Journal of Constitutional Law 415, 451–52.

applied by courts belonging to varied legal systems, and this awareness must be built into the reasoning provided by the ECtHR.

Proportionality analysis, with a broad, teleological character (mainly due to scrutiny of the legislative goals), provides an example of such a pattern. This, in turn, may be well understood and adopted across a broad range of legal cultures, while 'more formal types of arguments (e.g. textual interpretation) tend to be more dependent on the legal culture and language of a particular legal order, [and therefore] they travel less easily among different legal orders'.[50] In this way, proportionality analysis may be seen as a universal template: the language and methodology in which judges of different legal systems can recognize their reasoning as familiar and as conducted in a single, common register. Emily Crawford puts it well: '[T]he proportionality principle becomes self-perpetuating: as proportionality is given significant consideration by judges, so too do States, lawyers, governmental officials, and all other players in the field become more adept at utilizing the lexicon of proportionality analysis'.[51] There is a legitimating force to it in the same way in which doctors, priests, musicians, or computer experts from different countries can immediately recognize and validate each other's competence and authority. This universal, legitimating power of proportionality analysis may be seen as a password which provides an entry into the supranational conversation of judges and 'gives the legal system an entry card into the global community of judges'.[52]

The universal acceptance of proportionality analysis as a common matrix for evaluating rights restrictions has prevented the ECtHR's jurisprudence from collapsing into a 'lowest common denominator' approach, that is, a minimalist approach of erring on the side of the validation of the state-imposed restrictions that would effectively undermine the Court's legitimacy in the eyes of the general public. Rather, the internal workings of the proportionality analysis—with its in-built presumption against rights restrictions, displayed in the 'necessity' test (a test of the least restrictive alternatives)—favours a strong rights-protective approach and a ratcheting-up of the understandings of the European Convention's rights. Further, as proportionality analysis is underwritten by a highly rights-protective aspiration and a high degree of distrust in governmental intrusions into constitutional rights, the use of the proportionality analysis in international/supranational communication among judges is likely to produce a 'race to the top', whereby different courts pride themselves as being among the rights-protective league.[53] As courts aspire to be rights-protective,

[50] Miguel Poiares Maduro, 'Courts and Pluralism: Essay on a Theory of Judicial Adjudication in the Context of Legal and Constitutional Pluralism' in Jeffrey L Dunoff and Joel P Trachtman (eds), *Ruling the World? Constitutionalism, International Law, and Global Governance* (Cambridge University Press 2009) 356, 370.

[51] Emily Crawford, 'Proportionality' in Rüdiger Wolfrum (ed), *Max Planck Encyclopedia of Public International Law* (May 2011) para 7 <http://opil.ouplaw.com/view/10.1093/law:epil/9780199231690/law-9780199231690-e1459> accessed 8 April 2018.

[52] Moshe Cohen-Eliya and Iddo Porat, *Proportionality and Constitutional Culture* (Cambridge University Press 2013) 134.

[53] ibid 134–36.

the proportionality analysis provides a matrix for comparison and for making such claims credible.

What does the example of the ECtHR, as the most advanced supranational judicial body of today, tell us about the concept of legitimacy in the new constitutional architecture of the world? In particular, what can the ECtHR tell us about the relationship between supranational public reason and democracy-based legitimacy at the state level? One lesson that can be drawn is that, rather than justification-based legitimacy eclipsing democracy, there is potential for an important synergy. Democracy at state level supports supranational reason-giving (justificatory discipline) because states with multi-level governance retain their meaningful constitutional status as an important—although no longer exclusive—site of their legitimacy.

Vice versa, supranational public reason may also support and help improve democracy at a state level. This is best seen in the field of international human rights. As Joshua Cohen and Charles Sabel note: '[H]uman rights claims can be presented as elements of a global standard—*a global public reason*, itself part of global politics—that sets out conditions of acceptable treatment, requiring in particular that political societies assure conditions of membership for those who live in their territory'.[54] In engaging with international human rights, legal and constitutional actors at a state level commit themselves to transposing 'global standard[s]'—dubbed by Cohen and Sabel as 'global public reason'—to their state constitutional structures. For instance, an argument can be made that, when national constitutions make reference to international law and international standards—and, in particular, to international human rights law—they tacitly empower (confer legitimacy upon) transnational adjudicatory bodies to scrutinize national laws and decisions because those bodies are better positioned to ascertain and interpret transnational standards.[55] The ECtHR, for instance, by virtue of its position and expertise, is better placed to understand what the European standards *are* and whether they are sufficiently close to being consensual in order to restrict or exclude a state's margin of appreciation on the matter. In this way, the ECtHR engages directly with the domestic constitutional process. Through a sort of 'boomerang effect', the wider epistemic basis available to supranational bodies can subsequently enhance the range of information (eg 'best practices') and normativity (foreign and supranational standards) available to national judges and politicians and thus improve the quality of democratic decision-making at the national level.

Even where a well-established, state-based democracy gives proper effect to the majority opinion, it is often likely to be insensitive to minorities and will have inbuilt incentives to amend democratic procedures in ways that privilege the current political majority. These dysfunctions of nation-state-based democracy may, at least to some extent, be corrected by international human rights norms and through interventions of supranational institutions. In other words, transnational intervention

[54] Cohen and Sabel, 'Global Democracy?' (n 43) 788 (emphasis added).

[55] See Mattias Kumm, 'An Integrative Theory of Global Public Law: Cosmopolitan, Pluralist, Public Reason Oriented' (manuscript) 51–52. I am grateful to Professor Kumm for his kind permission to refer to and quote this unpublished paper.

may do to national democracy what John Hart Ely famously proclaimed to be the main function of judicial review within the United States' system of government: facilitate the representation of minorities and clear the channels of political change.[56] It can therefore protect national democracy against democratically adopted restrictions on the democratic system.

A transnationally driven enhancement of democracy can be seen to occur even more clearly in 'transitional' democracies. It is in such regimes that supranational human rights norms are of particular importance. Such norms do not ascertain a common denominator of the rights already universally recognized and protected at a national level (as was the tacit understanding behind the initial setting-up of the ECtHR system in 1950), but rather they identify an aspiration—serving as a critical measure of law reform—within a newly democratized state. Human rights standards, backed by supranational institutions, resonate with the incentives of some segments of the new leadership (often recruited from former dissidents and democratic opposition) to form an alliance with supranational bodies in countering a possible reversal to the bad old days when human rights were neglected.

Such standards are even more necessary in the cases of 'troubled', 'failed', or 'fragile' states. As Michel Rosenfeld noted, when analysing what he called 'the Internationally Grounded Model' of constitution-making, in such cases the incorporation of certain external norms and standards is accompanied by the fact that 'substantial decision making power over the substantive particulars of the constitution-in-the-making must be left in the hands of relevant political actors within the nation-state affected'.[57] Internationally sponsored/initiated constitution-making in troubled states may connect domestic state consolidation (including through constitution-making or reform) with the global space of continuously revised and updated standards and norms of governance.

International normativity may have diverse effects upon democratic practices at the state level. These effects can be good or bad. Some consequences—even where they strengthen the power of the executive (which will usually be in charge of implementing international standards and decisions)—may be beneficial, in democratic terms, by broadening stakeholders' impact on a decision. With respect to the United States, Robert Keohane et al note that 'the use of bilateral and multilateral forums to negotiate trade liberalization shifts control over the domestic trade agenda into the hands of the executive branch, which represents a broader national constituency than individual members of U.S. House of Representatives and Senate'.[58] This helps to diffuse the effect of small but powerful interest groups upon decision-making. In addition, international structures of norms and institutions provide an extra factor of visibility, accountability, and responsibility for state action. This is what can be called the 'straitjacket effect' of supranationalism, which often corrects national processes in the direction of liberal and democratic values.

[56] John Hart Ely, *Democracy and Distrust* (Harvard University Press 1980).

[57] Michel Rosenfeld, *The Identity of the Constitutional Subject* (Routledge 2010) 207.

[58] Robert O Keohane, Stephen Macedo, and Andrew Moravcsik, 'Democracy-Enhancing Multilateralism' (2009) 63 International Organization 1, 11.

At the end of the day, we should not see the growth of supranational normativity as necessarily antithetical to democratic legitimacy at the state level.[59] Reports of the 'death of the state' are definitely premature: national states remain key political actors in their territory, and that may not necessarily be a bad thing. Changes in the architecture of international politics which we witness today, and which are usually described as 'globalization', and—in particular—the emergence of new sites of non-state authority, go hand-in-hand with the persistence and often the entrenching of state powers. Indeed, when major human rights, economic, public health, environmental, and so on crises occur, the usual (and justified) aim of international intervention is directed towards creating and improving *state* capacity to deal with the crisis, rather than replacing state powers with those of international institutions. For instance, rather than bypassing or subverting states, the general model of assistance rendered by international bodies such as the World Bank or the UN Food and Agriculture Organization is to ensure that states are capable of fulfilling their responsibilities towards their citizens. This shows that states remain the primary form of territorial organization responsible for providing resources and satisfying the needs of the people.

This system may not necessarily last very long. It may well be that, in the long run (but subject to a proviso articulated in an oft-quoted Keynes saying), states will gradually give way to supranational authorities, which will dominate the global landscape without posing any serious competition to the status of states. In his ground-breaking history of international relations, published over twenty years ago, Hendrik Spruyt gestured to a state-decline hypothesis when he recalled 'that the fullest articulation of feudal organization and the church, both in a theoretical and practical sense, occurred shortly before their demise'.[60] He added that: 'Such articulation seems to occur exactly when institutional challenges arise. Changes in communications, economics, and the environment challenge the scope of state authority and thus create incentives for actors to alter the existing institutional arrangements.'[61]

Whether these alterations will mean the demise of states' powers is not something that can be predicted. (Spruyt notes, philosophically: 'In the long run, history sides with no one.')[62] For the time being, states are thought by many to be important, often indispensable, instruments for achieving 'the psychological and material conditions that ensure the survival of their inhabitants'.[63] Their symbolic appeal, often framed in national, religious, or ethnic terms, retains an attractive power with the effect of ensuring the persistence of these territorially organized entities. The existence of borders is reassuring to many people and resonates with the need for individual and group security and with their sense of identity. This is often informed by historically determined national borders and sovereignty-based pride. As long as many people feel secure in their reliance upon their states as the best

[59] I am grateful to Martin Krygier for discussions on this point.
[60] Hendrik Spruyt, *The Sovereign State and Its Competitors* (Princeton University Press 1994) 193.
[61] ibid. [62] ibid.
[63] Michael Reisman, 'Designing and Managing the Future of the State' (1997) 3 European Journal of International Law 409, 415.

guarantors of their needs—including material and bodily safety—they are much less inclined to trust that suprastate institutions can effectively provide such protection. As long as this holds, the survival of states in their current form is assured. But this is not to say that the search for grounds of supranational legitimacy is inconceivable. Supranational normativity, with its own new sites of legitimacy, may accompany and enhance democracy in nation states, which is often defective and imperfect.

D. Conclusion

The need to identify a persuasive conception of non-democracy-based legitimacy which transcends national borders arises where a persistent deficit in democracy at the supranational level is coupled with the emergence of supranational institutions wielding indisputable authority. Such a conception relies upon an understanding of legitimacy which is at the same time weak (justification-based), focused on specific norms and decisions, and subject-fragmented, that is, where the quality of legitimacy is conferred upon authoritative decisions by their addressees. The idea of public reason, extrapolated from Rawlsian public reason—as a pivot of his liberal principle of legitimacy (but in contrast to his own 'public reason of the Society of Peoples')—fulfils these requirements. Further, the norm-production of some supranational adjudicatory bodies, such as the ECtHR, may provide an exemplar of supranational public reason in action.

However, the above proposition requires a final caveat. I am not making a claim that the use of public reason is *the only* or even necessarily the most important factor in legitimating supranational authorities. There are a number of other essential factors which are dependent upon the type of institution that we consider. In the case of supranational adjudicatory bodies, a number of institutional factors (eg the selection and tenure of adjudicators, guarantees of their personal qualities, independence and impartiality) and procedural variables (eg guarantees of fairness, transparency, publicness and/or confidentiality, equal treatment of parties concerned, allowing third-party intervention, efficiency of secretariats or/and registrars, possibilities of appeal from decisions) exist. The pattern of reasoning used by decision-makers, including the pervasiveness of arguments matching the requirements of public reason, is one among the many factors which contribute to the overall legitimacy of supranational authorities.

IX

Who's Afraid of Suprastate Constitutional Theory?

Two Reasons to be Sceptical of the Sceptics

*Cormac Mac Amhlaigh**

A. Introduction

An entry in a recent *Handbook on Global Constitutionalism* written by a prominent international lawyer begins as follows:

> Constitutionalism-bashing has been *en vogue* for some time in international legal scholarship. International legal scholars have deployed an incredible amount of energy to discredit any pattern of argument, structure of thought, or conceptual framework that comes with constitutional overtones . . . [A] quick scan of the literature suffices to note that constitutionalism-bashing scholarship dramatically outweighs literature promoting constitutionalist thinking.[1]

The context for this constitutionalism-bashing, and suprastate[2] constitutional discourse more generally, is, of course, a reaction to the continued development of the globalization of states and the development and fortification of suprastate governance. This transition from a 'Westphalian order' of sovereign states to a 'post-Westphalian' order entails the demotion of the state from the centre of the political universe to one among a number of actors in a broader setting, where suprastate governing and adjudicatory bodies rival states for authority and influence.[3] Sovereignty,

* Earlier versions of this chapter were presented at the 'Legitimacy and the State' workshop at the University of Sydney School of Law in October 2016, the 'Globalization of Constitutional Law' workshop at Radzyner Law School, IDC Herzliya in June 2017, as well as at a meeting of the Irish and British Chapter of the International Society of Constitutional Law at Trinity College Dublin in September 2017. I am grateful to those present at these events for helpful comments on previous drafts.

[1] Jean d'Aspremont, 'International Legal Constitutionalism, Legal Forms and the Need for Villains' in Anthony F Lang and Antje Wiener (eds), *Handbook on Global Constitutionalism* (Edward Elgar 2017) 155.

[2] 'Suprastate' in this chapter is taken to mean simply 'beyond' or 'above' the state. As such, it includes any law or governing body beyond the state regardless of its formal classification as public international law or otherwise.

[3] Nico Krisch, *Beyond Constitutionalism: The Pluralist Structure of Postnational Law* (Oxford University Press 2010) 5.

Legitimacy: The State and Beyond. First Edition. Edited by Wojciech Sadurski, Michael Sevel, and Kevin Walton. Published 2019 by Oxford University Press.

if relevant to this worldview, is of a 'late'[4] form rather than the 'high sovereignty'[5] of the Westphalian age.

Against this backdrop, suprastate constitutionalism has emerged as one way of thinking about the myriad analytical and normative questions that such a 'post-Westphalian' transition poses. The contribution that constitutionalism purports to make to these developments relates to two particular 'anxieties of the international jurist': the evolution and growing power of suprastate governing bodies and the fragmentation of public international law.[6] Whereas they are usually treated as separate questions, they can be collapsed into one overarching concern which motivates global constitutionalism more generally: a broader concern with *international legitimacy* in an emerging post-Westphalian global order.[7] With respect to the first anxiety, constitutionalism is advanced as a way of tackling the legitimacy problems associated with the increasing power and influence of suprastate governing bodies, by ensuring that they respect constitutional values such as the rule of law or fundamental rights protections, often by prescribing enhanced judicial oversight of their activities.[8] The legitimacy concerns raised by the fragmentation of international law relate to the idea that the lack of a unified, comprehensive legal order at the international level risks undermining the role of law and, in particular, the legitimacy of legality in civilizing international relations.[9] Here, constitutionalism is offered as a framework with which to view the unity of the international legal order, elevating its status from a 'set'[10] of norms, to a full-blooded constitutional legal *system*.[11]

For suprastate constitutional sceptics, suprastate constitutionalists have the correct diagnosis with respect to the emergence of a post-Westphalian order, but they prescribe an incorrect remedy for these anxieties. They accuse suprastate

[4] Neil Walker, 'Late Sovereignty in the European Union' in Neil Walker (ed), *Sovereignty in Transition* (Hart Publishing 2003).

[5] Cormac Mac Amhlaigh, 'Late Sovereignty in Post-Integration Europe: Continuity and Change in a Constitutive Concept' in Rebecca Adler-Nissen and Ulrik Pram Gad (eds), *European Integration and Postcolonial Sovereignty Games: The EU Overseas Countries and Territories* (Routledge 2013) 42.

[6] Jan Klabbers, Anne Peters, and Geir Ulfstein, *The Constitutionalization of International Law* (Oxford University Press 2009) 18; Jeffrey L Dunoff and Joel P Trachtman (eds), *Ruling the World? Constitutionalism, International Law, and Global Governance* (Cambridge University Press 2009) 5–9.

[7] Cormac Mac Amhlaigh, 'Harmonising Global Constitutionalism' (2016) 5 Global Constitutionalism 173, 178–81.

[8] See, for example, Erika de Wet, 'The Constitutionalization of Public International Law' in Michel Rosenfeld and Andràs Sajó (eds), *The Oxford Handbook of Comparative Constitutional Law* (Oxford University Press 2012).

[9] A concern which dates back to Kant. See Immanuel Kant, 'Perpetual Peace: A Philosophical Sketch' in HS Reiss (ed), *Kant: Political Writings* (HB Nisbet tr, 2nd edn, Cambridge University Press 1991). For discussion, see Jürgen Habermas, *The Divided West* (Ciaran Cronin ed, Polity 2006) ch 8.

[10] HLA Hart, *The Concept of Law* (3rd edn, Oxford University Press 2012) 236. For discussion and critique, see Mehrdad Payandeh, 'The Concept of International Law in the Jurisprudence of H. L. A. Hart' (2011) 21 European Journal of International Law 967; Jeremy Waldron, 'International Law: "A Relatively Small and Unimportant" Part of Jurisprudence?' in Luís Duarte d'Almeida, James Edwards, and Andrea Dolcetti (eds), *Reading HLA Hart's* The Concept of Law (Hart Publishing 2013).

[11] Andreas Paulus, 'The International Legal System as a Constitution' in Jeffrey L Dunoff and Joel P Tractman (eds), *Ruling the World? Constitutionalism, International Law, and Global Governance* (Cambridge University Press 2009); Payandeh, 'The Concept of International Law in the Jurisprudence of H. L. A. Hart' (n 10); Waldron, 'International Law' (n 10).

constitutionalism of being unrealistic and potentially illegitimate.[12] Virtually all versions of suprastate constitutional scepticism accept that *some* forms of constitutionalism can play a *limited* role in the context of the legitimacy of suprastate governance, such as forms of constitutionalism promoting due process or some human rights protections. However, they argue that this form of constitutionalism—'constitutionalism lite'[13]—is not up to the task of tackling the profound legitimacy crises associated with suprastate governance. The types of constitutionalism that could, potentially, provide the relevant panacea to this problem—'foundational'[14] or demotic constitutionalism establishing the legitimate foundations of governing or public power—can have no part to play in this context primarily due to the radical dissimilarities between state-based law, politics and society, and its suprastate avatar. Thus, the core of the sceptical case regarding constitutionalism as a response to the legitimacy questions raised by the rise of suprastate governance fixates on one element of constitutional theory: the idea of a demos. Marshalling the concept of a demos to their cause, sceptics argue along the following lines: within the context of the legitimacy crisis of suprastate governance, if constitutionalism is to mean anything, it must entail the idea of a demos;[15] it is a fact that the suprastate political space, such as it is, whether at regional, international, or global levels, is marked by fragmentation, radically heterogeneous cultural, linguistic, political, historical, and religious outlooks, power asymmetries, insoluble disagreement, and weak institutional structures; in such a context, the notion of a demos, and therefore constitutionalism, makes little sense, given its association with strong commonalities and affinities of language, culture, history, nationality, or, more abstractly, an identification with a common political project[16] or 'felt need'[17] to do things in common. Any attempt to export this 'heavier' type of constitutionalism to the suprastate realm would result in hegemony, thereby further delegitimizing suprastate law and governance. It is therefore dismissed as 'radical' or 'wishful thinking',[18] a 'utopian' project,[19] in favour of other, more modest, 'realistic' alternatives, such as global administrative law,[20]

[12] Dieter Grimm, 'The Constitution in the Process of Denationalization' (2005) 12 Constellations 447; Dieter Grimm, 'Integration by Constitution' (2005) 3 International Journal of Constitutional Law 193; Martin Loughlin, 'What is Constitutionalisation?' in Petra Dobner and Martin Loughlin (eds), *The Twilight of Constitutionalism?* (Oxford University Press 2010); Martin Loughlin, 'Constitutional Pluralism: An Oxymoron?' (2014) 3 Global Constitutionalism 9; Krisch, *Beyond Constitutionalism* (n 3); Nico Krisch, 'Pouvoir Constituent *and* Pouvoir Irritant *in the Postnational Order*' (2016) 14 International Journal of Constitutional Law 657.

[13] Jan Klabbers, 'Constitutionalism Lite' (2004) 1 International Organizations Law Review 31.

[14] Krisch, *Beyond Constitutionalism* (n 3) 47.

[15] The concept of constituent power can be employed to mean the same thing, and both terms will be used interchangeably here. See Martin Loughlin, 'The Concept of Constituent Power' (2014) 13 European Journal of Political Theory 218.

[16] Krisch, *Beyond Constitutionalism* (n 3) 56.

[17] Jeremy Waldron, *Law and Disagreement* (Oxford University Press 1999) 102.

[18] Krisch, 'Pouvoir Constituent *and* Pouvoir Irritant *in the Postnational Order*' (n 12) 669.

[19] Krisch, *Beyond Constitutionalism* (n 3) 57.

[20] See, generally, Benedict Kingsbury, Nico Krisch, and Richard B Stewart, 'The Emergence of Global Administrative Law' (2005) 68 Law & Contemporary Problems 16; Nico Krisch, 'Global Administrative Law and the Constitutional Ambition' in Petra Dobner and Martin Loughlin (eds), *The Twilight of Constitutionalism?* (Oxford University Press 2010).

pluralism,[21] or reinvigorated domestic accountability for the exercise of foreign relations powers under state constitutions.[22]

This chapter will interrogate this suprastate constitutional scepticism regarding the use of constitutionalism, particularly in its 'heavier' forms, as a potential solution to the legitimacy concerns emerging from the post-Westphalian transition. It argues that we have reasons to be sceptical of the sceptical charge on two counts. First, if idealism or utopianism in normative theory is a flaw, excavating the normative claims which underpin the idea of a demos and demotic constitutionalism reveals that it, too, is susceptible to counterfactual, idealistic, or utopian tendencies, making the charge self-defeating by its own lights. Second, it argues that it is not even clear that idealism or utopianism is problematic in normative theory. Drawing on recent debates in political philosophy, the chapter argues that within certain parameters even radically idealistic theories can contribute to questions tackled by normative theory, including in the context of addressing the legitimacy questions posed by the post-Westphalian transition. Given that we have good reasons to doubt the sceptical charge against suprastate constitutionalism, the chapter concludes that we should be more sanguine about the contribution that constitutionalism in *all* its forms—whether 'lite', 'heavy', or somewhere in between—can make to addressing the challenges of legitimacy faced by contemporary suprastate law and governance.

The chapter will proceed as follows. Part B outlines the core claims of suprastate constitutional scepticism in terms of the charges of idealism and utopianism as well as elaborating on those claims by identifying the alleged problems with idealism in normative theory. Part C looks in more detail at the concept of a demos which informs suprastate constitutional scepticism and examines its key normative claims showing how, as normative theory, the notion of a demos itself entails (sometimes radically) idealized elements. Part D focuses more directly on the charge of idealism or utopianism in normative theory, outlining the objections and drawing on recent debates in political philosophy to argue that the charge of idealism in normative theory itself suffers from problems, given that all normative theory entails some idealistic elements and that a focus on purposes when considering the extent of idealized assumptions is a better way to evaluate particular normative theories. It then illustrates how, by linking idealization with purpose, constitutional theory can play a useful role as normative theory in the context of the legitimacy of the post-Westphalian transition with reference to extant suprastate constitutional theory.

B. What's Wrong with Suprastate Constitutionalism?

As the extract at the beginning of this chapter makes clear, suprastate constitutional scepticism is a thriving business. Indeed, barely had suprastate constitutionalism

[21] Krisch, *Beyond Constitutionalism* (n 3).

[22] See, for example, Anne-Marie Slaughter, 'Disaggregated Sovereignty: Towards Public Accountability of Global Government Networks' (2004) 39 Government and Opposition 159.

got off the ground in terms of conceptualizing suprastate law and politics in constitutional terms than the backlash began.[23] The scepticism straddles legal fields, with constitutional lawyers and international lawyers alike making common cause on the impossibilities of suprastate constitutionalism, based on its lack of realism or its utopian or hegemonic tendencies. A leading constitutional lawyer and prominent sceptic, Dieter Grimm, for example, has emphasized the unrealistic nature of suprastate constitutionalism, noting that the 'aspiration contained in the concept of constitutionalism'[24] cannot even be 'approximately realized'[25] at the suprastate level due to a lack of 'social integration'.[26] His conclusion is that the notion of suprastate constitutionalism still '*lacks a solid basis in reality*'.[27] Grimm is even pessimistic about the prospect of a suprastate constitutionalism *à venir*, arguing that there is no prospect of suprastate constitutionalism neither 'for the time being',[28] nor even 'in the long term'.[29] Another prominent constitutional lawyer and leading sceptic, Martin Loughlin, reviewing a particular strain of suprastate constitutional thought known as constitutional pluralism,[30] accuses one of its proponents of a direct attack on the 'inclusionary-exclusionary dynamic that lies at the core of any political understanding [and] the concept of the political'[31] for questioning the basis of a demos at national level as an obstacle to the idea of suprastate constitutionalism. He dismisses such a move as categorically unrealistic and accuses its proponents of deploying 'the tactic of *impossibilism*'.[32]

Among the international legal scholarly community, Nico Krisch has emerged as a prominent voice leading the charge against suprastate constitutionalism for its lack of realism and impractical nature. He argues that the suprastate sphere is a sphere of 'fate, not of constitution',[33] meaning that attempts to link this sphere to reason-based origins in the exercise of a constituent power or demos 'will ring utopian at best, illusory at worst'.[34] While not wholly dismissive of the idea of suprastate constitutionalism, he argues that, at least for the time being, we need to 'remain aware'[35] of the absence of satisfactory conditions for constitutionalism at the supra-level at

[23] For an overview in the European context, see JHH Weiler and Joel P Trachtman, 'European Constitutionalism and its Discontents' (1997) 17 Northwestern Journal of International Law & Business 354. See also Robert Howse and Kalypso Nicolaïdes, 'Legitimacy and Global Governance: Why Constitutionalizing the WTO is a Step Too Far' in Roger B Porter, Pierre Sauvé, Arvind Subramanian, and Americo Beviglia Zampetti (eds), *Efficiency, Equity and Legitimacy: The Multilateral Trading System at the Millennium* (Brookings Institute Press 2001). Of course, these developments relate primarily to post-war suprastate constitutional discourse which emerged initially in relation to the development of the European Union. International Constitutionalism has a longer pedigree, including, significantly, the Vienna School approaches of the interwar period. See Josef Laurenz Kunz, 'The "Vienna School" and International Law' (1933) 11 New York University Law Quarterly Review 370.

[24] Grimm, 'The Constitution in the Process of Denationalization' (n 12) 460. [25] ibid.

[26] Grimm, 'Integration by Constitution' (n 12) 208. [27] ibid (emphasis added).

[28] Grimm, 'The Constitution in the Process of Denationalization' (n 12) 460. [29] ibid.

[30] For an overview, see Cormac Mac Amhlaigh, 'Pluralising Constitutional Pluralism' in Nicole Roughan and Andrew Halpin (eds), *In Pursuit of Pluralist Jurisprudence* (Cambridge University Press 2017).

[31] Loughlin, 'Constitutional Pluralism: An Oxymoron?' (n 12) 28.

[32] ibid (emphasis added).

[33] Krisch, 'Pouvoir Constituent *and* Pouvoir Irritant *in the Postnational Order*' (n 12) 668.

[34] ibid. [35] ibid 677.

present, including the distinction that 'persists—and will long persist—between ideal and reality'[36] in respect of suprastate constitutionalism. As such, he concludes that suprastate constitutionalism can only 'find a home'[37] in the contemporary world as a set of 'highly *idealized assumptions* about the institutional structure of global governance—and even then, only with significant limitations'.[38]

Whereas it is clear that suprastate constitutional scepticism is founded on the perceived unrealistic, utopian, and hegemonic nature of the idea, what is less clear in the critical literature is precisely how and why this is so. While we do get some hints, for example, in Loughlin's charge of impossiblism, defined by the *Oxford English Dictionary* as a 'belief in ideas, especially on social reform, which cannot be reasonably put into practice',[39] for a clearer sense of the problems which a lack of realism in suprastate constitutional theory pose, we need to turn to methodological questions in political philosophy, where the problems with idealism in normative theory have been examined in more detail.

1. What's wrong with idealism in normative theory?

In order to understand the charge of idealism in normative theory, and particularly the reasons why it might be considered to be problematic, we need to define what we mean by 'idealism'. The terms 'ideal theory', 'non-ideal theory', 'utopianism', and 'realism' are often used interchangeably in the literature; however, a few, more nuanced, distinctions can be drawn with respect to these terms. A common approach in the literature is to distinguish between 'ideal' and 'non-ideal' theory. As with most trends in contemporary political theory and political philosophy, this distinction can be traced back to the influence of John Rawls's work. One of the distinctions Rawls drew in his *Theory of Justice* was that between ideal and non-ideal theories which reflected the two parts of this theory of justice.[40] The first part is aimed at working out 'the principles that characterize a well-ordered society under favourable conditions'.[41] This first 'ideal'[42] part 'presents a conception of a just society that we are to achieve if we can'[43] and, crucially for subsequent critiques, entails the assumption of '*strict compliance*'.[44]

The second part of the theory of justice, on the other hand, asks how this goal can be achieved, usually 'in gradual steps'.[45] This non-ideal theory looks for courses of action that are 'morally permissible and politically possible as well as likely to be effective'.[46] Moreover, it relates to the principles 'that govern how we are to deal with injustice'.[47] The idealism in the first part of the *Theory of Justice*, which makes it *ideal* theory, stems from the fact that the assumption of strict compliance envisages,

[36] ibid. [37] ibid 671. [38] ibid (emphasis added).

[39] *Oxford English Dictionary* (3rd edn, Oxford University Press 2012).

[40] John Rawls, *A Theory of Justice* (Harvard University Press 1971); see also A John Simmons, 'Ideal and Nonideal Theory' (2010) 38 Philosophy & Public Affairs 5.

[41] Rawls, *A Theory of Justice* (n 40) 216. [42] ibid. [43] ibid.

[44] ibid 145 (emphasis added).

[45] John Rawls, *The Law of Peoples* (Harvard University Press 1999) 89. [46] ibid.

[47] Rawls, *A Theory of Justice* (n 40) 8.

counterfactually, that everyone, in fact, accepts the principles of the theory of justice, helps to uphold just institutions, and acts precisely according to the dictates of justice.[48]

O'Neill develops the idea of idealism in normative theory by introducing a much relied-upon distinction between idealization in the premises of normative theory and 'abstraction'.[49] Abstraction relates to 'bracketing'[50] aspects of the real world in developing a normative theory, but, crucially, does not deny that those aspects are true of the real world. All reasoning abstracts in one sense or another and, as such, it is important, unavoidable, and useful.[51] Idealization in the premises of normative theory, on the other hand, is more problematic in that it can lead to 'falsehood'.[52] For O'Neill, an assumption or a theory idealizes 'when it ascribes predicates that are *false* of the case in hand, and so denies predicates that are true of that case'.[53] Assumptions about human capacities and capabilities such as 'rational choice or self-sufficiency or independence from others'[54] are not evidently traits of many, never mind all, humans and are, therefore, not mere abstractions, but a form of idealization. Any theory involving such idealized assumptions is an ideal theory.

More generally, political realism has a longer history, stretching back to Machiavelli and beyond, and is defined as a position in normative theory which does not 'seek to regiment politics through morality'.[55] Realists charge ideal theories, such as Rawls's, with attempting to specify 'pre-political'[56] normative commitments which are taken to float free of politics and enjoy 'antecedent authority'[57] over the political. In contrast to ideal theory, realist normative theory is primarily concerned with questions of feasibility.[58] As such, realism can be summarized as insisting upon a clear distinction between the norms of ethics and the norms of politics, as being concerned with more than merely questions of justice, as well as having an interest in political judgement.[59]

Generally speaking, then, the key issue with idealization in normative theory is, given that it includes false predicates,[60] that it leads to 'falsehood' and, therefore, produces theories which are 'fact-insensitive'[61] in respect of the real world in which we live. Two specific problems have been identified with this: first, such theories fail as a form of *practical reasoning* because they fail to provide action-guiding recommendations[62] and, second, they come at an *unacceptable moral cost*.[63]

With respect to the problem of practical reasoning (or lack thereof), O'Neill argues that normative theory qua practical reason aims at 'guidance rather than

[48] Simmons, 'Ideal and Nonideal Theory' (n 40) 8.

[49] Onora O'Neill, *Towards Justice and Virtue* (Cambridge University Press 1996) 40.

[50] ibid. [51] ibid 40. [52] ibid 41. [53] ibid (emphasis added).

[54] ibid.

[55] Enzo Rossi and Matt Sleat, 'Realism in Normative Political Theory' (2014) 9 Philosophy Compass 689.

[56] ibid 689. [57] ibid. [58] ibid 690. [59] ibid 691–94.

[60] O'Neill, *Towards Justice and Virtue* (n 49) 41.

[61] Colin Farrelly, 'Justice in Ideal Theory: A Refutation' (2007) 55 Political Studies 844, 846.

[62] Zofia Stemplowska, 'What's Ideal about Ideal Theory?' (2008) 34 Social Theory and Practice 319, 324.

[63] Charles Mills, '"Ideal Theory" as Ideology' (2005) 20 Hypatia 156.

explanation'[64] and 'seeks to guide action whose aim is to fit the world (in some measure) to its recommendations, rather than its conclusions to the world'.[65] By idealizing, a theory becomes unfeasible in that its prescriptions are too far removed from the realities on the ground, making it 'impotent'[66] or 'deficient'[67] normative theory.

Ideal theory has also come in for criticism based on the fact that the implementation of idealized normative theory can be morally perverse in creating more, rather than less, injustice. For example, Mills's critique of ideal theories argues that idealization ignores or is oblivious to oppression and power disequilibria in actual real-world societies.[68] The idealization in ideal theory thus comes at an unacceptable moral cost, in that it fails to recognize and factor-in that, in real-world societies, not all individuals enjoy the same levels of, for example, freedom and equality, due to inbuilt structural and institutional biases which have led to the disadvantaging of certain classes of society, whether it be women, racial minorities, the working class, or others.[69] In not seeing oppression in societies and institutions, ideal theory does not (need not) address this oppression. Indeed, in some cases, it may *exacerbate* it in claiming a higher moral authority for dominant structures and perspectives than they otherwise deserve. Ideal theory, Mills argues, therefore becomes a form of *ideology*—a 'distortional complex of ideas, values, norms and beliefs that reflects the non-representative interests and experiences of a small minority of [society]'.[70] Another, related, moral cost associated with ideal theory relates to what has been called the 'problem of second best'.[71] The problem here is that, if the prescriptions of a theory are too far removed from the realities on the ground, the theory becomes radical or revolutionary, requiring such structural change that even the attempt to implement the prescriptions of the theory would violate moral principles. The idea being expressed here is something along the lines of the road to hell being paved with ideal theory.[72]

In the case of suprastate constitutionalism, the idealization involved revolves around assuming facts about the suprastate realm which are false, namely that there is a level of social integration, solidarity, or reflexive self-identification as a political community at this level when, in reality, there is no such thing, such that any theories based on these assumptions will fail to provide action-guiding recommendations or will perpetuate or produce injustice. Thus, in the particular context of legitimacy in the post-Westphalian transition, constitutionalism is 'impotent'[73] as normative theory, given its reliance on false assumptions like a suprastate demos or political community. Furthermore, suprastate constitutionalism is potentially morally costly

[64] O'Neill, *Towards Justice and Virtue* (n 49) 42. [65] ibid.
[66] Farrelly, 'Justice in Ideal Theory' (n 61) 848. [67] ibid.
[68] Mills, '"Ideal Theory" as Ideology' (n 63) 168. [69] ibid. [70] ibid 172.
[71] David Estlund, 'Utopophobia' (2014) 42 Philosophy & Public Affairs 113, 125. See also RG Lipsey and Kelvin Lancaster, 'The General Theory of Second Best' (1956) 24 Review of Economic Studies 11.
[72] The original is 'the road to hell is paved with good intentions' and can be traced as far back as St Bernard of Clairvaux. See John Simpson and Jennifer Speake (eds), *The Oxford Dictionary of Proverbs* (6th edn, Oxford University Press 2008).
[73] Farrelly, 'Justice in Ideal Theory' (n 61) 848.

because it perpetuates structural injustices in the suprastate realm[74]—especially through 'economic constitutionalism',[75] as the more critical accounts argue—or because it makes prescriptions that would be so radical or revolutionary that moral principles would be invariably violated in the attempt to achieve such ideals.[76]

When viewed in this light, the challenges to suprastate constitutionalism seem daunting. Not only is the sceptical challenge seemingly robust, but it also seems to have the weight of contemporary political philosophy behind it. In the remainder of this chapter, I will argue that we have good reasons to be sceptical about the sceptical challenge to suprastate constitutionalism. The first reason to be sceptical about such scepticism relates to the chosen ground for the suprastate constitutional sceptical charge: the concept of a demos. The second reason for scepticism relates to a broader scepticism about the charges levelled at ideal theory by political philosophers more generally, which impacts upon the strength of the charges employed in suprastate constitutional scepticism.

C. What (Kind of Normative Theory) is a Demos?

The concept of a demos has a considerable historical pedigree and, even in contemporary political discourse, has been subject to a variety of meanings and uses. However, given the fact that the context of the current debate relates to questions of *legitimacy* at the suprastate level in a post-Westphalian transition, the conceptions of a demos at stake in these debates are necessarily, as Krisch emphasizes, 'normatively rich'[77] ones—that is, normative theories of a demos as opposed to purely descriptive, empirical, or historical accounts.[78] As such, as a theory of the legitimacy of governing authority, the concept of a demos cannot create an ought from an is; that is, normatively speaking, it cannot claim that a governing authority is legitimate

[74] In this regard, for example, Krisch argues that applying constitutionalism to the suprastate realm in the light of the idealization of its assumptions runs the risk of sanctifying that which ought not to be sanctified due to the normative costs involved. Such a move, he argues, 'represents a capitulation to contemporary circumstances when we should instead denounce the gap between our political ideals and what can currently be achieved. Only by naming that gap can we retain a sense for the challenge that constitutionalism … poses for the postnational space'. Krisch, *Beyond Constitutionalism* (n 3) 58.

[75] Kanishka Jayasuriya, 'Globalization, Sovereignty, and the Rule of Law: From Political to Economic Constitutionalism?' (2001) 8 Constellations 442; Stephen Gill and A Claire Cutler, 'New Constitutionalism and World Order: General Introduction' in Stephen Gill and A Claire Cutler (eds), *New Constitutionalism and World Order* (Cambridge University Press 2014); Loughlin, 'What is Constitutionalisation?' (n 12).

[76] Krisch, *Beyond Constitutionalism* (n 3) 54. [77] ibid 39.

[78] Some accounts of a demos and its cognates, such as constituent power, remain firmly in a descriptive register and are not of concern to us here. Some, for example, argue that a constituent power is an account of actual constitutional founding or constitutional development. It is a common trope in constitutional theory to posit the French and American Revolutions (and many since) and the constitutions to which they gave birth as the acts of historical constituent powers. More recently, Bruce Ackerman has attempted to explain constitutional change in the United States—'constitutional moments'—as exercises of a US constituent power. For discussion of the different uses of the concept, see Mattias Kumm, 'Constituent Power, Cosmopolitan Constitutionalism, and Post-Positivist law' (2016) 14 International Journal of Constitutional Law 697, 701. See also Loughlin, 'The Concept of Constituent Power' (n 15).

merely because it exists.[79] What this means, then, is that the claims of suprastate constitutional scepticism involving the concept of a demos must be attached to specific normative claims about what we ought to do. Thus, such normative statements must, at a minimum, prescribe particular courses of action.[80] As much is clear from the charges of 'impotence' levelled at ideal theory by its critics.[81] As Terry Macdonald notes, considering the concept of a demos in the context of the legitimacy of authority requires 'not only an empirical account of... social commonalities, but also a *normative* account of what kinds of political commonalities should count as politically significant in determining which social groups are entitled to democratic self-rule'.[82] This, therefore, necessitates closer scrutiny of the conception of demos and its normative use in suprastate constitutional scepticism.

The concept of a demos is used offensively by suprastate constitutional sceptics to support the charge of idealism in suprastate constitutional theory in two distinct but related ways: ontological and institutional. The ontological use of the concept of a demos to reject suprastate constitutionalism based on its false or idealized assumptions involves the stipulation of necessary and sufficient conditions of the concept and the application of that concept to suprastate governance to conclude that, in contrast to state-based societies, the conditions are far from suitable to support suprastate constitutionalism at this level. A classic version of the ontological use of the concept can be found in the *Maastricht* and *Lisbon* decisions of the German Federal Constitutional Court (GFCC).[83] While the Court found that, ultimately, German ratification of the Maastricht and Lisbon Treaties did not violate the right to vote and the democratic nature of the German state, its main line of argument was based on the fact that the European Union was not a competing source of democratic legitimacy for German political institutions and the German basic law.[84] This was due to the fact that democratic constitutional legitimacy presupposed a demos, defined as 'pre-legal'[85] conditions including 'language, history and culture'.[86] According to the Court, these factors create a 'cultural area'[87] sustaining a political

[79] I am adopting here, I think uncontroversially, a normative conception of legitimacy. Hence, we are not here concerned with purely descriptive accounts of legitimacy, such as those associated with Max Weber. See Max Weber, *Economy and Society* (Guenther Roth and Claus Wittich eds, University of California Press 1978). That suprastate constitutional sceptics assume a similar conception of legitimacy is evidenced by the fact that they see legitimacy problems arising in suprastate de facto authorities such as the European Union. If it were the case that obedience in fact was sufficient for the legitimacy of an authority along Weberian lines, then there would be little problem with suprastate authorities, as many can make plausible claims to be de facto authorities. See Mac Amhlaigh, 'Harmonising Global Constitutionalism' (n 7) 199. The problem is that they are not necessarily considered to be *legitimate* authorities in a normative sense. See Tom Christiano, 'Authority' in Edward N Zalta (ed), *The Stanford Encyclopedia of Philosophy* (spring edn, 2013) <https://plato.stanford.edu/archives/spr2013/entries/authority/> accessed 5 April 2018.

[80] Although not necessarily exclusively. See further below.

[81] Farrelly, 'Justice in Ideal Theory: A Refutation' (n 61) 845.

[82] Terry Macdonald, 'Boundaries beyond Borders: Delineating Democratic "Peoples" in a Globalizing World' (2003) 10 Democratization 173, 174 (emphasis added).

[83] 2 BvR 2134/92 and 2159/92 JZ 1993, 1100; [1994] 1 CMLR 57 (hereafter *Maastricht*). BverfG, 2 BE 2/08, 30 June 2009 (hereafter *Lisbon*).

[84] *Lisbon* (n 83) para 256.

[85] *Maastricht* (n 83) para 41l.

[86] *Lisbon* (n 83) para 227.

[87] ibid para 236.

community 'bound by ... tradition ... and convention',[88] something that was notably absent at the suprastate EU level. As such as a matter of empirical observation, then, as a commentator summarizes, the Court concluded that 'there is no European demos—not a people not a nation'.[89]

The institutional use of the concept of a demos to dismiss suprastate constitutionalism as utopian builds on the ontological use and involves the claim that current suprastate institutions and infrastructures are far from being able to express, manage, and support a suprastate demos. Krisch offers one such example. While he criticizes the GFCC's account of a demos as overwrought, he comes to similar conclusions regarding the societal barriers to a suprastate demos based on similar reasoning. In his account of the ontological use of a demos, he argues that suprastate constitutional theory must 'clarify what self-government through a constitution could mean'[90] in a space where there is 'no uncontested collective that could express its will in constitutional terms'.[91] This is all down to the 'power and wealth differentials, language and culture barriers, and the lack of identification of a common project'[92] at the suprastate level, which undermine the existence of the necessary 'pre-legal' conditions for suprastate constitutionalism. From this ontological premise regarding the suprastate realm, he argues that institutional factors present another, further, barrier to suprastate constitutionalism. If constitutions are tools to 'translate moral ideals into institutional practice',[93] Krisch argues certain institutional prerequisites are necessary to allow it to discharge this particular function. For Krisch, we don't need to fetishize the state to understand that it is the only form of political organization which has successfully claimed the monopoly of coercive legitimate force to which the comprehensive ambitions of constitutionalism could be attached.[94] The realities of the suprastate context are far removed from these conditions; they are characterized by forms of 'organic growth which are not steered by a definable centre but determined by the rationalities of social subsystems and the interests and position of particular actors'.[95] As such, the institutional challenges faced by constitutionalism in a global context are high, making the idea of suprastate constitutionalism 'utopian'.[96]

[88] ibid.

[89] JHH Weiler, 'Does Europe Need a Constitution? Demos, Telos and the German Maastricht Decision' (1995) 1 European Law Journal 219, 229. This view was reprised in the context of the European Union in more recent times by former British Prime Minister David Cameron in his fateful 'Bloomberg Speech', where he first committed to holding a referendum on the United Kingdom's EU membership, which ultimately led to the United Kingdom voting to leave the bloc in 2016: 'There is not, in my view, a single European demos. It is national parliaments, which are, and will remain, the true source of real democratic legitimacy and accountability in the EU.' David Cameron, 'EU Speech at Bloomberg' (23 January 2013) <https://www.gov.uk/government/speeches/eu-speech-at-bloomberg> accessed 5 April 2018.

[90] Krisch, *Beyond Constitutionalism* (n 3) 55.

[91] ibid.

[92] ibid 56.

[93] ibid 50.

[94] ibid 47–49. See also Grimm, 'The Constitution in the Process of Denationalization' (n 12) 459.

[95] Krisch, *Beyond Constitutionalism* (n 3) 54.

[96] ibid 55.

1. Whither the normative claim?

While it is clear that the use of a demos by sceptics speaks to a particular view of the empirical realities, both societal and institutional, which exist at the suprastate level, the precise normative significance of this state of affairs, and its relationship to constitutional theory, is less clear. That is, what types of normative claims are associated with this use of the demos?

A variety of normative claims can be based on the concept of a demos and its cognates, such as constituent power, depending on the specific context in question. For example, the concept can play a normative role in respect of questions of institutional design, the separation of powers, constitutional amendment or reform, representation, and decision-making.[97] In the context with which we are concerned here, however—the post-Westphalian transition and, in particular, the legitimacy issues associated with the demotion of states and the increasing power and influence of suprastate bodies—the claims associated with a normative theory of demos relate to the demarcation of legitimate *boundaries*, and particularly the boundary between state and suprastate governance. As much is clear from the use of the idea of demos in the suprastate constitutional sceptical accounts outlined above, where the boundaries of legitimate democratic communities are defined in terms of the particular 'pre-legal' features of that community which are assumed to be present in state-based communities, but not suprastate ones. In this context, then, the normative claims entailed in the idea of a demos relate to the question of where the legitimate boundaries of sovereign democratic communities *should* lie—in other words, which types of communities *should* be self-governing, should enjoy sovereignty.

Generally speaking, democratic theory contains two normative conceptions of a demos which justify normative claims surrounding the boundary question: a solidaristic conception and a jurisdictional conception.[98] The solidaristic account picks out the pre-political features of a particular group—empirical traits such as language, history, or culture—as normatively significant in two ways: as being per se normatively valuable or being valuable to achieve other normative ends, such as justice. Per se solidaristic accounts of democratic boundaries argue that it is only within groups which share, empirically, such features that political goods such as 'collective autonomy'[99] or republican ideals of self-governance can be achieved.[100] More instrumental defences of democratic boundaries rely on other values, such as justice, to delineate the boundaries of legitimate self-governing groups.[101] However, even if the concept of a demos is deemed to be a means to other ends, the claim is the same: only solidaristic groups sharing such empirical features constitute the legitimate objects of, for example, justice, as they are the only groups which enjoy

[97] For examples, see Joel Colón-Ríos, 'Five Conceptions of Constituent Power' (2014) 130 Law Quarterly Review 306.

[98] See Macdonald, 'Boundaries beyond Borders' (n 82). It should be noted that the terminology used here differs slightly from Macdonald's.

[99] David Miller, *On Nationality* (Oxford University Press 1995) 88–89.

[100] ibid.

[101] See Michael Walzer, *Spheres of Justice* (Oxford University Press 1983); Miller, *On Nationality* (n 99).

the requisite level of mutual understanding and mutual trust necessary to support justice-based institutions and initiatives.[102]

The jurisdictional account of legitimate democratic boundaries, on the other hand, looks at the empirical realities of power in the world and bases solutions to boundary problems on these empirical facts.[103] This account endorses an 'all-affected-interests' view of democratic boundaries—that is, that the boundaries of democracy are only legitimately drawn around all individuals who are affected by the exercise of that power in fact. As such, the jurisdictional account favours a more cosmopolitan approach to democratic boundaries, albeit that it is a bounded form of cosmopolitanism.[104]

This, then, reveals the crux of the normative claim embedded in accounts of constituent power or demos with respect to the boundary problem; that democratic boundaries *should* coincide with whichever of the two accounts of democracy the particular theory endorses. In the solidaristic case—that which is employed by suprastate constitutional sceptics—the claim becomes one that the boundaries of constitutional democracy *should* be based around state-based communities as they are the only types of communities which make plausible claims to enjoy the 'pre-legal' characteristics associated with a demos, and therefore the requisite level of solidarity for self-governance, justice, or constitutionalism. In the jurisdictional account, the boundaries of constitutional democracy *should* be redrawn to coincide with the way in which power is actually exercised in contemporary society, within and across state boundaries.

In considering the normative claims which underpin the use of a demos in the context of suprastate constitutionalism, and legitimacy beyond the state more generally in an emergent post-Westphalian world, the jurisdictional account initially appears to be the more radical of the two. This view, as noted, takes the exercise of power, whatever its formal status and however formally designated, as the starting point for the consideration of the legitimate boundaries of democracy and the identification of a demos for constitutional purposes. In the suprastate context, then, the demos or constituent power becomes merely those affected by the exercises of power, making the idea of a European demos eminently plausible.[105] Even a global demos could be concocted on this account in exercises of power with a global reach, such as certain decisions of the UN Security Council.[106] Viewed in this way, it can

[102] Walzer, *Spheres of Justice* (n 101).

[103] David Held is perhaps one of the best-known proponents of this conception of democracy. See, for example, David Held, *Democracy and the Global Order: From the Modern State to Cosmopolitan Governance* (Polity 1995).

[104] See, for example, Joshua Cohen and Charles Sabel, 'Directly Deliberative Polyarchy' (1997) 3 European Law Journal 313.

[105] See, for example, Chris Thornhill's recent work on transnational constituent power: Chris Thornhill, 'Contemporary Constitutionalism and the Dialectic of Constituent Power' (2012) 1 Global Constitutionalism 369; Chris Thornhill, *A Sociology of Transnational Constitutions: The Social Foundations of the Post-National Legal Structure* (Cambridge University Press 2016); Chris Thornhill, 'The Global Legal System and the Procedural Construction of Constituent Power' (2016) 5 Global Constitutionalism 405; Chris Thornhill, 'Rights and Constituent Power in the Global Constitution' (2014) 10 International Journal of Law in Context 357.

[106] In some ways, the jurisdictional account has a strong affinity with suprastate constitutional theory, a putative 'utopian' project which is divorced from the realities of suprastate law and governance.

be seen how suprastate constitutional scepticism presents itself as the more realistic account of suprastate governance.[107] Taking the solidaristic account of democratic boundaries, and its expression in state-based communities as a given, it argues that any attempt to replicate practices, institutions, and structures predicated on the features of solidaristic communities at the suprastate level, given its institutional weakness and the weak nature of cross-border or transnational solidarity, is wholly unrealistic or utopian.

However, on closer inspection, it is not clear that the solidaristic account employed by suprastate constitutional sceptics is any less radical or utopian than the jurisdictional account. A fundamental dogma of these sceptical positions is that states are the only legitimate governing arrangements for sovereign power or proper locus for democracy; the justification being that state-based societies enjoy or, at least best approximate the requisite degree of solidarity or homogeneity necessary for the existence of a demos based on the empirical features of that particular group. However, this is in itself a necessarily contingent matter. Some states could be said, empirically, to enjoy these features, but others not.[108] Moreover, the actual experience of statehood in the contemporary world betrays a large degree of variance in terms of the existence of these prerequisites and associated levels of solidarity; internally divided states, plurinational states, multicultural societies (which characterize most Western societies), multi-linguistic and ethnic federations are all features of many contemporary states, yet they fall short of the conditions considered necessary for the legitimate exercise of sovereign power or democracy by suprastate constitutional sceptics.[109] As such, there is a misalignment between the empirical realties of contemporary states and the ideal conditions stipulated by the concept of a demos. Furthermore, the realities of suprastate governance due to the post-Westphalian transition, which even suprastate constitutional sceptics adopt as a premise of theorizing transnational and global relations and structures, mean that there is a further misalignment between the contemporary status quo in terms of the boundaries of governance and groups sharing the pre-political features of the solidaristic account.

Thus, the solidaristic basis of suprastate constitutional scepticism itself runs into two problems when viewed in the light of the charges made against suprastate constitutionalism. First, the theory itself seems to rely on idealized assumptions about states in the real world. The fact that a good number, if not a majority, of state-based societies do not literally fulfil the criteria of a demos, and that other social groupings do, but are not formed around states, makes the assumptions that suprastate constitutional sceptics make about the legitimacy of states necessarily counterfactual or

[107] Krisch, *Beyond Constitutionalism* (n 3) ch 2.

[108] For example, recent referendums or attempted secession in Scotland in 2014 and Catalonia in 2017 question whether the boundaries of even reasonably stable and well-established states share the requisite level of solidarity entailed in the solidaristic (and therefore suprastate constitutional sceptical) account.

[109] This is not to mention the arbitrary boundaries of post-colonial states, where little if any consideration was given to the extent of solidarity in terms of common empirical features of social groups when the boundaries were drawn.

idealized.[110] Moreover, as the concept of a demos relies on idealized assumptions, it runs the risk of succumbing to the charges of impotence and moral cost outlined above. This is clear in the way that the prescriptions of the concept of a demos as a form of practical reasoning—that is, as making action-guiding recommendations—potentially entail a quite radical set of claims involving the redrawing of current boundaries to better reflect solidaristic communities based on these empirical criteria. Thus, for example, the solidaristic account of legitimate democratic boundaries could potentially prescribe that the boundaries of post-colonial states should be redrawn to better reflect the solidaristic groupings extant on these territories; that plurinational states should be split up to better reflect the different solidarities which exist on these territories; that multiculturalism should be halted or even reversed to better align democratic boundaries with solidaristic groupings; or, most relevant to the current context, that the entire post-Westphalian transition with its varieties of transnational governance should be radically redesigned or even dismantled to better align solidarity to democratic decision-making. One doesn't require a great deal of imagination to foresee the moral objections to such projects.

Of course, suprastate constitutional sceptics could counter argue that at least most states are more aligned with solidaristic communities on the whole than are not, and that redesigning boundaries according to the jurisdictional account would be more problematic. That is, one doesn't have to commit to a radical redesigning of sovereign boundaries or transnational governing arrangements in order to argue that there is more solidarity currently within state boundaries for just the types of reasons that theories of demos provide (common language, culture, history) than there would be if the boundaries were redesigned on purely jurisdictional lines in terms of transnational governance. As is often noted, arguably the majority of even EU member states currently enjoy a level of allegiance and authority much higher than EU institutions and enjoy more legitimacy than a hypothetical EU state ever would.[111] Again, however, all of this is a relative matter—it may be truer for some EU member states than others.[112] Furthermore, it supresses the normative claims associated with solidaristic accounts of a demos, failing to make the case for states as they currently exist and highlights that more needs to be done, including potentially dismantling state boundaries to achieve or at least approximate the alignment between sovereign power and societal solidarity based on the empirical features of a demos.

What all this serves to illustrate is that once the grounds of suprastate constitutional scepticism in terms of the normative claims associated with the concept

[110] As Macdonald notes, 'the theoretical demand [for alignment between solidarity and power] is not necessarily easily satisfied in practice'. Macdonald, 'Boundaries beyond Borders' (n 82) 177.

[111] See Krisch, *Beyond Constitutionalism* (n 3) 96.

[112] A fact borne out in the Eurobarometer results relied on by Krisch. For example, the most recent Eurobarometer data available at the time of writing from May 2017 shows a wide variance between member state citizens with respect to trusting EU institutions and having a positive image of the European Union. Eurobarometer, 'Public Opinion in the European Union' (May 2017) <http://ec.europa.eu/commfrontoffice/publicopinion/index.cfm/Survey/getSurveyDetail/instruments/STANDARD/surveyKy/2142> accessed 5 October 2018.

of a demos is interrogated, strong reasons for scepticism about this scepticism are revealed.

D. What's the Problem with Ideal Theory Anyway?

The second ground for scepticism relating to suprastate constitutional scepticism relates to the assumption that idealistic or utopian theory is, itself, problematic. As noted above, idealization in political theory is usually considered to be problematic because its fact-insensitivity can undermine action-guidingness and can be morally costly. However, normative theory must also not merely endorse the status quo; that is, it must do more than claim that what we should do about poverty, conflict, or helping refugees, or more closely related to the issue at hand, addressing the legitimacy problems in contemporary state and suprastate governance, is what we are already doing. Normative theory which merely endorses the status quo *also* comes at a moral cost, in that it is likely to mask or affirm actual injustices in the world which normative theory should make prescriptions to remedy.[113] As such, normative theory must 'make demands on the world' in some sense, albeit possibly not demands that run the risk of the dangers highlighted above. Normative theory, then, faces a particular Procrustean dilemma: idealize too little and we affirm extant structural injustice; idealize too much and the theory can fail to be action-guiding and/or can be morally costly. The question is: how do we go about resolving this particular Procrustean dilemma?

One tack would be to follow O'Neill's distinction between idealization and abstraction, and particularly the function of normative theory as giving reasons for action. As noted above, for O'Neill, normative theory qua practical reasoning aims at guidance rather than explanation,[114] the aim of such action-guidingness being to 'fit the world (in some measure) to its recommendations, rather than its conclusions to the world'.[115] Ideal theories fail to do this as they rely on false predicates, whereas theories that merely abstract can achieve these aims.

However, in assessing how much is too much (or how little is too little) in normative theory, the usefulness of O'Neill's distinction seems to run into problems. This is because it is not exactly clear what the difference between idealization and abstraction actually is or, at least, what the precise relevance of the distinction is for normative theory. To recap, for O'Neill an assumption or a theory idealizes 'when it ascribes predicates that are *false* of the case in hand, and so denies predicates that are true of that case',[116] whereas it abstracts when it brackets rather than denies predicates that are true of the issue at hand.[117] However, it is not clear how abstraction, by bracketing aspects of the real world, is not really (or also) a form of falsehood. Take, for example, one target of O'Neill's critique of ideal theory: rational choice theories,

[113] Such 'complacent realism', says Estlund, involves recommending that people and institutions 'be exactly as they are already'. Estlund, 'Utopophobia' (n 71) 115.

[114] O'Neill, *Towards Justice and Virtue* (n 49) 42.

[115] ibid.

[116] ibid 41 (emphasis added).

[117] ibid 40.

which see individuals as being truly equal and rational in their interactions with each other, which is common in economic modelling of human behaviour.[118] On one reading, we could say that this involves idealization, given that we know in reality that individuals are not actually free and equal to the same extent due to a variety of social factors (birth, sex, race, social status, wealth, and so on) and that they do not always act rationally. As such, these assumptions will contaminate the theory in the ways outlined above. However, in making assumptions about autonomous and equal individuals acting rationally, we *are* drawing on certain aspects of reality: that humans are autonomous mammals, that they have the capacity to reason and can interact in rational ways, albeit not all to the same extent and not all of the time. Thus, to take a model of autonomous rational humans interacting according to the dictates of reason is not necessarily a *misrepresentation*, that is, a false representation of social reality, but rather a *partial* one. As such, when presenting individuals in a theory as autonomous rational individuals interacting in, for example, commercial transactions according to the dictates of reason, rather than involving false predicates, we could be said to be *bracketing* the non-rational, non-autonomous aspects of human behaviour. That is, in making these assumptions about society, we are bracketing, rather than idealizing, certain aspects of an individual's situation in order to develop a particular theory. Thus, there seems to be little difference between idealizing and bracketing, as bracketing, like idealizing, seems to rely on a type of falsehood in the sense of not giving a completely accurate picture of the world.[119] Following on from this, there is a sense that all normative theories must rely on literally false assumptions in the form of *approximations* to reality[120] rather than literal descriptions of reality in order to be able to make advances on understanding what, for example, justice requires. This cannot mean that all theories are ideal theories and therefore useless, as then normative theory could only deal with very narrow and relatively simple problems.[121] If abstraction and idealization are forms of the same thing at least for the matters with which we are concerned here,[122] then we can see how some form of abstraction/idealization or, to use a more neutral term, *generalization*[123] is a necessary step in *any* normative theorizing. The question then remains: How much or little are we to *generalize* in normative theory?

[118] ibid 41.

[119] Hamlin and Stemplowska make a similar point. They offer the following example to highlight the problem: '[I]magine that we are concerned to include a treatment of the motivation of agents in our theory, and we recognise that in the "real world" there is considerable heterogeneity of motivation. Recognising the relevant degree of heterogeneity may make our model too unwieldy to be useful, so we consider adopting an assumption that limits the heterogeneity within the theory. This is clearly a false assumption, but is it an idealisation or an abstraction? One might answer that it is an abstraction if there is no reason to think that the assumption changes what we conclude from our theory. But how can we know?' They conclude that 'there is no straightforward, and perhaps no helpful, distinction between idealisation and abstraction'. They see it as a 'complex continuum'. Alan Hamlin and Zofia Stemplowska, 'Theory, Ideal Theory and the Theory of Ideals' (2012) 10 Political Studies Review 48, 50–51.

[120] Stemplowska, 'What's Ideal about Ideal Theory?' (n 62) 327.

[121] ibid.

[122] There may be instances where this is a useful distinction, such as in cases of 'deep impossibility', discussed below.

[123] Stemplowska, 'What's Ideal about Ideal Theory?' (n 62) 327.

We have already identified a 'floor' of the Procrustean dilemma in that normative theory cannot merely prescribe the status quo. With respect to a 'ceiling' of generalization, we can assume that the principle 'ought implies can'[124] sets a clear outer limit to generalization.[125] That is, we cannot be morally required to do things that are impossible for us to do. This rules out any theory which requires what Parfit calls the 'deeply impossible',[126] such as prescriptions that violate the laws of nature, such as that humans should fly unaided, or even a less demanding constraint, such as technical infeasibility,[127] which rules out prescriptions based on the likelihood of their being met, even if they are not strictly impossible.[128] However, the space between the 'floor' of a status quo bias and the 'ceiling' of 'technical constraints' is a potentially large one, which leaves potentially considerable latitude for generalization in normative theory. Within this space, then, there is much room for manoeuvre in terms of the generalizations made in the assumptions of normative theories and almost certainly more than critics of ideal theory assume.

Interrogating this space between the 'floor' and the 'ceiling' reveals that the relationship between purpose and generalization in the assumptions of normative theories is more complex than the simple 'action-guiding' criteria popular in critiques of ideal theory would suggest. First of all, while making action-guiding recommendations is clearly an important purpose of normative theory, it is a necessarily relative measure which will to some extent be informed by more specific motivations for the application of the theory. This, in turn, will have an impact on the level of generalization involved. If our stated purpose is to make specific recommendations in a particular policy area or even to decide a particular case at law based on, for example, moral principles, then the level of generalization required will be relatively low. However, if our purposes are the progressive realization of particular goals, such as the alleviation of poverty and malnutrition in a general sense, then the level of generalization of our theory will be necessarily higher. The variable nature of the action-guiding function of normative theory can be illustrated through an analogy with the implementation of human rights norms. Some human rights norms yield relatively specific prescriptions entailing limited levels of generalization, such as the right to life or prohibitions on torture or slavery.[129] Notwithstanding disagreement at the margins as to whether certain situations fit the relevant definitions, human rights norms such as these entail reasonably clear and direct action-guiding

[124] Commonly associated with Kant. See Immanuel Kant, *Groundwork of the Metaphysics of Morals* (Mary Gregor and Jens Timmerman eds, 2nd edn, Cambridge University Press 2012).

[125] See Estlund, 'Utopophobia' (n 71).

[126] Derek Parfit, *Reasons and Persons* (Oxford University Press 1986) 219.

[127] David Miller, *Justice for Earthlings* (Cambridge University Press 2013) 37.

[128] In fact, it is possibly in the range of deep impossibility or technical infeasibility where the idealization/abstraction distinction drawn by O'Neill can do some work. Assuming that humans can fly unaided is clearly a falsehood and cannot be rescued by claiming that flying humans is somehow 'bracketing' human ability in the manner outlined above. As such, it seems relevant to these outer constraints. However, in the context at hand, we are already working within these constraints so the distinction is, it is submitted, less relevant to the questions being addressed here.

[129] Arts 6, 7, and 8 respectively of the International Covenant on Civil and Political Rights 1966 <http://www.ohchr.org/EN/ProfessionalInterest/Pages/CCPR.aspx> accessed 5 October 2018.

recommendations, such as: do not arbitrarily deprive other humans of their life; do not intentionally inflict pain and suffering on individuals with a view to achieving certain outcomes; and so on. However, other rights, such as certain economic and social rights, are usually couched in more general terms, such as 'just and favourable conditions of work',[130] the 'right to an adequate standard of living ... including adequate food, clothing and housing',[131] and the right to 'the enjoyment of the highest attainable standard of physical and mental health'.[132] The attainment of these quite general goals are correspondingly achieved through their *progressive* realisation,[133] which does not yield recommendations as specific as the right to life or prohibitions on torture. Thus, whereas all of these human rights norms involve action-guiding recommendations, the level of generalization involved in each is quite different, as is the precise form of action-guiding recommendation.

Furthermore, there are good reasons for supposing that action-guiding recommendations are not necessarily the only conceivable purpose of normative theory within the floor and ceiling set by the Procrustean dilemma.[134] David Estlund, for example, makes one such case for what he terms 'hopeless aspirational theory'.[135] These are normative theories which are morally sound in that they do not transgress moral principles, and are technically achievable by humans as they are, but given other factors such as motivation, are unlikely to ever be achieved. He argues that such theories cannot be said to suffer from a defect in virtue of the fact that their prescriptions will never actually be met.[136] He identifies the terrain between the limits of status-quo bias and impossible theories as a 'noncomplacent nonutopian range of normative political theories'[137] and, while accepting that 'ought implies can', he argues that this does not entail the proposition that ought implies 'highly likely'.[138] As such, he argues it is important to separate probability from impossibility: the fact that it is improbable that something will happen does not make it impossible. This then brings theories which might be ruled out of the range of theories within the 'floor' and 'ceiling' of generalization on the grounds that they do not make action-guiding recommendations within the range as not being impossible, strictly speaking. Estlund argues that such theories can be normative in the sense of being *evaluative*, whether or not the evaluation itself guides action.[139] That is, normative theory can provide insights by suggesting that 'society would be better like this', which might be true 'whether or not there is anything it makes sense to do in the light of this fact'.[140]

Stemplowska further fleshes out this idea by outlining a number of roles for theories involving highly generalized assumptions and offering alternative purposes for

[130] Art 7 of the International Covenant on Economic, Social and Cultural Rights 1966 (ICESCR) <http://www.ohchr.org/EN/ProfessionalInterest/Pages/CESCR.aspx>.

[131] ibid Art 11. [132] ibid Art 12. [133] ibid Art 2.

[134] In this regard, Carens argues: 'There is no single correct starting point for reflection, no single correct set of presuppositions about what is possible ... The assumptions we adopt should depend ... on the purposes of our inquiry.' Joseph H Carens, 'Realistic and Idealistic Approaches to the Ethics of Migration' (1996) 30 International Migration Review 156, 169.

[135] See Estlund, 'Utopophobia' (n 71) 118. [136] See ibid 114. [137] See ibid 116.

[138] ibid. [139] ibid 121. [140] ibid.

normative theory beyond guiding action.[141] For example, she argues that highly generalized theories can help us see more clearly the actual real-world constraints on developing normative theories.[142] They can also help tease out the relationship between two principles or the values that underpin them, as this is easier to do in a radically simplified universe.[143] Furthermore, idealized theories, she contends, set out what is desirable when, for example, there is full compliance, and inform our non-ideal theories by forcing us to inquire if we could innovate in order to come closer to an ideal and whether we must depart from the ideal when we are presented with the facts on the ground.[144] Similarly to Estlund, she argues that idealized theory can also provide evaluative benchmarks to help orient ourselves in the real world by providing a metric to show how far we are from our stated aims and how much would need to be done to approximate them.[145] In short, Stemplowska concludes that highly generalized normative theory can have purposes such as uncovering, clarifying, and safeguarding our 'normative commitments',[146] even if it cannot provide specific action-guiding recommendations.

What these examples show is that normative theory can have purposes beyond an action-guiding function and that this impacts upon the level of generalization appropriate to a particular normative theory. Therefore, the key point in distinguishing between unproblematic and problematic normative theory is not, as the realists and suprastate constitutional sceptics have it, an unspecified arbitrary level of 'idealism', or even a failure to guide action. Rather, the distinction should be based on a theory being within the range of the 'floor' and 'ceiling' set by the exclusion of status quo bias and technical constraints, the extent to which the purposes of the theory are clearly specified, and the extent to which the level of generalization made in the assumptions of the theory are appropriate to that particular purpose. If we want very specific prescriptions about how to act in particular contexts, then our theories should be much more factually informed of the context, that is, rely on limited generalization. If we want to serve broad evaluative aims, our theories should generalize much more.

1. Suprastate constitutionalism as normative theory

Highlighting the fact that idealism or utopianism is not necessarily a flaw in normative theory doesn't just encourage us to move beyond low-level generalizations or specific action-guiding recommendations in looking at legitimacy questions at the suprastate level. It also serves to underline the role and relevance of extant suprastate constitutional theory and highlight the ways in which it can contribute to addressing problems of legitimacy in suprastate governance. Current uses of constitutionalism at the suprastate level betray a range of purposes and levels of generalization compatible with the broad range of purposes and levels of theorization identified above. Moreover, they include both 'heavier' and 'lighter' forms which make their

[141] Stemplowska, 'What's Ideal about Ideal Theory?' (n 62) 327–29. [142] ibid 337.
[143] ibid 328. [144] ibid 332. [145] ibid 336. [146] ibid 339.

own distinct contributions. The vindication of suprastate constitutional theory, both 'heavy' and 'lite', in this way can be illustrated by reference to two particular types of suprastate constitutional theory: theories of constitutionalization and 'world-order' constitutional theories.

Theories of 'constitutionalization'[147] or 'multi-level constitutionalism'[148] provide examples of low-generalizing normative theory which makes specific action-guiding recommendations in the context of the legitimacy questions associated with the post-Westphalian transition. The main thrust of these approaches involves taking suprastate governing structures as they are—usually set up through international treaties—and prescribing particular 'corrective' measures to their structures or practices to enhance their legitimacy.[149] What is clear in accounts of constitutionalization theories is that the prescriptions made are very sensitive to the governing body in question. Given the variety of suprastate governing bodies, the nature and extent of constitutionalization will vary from governing site to governing site. Related to this idea is the notion of 'multi-level constitutionalism'. This involves extrapolating from the legitimacy deficits of one specific site of governance, whether state or suprastate, to examine the interactions between them and see how they can be mutually reinforcing in terms of the legitimacy of their governing activities.[150] Multilevel constitutionalism therefore involves a composite of suprastate and state constitutionalism infused with values such as the rule of law, judicial review, human rights, the separation of powers, democracy, and a minimum of social security guarantees.[151]

The corrective or 'compensatory'[152] nature of these theories serves to highlight the relatively limited levels of generalization involved. Here, the purpose of the theory is well defined: compensating for specific legitimacy deficits at the state as well as suprastate level. In this regard, action-guiding recommendations are an important feature of these theories given that they attempt to prescribe courses of action for particular problems of legitimacy emerging in the particular sites of governance, whether state or suprastate. Peters outlines some of the practical uses of these approaches: providing guidelines for the interpretation of 'textually open international norms';[153] influencing the process of law-making; providing resources for institutional reform in, for example, the UN Security Council; critiquing the functioning of international institutions on good governance grounds as well as

[147] See Anne Peters, 'Compensatory Constitutionalism: The Function and Potential of Fundamental International Norms and Structures' (2006) 19 Leiden Journal of International Law 579, 583; Loughlin, 'What is Constitutionalisation?' (n 12).

[148] Ingolf Pernice, 'Multilevel Constitutionalism in the European Union' (2002) 27 European Law Review 511; Ernst Ulrich Petersmann, *Multilevel Constitutionalism for Multilevel Governance of Public Goods: Methodology Problems in International Law* (Bloomsbury 2017); Peters, 'Compensatory Constitutionalism' (n 147).

[149] See Klabbers et al, *The Constitutionalization of International Law* (n 6) ch 7; see also Krisch, *Beyond Constitutionalism* (n 3) 58.

[150] For a thorough development of this idea in theoretical terms, see Roughan's account of 'relative authority'. Nicole Roughan, *Authorities: Conflicts, Cooperation, and Transnational Legal Theory* (Oxford University Press 2013) chs 8, 10.

[151] Peters, 'Compensatory Constitutionalism' (n 147) 585.

[152] Klabbers et al, *The Constitutionalization of International Law* (n 6) 347.

[153] Peters, 'Compensatory Constitutionalism' (n 147) 606.

providing clarification for the role and status of international norms when they come into conflict with domestic constitutional norms.[154] All of these purposes are clearly feasible action-guiding recommendations and involve a concomitant low-level of generalization.[155]

However, even 'heavier' suprastate constitutional theories can be useful in the context of addressing legitimacy questions in suprastate law and governance. Habermas's project for a 'political constitution for a decentred world society'[156] provides one such example. Taking his starting point in Kant's project for perpetual peace, his model envisages three distinct, albeit connected, levels of law and governance: supranational, transnational, and national.[157] The 'supranational' level involves a world organization—similar to but not the same as the current United Nations—which would have 'vital but clearly circumstanced functions of security, peace and promoting human rights'.[158] The intermediate, 'transnational', level would involve cooperation on specific policy areas at a regional or continental level—the European Union is a model here—which would be 'equipped with a representative mandate to negotiate for whole continents and to wield the necessary powers of implementation for large territories'.[159] Finally, the national level equates with the current member states of the UN system. This tripartite structure also envisages two forms of citizenship: the citizens of extant sovereign states, which is the strongest site for democratic legitimacy, and a 'global public sphere and solidarity between world citizens'.[160] However, this global solidarity need not be particularly developed, it being sufficient that there is a shared 'moral outrage toward egregious human rights violations and manifest acts of aggression'.[161]

Habermas explicitly deals with questions of generalization in proposing his project. He notes that one of the reasons that led Kant to reject a global world state or 'republic of republics' and favour an association of peaceful republics was the fact that the former was too far detached from the contemporary (in Kant's time) state of relations between states.[162] Against this backdrop, Habermas attempts to provide an alternative account to Kant's, but expressly states that it serves merely as 'an illustration of a conceptual alternative to a world republic'[163] to show what is 'at least conceptually possible',[164] noting that such proposals are '*ahead of*'[165] existing global structures. He recognizes the 'powerlessness of a mere ought',[166] and that 'even well justified normative projects remain without consequence if reality does not meet them half way'.[167] As such, Habermas's account speaks directly to some of the roles for normative theory identified by Stemplowska and Estlund, such as visualizing alternative worlds which would be desirable even if they are never achieved,

[154] ibid 606–07. [155] Stemplowska, 'What's Ideal about Ideal Theory?' (n 62) 324.
[156] Habermas, *The Divided West* (n 9) 136. [157] ibid. [158] ibid.
[159] Jürgen Habermas, 'The Constitutionalization of International Law and the Legitimation Problems of a Constitution for World Society' (2008) 15 Constellations 444, 447.
[160] Habermas, *The Divided West* (n 9) 143. [161] ibid. [162] ibid 127.
[163] ibid 136. [164] ibid 144.
[165] Jürgen Habermas, 'A Political Constitution for the Pluralist World Society?' (2007) Journal of Chinese Philosophy 331, 335 (emphasis added).
[166] ibid 337. [167] ibid.

but also the problems associated with impossible ideal theory. Also, his proposals provide certain benchmarks for global governance for evaluative purposes, that is to see the possible ultimate goals that suprastate institution- and regime-building may aim towards, as well as providing a metric to assess the gap between the world as it is today, and the achievement of that ideal. Indeed, Habermas himself notes that much more work needs to be done in terms of legitimation, and particularly connecting the chain of legitimation from states to the supranational level, to achieve these aims.[168]

What these examples illustrate is that contemporary suprastate constitutional theorizing cannot be legitimately dismissed for entailing idealization or generalization. Rather, generalization is a necessary and useful aspect of suprastate constitutional theory. What requires attention are the purposes of the constitutional theory and, in particular, whether it aims at providing action-guiding recommendations or other purposes and whether or not it remains within morally acceptable parameters. Here, we can see that contemporary suprastate constitutional theory entails a variety of purposes for which different levels of generalization are required. In the light of the discussion above, these constitutional theories—and even 'heavier' ones—are perfectly defensible.

E. Conclusion

In this chapter, I have raised two reasons to be sceptical about suprastate constitutional scepticism and particularly its critique of the idealistic or utopian nature of suprastate constitutionalism. This critique centres around the concept of demos embedded in the concept of constitutionalism and the fragmented realities of suprastate society. However, the concept of a demos, when viewed through a normative register, itself entails idealistic and potentially utopian claims. Furthermore, recent interventions in political-philosophical debates on idealism in normative theory have shown that idealism is not in itself problematic, provided certain conditions are respected.

[168] ibid 338. In fact, in some senses, suprastate constitutional sceptics acknowledge the role that purposes and levels of generalization can play in constitutional theories addressing the legitimacy challenges involved in the post-Westphalian transition. Krisch, for example, in a remarkable admission, accepts that 'the notion of constituent power [doesn't] have to be abandoned on a *normative* plane. As we have seen in the proposals of [*inter alia*] Habermas, constituent power may well play a meaningful role in the construction of a future postnational order with a stronger basis in public autonomy' and that 'such a ... utopian ideal can also provide the basis for the continuing discursive relevance of constituent power as a justification of principled resistance'. Krisch, 'Pouvoir Constituent *and* Pouvoir Irritant *in the Postnational Order*' (n 12) 677 (emphasis in the original). This admission comes accompanied by a 'health warning' that such proposals need to remain aware of, and explicitly acknowledge, the gap between the theories and realities of the suprastate realm (ibid 677). There are two points to be made here. First, it is not clear how suprastate constitutional theory can operate on any other 'plane' than a normative one if we are concerned with questions of legitimacy in suprastate law and governance. Furthermore, the admission suggests that even suprastate constitutional sceptics themselves are starting to doubt the strength of their own objections to suprastate constitutionalism.

These grounds for scepticism about suprastate constitutional scepticism leave us with a sense of the renewed possibilities for constitutionalism in the context of addressing the legitimacy problems of the post-Westphalian transition. It encourages us to think in terms of suprastate constitutionalism rather than a single monolithic suprastate constitutionalism, in that the level of abstraction or idealization appropriate in this context will depend on the purpose of the particular constitutional theory advanced. This was illustrated by contrasting different types of suprastate constitutional theories, such as constitutionalization and world-order constitutional theories. In this way, the field of suprastate constitutionalism is not pre-emptively shut down by claims of idealism, but can explore solutions to ever more problems arising at this level with a variety of bespoke and innovative constitutional theories. Indeed, the range of possibilities of constitutional theories at the suprastate level means that suprastate constitutional theory will inevitably have an affinity with, if not be sympathetic to, some of the theories, such as pluralism or global administrative law, which are defined, in part, through their opposition to the very idea of suprastate constitutionalism. Suprastate constitutional theory is more versatile than is commonly thought and provides an important normative resource in thinking about legitimacy in the post-Westphalian transition as it enters a particularly turbulent era.

X

Perfectionist Liberalism and the Legitimacy of International Law

Michael Sevel

The dominant approach to liberal political philosophy has been based on the general idea that, when faced with a diverse society, in which citizens pursue complex and incompatible conceptions of a good life, the state ought to abstain from expressing commitment to, but, more importantly, abstain from acting upon and in pursuit of, any of them. That is, in order to be legitimate, a state in governing must remain neutral among all of those conceptions. Given the profound influence of this approach over the last half century, through the work of Rawls, Larmore, and others,[1] the opposing (and much older) approach of perfectionism has often, and perhaps unfairly, been defined negatively: as simply the rejection of state neutrality in determining the legitimacy of the state and its organs. A more robust formulation, however, is that a legitimate state tries, in the adoption of laws and policies, to realize valuable forms of life for its citizens, where 'valuable' references something other than subjective or relativized standards.[2]

Perhaps the leading defender of perfectionist liberalism in recent times is Joseph Raz, who has sporadically developed a distinctive version of the theory over the last thirty years.[3] We will examine the details of Raz's theory, but as a general matter, it

[1] John Rawls, *A Theory of Justice* (rev edn, Harvard University Press 1999); John Rawls, *Political Liberalism* (Columbia University Press 2005); Charles Larmore, *The Morals of Modernity* (Cambridge University Press 1996); Thomas Nagel, 'Moral Conflict and Political Legitimacy' (1987) 16 Philosophy and Public Affairs 215.

[2] The question of whether perfectionist liberalism requires commitment to some, or any, form of moral realism (roughly, that there are objective, mind-independent moral facts), or whether it is compatible with other, more sceptical views in metaethics, has received scant attention in the liberalism literature. I note, however, that the leading proponents of perfectionism over the last century, from TH Green and Hobhouse to Raz, have all been moral realists of various sorts. Settling the issue will not matter for my purposes here.

[3] See Joseph Raz, *The Morality of Freedom* (Clarendon Press 1986); Joseph Raz, 'Autonomy, Toleration, and the Harm Principle' in Ruth Gavison (ed), *Issues in Contemporary Legal Philosophy* (Oxford University Press 1987); Joseph Raz, 'Facing Up' (1989) 62 Southern California Law Review 1230, 1230–36; Joseph Raz, *Ethics in the Public Domain* (Oxford University Press 1994); Joseph Raz, 'On Respect, Authority, and Neutrality: A Response' (2010) 120 Ethics 279; Joseph Raz, 'Human Rights in the Emerging World Order' (2010) 1 Transnational Legal Theory 31, 41–47; Joseph Raz, 'Comments on *The Morality of Freedom*' (2016) 14 Jerusalem Review of Legal Studies 169; Joseph Raz, 'Why the State?' in Andrew Halpin and Nicole Roughan (eds), *In Pursuit of Pluralist Jurisprudence*

Legitimacy: The State and Beyond. First Edition. Edited by Wojciech Sadurski, Michael Sevel, and Kevin Walton. Published 2019 by Oxford University Press.

is worth noting that a salient feature of the general characterization of perfectionism just given is that it is put forth as a theory of legitimacy only of the *state* and its institutions. And while proponents of state neutrality have recently extended their theories to the principles of legitimacy of international law and institutions,[4] perfectionists such as Raz have said very little about the relevance of their theories to such questions. Indeed, Raz's influential ideas in legal and political philosophy have been applied in the international realm (by others) in only two, quite narrow ways. First, his general theory of (state-based) law has been considered as an explanation of the nature of international and transnational law.[5] Second, and more commonly, his much-discussed 'service conception' of authority, and the complex theory of reasons which underwrite it, has been straightforwardly extended to explain the normativity and structure of various aspects of international law and institutions.[6] And to the extent that Raz himself has considered international law at all, it has been more in a descriptive or conceptual, rather than a normative, mode.[7]

And yet, there are reasons to think that Raz's perfectionism can naturally be extended to the explanation and justification of international law and institutions. For example, he characterizes his political philosophy as a 'liberal foundation for a political morality', that part of morality which governs the actions of political institutions.[8] Even attentive readers presume that 'political institutions' is here limited to those of the state and its organs,[9] but Raz is clear that the term encompasses 'all public authorities', which may include ones which are not constitutive parts of state-based legal systems—for example, those within religions, sports leagues,

(Cambridge University Press 2017); Joseph Raz, 'The Future of State Sovereignty', Chapter IV in this volume.

[4] See, for example, DAJ Richards, 'International Distributive Justice' in J Pennock and J Chapman (eds), *Ethics, Economics, and the Law* (New York University Press 1982); Thomas Pogge, *Realizing Rawls* (Cornell University Press 1989) 211–80; Thomas Nagel, 'The Problem of Global Justice' (2005) 33 Philosophy and Public Affairs 113; Andreas Follesdal, 'Justice, Stability, and Toleration in a Federation of Well-Ordered Peoples' in Rex Martin and David A Reidy (eds), *Rawls's Law of Peoples: A Realistic Utopia?* (Blackwell Publishing 2006).

[5] See, for example, Keith Culver and Michael Giudice, *Legality's Borders: An Essay in General Jurisprudence* (Oxford University Press 2010).

[6] Samantha Besson, 'Theorizing the Sources of International Law' in Samantha Besson and John Tasioulas (eds), *The Philosophy of International* Law (Oxford University Press 2010); Allen Buchanan, 'The Legitimacy of International Law' in Samantha Besson and John Tasioulas (eds), *The Philosophy of International* Law (Oxford University Press 2010); John Tasioulas, 'The Legitimacy of International Law' in Samantha Besson and John Tasioulas (eds), *The Philosophy of International* Law (Oxford University Press 2010); Samantha Besson, 'The Authority of International Law-Lifting the State Veil' (2009) 31 Sydney Law Review 343; Nicole Roughan, 'Mind the Gaps: Authority and Legality in International Law' (2016) 27 European Journal of International Law 329; Richard Collins, 'Sources and the Legitimate Authority of International Law: A Challenge to the "Standard View"?' in Samantha Besson and Jean d'Aspremont (eds), *The Oxford Handbook of the Sources of International Law* (Oxford University Press 2017); Andreas Follesdal, 'The Legitimate Authority of International Courts and Its Limits: A Challenge to Raz's Service Conception?' in Patrick Capps and Henrik Palmer Olsen (eds), *Legal Authority beyond the State* (Cambridge University Press 2018).

[7] See Raz, 'Why the State?' (n 3); and Raz, 'The Future of State Sovereignty' (n 3). I use the descriptive/normative distinction in the sense explained in Buchanan, 'The Legitimacy of International Law' (n 6).

[8] Raz, *The Morality of Freedom* (n 3) 3.

[9] See, for example, Thomas Nagel, 'Getting on with Each Other' (1994) 16 London Review of Books 12; George Sher, *Beyond Neutrality: Perfectionism and Politics* (Cambridge University Press 1997).

corporations, or other transnational institutions that claim authority over some community or other.[10] Thus, from the start, his much-discussed account of legitimate practical authority extends in principle to non-state-based legal authorities, such as international courts or transnational commercial arbitration panels. And although that account is often discussed (particularly by legal philosophers) in isolation from Raz's political philosophy,[11] the service conception is explicitly put forth as an essential part of a broader perfectionist liberalism, a body of principles which 'require[s] governments to protect and promote individual freedom' and well-being, such that 'violation of the principles of freedom may undermine the legitimacy of the authority'.[12] Perfectionist principles are therefore 'part of a view of the foundations of legitimacy of political authorities'.[13] The theoretical motivations of Raz's perfectionist liberalism, therefore, in respect of both its theory of authority and broader political principles of legitimacy, seem *ex ante* suitable for application to the international and transnational domains.

However, it may be thought that the core idea of perfectionism—that political authorities should act on and favour one particular conception of the good life—is precisely what makes it problematic as a framework for justifying and explaining legal institutions beyond the state. Just as such partiality within the state may ground a charge of some form of authoritarianism (in the coercive enforcement of principles based on the perfectionist's preferred morality),[14] the objection seems more acute in the case of international legal authorities. Such authorities, especially those with general jurisdiction like the International Court of Justice, run the risk of being even more 'morally authoritarian' in their tendencies, in virtue of the fact that they are charged with considering an even wider diversity of conceptions of the good life than courts within states, that is, in principle the full extent of the diversity of such conceptions in existence across the world at a given time.

Raz responds to the worry about authoritarianism within the state by advocating a strong form of moral pluralism, and complementary, mutually reinforcing conceptions of autonomy and toleration. But how such views address the moral diversity across state boundaries is unclear and so will be the focus of my discussion. Not surprisingly, many of the same objections to perfectionism within the state also apply when extended beyond it. I will consider a set of closely related and now familiar objections to perfectionism from the point of view of Rawlsian political

[10] cf Raz, *The Morality of Freedom* (n 3) 4–5, where Raz claims that private organizations such as corporations and trade unions 'are like public authorities'; but see also Raz, *Ethics in the Public Domain* (n 3) 34, in which public authorities are clearly distinguished as a broader class than state-based, legal ones: 'Typically governments and other public authorities have duties to protect the common goods of a community.'

[11] See, for example, Kenneth Ehrenberg, 'Joseph Raz's Theory of Authority' (2011) 6 Philosophy Compass 884; Scott Hershovitz, 'The Role of Authority' (2011) 11 Philosophers' Imprint 1; Scott Shapiro, 'Authority' in Jules Coleman and Scott Shapiro (eds), *The Oxford Handbook of Jurisprudence and Philosophy of Law* (Oxford University Press 2002).

[12] Raz, *The Morality of Freedom* (n 3) 21. [13] ibid.

[14] George Crowder, *Liberalism and Value Pluralism* (Continuum 2002) 202. Raz acknowledges this sort of worry in *The Morality of Freedom* (n 3) 412: 'This may sound very rigoristic and paternalistic. It conjures images of the state playing big brother forcing or manipulating people to do what it considers good for them against their will.'

liberalism: that the kind of strong moral pluralism for which Raz argues, as a necessary part of his broader theory, is inherently less stable politically than other kinds of liberalism which advocate state neutrality, and that by privileging the autonomous life as (conditionally) valuable, perfectionism has the effect of 'denigrating and expressively subordinating many citizens' who hold contrary, non-perfectionist moral views and thus of disrespecting them.[15] I argue that these objections do not succeed in respect of state government, but that even if they are plausible in that case, they have considerably less force in the international context. This is owing to familiar features of international institutions, such as limited jurisdiction and lack of formal enforcement mechanisms, the significance of which is cast in a new light given their distinctive function in perfectionist liberal theory. I begin by setting out the essential features of Raz's state-based perfectionist liberalism, and then suggest how the theory may be extended to international legal institutions. I then consider the Rawlsian objections to, first, Raz's state-based perfectionism, and then in relation to the internationalized version of the theory as I have developed it. The overall aim is to show that Raz's perfectionism is less vulnerable to Rawlsian objections than often thought, and even less so in the case of perfectionist liberalism as applied to international law and institutions.

A. Raz's Perfectionism: A Primer

Most aspects of Raz's perfectionist political theory have been critically discussed over the last three decades, so for present purposes we need not delve too deeply into matters of interpretation except when necessary. As is often the case in Raz's thought, his political theory consists of several interlocking and mutually supporting views which are not easily severable from his views in moral and legal philosophy. We may start, then, with the notion of a person's well-being, the promotion of which Raz says is 'the pivotal ethical precept of public action',[16] and so is central to his perfectionist political theory as it applies to the governments of states. Raz characterizes a person's well-being as the whole-hearted, successful pursuit of valuable activities, goals, or projects by a person over the course of that person's life.[17] Such valuable or worthwhile goals must (largely) be chosen by the person whose goals they are, and so not forced upon them, in order for that person to lead a life of their choosing, that is, in order to be the author of her life.[18] Deliberating about such worthwhile goals, as well as choosing and pursuing them, are the primary ways in which persons engage their faculty of reason, and thereby display activity rather than passivity, activity being one of the marks of personhood.[19]

[15] Martha Nussbaum, 'Perfectionist Liberalism and Political Liberalism' (2011) 39 Philosophy and Public Affairs 3, 38.

[16] Raz, *Ethics in the Public Domain* (n 3) vi.

[17] ibid 3; see also Raz, *The Morality of Freedom* (n 3) 308–09; Joseph Raz, *Engaging Reason* (Oxford University Press 1999) 306–07; Raz, 'The Role of Well-Being' (2004) 18 Philosophical Perspectives 269.

[18] Raz, *The Morality of Freedom* (n 3) 306.

[19] Raz, *Engaging Reason* (n 17) 5–21.

In order for it to be possible for a person to realize their well-being, it must be the case that the goals or projects adopted are several and varied, and that they are in fact chosen among a range of (again, valuable) options. And so, for example, the tragic figure from Greek mythology, Sisyphus, who was condemned to the underworld to roll a boulder uphill over and over again for all eternity, cannot achieve any reasonable degree of well-being because, while there are some trivial opportunities for free choice (for example, how often and how fast to push the boulder uphill, and so on), his long-term life options are limited to only one.[20] The adequacy of a particular range of options is determined by not only their number, but also variety, along a number of metrics, including both long- and short-term options, and ones which engage our emotional, physical, and intellectual capacities, among others.[21] Such options (as diverse as what to have for dinner, to one's hobbies, to choosing one's friends and occupation) are typically available to a person via a comprehensive set of practices, norms, and attitudes which constitute a culture.[22]

The state of affairs in which persons have an adequate range of worthwhile options available to them over time Raz calls personal autonomy,[23] the protection and promotion of which is of central concern to legitimate political authorities. Autonomy itself does not guarantee the well-being of the autonomous person; a person who achieves well-being must act on it or take advantage of it, that is, use the autonomy available to them to both choose worthwhile options and, importantly, achieve some level of success in pursuit of them. The prospect of achieving well-being is a source of what Raz calls 'action reasons', reasons for the performance of actions by particular agents; these are reasons which only the person whose well-being is at issue can act on. A person recognizing and responding to the reasons arising from one's own projects contributes to living an autonomous life in that one thereby is (partly) the author of one's life.

Now, the plurality of worthwhile options required for a person to live autonomously, for all that has been said so far, may be thought to be of only a mundane sort, that is, an array of various options within a cultural milieu which are incompatible only in the sense that a person cannot pursue all of them at the same time, or even in the same life, such that the reasons one has to pursue them may always conflict.[24]

[20] cf Raz's examples of 'the man in the pit' and 'the hounded woman', illustrating the same problem, in *The Morality of Freedom* (n 3) 373–74.

[21] 'To be autonomous and have an autonomous life, a person must have options which enable him to sustain throughout his life activities taken together, exercise all the capacities human beings have an innate drive to exercise, as well as to decline to develop any of them.' Raz, *The Morality of Freedom* (n 3) 375.

[22] See especially Raz, *Ethics in the Public Domain* (n 3) 170–91; and Avishai Margalit and Joseph Raz, 'National Self-Determination' (1990) 87 The Journal of Philosophy 439, 448. cf Will Kymlicka, *Multicultural Citizenship* (Oxford University Press 1995) 76. Whether a self-contained culture is required to deliver a comprehensive set of valuable options is contested in Jeremy Waldron, 'Two Conceptions of Self Determination' in Samantha Besson and John Tasioulas (eds), *The Philosophy of International Law* (Oxford University Press 2010) 401–06.

[23] Raz, 'Autonomy, Toleration, and the Harm Principle' (n 3) 314–15; Raz, *The Morality of Freedom* (n 3) 378–79.

[24] Raz calls this 'weak moral pluralism': Raz, *The Morality of Freedom* (n 3) 396. Nussbaum calls the same view 'internal pluralism': Nussbaum, 'Perfectionist Liberalism and Political Liberalism' (n 15) 9.

But Raz argues for a stronger view. The various options constitutive of autonomy are commonly, he claims, strongly incommensurable with each other. That is, between two options, if they are incommensurable, it is true of them that neither is more valuable (and thus choiceworthy) than the other, nor are they of equal value.[25] The strong moral pluralism he advocates is the view that 'there are various forms and styles of life which exemplify different virtues and which are incompatible' and yet are all morally valuable.[26] Raz's pluralism is strong in another sense. If there are, as he claims, plural, incompatible, and yet valuable, forms of life which require and cultivate different (and, again, incommensurable) virtues, then persons leading these lives of incompatible virtue will be disposed to conflict with and be intolerant of one another. The cultivation of a given set of virtues suitable to one form of life seems to have the invariable side effect of creating a tendency in the person who cultivates them to view other forms of life with disdain and disapproval. For example, philosophers tend to regard lawyers as fickle-minded and hasty thinkers; lawyers will regard philosophers as indecisive and impractical. Plumbers will regard both as lost in abstractions and lacking in 'common sense'. Bankers will, in turn, regard all three ways of life as less significant than their chosen vocation and advantageous skills in a capitalist society. And so on.[27] Raz uses the term 'competitive pluralism' to refer to this situation in which persons pursuing valuable and incompatible ways of life have a tendency to feel (and in some form express) intolerance and animosity towards each other on the basis that each tries to cultivate valuable but incompatible virtues which will enable their respective successes in their own lives, but will also ground criticism of others who cultivate different, incompatible virtues.[28] Raz runs an argument that autonomy, construed as the availability of a sufficient range of valuable options, *requires* this kind of pluralism, although that argument need not detain us here.[29] He further argues that the animosity and divisiveness that is the inevitable side effect of competitive pluralism combined with the value of autonomy, requires the implementation (and perhaps coercive enforcement) of a principle of toleration.

How does this collection of views justify and figure into the actions and legitimacy of the political authorities of states? Raz has perhaps been most influential as a

[25] Raz, *The Morality of Freedom* (n 3) 322–23; Raz, *Engaging Reason* (n 17) 66.

[26] Raz, 'Autonomy, Toleration, and the Harm Principle' (n 3) 316. Although he does not discuss it, Raz presumably accepts that incommensurability holds not only between options within a culture, but also between options *across* cultures, for example, between Christian and Buddhist marriage customs. This is significant in the context of legal governance both in multicultural societies and, as will be discussed below, in legal frameworks applying to and across states.

[27] I use examples of occupation, but conflicts may arise in regard to virtually any life project—for example, religion, hobbies, how one raises one's children, and many other cultural practices. See Catriona McKinnon, 'Tolerance and the Character of Pluralism' in Catriona McKinnon and Dario Castiglione (eds), *The Culture of Toleration in Diverse Societies* (Manchester University Press 2003) 65.

[28] Again, such conflict can arise not only among people pursuing incompatible lives within a single culture, but perhaps more dramatically among people, either in a single society or across societies, pursuing goals within distinct cultures.

[29] At times, Raz suggests the ultimate basis of this connection between autonomy and competitive pluralism is rooted in the nature of the potentiality of human capacities, each of which can be developed in an indefinite number of worthwhile and incompatible ways. See, for example, n 21 and Raz, 'Autonomy, Toleration, and the Harm Principle' (n 3) 315.

theorist of practical authority; his 'service conception' has been critically discussed among legal philosophers for decades.[30] The relevant aspect of that conception for present purposes is the 'normal justification thesis', according to which an authority is legitimate only if a putative subject, by recognizing and acting on its directives as pre-emptive reasons, achieves greater conformity to the reasons which apply to her independently of those directives.[31] Raz and others have sometimes claimed that the theory is nearly as simple as this, and that it may be evaluated independently of any other arguments in moral and political philosophy. The claim is dubious,[32] and the reasons why are most salient in the present context. To be sure, so far as the service conception goes, the political authorities of states issue binding directives to their citizens which are backed up by reasons of some sort, reasons which justify those directives and (indirectly, over time) render the issuing authorities legitimate. But if only that were required, an authority would satisfy its conditions for legitimacy by offering its subjects only one option, or only one circumscribed set of options, for example, compulsory education, followed by military service, and a strict regime of options thereafter, akin to that provided to the 'guardian' class in Plato's *Republic*,[33] so long as that option or set of options were justified by the subjects' background reasons. It should be clear, however, given what has been said so far regarding the nature of autonomy and well-being, obedient persons living under such an authority would likely not be able to live an autonomous life to any great extent and thus unable to enjoy a reasonable degree of well-being.

So, in light of the pluralism required for autonomy and the idea that autonomy is at least an enabling, necessary condition of personal well-being, legitimate authorities of the state must do substantially more than simply help their subjects conform to some reasons or other that apply to them. In a perfectionist society, authorities (like everyone else) are under a duty to facilitate the well-being of people.[34] But if the achievement of well-being is ultimately in the hands of the persons whose well-being it is, the facilitation of it by political authorities will be at most indirect.[35] The authorities of the state must play what may be called a supervisory (and

[30] See Kenneth Ehrenberg, 'Critical Reception of Raz's Theory of Authority' (2011) 6 Philosophy Compass 777.

[31] Raz, *The Morality of Freedom* (n 3) 53; Joseph Raz, *Between Authority and Interpretation: On the Theory of Law and Practical Reason* (Oxford University Press 2009) 136–37.

[32] See Michael Sevel, 'The Constitution of Authority' (2014) 5 Jurisprudence 430.

[33] See Plato, 'Republic' in John Cooper (ed), *Plato: Complete Works* (GMA Grube and CDC Reeve trs, Hackett Publishing 1997) 376d–427c.

[34] Raz, *Ethics in the Public Domain* (n 3) 9. This should not be confused with the idea that legitimate authorities have a duty to govern, much less a duty to govern in a particular way, as the Thomist tradition has it. See Leslie Green, 'The Duty to Govern' (2007) 13 Legal Theory 165.

[35] Raz, *The Morality of Freedom* (n 3) 407. This is the sense in which Raz disagrees with Aristotle's famous claim that citizens can be made virtuous by laws which force them to engage in the habits of virtuous people. See Aristotle, 'Nichomachean Ethics' in Jonathan Barnes (ed), *The Complete Works of Aristotle*, vol 2 (WD Ross and JO Urmson trs, Princeton University Press 1984), 1179b30–80a10. For Raz, obeying the laws made by legitimate authorities will make one more *rational*, in the sense of acting in greater conformity with the reasons one has; but whether a person leads an autonomous life with a sufficient degree of well-being in large part will depend on the efforts and success of that person in her chosen goals and projects, explainable only by reference to far more than the requirements of governments.

coordinative) role in ensuring the autonomy of its citizens—that is, ensuring that its citizens have an adequate range of worthwhile options to choose from, throughout their lives and in every area of life (social relations, work, recreation, and so on), so that well-being is at least possible for them.[36] This is the deeper significance of Raz's repeated insistence that legal authorities are comprehensive, in the sense that their claim to legitimacy includes the right to regulate, in principle, all forms of behaviour.[37] Anything short of comprehensiveness in this regard would severely hinder an authority's capacity to promote and secure autonomy for its citizens, to ensure the availability to them of an adequate range of worthwhile options.

In order to secure autonomy, perfectionist political authorities must also embrace competitive pluralism; they must govern in accordance with the view that there are many incompatible and valuable forms of life to be lived by their citizens, both within and across cultures. The imposition of only one such way of life (or the prohibition of all but one) would be stifling from the perspective of well-being and therefore likely harmful to those citizens.[38] In multicultural societies, there are additional tasks for legitimate political authorities. In such societies, the fact of competitive pluralism may require them to take action to protect, preserve, and sustain minority cultures whose participants want them preserved.[39] Perfectionist authorities will also govern in accordance with a principle of toleration which is compatible with and reflective of a competitive pluralist society, that is, a principle that takes into account the ongoing potential conflict involved in citizens being disposed to discount and even resent each other's forms of life and respective virtues. But importantly, as Raz points out, legitimate authorities may act 'in accordance with' pluralism without avowing it, much less publicly endorsing it; as he puts it, authorities can respect pluralism without recognizing it.[40]

B. Perfectionism beyond the State

How might this complex account of the legitimacy of the perfectionist state extend to international legal institutions? We may start by reiterating the obvious point that like many forms of liberal political philosophy, Raz's perfectionism is based on the value of personal well-being and what makes it possible: personal autonomy

[36] Raz, *The Morality of Freedom* (n 3) 133, 417. For helpful discussion of this point, see Denise Meyerson, 'Three Versions of Liberal Tolerance: Dworkin, Rawls, Raz' (2012) 3 Jurisprudence 37, 52–59.

[37] Joseph Raz, *Practical Reason and Norms* (2nd edn, Oxford University Press 1990) 150–51; Joseph Raz, *The Authority of Law* (2nd edn, Oxford University Press 2009) 116–17; Raz, *The Morality of Freedom* (n 3) 4.

[38] Raz, *The Morality of Freedom* (n 3) 161. Raz does not elaborate on the precise role of perfectionist principles in the exercise of political authority; I discuss it below.

[39] Raz, *Ethics in the Public Domain* (n 3) 180–83.

[40] Raz, 'The Future of State Sovereignty' (n 3) 80. This corresponds to an important, recurring distinction in Raz's thought between conforming to and complying with a reason. See Raz, *Practical Reason and Norms* (n 37) 178–79. See also his discussion of the structure of the reasons for respecting persons in Joseph Raz, *Value, Respect, and Attachment* (Oxford University Press 2001) 160–64.

and individual freedom.[41] And that, in addition to the theoretical emphasis, already noted, on public authorities generally rather than the legal authorities only of the state, may suggest an approach to the question from something like a cosmopolitan point of view, according to which the autonomy and well-being of each person within a set of states, or all states, are, in principle, the direct concern of international legal institutions, such as international courts, or legislative institutions, such as the European Parliament. A justification of such institutions would then be thoroughly individualistic, that is, would depend on whether their actions promote and protect the autonomy of individual persons across state boundaries.

However, the first obstacle of extending perfectionism to the international legal arena is encountered even here. As we have seen, perfectionist state governments achieve legitimacy by not only satisfying the abstract normal justification thesis, but by going much further, to protect the autonomy of its citizens by providing them with a sufficient range of morally acceptable and incompatible options and ways of life. The state and its institutions ensure this in part by exhibiting (for example, by claiming) comprehensiveness in its authority: the capacity to, in principle, regulate all forms of behaviour of its citizens. Comprehensive authority in this sense is, however, precisely what international legal institutions lack.[42] The European Court of Human Rights, for example, proceeds on a case-by-case basis, enforcing and protecting only the rights set out in the Convention and Protocols which established it. Through the lens of Raz's perfectionism, the Court considers highly circumscribed aspects of the autonomy of particular litigants in disputes before it, for example, a person's right to engage in religious practices or to immigrate to a neighbouring country which would greatly affect the options open to them. In this way, the Court's capacity to promote and protect the autonomy of those persons—which, recall, requires creating or sustaining an adequate range of worthwhile options across time, indeed across the life of a person—is severely limited. The same would seem to be the case with every other international tribunal. Even the International Court of Justice may consider whether particular plaintiffs (which are always states, occasionally ones representing non-state interests) are being oppressed or unfairly treated in terms of whether particular options are available to its citizens or not. For example, the Court may consider whether a state has exclusive fishing rights within its coastal waters, such that its determination may substantially affect the availability of a broad range of cultural options constitutive of the autonomy of many citizens of a particular state.[43] It may be thought that the problem of lack of comprehensive authority applies only to tribunals. But international legislative and administrative institutions suffer the same problem. Institutions such as the World Trade Organization, the Pan-African Parliament, or the International Seabed Authority

[41] Raz, *The Morality of Freedom* (n 3) 18, 265–66, 369–72.

[42] See Culver and Giudice, *Legality's Borders* (n 5) 134. See also Jeremy Waldron, 'International Law: "A Relatively Small and Unimportant" Part of Jurisprudence?' in Luís Duarte d'Almeida, James Edwards, and Andrea Dolcetti (eds), *Reading HLA Hart's* The Concept of Law (Hart Publishing 2013).

[43] See, for example, the influential Anglo-Norwegian Fisheries Case, *The United Kingdom v Norway* [1951] ICJ Rep 116, which determined the maritime boundary between the two countries for the purpose of determining exclusive fishing rights.

are all, in different ways, considerably limited in their capacities to affect the autonomy and well-being of individual persons, due in part to their distinct purposes and roles within a larger institutional framework. But all these common examples reinforce the present point, that the capacity of international legal authorities to successfully act on and implement perfectionist principles is severely limited as compared to that of a state; it would seem then that their legitimacy, insofar as it depends on such action and implementation, is either quite weak or not achievable at all.

Given the lack of even claimed comprehensive authority by international institutions, a slightly different explanation of how they may discharge their perfectionist function of promoting autonomy may be available. It has recently been argued that a plurality of authorities which overlap in some way in their respective legitimate domains may be subject to principles of cooperation and coordination, principles which are additional to the ones operative in isolation from outside authorities.[44] In the present context, such cooperation and coordination would proceed between state and international legal institutions with the aim of protecting and promoting the personal autonomy of citizens in and across states. But as Raz points out, direct promotion of the autonomy of citizens within states by international institutions may be an inadequate way to enhance the legitimacy of such institutions, due primarily to the enduring importance of state sovereignty. Any reasonable principle of subsidiarity would require that states primarily (and perhaps exclusively) are charged with the task of maintaining the kind of pluralism required for autonomy.[45]

And yet, he argues that full recognition of (and not just respect for) the truth of pluralism by international institutions may indirectly serve as the basis of their legitimacy, by inspiring loyalty and solidarity in respect of them on the part of people around the world. But how is recognition of value-pluralism by international institutions supposed to affect—that is to say, improve—international relations and thereby improve legitimacy? To what extent is pluralism's role within states to be reproduced *among* states? Is the aim ultimately to work towards a fully perfectionist world government by way of a maximally developed international legal order? As we have seen, the immediate subjects of international institutions are still, in an overwhelming number of cases, states rather than persons. This seems to cast doubt on what I called earlier the broadly cosmopolitan approach. If state-based perfectionist liberalism is to be extended relatively seamlessly to international institutions, then the embrace of value-pluralism by those institutions would seem to serve the purpose of promoting the autonomy of *states*, in order for the *states* themselves to have an adequate range of valuable options from which to choose, in pursuit of some kind of statist well-being. But state autonomy in this sense is not obviously valuable; nor are states the bearers of well-being in any relevant sense.

But if we are led back to a cosmopolitan picture, in which the recognition of value-pluralism of international institutions is meant to enhance their legitimacy in relation to the *citizens* of states directly, and without a view to shaping a

[44] Nicole Roughan, *Authorities: Conflicts, Cooperation, and Transnational Legal Theory* (Oxford University Press 2013) 51–57.

[45] Raz, 'The Future of State Sovereignty' (n 3) 77–78.

comprehensive liberal international political order, then it is less clear how this would work. Again, individuals are rarely governed directly by international institutions, such that their recognition of value-pluralism would have such a direct effect on their available options in pursuit of well-being. Some international courts (for example, the European Court of Human Rights) have jurisdiction over individual complaints alleging human rights violations, and so can have such a direct supervisory function in regard to a citizen's autonomy. The Court could embrace pluralism and thereby inspire loyalty and solidarity among the class of successful plaintiffs. But the case-by-case influence, even over time, would be negligible. There are other sorts of examples: the United Nations recently formed the International Commission against Impunity in Guatemala (CICIG), part of a novel effort to fight corruption in Latin American governments. The Commission's investigations have led to the resignation and arrest of both the president and vice-president of the country, which has been met with widespread praise from ordinary citizens. Such efforts may lead to an overall increase in loyalty and solidary towards the United Nations on the part of Guatemalan citizens.[46] But this is also a rare example, and one which does not obviously require the recognition of the truth of pluralism.

These examples do not, however, directly counter Raz's argument that once a reasonable principle of subsidiarity is observed, which may limit the protection of pluralism to primarily a task for state governments, the best way for international institutions to gain legitimacy is to recognize the truth of competitive pluralism and to act on the basis of it. By recognizing, and not just respecting, pluralism, such institutions would address a set of recurring challenges to the legitimacy of international law and institutions: that the membership of such institutions are not representative of the community of states, that they are controlled by the rich and powerful states in their own interests, and so on.[47] Institutions based on pluralist principles may curb these tendencies, by inspiring a sense of identity with them on the part of citizens around the world.[48]

C. International Perfectionism and Respecting Persons

I turn now to consider recent objections to Raz's perfectionist liberalism as it applies within the state, recently made by Martha Nussbaum,[49] to then see whether the

[46] Interestingly, the Commission has recently come under criticism, precisely for contributing to corruption within the Guatemalan legal system. See Mary Anastasia O'Grady, 'A Crisis in Guatemala, Abetted by the U.N.' *Wall Street Journal* (New York, 22 April 2018) <https://www.wsj.com/articles/a-crisis-in-guatemala-abetted-by-the-u-n-1524420935> accessed 25 April 2018.

[47] See, for example, Buchanan, 'The Legitimacy of International Law' (n 6) 85–87; and Mohammed Ayoob, 'Humanitarian Intervention and State Sovereignty' (2002) 6 The International Journal of Human Rights 81.

[48] Raz, 'The Future of State Sovereignty' (n 3) 80–81. Raz spends little time exploring the ways in which international institutions may recognize pluralism, but we may suppose paradigmatic examples include explicitly citing perfectionist principles, or claims reflecting them, as the grounds of legislation, judicial reasoning, or administrative decisions.

[49] Nussbaum, 'Perfectionist Liberalism and Political Liberalism' (n 15).

objections may be plausibly refashioned to apply to its international form as characterized thus far. Nussbaum's objections are inspired by a rival account of liberalism, the political liberalism of Rawls and Larmore, which famously requires state neutrality among citizens' conceptions of the good life. She begins by noting the potential danger of governance according to a kind of 'monism' about value. This is when the state acts on the basis of the view that there is only one correct moral conception of the good life, and citizens' conduct and the policies and law that govern it are to be judged and shaped by that conception. This is similar to the danger of 'moral authoritarianism' noted earlier.[50] The real danger, Nussbaum claims, is that the state may, as a result, act on the belief that it has licence to coerce deviant citizens into adopting that conception and for them to live their lives according to it, severely curtailing individual freedom contrary to the spirit of liberalism.

Nussbaum credits Raz with presenting an attractive alternative to political liberalism which addresses this political danger of the state embracing 'monism' about value. Governance based on the truth of competitive pluralism, that there are multiple incompatible and morally valuable forms of life, is intended to diffuse this problem, both from a political and a philosophical perspective. If the legal and political institutions of a state govern according to this view, and implement a complementary doctrine of tolerance, then persons who pursue incompatible lives and virtues will not only be free to do so, but their pursuits will be tolerated by others, because of either the mutual recognition of one another's life projects as worthwhile, or at least the mutual withholding of animosity and disapproval of incompatible forms of life. And yet Nussbaum argues that Raz's perfectionism is far more problematic than Rawlsian-style approach, which recommends state neutrality. Her objection is rooted in the claim that pluralism is itself a form of monism: an alleged moral truth which everyone should therefore accept. But, she argues, nearly all comprehensive conceptions of the good life are not compatible with, much less committed to, any sort of pluralism, much less Raz's sort. This includes most religious views which may tolerate a modest kind of pluralism, but which fall far short of Raz's more radical and comprehensive competitive pluralism. Raz, therefore, wants 'to build liberal society on a set of views that virtually none of its members actually holds'.[51]

Nussbaum understands Raz's view to be that 'the government will be licensed to try to convert you to the correct view' of pluralism. This, she further claims, is an instance of the 'expressive subordination' of persons who hold comprehensive moral views which are incompatible with the alleged state-endorsed pluralism. Since the institutions of a perfectionist society are built on principles of pluralism, which persons with monistic conceptions of the good life (for example, orthodox religious Jews or Roman Catholics) ultimately reject, then Nussbaum claims those citizens are made to be second-class citizens who hold inferior moral views, which is itself a form of disrespect for persons.[52] She imputes to Raz the view that 'if [citizens] do not accept the fact of pluralism and the ideal of autonomy, it is fine to treat

[50] See above n 14 and accompanying text.

[51] Nussbaum, 'Perfectionist Liberalism and Political Liberalism' (n 15) 34.

[52] ibid 35.

them unequally'.[53] Rawlsian political liberalism, by contrast, is committed to equal respect for persons, that is, to adhering to the Kantian principle of treating persons as ends in themselves, which requires people with conflicting conceptions of the good to find their own way through life and 'to have liberty to pursue commitments that lie at the core of their identity, provided that they do not violate the rights of others and that no other compelling state interest intervenes'.[54] For this reason, Nussbaum claims, Rawlsian liberalism does a better job of ensuring political stability than Raz's perfectionism, which is inherently at odds with the comprehensive doctrines of many people (and cultural minorities) in any liberal society.

To take the last point first: there is an immediate difficulty in assessing the objection that Raz's (state-based) perfectionism violates Kantian respect for persons. The difficulty is that Nussbaum and Raz hold fundamentally divergent understandings of respect and its role and importance in moral philosophy. Raz has long argued against the very notion of Kantian respect, as a moral principle which applies univocally across contexts, and which holds (or ought to hold) a privileged (and on some accounts indefeasible) status in both our moral theory and practical reasoning.[55] He argues, in short, that a principle of Kantian respect is not an independent and discrete source of reasons for action. On his view, in most cases, respect is *shown* to people by simply doing what we have good reason to do in regard to them in a given set of circumstances:

> After all we respect people if we treat them as they should morally be treated. But that means that the way they should morally be treated is determined by other considerations (they should not be made to suffer, should be helped in their valuable endeavours, should be protected from destitution, and so on). Once these considerations are determined we know what we ought to do. They are moral reasons, and we should follow them. A byproduct of following them, a byproduct of doing our moral duty, is that we will be respecting people. If that is so then there are no duties of respect as such. Respect is what we show when we do what we otherwise have reason to do ... We will respect people willy nilly, simply by doing what we have non-respect-based reasons to do.[56]

Nussbaum and others working in the Kantian, and more broadly constructivist, tradition clearly do not share this point of view; they view respect for persons as a bedrock moral principle. In addition to this eliminativist argument against Kantian respect, Raz separately argues against the more general idea of universal moral principles which apply to all persons everywhere, and in an invariant way.[57] Assessing the merits of these arguments is a topic for another occasion, but this deeper (and

[53] ibid. [54] ibid 17.

[55] See Raz, *Value, Respect, and Attachment* (n 40) 124–75; Joseph Raz, 'On Frankfurt's Explanation of Respect for Persons' in Sarah Buss and Lee Overton (eds), *Contours of Agency: Essays on Themes from Harry Frankfurt* (MIT Press 2002) 299; Raz, 'On Respect, Authority, and Neutrality: A Response' (n 3) 279–85. Raz follows, and expands upon, the critical arguments made earlier in WK Frankena, 'The Ethics of Respect for Persons' (1986) 14 Philosophical Topics 149.

[56] Raz, 'On Frankfurt's Explanation of Respect for Persons' (n 55) 301.

[57] See especially his argument against human rights principles, which are often claimed to be of just this sort: Raz, *Value, Respect, and Attachment* (n 40) 41–60; Raz, 'Human Rights in the Emerging World Order' (n 3).

relevant) disagreement goes entirely unnoticed by Nussbaum, and yet taking it into account is essential in determining who has the more plausible view on the question of perfectionism.

But what is more significant is Nussbaum's explanation of *why* perfectionist liberalism disrespects persons: because it requires the acceptance of the truth of competitive pluralism. Nussbaum is equivocal as to how she understands Raz on this crucial point. At times, she reads him as suggesting that only (presumably legal) officials need to believe in competitive pluralism, in order to enact and justify state policies which provide an adequate range of valuable options to citizens, as well as to justify tolerance as an appropriate attitude to have in regards to ways of life incompatible with our own.[58] Elsewhere, she attributes to Raz the more radical idea that *everyone* in a society should believe the normative truth of pluralism ('people should believe in the truth of pluralism so that they happily extend autonomy to others').[59] But it is striking that Raz nowhere in his voluminous writings makes either of these claims. At one point, Raz does suggest, without explanation, that 'given human nature, autonomy can only be realized within a community which endorses a competitive pluralistic morality'.[60] But the claim is multiply ambiguous. Raz here does not clearly claim that each member of a community must endorse pluralism, nor does he explain what exactly that endorsement consists. Rather, he seems to say that the community as a whole must organize itself on the basis of pluralism, which of course could be achieved in a variety of ways in which pluralistic principles would play different roles. In any case, Nussbaum's very strong interpretation of the remark, which generates the objection, is dubious, given Raz's other explicit (and clearer) theoretical commitments.

For example, it is not even clear, on Raz's view, that *anyone* must fully endorse competitive pluralism in a society which realizes perfectionist liberalism, in the sense that the normative proposition that there are multiple, incompatible, and valuable ways of life must be incorporated into the comprehensive moral conceptions of the persons in that society. This is so for two reasons. First, as we have already seen, Raz argues that a state can respect pluralism without recognizing it.[61] That is, a government can enact laws and implement policies which in fact realize the personal autonomy of its citizens, but for reasons unrelated either to the substance of pluralist principles or anyone's endorsement of them. The (true) justification of those laws and policies may be ultimately grounded in the truth of pluralism, and yet that justification is implicit and indirect.[62] Of course, the putative justification given by a legal institution for a law or policy—an appeal to constitutional principles,

[58] Nussbaum, 'Perfectionist Liberalism and Political Liberalism' (n 15) 14. [59] ibid 12.

[60] Raz, *The Morality of Freedom* (n 3) 406. The remark is repeated verbatim in an essay published a year later in Raz, 'Autonomy, Toleration, and the Harm Principle' (n 3) 322.

[61] See above n 40, and accompanying text.

[62] This structure of justification has long been taken for granted among writers in moral philosophy in arguing for various forms of rule-consequentialism. Raz has often relied on a form of indirect justification, for example, in his account of legitimate authority: see Joseph Raz, 'The Force of Number' (2004) 54 Royal Institute of Philosophy Supplement 245, 247n5.

for example—is another matter entirely, and may not itself follow from or reflect pluralist principles, much less a manifest, conscious endorsement of such principles.

Second, even if a stronger reading of Raz's views is warranted, according to which the truth of pluralism must figure in the political discourse of a perfectionist, liberal society, and more specifically as explicit justification for government action (court decisions, administrative actions, legislative enactments, and so on), the actual endorsement of pluralism is still not required, contrary to what Nussbaum claims. Raz has long argued that there is a kind of judgement one can make when applying a set or system of norms or reasons which is, on the one hand, not a description of those norms nor, on the other, expressive of a full-blooded moral commitment to those norms by those who make them. Raz calls these 'detached normative statements', or statements made from the point of view of that set or system of norms.[63] Raz thinks that statements of this kind are endemic to legal reasoning, and indeed any reasoning that involves rules or general norms.[64] The relevance of this kind of judgement to answering part of Nussbaum's objection is straightforward. Even if, as she suggests, a 'belief' in Razian pluralism is required on the part of the legal and political actors of a society, Raz may respond that such a belief and the statements expressing it need only be of the detached sort, that is, in accordance with the truth of pluralism without a full-blooded moral endorsement of that truth. So, for example, a Catholic judge may reason in favour of a prohibition on prayer sponsored by officials of public schools in accordance with a kind of pluralism which values Razian personal autonomy, in order to ensure an adequate range of relevant, worthwhile options for school children, without himself morally endorsing and accepting such a restriction on religious liberty.[65] Detached normative assessment thus creates the possibility of a government which takes political action based on perfectionist principles without it being necessary for the officials of that government, particularly those who apply and interpret the laws and policies pursuant to that action, to commit to those principles in the sense of incorporating them into their own conceptions of the good life. Raz's argument is compatible both with this interpretation, as well as with the one Nussbaum imputes to him, that perfectionist principles are explicitly written into the laws, are cited in justifications of public action, such as in court opinions, legislation, and so on, and are embraced by citizens and officials alike.

For these reasons, it is not necessary on Raz's picture that either the legal officials of a society or its citizens need to integrate the principles of competitive pluralism into their comprehensive conceptions of the good life. And if such integration is not necessary, it is difficult to see how a government which achieves legitimacy on perfectionist principles thereby disrespects its citizens whose comprehensive doctrines neither include nor accommodate the truth of competitive pluralism. Perfectionist

[63] See Joseph Raz, *The Concept of a Legal* System (2nd edn, Clarendon Press 1980) 234–38; Raz, *Practical Reason and Norms* (n 37) 170–77; Raz, *The Authority of Law* (n 37) 154–57, 299–308. This is an important way in which he diverges from his fellow legal positivist, HLA Hart. See Kevin Toh, 'Raz on Detachment, Acceptance and Describability' (2007) 27 Oxford Journal of Legal Studies 403.

[64] cf his example of a Catholic, who is an expert in Rabbinical law, offering practical advice to an ill-informed orthodox religious Jew: Raz, *The Authority of Law* (n 37) 156–57.

[65] See, for example, the US Supreme Court case of *Lee v Weisman* 505 US 577 (1992).

liberalism, as far as it goes, does not license, much less require, 'expressive subordination' of citizens who do not recognize and endorse its principles, unless those citizens pursue, or desire to pursue, options and projects which are without genuine value. Neither Raz nor any other writer in the perfectionist literature has claimed that 'monistic' (for example, religious) conceptions of the good are *ipso facto* worthless because they are not themselves pluralistic, and therefore impermissible in a pluralist society—precisely the contrary.

I have argued that Nussbaum's Rawlsian objections to perfectionist liberalism as applied to the state fail. Let us assume, however, that they succeed in the context of the state. Do they serve as plausible objections against perfectionist international legal institutions, as characterized in the previous section? Not surprisingly, the differences already noted in extending perfectionist principles to those institutions are relevant to assessing the strength of the objections. Given Raz's claim that, due to the principle of subsidiarity and international institutions' already fragmented and incomplete jurisdiction, these institutions must recognize the truth of pluralism and be openly governed by it in order to inspire loyalty and solidarity on the part of citizens across states, it may be thought that they run a greater risk of disrespecting citizens whose comprehensive moral doctrines do not include a commitment to pluralism. If, for example, international courts must openly and explicitly embrace pluralistic principles, including a principle of toleration, in their case-by-case reasoning, it might be thought that they will inevitably engage in just the sort of expressive subordination of citizens' moral views which Nussbaum cautions against.

A familiar difference between state-based and international legal institutions, including courts, is that they usually directly regulate the behaviour of states and not that of individual citizens. And again, perhaps the objection could be generalized to assert that international legal authorities which recognize the truth of pluralism may expressively subordinate the values of states which do not embrace pluralism (for example, religious states). However, it is not clear how Nussbaum's conception of expressive subordination would be adapted to apply directly to states, since, as she says, it relates essentially to the lack of equality or standing of citizens within a society.[66] For the same reason, it is unclear how the objection would apply to the adjudication of disputes between states and citizens by international courts; for example, it opens the possibility of an international court expressively subordinating a citizen's comprehensive moral doctrine to that of the state's. It is unclear from Nussbaum's discussion whether this kind of disrespect (assuming it could be such) by an international institution is of the same significance and gravity as that expressed by a state in regard to its own citizens.

Of course, evidence would have to be adduced to show that international institutions acting on pluralist principles necessarily engage in such disrespect. Actual practice indicates they do not. For example, the European Court of Human Rights, in finding that a national prohibition on women wearing face-coverings in Belgium did not violate the European Convention on Human Rights, arguably relied on the

[66] Nussbaum, 'Perfectionist Liberalism and Political Liberalism' (n 15) 35.

principles of pluralism (among others, including the margin of appreciation, consistent with Raz's discussion of a suitable principle of subsidiarity), which can be read as justifying the relevant Articles, in reaching its decision.[67] While the Court ultimately found in favour of the state and against the citizen plaintiff, it explicitly recognized the plaintiff's right to wear the veil under Articles 8 and 9 of the Convention, but concluded that Belgium's interest in banning its use outweighed that right. One would think that the Court's unequivocal recognition of the plaintiff's right to wear the covering, alongside the interests of Belgium to regulate it, is both consistent with pluralistic principles and runs counter to any charge of disrespect. But it is not clear from Nussbaum's discussion whether disrespect can be expressed by a legal authority only in its outcomes (the plain meaning of statutes, the narrow dispositions of cases, and so on) or also in its reasoning, independently of the outcome.[68] In either case, the Court in the Belgian case at least attempts to avoid both by recognizing the value of both a widespread cultural practice (women wearing face-coverings) and curtailing that practice to ensure adequate options for those who are not disposed to participate in the practice.

D. Conclusion

I have argued for one way in which Raz's perfectionist liberalism can be extended to explain and justify the legitimacy of international legal institutions, and that one common objection to it in the context of the state fails. But even if we are to grant its force in regard to state government, it has considerably less force in the international context. The objection fails partly due to a lack of appreciation of the explanatory power of Raz's complex moral and legal philosophy, some parts of which are rarely discussed in connection with his perfectionism. But the objection also fails on the merits, since the kind of disrespect to citizens allegedly consequent on the state embracing pluralism is not reflected in the actual practice of international legal institutions: consistent with Raz's suggestion, such institutions must explicitly recognize the truth of pluralism and, as we see in the veil ban case, their recognition of the validity and value of incompatible ways of life is sometimes explicitly incorporated into the reasons for applying or making law in the circumstances. More importantly, the objections fail because the moral equality of citizens (that is, among citizens) is not at issue in the relevant way in that context. There is, of course, more to be said in defence of a pluralist, perfectionist approach to political legitimacy, both within the state and beyond, and its advantages over a Rawlsian, political approach, but a broader assessment must wait for another occasion.

[67] *Dakir v Belgium*, App no 4619/12, 11 July 2017.

[68] Nussbaum finds the distinction between perfectionism in content and grounds of content as drawn in Peter DeMarneffe, 'Liberalism, Liberty, and Neutrality' (1990) 19 Philosophy and Public Affairs 253 important, a distinction which would illuminate this issue, but she not does discuss it in any detail in regard to the present point: Nussbaum, 'Perfectionist Liberalism and Political Liberalism' (n 15) 6n8.

XI

Legitimacy Criticisms of International Courts

Not Only Fuzzy Rhetoric?

*Andreas Follesdal**

A. Overview

Since the end of the Cold War, states have established a cascade of international and regional courts and tribunals (ICs). They have been inter alia set up to protect human rights, settle investment disputes between states and foreign nationals, establish the rule of law, promote global trade, and bring closure to past atrocities. Their increase in number and influence has not fuelled general popularity. To the contrary, they endure wide-ranging criticisms that they are *illegitimate*. The present chapter considers what we are to make of such objections.

Some scholars of international law warn that the term 'legitimacy' often appears devoid of meaning, a mere emotive venting of distaste:

> Increasingly the fuzziness and indeterminacy of 'legitimacy-speak' has seemed to allow us to break free from disciplinary constraints and to assert and impose our own moral intuitions, shared or unshared, on various target audiences.[1]

* This chapter was written under the auspices of ERC Advanced Grant 269841—MultiRights: On the Legitimacy of Multi-Level Human Rights Judiciary; and partly supported by the Research Council of Norway through its Centres of Excellence Funding Scheme, project number 223274—PluriCourts: The Legitimacy of the International Judiciary. The present version has benefited from comments on several occasions, including the inaugural conference of iCourts, Copenhagen, 15 September 2012; a 'Concepts and Methods' workshop in Oslo September 2013; a PluriCourts Workshop in Barcelona, 15 February 2015; a Justitia Amplificata workshop on 'International Legitimacy and Law' and its Annual Conference on 'The Challenges of Global Pluralism', Frankfurt, 16–17 July 2015; the IVR workshop on the legitimacy of international institutions, 28 July 2015; and the conference on the legitimacy of the state, Sydney, 14 October 2016. I am especially grateful to Nathan Adams, Joseph Raz, Geir Ulfstein, and the editors of this volume for constructive suggestions. *Justitia Amplificata* provided excellent working conditions to drastically improve this chapter.

[1] James Crawford, 'The Problems of Legitimacy-Speak' (2004) 98 Proceedings of the American Society of International Law 271, 271. I owe this reference to Christopher A Thomas, 'The Uses and Abuses of Legitimacy in International Law' (2014) 34 Oxford Journal of Legal Studies 729.

Legitimacy: The State and Beyond. First Edition. Edited by Wojciech Sadurski, Michael Sevel, and Kevin Walton. Published 2019 by Oxford University Press.

Indeed, some of those discussing the moral permissibility of military intervention in Kosovo or Iraq may use the term 'illegitimacy' for emphasis alone. And some political actors 'may call something legitimate or illegitimate ... because they like or do not like it and are grasping for an authoritative way to express that emotion'.[2] Indeed, some authors go further, claiming that the term is *intentionally* void of normative substance. Its main function is as a politically suspect instrument of rhetoric manipulation—'to ensure a warm feeling in the audience'.[3]

Another, less emotive and rhetorically manipulative analysis of the manifold uses of 'legitimacy' might hold that they are *homonyms*—identically spelled, but with drastically different meanings.

The account sketched here defends a third response, one limited to criticisms concerning ICs in particular and not international law in general, or concerns about illegal warfare. Many of these charges of illegitimacy relate to each other in complex ways—differently in fields ranging from human rights to trade. This is not to deny that some talk of the illegitimacy of ICs is inaccurate or wrong. On the contrary, it is possible and indeed valuable to develop a coherent account that connects several various usages, so as to specify better, worse, and downright *mistaken* claims concerning the legitimacy of ICs. This response will bring some order and connection among what appears to be isolated usages. It can explain how claims about legitimacy may be *mistaken*, and thereby disproves the first, emotivist account. This account of normatively justifiable ICs may also guide prescriptions for how to increase their legitimacy by changing some institutions, informing some actors' legitimation strategies, and possibly even shaping some 'civilly disobedient' violations of ICs' judgements.

Some point to the lack of *social legitimacy* among important agents who deny the authority of an IC as *rightful*. This lack raises a related concern that states will therefore fail to *comply*—which some fear may, in turn, reduce the IC's legitimacy further.[4] Other talk of illegitimacy invokes legal considerations, such as the *illegality* of an IC's 'dynamic' treaty interpretation, beyond the text originally consented to by states. Other examples of illegitimacy include the lack of *causal effectiveness* or performance in securing the objectives of the treaties. Finally, some critics use 'legitimacy' in a normative sense, holding that an IC lacks normative *justifiability*: without a normative justification for the authority of the IC, its subjects have no moral duty to defer to its judgements or interpretations.

[2] Thomas, 'The Uses and Abuses of Legitimacy in International Law' (n 1) 732.

[3] Martti Koskenniemi, 'Miserable Comforters: International Relations as New Natural Law' (2009) 15 European Journal of International Relations 395, 409–10; cf Martti Koskenniemi, 'Human Rights and Cultural Diversity: A Study on the Politics of Human Rights in International Institutions' in Eyassu Gayim, Päiti Leino, and Miko Lempinen (eds), *Human Rights and Institutional Politics: The EU, UN and Other International Institutions* (The Erik Castrén Institute of Human Rights and International Law 2005).

[4] Clifford Carrubba, 'A Model of the Endogenous Development of Judicial Institutions in Federal and International Systems' (2009) 71 Journal of Politics 55; Daniel Bodansky, 'Legitimacy in International Law and International Relations' in Jeffrey L Dunoff and Mark A Pollack (eds), *Interdisciplinary Perspectives on International Law and International Relations: The State of the Art* (Cambridge University Press 2012) 323.

I shall argue that *normative legitimacy* provides helpful unity to many of the canvassed forms of legitimacy. The particular substantive normative conception of global justice to be respected and promoted by these institutions is not central to this task. I develop the outline of a theory by drawing on Joseph Raz's 'service conception' of normatively legitimate authority, David Easton's 'systems analysis', and a cosmopolitan normative theory. The first two of these accounts originally apply to the political authority of the state, so we need to reconsider the arguments with great care when we extrapolate to ICs that have several distinct features.

On this account, the central concept of legitimacy for ICs is normative. Each of the other forms of legitimacy often contributes to, and sometimes draws on, the normative justifiability of the international judiciary. But the forms of legitimacy matter in different ways for the normative justifiability of ICs on various issues, be it human rights, trade, investment, or international criminal law—in part due to the different functions, objectives, and interconnected roles of each IC, and the problem types they address. The legitimate authority of ICs is a matter of why and when their judgements or recommendations should count as defeasible reasons for other actors deciding what to do.

ICs do not often issue commands, but rather serve several other functions. They typically *adjudicate disputes*, among states but also between states and private parties, such as citizens or investors, based on an agreed treaty. ICs also engage in the *interpretation* and *specification* of laws, and—some would argue—even *law-making*. Thus, the issue is not only the *judicial* legitimacy of these courts, but also their legitimate role in specifying treaties and shaping other actors' expectations of others' future actions more broadly.

The actors over which the IC claims authority may include domestic courts, legislatures, administrations, civil society bodies, and other states. They must decide not simply whether to obey, but often whether to defer to an IC when they interpret treaties, balance legal norms, shape new pieces of legislation, bring cases, or urge reforms.

ICs interact with other bodies in complex and different ways. The European Court of Human Rights (ECtHR) serves subsidiary roles of support and review of the domestic judiciary. World Trade Organization (WTO) panels *replace* domestic dispute resolution bodies. These complexities add to the challenges of answering the question: Why defer to ICs' judgements? Importantly, ICs lack the direct authority to initiate sanctions, but must rely on other actors and their perception of the ICs' legitimacy.

Section B sketches relevant aspects of Raz's account of legitimate authority: the service conception. Section C lays out some normative standards relevant for the ICs. The next sections then elaborate why, on the service conception, various legitimacy conceptions matter for normative legitimacy: why legality matters (section D), including some reasons for the (limited) significance of state consent—even by rogue states. Section E starts to explore why and when *actual compliance* is important, but not always decisive.

B. Raz's Service Conception of Legitimate Authority

Joseph Raz's 'service' account of when *political* authorities are normatively legitimate is a helpful starting point to bring order to the disparate claims about the legitimacy of various ICs.

The puzzle that motivates Raz's account concerns involuntary political authority, typically the state. He asks why an agent has an obligation to obey a command that the agent has not consented to, especially because the obligation is somewhat 'content independent' and holds even when the command is contrary to what the agent otherwise has reasons to do, or the command is unwise or somewhat unjust.

In brief, Raz holds that a legitimate authority *for* an agent is one that helps that agent to do the right thing, so that the agent acts better according to those reasons the agent has independent of the authority:

> The suggestion of the service conception is that the moral question is answered when two conditions are met, and regarding matters with respect to which they are met: First, that the subject would better conform to reasons that apply to him anyway (that is, to reasons other than the directives of the authority) if he intends to be guided by the authority's directives than if he does not (I will refer to it as the normal justification thesis or condition). Second, that the matters regarding which the first condition is met are such that with respect to them it is better to conform to reason than to decide for oneself, unaided by authority (I will refer to it as the independence condition).[5]

This account of legitimate authority has several helpful features. It asks us to assess an institution in terms of its long-term pattern of decisions and their effects, rather than insist that every particular decision actually helps the agent. An IC can thus be a legitimate authority—and merit deference to its judgements—even though it makes some poor particular judgements. Such an authority is legitimate for an actor only if the pattern or trend of its judgements is likely to yield better outcomes than if the actor tried itself. At the same time, there may be special cases of bad judgements where 'civil disobedience' or similar responses may be appropriate.[6] This relationship between the correctness of individual outcomes and the legitimacy of the institution is one source of what Easton terms 'diffuse support' for an institution:

> [I]n every system, part of the readiness to tolerate outputs that are perceived to run contrary to one's wants and demands, flows from a general or diffuse attachment to regime and community.[7]

[5] Joseph Raz, 'The Problem of Authority: Revisiting the Service Conception' (2006) 90 Minnesota Law Review 1003, 1014.

[6] Andreas Follesdal, 'Law Making by Law Breaking? A Theory of Parliamentary Civil Disobedience against International Human Rights Courts' in Matthew Saul, Andreas Follesdal, and Geir Ulfstein (eds), *The International Human Rights Judiciary and National Parliaments: Europe and beyond* (Cambridge University Press 2017); Andreas Follesdal, 'The Legitimate Authority of International Courts and its Limits: A Challenge to Raz's Service Conception?' in Patrick Capps, Henrik Palmer Olsen, and Stuart Toddington (eds), *Legal Authority beyond the State* (Cambridge University Press 2017).

[7] David Easton, *A Systems Analysis of Political Life* (Wiley 1965) 272.

This diffuse support is a

reservoir of favorable attitudes or good will that help members to accept or tolerate outputs to which they are opposed or the effects of which they see as damaging to their wants.[8]

The service conception insists that an authority's claim to legitimacy as regards any particular agent is only correct if it actually provides this service to that agent—over the long run, if not in every particular instance.

The account also distinguishes between the reasons the agent actually has for acting, and the preferences the agent has:

[S]ince the goals people actually have need not be desirable, coordination aimed at securing these goals need not be desirable either. The coordinated schemes of action that political authorities should pursue are those to which people should be committed, or those needed to secure goals that people should have, which are not always the goals which they do have.[9]

This account allows us to discern how and when an IC may be legitimate for some actors and some issues, but not for others.

This account can also guide our judgement in non-ideal situations. It lets us differentiate between the policy preferences a government—or an IC—actually has, and the reasons which state or IC policies *should* pursue. For instance, states may have good reason to respect, protect, and promote some interests of individuals who are citizens of other states, although a government may hold that its only obligations are towards its own citizens. ICs may thus have to accommodate both sorts of claims.

Furthermore, the service conception can regard legitimacy as scalar rather than either-or, depending on the extent to which an IC provides a service to subjects and whether alternative institutions might provide even better services.

This perspective may also shed light on whether and when an IC may be legitimate when it interacts with deeply unjust states, for example, insofar as it assists in reducing injustice.

The second condition of the service conception, that of independence, may help frame discussions about the normative case for sovereignty, the reasons for state consent, and its limits.

Raz's account only offers a schema or generic framework for more specific arguments concerning any particular institution that claims authority. Among the generic services listed by Raz, several may apply to ICs: an authority may be *wiser* than the agent; have *steadier will* because it is less subject to bias or weakness; *avoid self-defeating strategies; reduce decision-making costs*; or be *better positioned* to overcome coordination problems.[10] For various ICs, the last four are particularly relevant. Note that which services an authority offers must be determined in each case. It is not always easy to determine those services: they may depart from what states intended when they established the IC. And an IC may be discovered to provide several services or perform several functions.

[8] ibid 273. [9] Raz, 'The Problem of Authority' (n 5) 1032.
[10] Joseph Raz, *The Morality of Freedom* (Oxford University Press 1986) 75.

Several ICs may provide states with a 'steadier will', allowing states to credibly commit themselves in the eyes of other audiences. The Arbitration Panels under the International Centre for Settlement of Investment Disputes (ICSID) provide this service when they adjudicate disputes between a contracting state and a national of another contracting state. The International Criminal Court and human rights ICs such as the European and the Inter-American Courts of Human Rights arguably offer similar 'self-commitment' services, whereby state governments and legislators can express their commitment to various norms.[11] Legislatures may enhance their own credibility as a rule-of-law, human-rights-respecting political system, in the eyes of their own citizens and other states—for example, within the European Union. By submitting to an IC, they may also reduce the risk that their successors violate human rights.[12] The ICs offer such services by considering allegations of violations and by reviewing whether national laws and practices are consistent with the relevant conventions.

Several ICs are *better placed* than states to address collective action problems. They can reduce the likelihood that states will engage in free-riding which risks unravelling the collaboration. The WTO dispute settlement system for trade and the Court of Justice of the European Union (CJEU) help states to secure 'collective action over some set of policies among a set of states'.[13] They monitor compliance, review whether administrative authorities have implemented rules correctly, and may adjudicate disputes in a more impartial manner that states could themselves. The ICs thereby reduce the free-rider problems that might prevent the trade regimes every state would prefer. Similarly, one reason many states originally agreed to the European Convention on Human Rights may have been to address another collective action problem: to prevent future governments from violating human rights.

Another role of many ICs is to specify and make law, and thus stabilize the expectations of various parties. Many argue that these ICs then, in effect, not only interpret and apply, but *make* international law. This law-making function creates further legitimacy challenges.[14] This function may be more pronounced and influential for those ICs whose judgements actually set precedents and for those ICs that provide public justifications which enable predictions about future judgements. On the other hand, the law-making role may be less prominent for investment dispute tribunals insofar as they actually interpret their treaties as 'self-contained' and honour the parties' autonomy—without drawing on, for example, human rights

[11] Karen J Alter, 'Delegating to International Courts: Self-Binding Vs. Other-Binding Delegation' (2008) 71 Law and Contemporary Problems 37, 45.

[12] Andrew Moravcsik, 'The Origins of Human Rights Regimes: Democratic Delegation in Postwar Europe' (2000) 54 International Organization 217.

[13] Clifford J Carrubba and Matthew Gabel, 'Courts, Compliance, and the Quest for Legitimacy in International Law' (2013) 14 Theoretical Inquiries in Law 505, 513.

[14] Jose Alvarez, *International Organizations as Law-Makers* (Oxford University Press 2006); Joost Pauwelyn and Manfred Elsig, 'The Politics of Treaty Interpretation: Variations and Explanations across International Tribunals' in Jeffrey L Dunoff and Mark A Pollack (eds), *Interdisciplinary Perspectives on International Law and International Relations: The State of the Art* (Cambridge University Press 2012); Armin von Bogdandy and Ingo Venzke, 'Beyond Dispute: International Judicial Institutions as Lawmakers' (2011) 12 German Law Journal 979.

or environmental treaties—although whether the tribunals actually do this is contested.[15] Other ICs engage in 'systemic interpretation', drawing on other treaties. They may thereby reduce the alleged 'fragmentation' of international law. A central challenge is that there are several ways to bring order and reduce potential conflicts, thus raising the issue of which extra-legal norms and values judges should draw on.[16]

Such interpretation and law-making may combine several of the five services. States are often unable or unwilling to specify treaties fully, preferring to agree to 'deliberately incomplete contracts', the gaps in which the judges must be understood to have a mandate to fill.[17] Examples of such vague phrases are the exceptions to trade agreements on the basis of states' claims about 'Public Morals' or as 'necessary to protect human, animal or plant life or health'.[18] States *reduce their decision-making costs* when they use such terms and delegate the remaining law-making task to an IC which is sufficiently impartial among the parties to a particular conflict.

Of course, these outlines of argument types do not show that any particular IC exercises legitimate authority. The sketches only indicate premises that must be substantiated, if an IC's claim to authority is to be normatively correct.

Several conditions must be satisfied to some extent for the service conception to support such claims.

The patterns of judgements and interpretations issued by an IC should help actors to act better according to the reasons they really have. A central concern is whether an IC will indeed provide such a service and, if so, the likelihood thereof. The treaty must be sufficiently in accordance with the reasons states have to act. The IC may sometimes make mistakes, so we must look at the general trends of the IC's judgements. Several features of the institution are relevant to determine how robust such claims to service are. The states must succeed in setting up and maintaining the IC as sufficiently impartial among the parties to secure the service. There must be sufficient checks and accountability mechanisms to trust the IC not to abuse its independence, but instead interpret in light of the 'object and purpose of the treaty',[19] and the IC must be better positioned or have a steadier will than the states engaged in the dispute or involved in development of the law, or such like. So, how are the judges selected to ensure impartial will and independence? Which procedures do they abide by to reduce the risks that the judges will abuse their authority? If there are no mechanisms to ensure that the 'cosmopolitan-minded lawyers'[20] remain just that, the service arguments for the legitimacy of ICs will not hold.

[15] Pauwelyn and Elsig, 'The Politics of Treaty Interpretation' (n 14).

[16] Jose Alvarez, 'Beware Boundary Crossing' in Tsvi Kahana and Anat Scolnicov (eds), *Boundaries of State, Boundaries of Rights: Human Rights, Private Actors, and Positive Obligations* (Cambridge University Press 2016).

[17] Pauwelyn and Elsig, 'The Politics of Treaty Interpretation' (n 14).

[18] General Agreement on Tariffs and Trade 1994 (GATT 1994), XXa, XXb <https://www.wto.org/english/docs_e/legal_e/06-gatt_e.htm> accessed 6 April 2018.

[19] Vienna Convention on the Law of Treaties (opened for signature 23 May 1969, entered into force 27 January 1980) 1155 United Nations Treaty Series 331, Art 31(1).

[20] Martti Koskenniemi, 'The Fate of Public International Law: Between Technique and Politics' (2007) 70 Modern Law Review 1.

The following sections indicate how the service conception brings some unity to various illegitimacy objections by considering why the legality of ICs and compliance with ICs' judgements matter for their normative legitimacy. Before that, a brief sketch of the normative premises that inform the present account is helpful, to indicate which reasons the various actors have for acting.

C. Some Cosmopolitan Normative Standards

One reason why this service account can help structure the perplexing discussions of legitimacy is that it provides a fairly open schema for arguments. It allows a variety of actors and is agnostic concerning which ultimate reasons they have for action. In this brief overview, the main focus is on states as actors, but recall that ICs must simultaneously handle potentially conflicting expectations from other actors, both *within* states, such as domestic judiciaries, and *outside* states, such as NGOs and other international organizations.

Some comments are required on the reasons these actors, in particular states, have. To fix ideas, I draw on normative premises from the tradition of normative cosmopolitanism. Fellow travellers of this broadly Kantian tradition include Brian Barry, Simon Caney, Martha Nussbaum, John Rawls, and Jeremy Waldron.[21] These premises are, of course, open to challenge, but not simply on the grounds that they constitute normative claims or that some parties may disagree with them. More salient objections might be that *other* sets of normative premises are more defensible, because they match a more credible set of moral judgements overall, in reflective equilibrium.[22]

I here posit four interests of individuals that domestic, regional, and international institutions as a whole should protect and promote. This is not meant as an exhaustive list, and alternative normative theories may accept somewhat different lists. Moreover, each of the institutions need not satisfy and promote the four standards listed; rather, the institutions as a whole must do so.

[21] Martha C Nussbaum, 'Patriotism and Cosmopolitanism' in Joshua Cohen (ed), *For Love of Country: Debating the Limits of Patriotism* (Beacon Press 1996); Jeremy Waldron, 'Theoretical Foundations of Liberalism' (1987) 37 Philosophical Quarterly 127, 139; John Rawls, *A Theory of Justice* (Harvard University Press 1971); Brian Barry, *Theories of Justice: A Treatise on Social Justice* (University of California Press 1989); Rainer Forst, *The Right to Justification: Elements of a Constructivist Theory of Justice* (Jeffrey Flynn tr, Columbia University Press 2012); Simon Caney, *Justice beyond Borders* (Oxford University Press 2005); Simon Caney, 'Cosmopolitan Justice and Institutional Design: An Egalitarian Liberal Conception of Global Governance' (2006) 32 Social Theory and Practice 725. cf Samuel Scheffler, 'Conceptions of Cosmopolitanism' (1999) 11 Utilitas 255.

[22] Norman Daniels, 'Reflective Equilibrium' in Edward N Zalta (ed), *The Stanford Encyclopedia of Philosophy* (spring edn, 2018) <https://plato.stanford.edu/archives/spr2018/entries/reflective-equilibrium/> accessed 6 April 2018; Andreas Follesdal, 'Methods of Philosophical Research on Human Rights' in Fons Coomans, Menno Kamminga, and Fred Grunfeld (eds), *Methods of Human Rights Research* (Intersentia 2009); Martha C Nussbaum, 'Valuing Values: A Case of Reasoned Commitment' (1994) 6 Yale Journal of Law and the Humanities 197; Thomas M Scanlon, 'The Aims and Authority of Moral Theory' (1992) 12 Oxford Journal of Legal Studies 3.

These norms are familiar from various *cosmopolitan* normative theories. Such normative cosmopolitanism should not be confused with versions of cosmopolitanism that require many globally shared institutions and centralized world government.[23] Rather, the central point concerns to whom justification is owed: the set of institutions as a whole must be justifiable to all individuals who are its subjects, as political equals. The institutions should be arranged so as to respect, protect, and further the interests of individuals globally.

The first interest is to be able to satisfy one's vital needs for physical survival and basic well-being, such as not to be tortured.

The second is to be protected from the arbitrary use of political authority and coercive power, be it from domestic rulers, private actors, or international institutions. This interest in 'non-domination' has found expression in a wide range of Western writings.[24] Legal mechanisms that provide such protection include requirements of legality, checks and balances to ensure accountability, and respect for the rule of law—to ensure that authority is exercised only within certain domains. Our interest in non-domination also supports the interest of our states in impartial, rule-guided dispute resolution by peaceful means. ICs can help provide such non-domination, both in protecting individuals against human rights abuses by their own government and in ensuring that powerful states abide by treaties that benefit other parties. However, ICs can themselves also become new sources of domination unless they are checked and constrained by formal means as well as professional norms.

A third interest is the ability to make longer-term plans with some expectation of success, including being able to rely on general compliance with legal rules. This interest supports similar requirements as the interest in non-domination, such as legality, the rule of law, and non-retroactivity.

A fourth interest is to have actual influence over the institutions and rules that affect individuals' opportunities, aspirations, and life plans. This has several aspects. One is due to the interest in having valuable outcomes brought about. A second concern is to have a public expression that all adults are treated as equals. This interest justifies some procedures that give all affected adults levers of democratic decision-making.

The following reflections assume that respect for and promotion of these and other interests of individuals are the ultimate relevant reasons for assessing claims to legitimate political and legal authority, including both of states and of ICs.

According to the service conception, the legitimacy of an institution, such as an IC, for a state is a question of the legitimate authority of the institution over that state. This in turn is a matter of whether the institution helps the state act better in accordance with the reasons the state already has, ultimately based on the concern

[23] cf Thomas Nagel, 'The Problem of Global Justice' (2005) 33 Philosophy and Public Affairs 113–47. Several cosmopolitan theories make no such claims: cf Charles R Beitz, 'Cosmopolitanism Liberalism and the States System' in Chris Brown (ed), *Political Restructuring in Europe: Ethical Perspectives* (Routledge 1994); Thomas W Pogge, 'Cosmopolitanism and Sovereignty' (1992) 103 Ethics 48.

[24] Quintin Skinner, *Liberty before Liberalism* (Cambridge University Press 1998); Philip Pettit, *Republicanism: A Theory of Freedom and Government* (Oxford University Press 1997).

to respect and promote the interests of individuals. Whether in fact such arguments hold for any particular ICs remains to be argued.

Note that from this normative perspective, there is no fundamental assumption that states' reasons to act are limited only to respecting and promoting the interests of their own citizens. Given the opportunities and benefits that a state system establishes, a defensible delineation of sovereignty would arguably include among the objectives of states the protection and promotion of foreigners' interests—to some extent. The salient issue from this perspective is not whether to temper states' priority towards their own citizens with some duties to mankind in general, but the scope and form of the latter.[25]

The following sections indicate how this conception of normative legitimacy provides some unity among the various other forms of legitimacy. The normative legitimacy of ICs often depends on the *legality* of ICs and *general compliance* with their judgements and interpretations, but to different extents and in different ways depending on the IC. Some of these relations will depend on accepting most or parts of the general normative account sketched above, such as the interest in non-domination, while other relations may hold across a broader range of normative theories.

D. Why Legality and State Consent Matters for Normative Justifiability

Several authors note that central requirements of legitimacy for ICs are that they must act according to their legal mandate as agreed in the relevant treaty by the state parties and that they must adjudicate according to standards of legal validity.[26]

This account agrees that there are often good reasons to value state consent and legality. An IC that exceeds its mandate delineated by state consent, violates standard legal methods or decision procedures, or overrides institutional checks may foster suspicion that it is unlikely to reliably provide the requisite service of impartial dispute resolution according to legal method.[27] Thus, compliance with norms of legality and the rule of law are generally necessary for ICs to be legitimate according to the service conception. It is when ICs remain loyal to their mandate and follow agreed criteria for treaty interpretation that they can provide a steadier will than states can on their own and help address coordination problems. And it is when the ICs abide by these norms that they protect against state domination over citizens and bolster parties' mutual expectations that states will honour their commitments.

[25] Nussbaum, 'Patriotism and Cosmopolitanism' (n 21); David Miller, *National Responsibility and Global Justice* (Oxford University Press 2007); Caney, *Justice beyond Borders* (n 21).

[26] Allen Buchanan and Robert O Keohane, 'The Legitimacy of Global Governance Institutions' (2006) 20 Ethics and International Affairs 405, 412; Daniel Bodansky, 'The Legitimacy of International Governance: A Coming Challenge for International Environmental Law?' (1999) 93 American Journal of International Law 596, 624.

[27] Yuval Shany, *Assessing the Effectiveness of International Courts* (Oxford University Press 2013) 142–43.

It is also important that ICs themselves abide by rule of law standards lest they themselves become new sources of domination. This fear of discretionary 'rule of lawyers' is one reason for several scholars' concern about domestic judicial review in general.[28] Some worry that these risks, familiar from domestic settings, are even greater for ICs. They are not curbed by an established, carefully crafted, and fine-tuned system of checks and balances from a comprehensive perspective in anything like a global constitutional convention. Instead, each IC is typically agreed to address one kind of concern, often without attention to systemic issues.

Several authors have come to question the general normative justifications for this role of state consent in international law.[29] State consent is an important feature of much of international law, but is not a necessary condition for all obligations of states: the Statute of the International Court of Justice also recognizes other sources of international law, including customary state practice, general principles of law common to many countries, domestic judicial decisions, and legal scholarship.[30] Yet, for discussions of the legitimacy of ICs, state consent arises in several ways which require some more attention to the normative significance of such consent. For instance, should judges of ICs adjudicate at odds with the explicit mandate that states have given to them and be guided by the objectives states *should* have? Should ICs interpret treaties in light of other treaties to which some of the state parties have not agreed, if the states ought to have consented to these?

One important topic where the normative role of state consent is challenged is the ICs' practice of 'dynamic' or 'evolutive' interpretations of treaties, clearly beyond what states agreed. Several factors mitigate this apparent conflict. Some dynamic interpretation may be required if, in new circumstances, the IC is to promote the objectives the states have agreed to pursue. Such interpretations may be unavoidable—and foreseeable by states, especially when the states have insisted that formal treaty change would require unanimity and hence be very cumbersome. In contrast, some treaties, such as the European Union's Lisbon Treaty, allow treaty changes and secondary law-making in some areas, for example, by means of complex qualified majority voting.[31] Furthermore, interpretation of a treaty 'in light of its object and purpose' is explicitly sanctioned by the Vienna Convention on the Law of Treaties.[32] States therefore authorized the IC to interpret its treaty thus when they agreed the treaty as a drastically incomplete contract.

[28] Jeremy Waldron, 'The Core of the Case against Judicial Review' (2006) 115 Yale Law Journal 1346; Richard Bellamy, *Political Constitutionalism: A Republican Defence of the Constitutionality of Democracy* (Cambridge University Press 2007).

[29] Matthew Lister, 'The Legitimating Role of Consent in International Law' (2011) 11 Chicago Journal of International Law 663; Ronald Dworkin, 'A New Philosophy for International Law' (2013) 41 Philosophy and Public Affairs 2; but cf Thomas Christiano, 'Ronald Dworkin, State Consent, and Progressive Cosmopolitanism' in Wil Waluchow and Stefan Sciaraffa (eds), *The Legacy of Ronald Dworkin* (Oxford University Press 2016).

[30] Statute of the International Court of Justice, Art 38(1) <http://www.icj-cij.org/en/statute> accessed 6 April 2018.

[31] Treaty of Lisbon, Amending the Treaty on European Union and the Treaty Establishing the European Community (signed 13 December 2007, entered in to force 1 December 2009) (2007) 50 Official Journal of the European Union 2007/C 306/01, Art 16(3)–(4).

[32] Vienna Convention on the Law of Treaties (n 19) Art 31(1).

These factors reduce but do not remove the charge that ICs sometimes go beyond the mandate states consented to when they interpret or make law. They may, for instance, be guided by interpretations of other treaties which some of the states have not consented to. What are we to make of this?

One reason to favour such interpretive practice by an IC is that a legitimate IC must be checked and guided so as both to reduce the risk of domination by the IC itself and to ensure that its interpretations and law-making respect and promote the best interests of the individuals ultimately subject to the rules. Domestically, democratic control and judicial review are important guides and checks that promote these ends. There must be institutional mechanisms with similar effects in place for ICs for their law-making to be legitimate. When judges of an IC seek to draw on other treaties, they arguably show that they limit their discretion to reduce the risk of domination by that IC itself.

Furthermore, while some norms should only bind states which have consented, others may be of the sort that states should consent to.[33] The former may include states' obligations towards their own citizens and foreigners which they should be free to negotiate the details of as concerns the division of benefits and burdens. But other obligations may hold regardless of consent. I submit that the latter include some human rights requirements insofar as they provide effective protection[34] and being subject to the jurisdiction of the International Criminal Court (ICC) for genocide, crimes against humanity, and war crimes. If the ICC in fact does deter such crimes,[35] all states should consent to such normatively obligatory limitations to sovereignty. Interpretations done by such normatively obligatory courts would arguably be appropriate for judges of other ICs to rely on when adjudicating disputes, even where one state has not agreed to the former IC.

E. Why General Compliance May Matter for the Normative Legitimacy of ICs

I now move to consider why *compliance* with IC judgements by states is often, but not always, relevant for the normative legitimacy of some ICs. Several authors note that 'legitimacy enhances compliance and compliance enhances legitimacy'.[36] Consider how this may apply to some—but not all—ICs.

Several ICs actually provide the proclaimed service only under conditions of close-to-general compliance by the relevant subjects. This holds most obviously for

[33] For arguments to this effect, see Christiano, 'Ronald Dworkin, State Consent, and Progressive Cosmopolitanism' (n 29).

[34] Beth A Simmons, *Mobilizing for Human Rights: International Law in Domestic Politics* (Cambridge University Press 2009).

[35] cf Beth Simmons and Allison Danner, 'Credible Commitments and the International Criminal Court' (2010) 64 International Organization 225.

[36] Carrubba and Gabel, 'Courts, Compliance, and the Quest for Legitimacy in International Law' (n 13) 509.

the ICs that serve to reduce the risks of 'free rider' or 'prisoners' dilemma' collective action problems. ICs may monitor parties' compliance and issue statements concerning whether they do, in fact, comply. For the WTO, the Dispute Settlement Mechanism may also authorize retaliation by other states against violators.[37] An IC that is set up to address such problems can only succeed if it *in fact* commands general compliance. Otherwise, actors do not have a reason grounded in the service conception to defer to the IC. Note that states may still have reasons to comply, for example to honour several other actors' good-faith expectations—but these reasons are not due to the authority of the IC. So, persistent free-riding among state signatories, especially if it shifts excessive burdens onto compliers, challenges the normative legitimacy of this kind of IC.

For other ICs, general compliance does not appear so directly crucial for their normative legitimacy. Consider regional human rights courts, such as the ECtHR. It arguably provides two services. First, it helps states give other parties, such as citizens and other states, assurance of their commitment to human rights and the rule of law. Second, it helps states bolster human rights in other states in the region, thus contributing to states' obligations to protect and promote the four interests of those who live outside that state.

These services by human rights ICs are less vulnerable to partial non-compliance. Thus, even if some states fail to honour judgements against them, these ICs may be normatively legitimate. For instance, the systemic failures of a few European states in their human rights obligations do not directly affect the legitimacy of the ECtHR. To the contrary, single instances of blatant non-compliance often hurt the reputation of the country as a rule-of-law, human-rights-complying state. Thus, the large backlog of the ECtHR—67,000 applications pending before a judicial formation in March 2016—is arguably mainly a challenge to the legitimacy of the five states accused in two-thirds of these cases: the Ukraine, Russia, Turkey, Italy, and Hungary.[38] Their reputation as rule-of-law-respecting states is at risk. This may arguably also be the consequence of the United Kingdom's refusal to comply with the ECtHR's ruling to reconsider a blanket ban against prisoners' right to vote.[39]

However, if non-compliance becomes sufficiently widespread, or if the IC's reputation is less secure, the IC's normative legitimacy may also be challenged. If Venezuela fails to defer to the Inter-American Court of Human Rights—and even exits the American Convention on Human Rights—both the state and that Court may suffer in terms of normative legitimacy. Indeed, 'a noisy act of noncompliance

[37] Robert W Staiger, 'Report on the International Trade Regime for the International Task Force on Global Public Goods' (Final Draft, 5 February 2004) <http://www.dartmouth.edu/~rstaiger/global.public.goods.paper.020504.pdf> accessed 6 April 2018.

[38] European Court of Human Rights, 'Annual Report 2015' 187 <http://www.echr.coe.int/Documents/Annual_Report_2015_ENG.pdf> accessed 6 April 2018.

[39] Joint Committee on the Draft Voting Eligibility (Prisoners) Bill, *Draft Voting Eligibility (Prisoners) Bill Report* (2013–14, HL Paper 103, HC 924) paras 229, 235. I owe these and the following references to the Joint Committee Report to Edward Bates, 'Democratic Override (or Rejection) and the Authority of the Strasbourg Court: The UK Parliament and Prisoner Voting' in Matthew Saul, Andreas Follesdal, and Geir Ulfstein (eds), *The International Human Rights Judiciary and National Parliaments* (Cambridge University Press 2017).

by a powerful state that occurs early in a tribunal's life may devastate its legitimacy'.[40] Another challenge to the ECtHR arises as more states, including Russia, refer to the United Kingdom's refusal to justify their own non-compliance with the ECtHR. This may threaten the European human rights protection system as a whole—thus challenging both of the services provided by the ECtHR.[41] The legitimacy of the ECtHR would then unravel: it would neither serve to credibly commit the states nor promote human rights compliance—although the substantive norms applied by the Court are normatively sound and the Court satisfies all legality requirements. While continued political opposition by only one or a few states may not prevent a human rights IC from providing its service, *widespread* non-compliance may render the IC illegitimate on the service conception.

The upshot of the discussions of legality and general compliance is that the service account helps to explain why and when conceptions of legitimacy as legality and as general compliance also matter for the normative legitimacy of ICs. In order to provide the requisite services, they must act according to standards of legality and several of them must also enjoy sufficient compliance by states. Note also that some of the services are more vulnerable to partial non-compliance than others, thus requiring case-specific arguments concerning the various services provided by each IC.

F. Conclusion: Is Normative Legitimacy Fuzzy and Indeterminate?

The upshot of my argument is that there are several ways to reduce the apparently diffuse and conflicting claims about the legitimacy of ICs, based on the service conception and normative cosmopolitanism. Several of the concepts of legitimacy canvassed—legality, social acceptance, and compliance—are relevant for normative legitimacy. The apparent confusion in usage is partly due to the complex relationships between these aspects, which differ among the various ICs. Some ICs—for example, in trade—promote their laudable objectives only if most states comply. Others—such as human rights ICs—may bring important benefits, even if several states fail to comply. Another source of confusion is due to the complex interdependence between ICs and other actors, such as states, that affect the impact of ICs. These complexities caution us against drawing general conclusions about necessary or sufficient conditions for rendering an IC more normatively legitimate or what to make of an IC which fulfils some, but not all, of these aspects. Some ICs may gain in normative legitimacy if they are complied with more, but this is not necessary. ICs may improve their normative legitimacy if they help to secure desired outcomes on the ground—but only if those outcomes are justifiable.

Many of these discussions about the legitimacy of international courts and tribunals and the lack thereof should thus not be dismissed as unhelpful, unscientific, or mere manipulation by new rhetorical means.

[40] Laurence Helfer and Anne-Marie Slaughter, 'Why States Create International Tribunals: A Response to Professors Posner and Yoo' (2005) 93 California Law Review 93, 899, 952.

[41] Joint Committee, *Report* (n 39) para 230. See also paras 109–10.

This is not to say that all claims about the illegitimacy of ICs are sound. That would indeed be surprising, given that those who lose cases decided by ICs are likely to protest—and may want to use 'illegitimacy' only in an emotive sense.

I submit that the account sketched above helps to assess such opposition to ICs, by throwing light on the relevant claims: Is the concern that the treaty is imposed by force rather than by consent, that the legal reasoning is flawed, or that the intended outcomes don't arise? Some of these claims may have to be substantiated by empirical, legal, or normative premises. This account may thus lead us to reject some such claims of illegitimacy as *mistaken* rather than mere venting of displeasure—a conclusion which also challenges the dismissal of 'legitimacy talk' as mere emotivism.

I submit that this framework, drawing on the service conception, may allow a more constructive approach: to foster more reasoned assessment of ICs and of the multiple, partially conflicting proposals for their reform.

Index

The manufacturer's authorised representative in the EU for product safety is Oxford University Press España S.A. of El Parque Empresarial San Fernando de Henares, Avenida de Castilla, 2 - 28830 Madrid (www.oup.es/en or product.safety@oup.com). OUP España S.A. also acts as importer into Spain of products made by the manufacturer.
Printed and bound by CPI Group (UK) Ltd, Croydon, CR0 4YY
14/09/2026
02216306-0004